Ernst by Frederick Tatham, England, 1844
(from a picture once owned by W.E. Hill and Sons)

HEINRICH WILHELM ERNST: VIRTUOSO VIOLINIST

To Marie

Heinrich Wilhelm Ernst:
Virtuoso Violinist

M.W. ROWE
Birkbeck College, University of London, UK

ASHGATE

© M.W. Rowe 2008

All rights reserved. No part of this publication may be reproduced, stored in a retrieval system or transmitted in any form or by any means, electronic, mechanical, photocopying, recording or otherwise without the prior permission of the publisher.

M.W. Rowe has asserted his moral right under the Copyright, Designs and Patents Act, 1988, to be identified as the author of this work.

Published by
Ashgate Publishing Limited
Gower House
Croft Road
Aldershot
Hampshire GU11 3HR
England

Ashgate Publishing Company
Suite 420
101 Cherry Street
Burlington, VT 05401-4405
USA

www.ashgate.com

British Library Cataloguing in Publication Data
Rowe, Mark W.
  Heinrich Wilhelm Ernst : virtuoso violinist
  1. Ernst, Heinrich Wilhelm, 1812–1865 2. Violinists – Biography
  I. Title
  787.2'092

Library of Congress Cataloging-in-Publication Data
Rowe, Mark W.
  Heinrich Wilhelm Ernst : virtuoso violinist / by Mark W. Rowe.
    p. cm.
  Includes discography (p. 291), bibliographical references (p. 297), and index.
  ISBN 978-0-7546-6340-9 (alk. paper)
  1. Ernst, Heinrich Wilhelm, 1812–1865. 2. Violinists – Biography. I. Title.

  ML418.E72R68 2008
  787.2092–dc22
  [B]
                                                                    2007050607

ISBN 978-0-7546-6340-9

Bach font developed by © Yo Tomita.

Printed and bound in Great Britain by
MPG Books Ltd, Bodmin, Cornwall.

Contents

List of Illustrations and Figures	ix
List of Music Examples	xi
References and Abbreviations	xiii
Preface	xv
Permissions and Acknowledgements	xix

1	Introduction	1

Part I   Apprenticeship

2	Brünn: 1812–25	15
3	Vienna: 1825–28	27
4	From Vienna to Paris: 1828–31	37
5	Paris: 1831–36	49
6	Paganini and Marseilles: 1837	59

Part II   Early Tours

7	Holland, Germany and the Austrian Empire: 1837–40	69
8	Paris and Vieuxtemps: 1841	83
9	Germany, Poland and Paris: 1841–42	93
10	The Low Countries, Germany and Scandinavia: 1842–43	101
11	England, Sivori, and King Ernest: 1843	113
12	Mendelssohn, Joachim and the Philharmonic: 1844	125
13	New Repertoire: 1845–46	135
14	Russia and Revolution: 1847–49	153

Part III   Later Tours

15	The Elite and the Popular: 1849	167
16	Beethoven and the Classics: 1850–51	175
17	Amélie: 1852–53	189
18	Changing Fashions: 1854–55	199
19	Decline: 1856–57	213

Part IV   Retirement

20	Nice, Vienna, and the B♭ Major String Quartet: 1858–62	225
21	Bulwer Lytton and the Last Journey to England: 1862–63	235
22	Norfolk, London, and the A Major String Quartet: 1864	247
23	Last Days in Paris and Nice: 1864–65	259
24	Epilogue	271

Appendix: The Main Themes of Ernst's Lost A Major String Quartet	275
List of Works by H.W. Ernst	283
H.W. Ernst: Discography	291
Bibliography of Works Quoted or Referred to in the Text	297
Index	309

List of Illustrations and Figures

Frontispiece   Ernst by Frederick Tatham, England, 1844 (from a picture once owned by W.E. Hill and Sons)

Plates

I   Ernst's birthplace in Brno (Amely Heller, *H.W. Ernst im Urteile seiner Zeitgenossen* (Linthicum Heights, Swand Publications, 1986), p.10)
II   The Augustinian Monastery in Brno (by permission of the Augustinian Abbey, Brno)
III   The young Ernst by Teltscher, Vienna, 1827 (by permission of Österreichische Nationalbibliothek, Vienna)
IV   Ernst rehearsing with Chopin, by Delacroix, 1841 (by permission of the Rijksmuseum, Amsterdam)
V   Ernst and the other leading violinists of Paris, by Maurin, *c.*1841–42 (Heller, *H.W. Ernst im Urteile seiner Zeitgenossen*, p.30)
VI   Ernst by Kriehuber, Vienna, 1846 (by permission of Österreichische Nationalbibliothek, Vienna)
VII   Ernst by Prinzhofer, Vienna, 1846 (by permission of Österreichische Nationalbibliothek, Vienna)
VIII   *Ein Matinée bei Liszt*, by Kriehuber, Vienna, spring 1846 (by permission of Österreichische Nationalbibliothek, Vienna)
IX   Ernst, a drawing by J.-J.-B. Laurens, 24 February 1853 (by permission of Bibliothèque Inguimbertine, Carpentras, France)
X   Ernst in Vienna, *c.*1854 (from the *Strad*, 1910)
XI   Amélie-Siona Ernst, *c.*1854 (by permission of www.knebworthhouse.com)
XII   Ernst and his wife, Vienna, *c.*1854 (by permission of www.knebworthhouse.com)
XIII   The only photograph of Ernst playing, *c.*1855 (by permission of California Classic Books)
XIV   A mortally ill Ernst, *c.*1864 (Heller, *H.W. Ernst im Urteile seiner Zeitgenossen*, p.44)
XV   The London Beethoven Quartet Society from Andreas Moser, *Joseph Joachim*, trans. Lilla Durham (London: Philip Welby, 1901), p.288
XVI   The same photograph, London, 6 June 1864, as it appears in Heller, *H.W. Ernst im Urteile seiner Zeitgenossen*, p.32
XVII   A sculpture of Ernst's left hand made by his wife in the 1860s (by permission of Musée Massena, Nice)

XVIII	The rue St François de Paule in Nice (a photograph by the author)
XIX	Ernst's grave in Nice (a photograph by the author)
XX	The bronze relief on Ernst's grave (a photograph by the author)

Figures

| 1 | Jakob Ernst's first family and their descendants | 14 |
| 2 | Jakob Ernst's second family with that of Amélie-Siona Lévy | 14 |

List of Music Examples

6.1	Ernst, *The Carnival of Venice*, op.18, bars 243–248	65
7.1	Ernst, *Elegy*, op.10, bars 14–16	69
7.2	Ernst, *Elegy*, op.10, bars 1–5	69
7.3	Ernst, *Elegy*, op.10, bars 31–32	69
9.1	Ernst, *Le Roi des Aulnes: Grand Caprice*, op.26, bars 58–60	97
9.2	Ernst, *Feuillet D'Album*, bars 1–6	99
13.1	Ernst, *Hungarian Airs*, op.22, bars 57–59	137
13.2	Ernst, *Hungarian Airs*, op.22, bars 68–70	137
13.3	Ernst, *Hungarian Airs*, op.22, bar 13	138
13.4	Elgar, Violin Sonata in E minor, op.82, first movement, bars 170–172	138
13.5	Elgar, Violin Concerto in B minor, op.61, second movement, bars 93–94	138
13.6	Ernst, Concerto, op.23, bars 1–9	140
13.7	Ernst, Concerto, op.23, bars 9–11	140
13.8	Ernst, Concerto, op.23, bars 11–13	140
13.9	Ernst, Concerto, op.23, bars 13–15	140
13.10	Ernst, Concerto, op.23, bars 24–26	140
13.11	Ernst, Concerto, op.23, bars 30–32	141
13.12	Ernst, Concerto, op.23, bars 55–57	141
13.13	Ernst, Concerto, op.23, bars 58–65	141
13.14	Ernst, Concerto, op.23, bars 65–73	141
13.15	Ernst, Concerto, op.23, bars 73–80	142
13.16	Ernst, Concerto, op.23, bars 93–95	142
13.17	Ernst, Concerto, op.23, bars 96–102	142
13.18	Ernst, Concerto, op.23, bars 437–439	144
13.19	Ernst, Concerto, op.23, bars 24–25	145
13.20	Brahms, Serenade no.1 in D major, op.11, first movement, bars 200–202	146
13.21	Ernst, Concerto, op.23, bars 100–104	146
13.22	Brahms, Piano Concerto no.1 in D minor, op.15, first movement, bars 91–96	146
13.23	Ernst, Concerto, op.23, bars 323–324	147
13.24	Brahms, Violin Concerto in D major, op.77, first movement, bars 491–492	147
13.25	Ernst, Concerto, op.23, bars 438–441	148

13.26	Sibelius, Violin Concerto in D minor, op.47, first movement, bars 447–456	148
14.1	Ernst, Concerto, op.23, bars 1–9	162
14.2	Liszt, *Grosses Konzertsolo*, bars 1–6	163
22.1	Ernst, *Polyphonic Study*, no.1, bars 35–40	251
22.2	Ernst, *Polyphonic Study*, no.2, bars 56 62	251
22.3	Wieniawski, *Etude, L'Ecole Moderne*, op.10, no.3, bars 1–2	252
22.4	Ernst, *Polyphonic Study*, no.3, bars 1–2	252
22.5	Ernst, *Polyphonic Study*, no.6, variation 2, bars 39–42	253
22.6	Ernst, *Polyphonic Study*, no.6, variation 3, bars 11–17	253
22.7	Wieniawski, *Les Arpèges, L'Ecole Moderne*, op.10, no.9, variation 3, bars 1–2	254
22.8	Ernst, *Polyphonic Study*, no.6, variation 4, bars 1–2	254
22.9	Ernst, *Polyphonic Study*, no.6, finale, bars 14–15	254

References and Abbreviations

The key to all abbreviations is found in the bibliography. This is in alphabetical order.

All references are given in square brackets immediately after a mention or quotation in the text; some esoteric pieces of information are also referred to in this way.

The abbreviation for a book is followed by the page number; in multi-volume works, the page number is preceded by the volume number in roman numerals.

References to journals are given by date and page number thus: [MW:24/6/53:294] where 53 denotes 1853. Journals mentioned only once are not abbreviated.

References in one place to two or more sources are separated by a full stop. Dates and page numbers from different issues of one journal are separated by semi-colons. Where one journal quotes another, the name of the journal quoted is separated from the other by a colon.

As I mention in the preface, EOC is a shortened English translation of EUZ which itself is an expanded version of HWE. As EOC is the most accessible, I take my references from there, only taking information from the others when it is not included in EOC.

Superscript numbers refer only to footnotes.

Preface

When I was eighteen, I worked in the shop of a small music museum. Along with the usual bees-wax candles, pot-pourris and records, there was a table with secondhand sheet music and books. I remember picking up a copy of a piece called *Hungarian Airs* by Ernst – a composer of whom I had never heard – and being staggered by the difficulty of the music I saw. Not only could I not play it, I had no idea how it could be played. Putting it down, I then picked up a dullish-looking memoir and opened it at random. I was very surprised to see a sentence about Ernst. It said that the writer had seen the dying artist in Oxford Street, walking with evident difficulty, and that Ernst's yellow face and bent posture had upset him for days. It seemed very remarkable to stumble, within successive minutes, on two items to do with Ernst, having never come across him before, and I naturally wondered what events had caused the writer of such extravagant and extrovert music to fall into this miserable condition. The present book is in part an attempt to answer this thirty-year-old question.

In succeeding years, I tried to play *Hungarian Airs*, and read the deeply admiring accounts of Ernst by Hallé and Berlioz. But it was when I saw the reference to him in Tolstoy's *The Kreutzer Sonata* and immediately heard (another coincidence) Sherban Lupu's recording of the *Rondo Papageno* – surely one of the most *cheerful* and invigorating pieces ever written – that I decided to find out more about him. I was at a slight impasse in my normal academic work, and when I discovered that encyclopaedia entries were the fullest accounts of him that were readily available, the mania for research took hold. Since then, every secondhand bookshop has had to be searched, every likely museum written to, all important Ernst sites visited. I have never felt so strongly that a subject chose me rather than vice versa, and few hours in the last ten years have passed without at least one thought about him passing through my head.

The ideal Ernst-researcher should be able to speak French, German, Czech, Danish, Hungarian, Norwegian, Swedish, Flemish and Russian; have a clear understanding of nineteenth-century European political and cultural history; a firm grasp of the less well documented reaches of musical history; know how to decipher early nineteenth-century German handwriting; have the money and leisure to spend his time browsing in dusty European archives; be a fluent pianist and an outstanding violin virtuoso. I realize how far my qualifications fall short of these; my only consolation is that no one has all of them.

Because of these unreasonable demands, I have needed a good deal of help from other people, and I have always been gratified by the readiness and interest with which they responded to my requests. I was lucky enough to teach in an institution with many fine linguists and I would particularly like to thank the following. For help with French: Philippa Bosworth, Stephen Bosworth, Pierre-Louis Coudray, Damien Duboerf, Hélène Knights, Steven Nesom and Marianne Peel. For translations from

German: Christian Piller, Anthony Price, Renate Demmer, Esther Gyamarti, Oliver Radley-Gardner, and particularly David Galloway. For translations from Czech: Monika Betzler.

Reading early nineteenth-century German handwriting is a rare specialist skill, and I am grateful to Peter Ward Jones, of the Bodleian Library, Oxford, for deciphering Ernst's letters to Hallé, Joachim and Schlésinger, and for pointing me in the direction of some of the most important recent American research. Professor Wilma Iggers was kind enough to decipher Ernst's earliest surviving letter, and extract some important information from the documents deposited in the Brno archives.

Jan Pěčka did some of the first scholarly research on Ernst in the 1950s, and he has been unstinting in his help, giving me both sound advice and copies of many rare and important documents. I speak no Czech and he speaks little English, but our joint Ernst enthusiasm has allowed us to overcome this barrier.

The Keeper of Portraits and Performance History at the Royal College of Music, Oliver Davies, gave me much helpful advice in the very early days of my research and drew my attention to the picture on the cover. Clare Fleck, the archivist at Knebworth, was kind enough to guide me round the records and give me a personal tour of the house. Dr Andrew Brown at Cambridge University Press expertly assisted me with the Bulwer Lytton literature and drew several obscure memoirs to my attention.

I received valuable assistance on medical matters from my uncle, Professor David C. Taylor, who diagnosed Ernst's condition, and from Donald Everson, who also discovered some useful information about Ernst recordings. By insisting that I consider the agendas of Ernst's reviewers, Professor Katherine Ellis, who read my first essay on the violinist, saved me from taking much prejudice at face value. I am also very grateful to my music teachers at Cranbrook School – Cecil Irwin, John Williams and David Murphy – for fostering my early interests, and my violin teacher, Launa Carpenter, for giving me the technique to play at least some of Ernst's music. She regularly raised an eyebrow at my taste for superficial music, but at least she can now see it was deep-seated.

I am also grateful to my colleagues, John Cullen, Margaret Sawyer and Fenella Clements, for jointly engaging with me in the demanding task of performing Ernst's quartet in B♭ op.26 in the spring of 2004. I think this was probably the first public performance for 140 years. I would also like to thank David Lang, with whom I've played violin and piano works for many years, for accompanying a performance of the *Elegy* op.10 on an earlier occasion. My colleagues in the English department at Pocklington School, who heard a good deal more about Ernst than they would have liked, were most forbearing.

Finally, I would like to thank my wife, Marie McGinn, for humouring and tolerating my enthusiasms. She endured many Ernst-related expeditions, attended my lectures, and waited – for the most part patiently – while I regularly sorted through stacks of dusty music. She also found Ernst's grave and birthplace before I did, and made some important suggestions about the structure of Ernst's family. Alan Heaven has helped me decipher many poorly photocopied, stained, blotted and otherwise illegible letters by people writing hastily in their second or third language.

His vivifying interest and encouragement remain as important to me now as they were twenty years ago.

M.W. Rowe
Kensington

Permissions and Acknowledgements

Hundreds of librarians, archivists and publishers from all over Britain, Europe and America responded to my requests for information. I am indebted to all of them, but perhaps I could give special thanks to the following people who supplied me with notably valuable leads, or material on Ernst's life, works and family: Cl. Alméras, Bibliothèque Inguimbertine, Archives et Musée de Carpentras; Mlle Amadei, Conseil General des Alpes-Maritimes; Mrs C.A. Banks, British Library; Dr Thomas Bardelle, Niedersächsisches Hauptstaatsarchiv, Hanover; Dr Günter Brosche, Österreichische Nationalbibliothek; Professor Arden Bucholz; PhDr Eva Drasarova, Director of Central State Archives, Prague; Elizabeth Fielden, The Fitzwilliam Museum, Cambridge; Helen Foster, Henry Watson Music Library, Manchester; Stephen M. Fry, University of California, Los Angeles; V. Hamáčková, Jewish Museum, Prague; Jill Hughes, Taylorian Institute Library, Oxford; Dr Mary Harcup, Malvern; Herr Krause, Leipziger Städtische Bibliotheken; Sophie Levy, Conservatoire de Paris, Cité de la musique; Dr Heinz von Loesch, Staatliches Institut für Musikforschung Preussischer Kulturebesitz, Berlin; Madame Catherine Massip, Directeur, Bibliothèque nationale de France, Département de la Musique; Dr Chris Maunder, the College of Ripon and York St John; PhDr František Novak, Director Archiv Města Brna; Father Richard Price, Heythrop College; Ruth Pyle, Hertfordshire Records Office, County Hall, Hertford; Mgr Simona Romportlova, Moravian Museum, Brno; M. Luc Thevenon, Conservateur en Chef, Musée d'Art et d'Histoire, Nice; J. Rigbie Turner, Pierpont Morgan Library, New York; Professor Alan Walker, McMaster University; Ágnes Watzatka, Franz Liszt Memorial Museum and Research Centre, Budapest. Over many years, the staff at York University Library, the London Library, and the Library of the Royal College of Music have been a great asset to my research, and have tirelessly responded to my requests for yet more obscure and hard to locate foreign books.

I would also like to thank the following people and organizations for permission to reproduce material: David Cairns; Lytton Enterprises Ltd, www.knebworthhouse.com; Lord Cobbold; the Osterreichische Nationalbibliothek; Hertfordshire Archives and Local Studies; Christel Wallbaum of H. Barons, London; the British Library; Harper-Collins; the Orion Publishing Group; Harcourt, Brace, Jovanovic; Universitätsbibliothek Frankfurt am Main; the Pierpont Morgan Library, New York; Librairie Droz, Geneva.; Manchester Archives and Local Studies, Central Library; Peter Ward Jones, the Bodleian Library, Oxford; Ariane Todes, editor of the *Strad* magazine; California Classic Books; the Bibliothèque Nationale, Paris; Oxford University Press; Niedersächsisches Hauptstaatsarchiv, Hanover; Paul Hamlyn; Hachette Livre; the archives of Stadt Leipzig; Staatliches Institut für Musikforschung Preussischer Kultursitz, Berlin; the Augustinian Monastery, Brno; the Rijksmuseum, Amsterdam; Bibliothèque Inguimbertine Archives et Musées de Carpentras, France; Musée Massena, Nice.

Every attempt has been made to trace all the copyright holders, but if any have been inadvertently overlooked, please contact the publishers.

In Art, a difficulty overcome is beautiful.
Saint-Saëns

Chapter 1

Introduction

I

For Joachim, Ernst was 'the greatest violinist I ever heard; he towered above the others ... [He] became my ideal of a performer, even surpassing in many respects the ideal I had imagined for myself' [GV:519, 533]; for Berlioz, he was 'one of the artists whom I love the most, and with whose talent I am most *sympathetique*'. [CGB:III:628] For Schumann, he was the only violinist able 'to win over all parties whenever he pleases' [SMM:162]; for Liszt, his playing was 'admirable' [LOFL: I:65–6]; for Heine, he was 'perhaps the greatest violinist of our time.' [HS:380] Several reviewers with recent memories of Paganini preferred Ernst to the great Italian, and in 1884, reviewing over thirty years of concert-going, the Reverend H.R. Haweis wrote: '[If], looking back and up to the present hour, I am asked to name off hand, the greatest players – the very greatest I ever heard – I say at once Ernst, Liszt, Rubinstein.' [MML:34]

Besides being one of the most expressive and technically gifted of all nineteenth-century violinists, there are several other reasons for thinking Ernst important. He successfully advised Schumann to take up music professionally, and saved the career of the young Joachim. He performed with Mendelssohn, Chopin, Liszt, Wagner, Alkan and Clara Schumann, and gave five pioneering performances of *Harold in Italy* with Berlioz. He developed several new violin techniques – particularly in the areas of left-hand pizzicato and artificial harmonics. He was the first Jewish touring violin virtuoso of any importance; the form and pattern for countless others. He composed two of the nineteenth-century's best loved pieces – the burlesque variations on the *Carnival of Venice*, and the *Elegy* – and two other pieces of more lasting consequence: a set of studies which leads directly into Ysaÿe's *Sonates pour violon seul*; and a concerto that was a profound influence on Liszt's B minor piano sonata, and still in the repertoires of Enescu, Szigeti, Heifetz, Milstein, Menuhin and Stern in the first half of the twentieth century. Finally, Ernst was the early nineteenth-century violinist who did most to make Beethoven's late quartets widely known and appreciated. This was especially true in England where he led many performances at the Beethoven Quartet Society, the Musical Union and the Manchester Classical Chamber Concerts in the 1840s and '50s.

This naturally raises the question: why have only violin specialists and the best informed musicologists heard of Ernst? The main reason is lack of evidence about his life and character. The problem is not of recent origin because even his closest colleagues seem to have known little about him. 'At the moment of writing,' wrote Ernst's friend Chorley in the violinist's obituary, 'we are without any biographical data,' [A:21/10/1865:541] and the situation never improved: 'Few precise documents exist regarding this eminent violinist,' lamented Alberto Bachmann in his *Les grands violonistes du passé* in 1913. [GVP:82]

Perhaps the most telling symptom of this almost universal ignorance is the entry for Ernst in George Dubourg's *The Violin*. The book is well informed – it contains information about some players ignored by similar texts – and was first published in 1853 when Ernst was one of the most famous living violinists. But in his chapter, 'The German School,' when he reaches the moment for his entry on Ernst, Dubourg turns to poetry:

> Vainly, oh Pen! expectant here thou turn'st
> To trace the doings of Teutonic ERNST –
> To show what praise he won, what hearts he moved,
> What realms he traversed, and what trials he proved.
> Wanting the *records* that should speak his fame,
> Prose fails – and Verse, alas! but gives *his name*.
> So, in life's common round, when just aware
> That one whom we have longed to *know* is near –
> To see him, hear him, *chat* with him, prepared,
> We find he's gone, and has but *left his card!* [DV:185]

There are many reasons for this lack of evidence. Ernst did not like writing, did not teach, and had no children; and apart from his student days and a few unhappy weeks in Hesse-Kassel and Hanover, he was never a member of an orchestra, ensemble or institution. In addition, being a rich, agreeable and independent man who liked to avoid disputes, he had only one protracted public row, and never made a court appearance of any kind. All these facts deprive us of immediate memories and documentation.

These problems are compounded by two further difficulties. First, the old Austrian Empire saw the birth of many famous musicians, and clearly these absorbed the interest of musicologists in the region. More minor figures, who might have been written about elsewhere, consequently languished. Second, by the time of his death, Ernst had gone severely out of fashion, not appeared on a public stage for eight years, and been playing below his best for at least three years before that. Accordingly, obituaries were few, and his entries in the first serious histories of the violin – written towards the end of the nineteenth and the beginning of the twentieth century – are scant and less than generous. [VIM:475–6]

It sometimes seems as if history itself were conspiring to keep Ernst's name out of view. The most obvious and terrible manifestation of this is the Nazi holocaust which slaughtered most of European Jewry, killed Ernst's surviving family, and scattered and destroyed their possessions. Until the Second World War, Ernst's name was kept alive by his family and other members of the Jewish community in Brno. After the war, there was no family and virtually no Jewish community to recall him.

There has also been a certain amount of quotidian bad luck. His English friends, J.W. Davison (music critic of *The Times*) and Edward Bulwer Lytton (the novelist), were famous men in their day, but their reputations have sunk with few traces, and only a handful of scholars are interested in their friends and associates. Some contemporaries, like Julius Benedict, died before they could discuss Ernst in their memoirs; others, like Hallé, unaccountably omitted important events relating to him. All the documents from the early years of the Vienna Conservatoire have been lost, and in 1964 a serious fire consumed the archives of his English publisher, Chappell. His birthplace was destroyed during the Second World War, and when the war ended, the street in Nice named after him was renamed.

More than most, he has been subject to the erasures of political geography. Ernst was a cosmopolitan creature who felt deeply at home in borderlands, and as states wax and wane, institutions are changed and records thrown away. Brno, where he was born, was part of the Austrian Empire but became part of Czechoslovakia and then the Czech Republic. Nice, where he died, was once part of Piedmont-Sardinia but became part of France. Alsace, where his wife came from, was once part of France, then became part of Germany, and then became part of France again. Even the village of Narford in Norfolk, where he stayed for several months in the 1860s, has a peculiarly remitting existence. It is shown on some maps but not on others, and signposts to it run out in an altogether baffling way, so that even the most committed Ernst-researcher finds himself heading off into East Anglian vacancy.

II

Ernst's character, and the cultural background which formed it, must also be held partially responsible for his present invisibility, and they are worth looking at in their own rights.

He knew from childhood that he would eventually have to leave his birthplace permanently – because of the Moravian Familiant Law – and this knowledge prevented the formation of any patriotic feeling and, more importantly, any sense of home. Even when he was married and terribly ill, he never abandoned the nomadic form of life which he established in the late 1830s, moving from one hotel room or rented apartment to another every few months at most. This lifestyle undoubtedly helped undermine his health, and it also meant that he never stayed in one place long enough, either to compose a good deal himself, or collaborate with another composer on an important violin composition. For the biographer, it means that even his best friends were rarely in his company for long, and surviving documents are scattered throughout northern Europe.

But the cultural influence went deeper than this. In much of early nineteenth-century Europe, the Jews were harshly persecuted. Their lives were hedged around with legal restrictions, they were subject to punitive taxation, and they were frequently victims of abuse. Life had been like this – and worse – for centuries.

Given the severity of this anti-Semitism, it was foreseeable that more fortunate Jews would begin to develop a habit of elusiveness, enjoy the prosperous present, avoid documentation, cover their traces, and never give more information about themselves than was strictly necessary. These habits soon became second nature. A recent historian of the Rothschild family remarks that, although spectacularly rich, they were not deeply interested in their own past or future: 'They kept no muniment room. They were not interested in their own history. They were respectful towards their ancestors, as a matter of good form, and they prudently thought about tomorrow. But they lived for the present and did not care deeply about past or future.' [HJ:314]

Ernst assimilated the same outlook. He was impulsive and spontaneous, reacting with powerful emotion to the present moment, but he gave little thought to his own future (he never, for example, saved any money), and he seems to have cared little about posterity. Nor did he seem particularly interested in his own past. Friends were told very little about it, and his letters almost never mention an event which happened more than a few years before. Such details as he was prepared to give away, like those on his marriage certificate, become a little vaguer and more elevated. His father, who was a retired café-owner, becomes a 'gentleman'; his own profession becomes 'Artist'; and his wife, and probably he himself, revised their ages downwards. [MC]

Ernst had all the equipment necessary to survive in a hostile world. His livelihood depended on superior talent and education, and he ensured that his dependency on other musicians or administrators was minimal. He had virtually no physical property which could be taken from him, his obsessively peripatetic style of living ensured that prejudice could never effectively build against him, and he was ready to move on at a moment's notice. He was therefore as invulnerable to anti-Semitism was it was possible to be. In addition, his wit, self-deprecating charm, generosity and kindness meant he was rarely likely to be the target of hatred or animosity, and allowed him to be friendly with an enormous number of people, many of whom hated one another. To a certain extent these virtues made him harder to know because the inner man was shrouded by a bright miasma of sympathetic and elusive charm.

People's responses to Ernst were deeply personal: 'While talking of Ernst, I have entirely lost sight of the editorial plural', wrote a critic in the *Musical World* [MW:12/1/50:18], and the violinist had an extraordinary ability to turn attention away from himself and back onto the people with whom he was interacting. This is clear in his letters, which frequently say nothing about himself or his affairs, but are full of extravagant sympathy and interest in his correspondent. It is also striking how frequently reports speak less of Ernst than of his effects on others. This is even reflected in the titles of the few books and theses written about him: *Ernst in the Opinion of his Contemporaries*, 'The Life and Works of Heinrich Wilhelm Ernst with Emphasis on his Reception as Violinist and Composer'. Somehow, Ernst blends into his reception.

This is all too evident when the people writing are recounting their own experiences of his playing. When critics describe the playing of Vieuxtemps, they talk about his imposing tone, his splendid staccato, the accuracy of his intonation; when they describe Ernst, they soon become wholly absorbed in their own fantasies. Berlioz's account of the effect of Ernst's music on his own experiential memory, with its invocation of E.T.A. Hoffmann, is a good case in point. (See p.155.) Heine takes off into world of fanciful Arthurian romance while listening to Ernst; and there is a most extraordinary passage in one of Haweis's books that recounts the visions conjured up by the violinist's playing. (See pp.125–26 and 206–7.) In all these cases, hard and interesting facts about him and his playing dissolve into whimsical and emotional day-dreaming. Dubourg's poem is emblematic of the way Ernst is recalled: the shift to the more emotional medium of verse; the emphasis on the writer's feelings of great friendliness and warmth; Ernst's mannerly absence; the complete lack of facts. One sometimes has the impression of a man who politely abstained from history.[1]

Some of Ernst's elusiveness must also be ascribed to his artistic nature. Contemporaries were agreed that Ernst was distinguished from most of his fellow violinists by being able to excel at both virtuoso and classical music. ('Classical music' for the mid-nineteenth century meant the works of Haydn, Mozart, Beethoven, Hummel and Spohr, particularly their chamber music). The critic of the *Morning Post* put the matter naively and pithily: 'Ernst is the greatest living violinist, for he can do everything.' [MW:5/1/50:2]

Contemporaries were also surprised at the kind of differentiation which Ernst could make between one kind of chamber music and another. Davison wrote: 'It was a real treat to connoisseurs to hear Herr Ernst's fine and expressive reading of [Mendelssohn's quartet in E♭, op.12] and to remark the entire distinction which he made between it and the more primitive work of the genial and prolific Mozart. [Quartet in B♭, probably K.458]. Herr Ernst, in short, is a subtle actor; and the various quartets, etc, of the great masters to him are much the same as the different characters of Shakespeare to such a comedian [i.e. actor] as Macready.'[2] [MW:17/2/55:107]

The actor's ability to project himself sympathetically into any kind of work or personality is characteristic of a certain kind of artistic nature. The poet, observed Keats, is a man '*without* identity' [KL:157–8], a man who is simply a 'thoroughfare for all thoughts'. [KL:326] Unlike the self-sufficient 'man of power', the artist does not impose his personality on others, but takes on another person's personality and imaginatively entertains their feelings and circumstances. The artist is without identity because there are an infinite number he can assume. Perhaps the reason why Ernst did not want to be an orchestral leader or a teacher was that these roles would force him to act like a man of power; both musical roles demand a fixed and definite identity which has to be asserted on and against other people. One suspects that, like Keats and Wordsworth, he found wise passiveness the key to self-understanding and to the understanding of others. [KL:53]

We can see the same disposition of mind in his sense of humour. Invariably, in the few examples that have come down to us, this involves Ernst projecting an imagined identity onto a person or set of circumstances, and then acting as if that identity were real. He treats the young and unqualified Reinecke as if he were a venerable *Kapellmeister*; he pretends to Schindler that another friend's house is a restaurant; he persuades Bulwer Lytton that the visiting piano virtuoso Sigismond Thalberg is a magician; he pretends that a curl of hair can be reattached to his head. This is also the core of his irony, since irony (unlike sarcasm) requires the creation

---

[1] In some ways the case of Ernst resembles that of Alkan. Both were super-virtuosi preoccupied with writing exceedingly difficult music, and both have suffered a long period of neglect from musicologists. (I would say that Ernst Studies now is in about the same condition as Alkan Studies in 1960.) During their lifetimes, Alkan remained virtually invisible by living a life that was largely private; Ernst pulled off the more difficult trick of remaining invisible by living a life that was almost wholly public.

[2] I overlook Davison's characteristically nineteenth-century assessment of Mozart.

of an entertained persona or circumstance which can then be discreetly signalled and lightly discarded.

It is also the core of his sympathy, since this too requires one to entertain the circumstances of another, experience the world as he does, and want to relieve his misfortunes. Ernst was a modest man who was famously sympathetic and generous to those he knew. He hugged and comforted Berlioz in St Petersburg when the latter was overcome by excitement and nerves; he gave up a large part of his fortune to his half-brother who had run into serious debt; he thought nothing of taking sixty people to a restaurant. [EUZ:56] He was also famously sympathetic to people he did not know, and his charitable work was frequently cause for comment in the press. He gave money to the victims of the Hamburg fire and other public disasters, and even at the end of his life, when he was severely impoverished himself, he still regularly gave money to the poor of Nice. As in the case of his artistic virtues, it is natural to speak of his moral virtues in terms of the self and denial of the self: we call a modest man 'self-effacing'; we call a charitable man 'selfless'. In all cases, an egotistic hardness of outline is avoided.

Although witty, sympathetic and intelligent, Ernst was not an intellectual. His life at one period, according to Hallé, was 'the same eating and drinking parties, the same chess and whist parties,' [LLCH:244] and it is reasonable to assume that it was like this most of the time. His letters rarely discuss music; the only book he ever mentions is a book on whist; and the only poetry he quotes is a passage from Schiller which was recited, in his presence, by his wife a short time before. Judaism as a religion seems to have meant nothing to him, and he showed no haste to convert to Christianity either. Only in the late 1850s or early '60s did he convert to Catholicism, but this was entirely under the influence of his deeply religious wife. Moral and political ambitions seem to have been equally lacking. He writes on one occasion to his half-brother: 'I don't offend anyone when I only benefit myself and do no harm. I desire no more than that.' [EOC:11]

With illness and age, wise passiveness turned into passivity. In a letter to Davison, written while on holiday in France, he remarks: 'It has always been my idea of supreme happiness not to earn my living with my intelligence, with my soul, or even with my fingers.' [BL] And the same passivity is described in several obituaries: 'He was rather passive than energetic, more subject to an impression than able to rule it,' says the *Neue Berliner Musik-Zeitung* [MW:4/11/65:690], and there is a hint of disapproval in the *Athenaeum*'s description of the same trait: 'A certain languor of temperament, approaching to indolence, and in late years aggravated by illness, prevented him doing full justice to his powers, either as a creative musician or a member of society …' [A:21/10/65:541]

In some ways, his life of travel ministered to this characteristic. Staying in one place looks like doing nothing and being passive, whereas travelling looks like doing something and being active. But this is misleading. In the first place, travelling in the mid-nineteenth century, was more or less the sedentary occupation it is today, and consisted largely of waiting, sitting, eating, and looking out of the window. In the second, if a performing musician stays in one place, he has constantly to change and develop his repertoire, otherwise his audience will grow bored and disappear. Furthermore, to prevent himself from becoming stale, he has constantly to look within himself for change, and this often means developing joint projects with others. But if a musician is always travelling, then collaborative projects become more problematic, and he no longer has to look inside himself for variety. He can constantly play the same repertoire to different audiences, and boredom is kept at bay for him by frequently changing scenes and people. In other words, if Ernst had stayed in one place, he would have had to join something, develop something, change something – all things he was distinctly disinclined to do.

His intellectual passivity had an effect on his career. He certainly continued to play the same handful of pieces for far too long, but the problem was more deep-seated. In Paris in the 1830s and '40s, he showed no interest in either the nationalist or socialist ideas that meant so much to musicians like Chopin and Liszt. Without a sense of home or country, one can quite see why nationalism had little appeal, but it is less obvious why the socialist ideas meant nothing to him. Perhaps it was because his origins were Jewish and the socialisms of Saint-Simon and Lamennais were profoundly Christian in inspiration; perhaps it was because Ernst did not want to create problems with potential patrons, and was largely concerned to fit in with society as he found it. After 1850, when music became increasingly nationalistic, literary and historical in inspiration, and when the role of the virtuoso changed from that of dazzling entertainer to interpreter of the masters, Ernst in his solo repertoire was insufficiently responsive to these changes and his reputation suffered.

His irenic, complaisant nature meant he was rarely the *first* to do anything, but he was quick to assimilate and improve on the work of others. By the time he came to programme the Beethoven and Mendelssohn concertos others had played them before, but everyone agreed that he played them much better than his predecessors. He was not the first nineteenth-century violin virtuoso to compose an operatic fantasy, a set of studies, or a virtuoso concerto, but there are good grounds for saying that his works are amongst the very best of their kind. And the sheer technical ingenuity and difficulty of his compositions reveals a kind of genius, and outdistances all but a handful of pieces by his contemporaries.

The successes of his early years seem due in large measure to finding himself in the right place and at the right time. The musical education on offer at the Augustinian monastery in Brno was one of the best available in Europe; the Vienna of Beethoven, Schubert and Paganini could not have been more exciting; Paris in the 1830s and '40s was the centre of instrumental virtuosity. After the 1848 Revolution, however, he seems to have lost his way. While the fundamentals of composition were being explored in Leipzig and Weimar, he initially found himself receiving bouquets for evenings of music and recitation in the south of France, and then playing quartets in musically reactionary England. If those around him were not of the first quality, then Ernst does not seem to have been capable of seizing the initiative himself. Even the important role he played in making the late Beethoven quartets known in England was largely because Hallé in Manchester, and Ella, Alsager, and Rousselot in London, had already set up the necessary institutions.

As a young man, Ernst was certainly determined and intensely ambitious. Nothing else can explain how, by the age of sixteen, he was in a position to place himself in direct competition with Paganini, or make a name for himself within a few years in the intensely competitive atmosphere of Paris in the 1830s. His early letters are full of the heady delights of his own successes, and, on a couple of occasions when conflict was unavoidable, he displayed what Aristotle would call a sense of proper pride. He was also remarkably good at what we now think of as public relations, marketing, networking – even merchandizing. Two significant tussles with Paganini and Sivori were won because he knew that sincerely working for the good of others, and not thinking about himself, was the best way, ultimately, to promote his own cause. The genuine demonstrations of concern and sympathy in his letters make the recipients all the more receptive to news of his own plans and achievements, and all the more inclined to offer help and support.

Like many slightly unintellectual and indolent people, he readily acquired skills and could be galvanized by technical problems. His phenomenal violin technique and fluent piano-playing demonstrate this clearly enough. Another manifestation was the excellence of his written French, which Berlioz jokingly described as indecent, and his fondness for games and puzzles. Hiller recalled evenings of whist with Ferdinand David; Liszt described some hundred rubbers of the same game with Ernst in Weimar; the violinist's letters to Hallé (and Hallé's notebooks) are full of moves for their games of postal chess; Berlioz was exasperated by the way Ernst sat up all night at the chessboard with Louis Blanc, the exiled revolutionary.

The self-absorbed determination not to be beaten by any obstacle, and the desire to write pieces that challenged even his own transcendental technique, were seen by one London reviewer as an integral feature of his approach to composing and performing. 'The variations were original,' noted the *Morning Advertiser* in 1849, 'and yet, amid all their eccentricity, they were always distinguished by exquisitely sweet and expressive notes. In fact, he seemed to be revelling, so to speak, in instrumental "puzzles" – puzzles that would perplex and confound others, but were surmounted by him with facility, precision, and elegance.' [MW:1/12/49:739] Several of his best known compositions are also motivated by a desire to overcome an obstacle or solve a puzzle. His arrangement of the *Erlking* for solo violin seems to be prompted by the question: is it possible to transcribe the two hands of the pianist, and the four characters impersonated by the singer, for just four strings? And his arrangement of *The Last Rose of Summer* seems to be prompted by the equally perverse desire to use a slight, nostalgic Irish air as the basis for the most technically demanding set of variations ever written for the instrument. It is notable that these two pieces, currently his most widely played, are both arrangements. His creative impulses, as we might expect, tended to be ingenious rather than original.[3]

---

3   Many features of Ernst's personality – an extreme sensitivity to others, an ability to understand other people's ideas better than they understand them themselves, a certain lack of originality, an acceptance of the world as it is, a desire to conform and assimilate – were later generalized into characteristically Jewish personality-traits by a number of philosophers who were either Jewish themselves or of Jewish origin. [See WCV: 3e,4e,14e–19e, 23e, 42e; LIB:34–5, 184–5; JSE:18–42] All these ideas, of course, may be influenced by anti-Semitic propaganda; in particular, Wagner's widely influential 'Judaism in Music'. Although Ernst is not named in this article, he had many of the traits which Wagner labelled as characteristically Jewish, and Wagner may well have had him in mind as he wrote. In the early 1850s, Ernst was one of the most famous Jewish performers in Europe; he had been celebrated and successful in

He revelled in technical risk. The music of Vieuxtemps and Wieniawski usually sounds more difficult than it is; Ernst belongs to a select group of composers (it includes Henselt and Brahms) whose music is much more difficult than it sounds. As Ernst largely played his own music, some of his celebrated unevenness may be put down to the difficulty of his own compositions, especially when we consider that, in the early nineteenth century, virtuosi made a number of short appearances at concerts without any chance to warm up. John Ella, the English impresario, tells an instructive story:

> [Deloffre the] late *chef d'orchestre* at the Opéra Comique, in Paris, was principal second violin, for several seasons, at the Musical Union. On quitting London for his present appointment, Ernst justly remarked that I had lost an excellent second, a most conscientious musician, and a thorough artist. To which I added, 'and a safe one, who never played a wrong note or made a mistake.' Ernst humorously replied, 'I should be sorry were you to pay *me* such a compliment.' The daring impulsive genius of Ernst occasionally led him to daring flight,
>
> > 'Which, without passing thro' the judgment, gains
> > The heart, and all its end at once attains.' [MSAH:281]

Aside from a further recourse to poetry, it is significant that both Ella and the London critic, when speaking of Ernst's daring impulsiveness and interest in puzzles, also speak of his sweetness, expressiveness and power of speaking to the heart. In him, it would seem, ingenuity, risk and sweetness were not only naturally combined but mutually supportive.

III

Besides information, biography thrives on connections, influences, close relationships, institutional membership, ideas and development, and I will not deny that lack of all these things has made writing Ernst's biography problematic. However, I have only been able to write it at all thanks to a select group of writers and scholars who went before me.

In the nineteenth century, these include Ernst's friend Dr Leone, whose *H.W. Ernst: Eine Biographische Skizze* [*A Biographical Sketch*] of 1847 is one of the few sources of information about Ernst's childhood [HWE], although it can be usefully supplemented by the lengthy nineteenth-century pamphlets and encyclopaedia entries of Pohl, Deutsch and D'Elvert. [ADB. D. GMM] Amongst Ernst's fellow musicians, there are brief mentions of him in letters by Mendelssohn, Berlioz and Liszt, and good accounts in Berlioz's *Memoirs* and essay on Ernst, Hallé's *Life and Letters*, and Reinecke's 'A Half-Forgotten Prince of Violinists'. [BM. JD:27/1/52. LLCH. HFPV] Short articles from the turn of the century usually only summarize encyclopaedia entries, but an exception can be made for Authur M. Abell's 'Famous Violinists of the Past VIII: Heinrich Ernst and Charles De Beriot'. [FVP]

Paris when Wagner was not; and, although they met several times, there was no great warmth between them.

In the twentieth century, Amely Heller's *H.W. Ernst im urteile seiner Zeitgenossen* [*H.W. Ernst in the Opinion of his Contemporaries*], self-published in 1905, is also an essential but problematic work. [EUZ] I assume she did not attempt (or at least did not succeed) in publishing it commercially because almost the entire biographical part was copied out word for word from Leone's by then obscure pamphlet. The main value of the work is that she reproduces a number of letters which Ernst wrote to his half-brother Johann, a few miscellaneous poems and articles, and some slightly unreliable details about Ernst's family home and background.[4] She obtained her unreliable details from Johann's daughter Josephine, who had a remarkably long life – from 9 May 1836 to 20 September 1930 – and her documentation from Josephine's two sons, a chemist also called Heinrich who owned Ernst's school violin, and a lawyer called Ludwig who looked after his surviving letters and documents.[5] [NJC. EUZ:57]

The first person to show that Josephine's details were often incorrect was Jan Pěcka in his pioneering thesis 'Heinrich Wilhelm Ernst' of 1958, a work which has still not been translated from Czech, and is still unfortunately confined to its institution. [JP] Pěcka's major discovery was a file of legal documents deposited in the Brno archives, including *Sperre-relations* (Austrian Empire documents giving details of the estates of the dead), legal depositions, and Ernst's father's will. From these, Pěcka was able to see that Ernst's father had married twice, that Ernst's accepted birth date is incorrect, and that Josephine and Heller got the sexes and number of his siblings wrong. He also came close to deciphering Ernst's mother's Christian name (he read it as 'Charlota') although her surname still escaped him. Ten years after writing this thesis, the Russian invasion of Czechoslovakia resulted in Pěcka's being forced to abandon his research and work as a caretaker for twenty years. I am pleased to say that he has now taken up his research again, and has recently published a short piece on Ernst and Brno. [MI:93]

In 1983, Boris Schwarz usefully expanded his two previous encyclopaedia entries on Ernst by devoting four and a half pages to him in *Great Masters of the Violin*. [G1&2. MGG1. GMV] Edward Sainati published two of Ernst's letters to the sculptor Dantan in the *Strad* in 1985; and in 1986, Samual Wolf edited a version of Heller's book, translated by Roberta Franke, and published as a typescript by Swand Publications. [IC. EOC] Heller's material is reduced by at least a third, but the loss is compensated for by a very useful set of notes and annotations.

These publications were the immediate forerunners of the most recent and significant contribution to the Ernst literature, Fan Elun's unpublished Cornell PhD thesis, 'The Life and Works of Heinrich Wilhelm Ernst (1814–1865) with Emphasis on his Reception as Violinist and Composer', submitted in 1993. [E] This is a most careful, reliable and conscientious piece of work. By a systematic reading of the

---

4   According to Heller, Ernst's father lived from 1770 to 1830, and had one wife, Barbara Ernst, with whom he had six sons and two daughters, including Heinrich Ernst. [EOC:4] For the correct account of Ernst's family, see Chapter 2.

5   The mystery as to why Josephine retained the surname 'Ernst' after marriage is resolved when we discover she is buried next to Adolf Ernst (died 1 May 1898). He was almost certainly her husband, and possibly a cousin. [NJC]

music press and nineteenth-century reference books, Elun establishes for the first time a reliable chronology of Ernst's life, and shows that a number of stories about Ernst – for example that he played with Joachim in London in 1859 – are myths. It has been constantly at my elbow and has supplied a framework, and many detailed references, for this book. I could not have written it without him.

The most recent substantial contribution to the literature is Tobias Wilczkowski's 2006 thesis, 'Heinrich Wilhelm Ernst: En stor violinist I skuggan av Paganini' ['A Great Violinist in the Shadow of Paganini'], from Uppsala University. [TW] This contains no new biographical information (apart from some Scandinavian newspaper reviews) but it considers some cases where Ernst's technical innovations in violin technique go beyond Paganini's.

IV

This book was originally much longer, but the economics of publishing made me see it was necessary to delete 80,000 words. Consequently, most of the social and political background, descriptions of the places where Ernst lived and played, and portraits of his friends and colleagues, have been removed. I have not, however, deleted any information about Ernst, and wherever possible I have tried to keep my quotations from nineteenth-century sources. This is partly because there is so little primary material about Ernst which is readily available, but mainly because I want to preserve the tone of the originals. Tone is largely conveyed by style, and consequently, paraphrasing away the style of a letter or review destroys most of its interest. Many of Ernst's letters were written directly after concerts, and I want to retain his sense of excitement; many reviews were written with the glorious sound of Ernst's Stradivarius still singing in the critics' ears, and I want to preserve their sense of wonder and pleasure, as well as the distinctive flavour of the nineteenth-century sensibilities which experienced it.

PART I
Apprenticeship

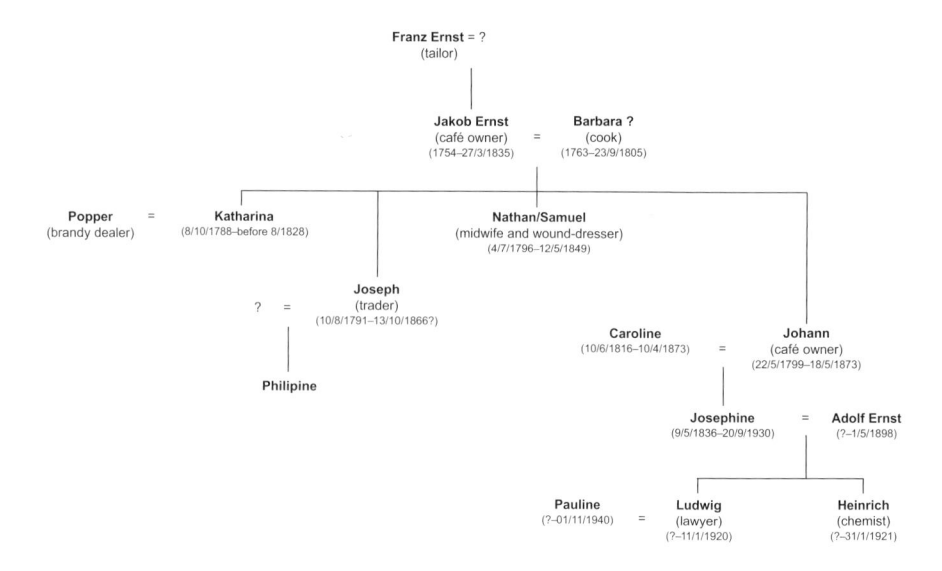

```
                          Franz Ernst = ?
                              (tailor)
                                 |
                           Jakob Ernst    =    Barbara ?
                          (café owner)           (cook)
                        (1754–27/3/1835)    (1763–23/9/1805)
                                 |
         ┌───────────────────────┴───────────────────────┐
Popper  =  Katharina                          Nathan/Samuel
(brandy dealer) (8/10/1788–before 8/1828)   (midwife and wound-dresser)
                                                (4/7/1796–12/5/1849)
                         Joseph
              ?   =     (trader)
                   (10/8/1791–13/10/1866?)
                         |                    Caroline              Johann
                      Philipine          (10/6/1816–10/4/1873)  =  (café owner)
                                                              (22/5/1799–18/5/1873)
                                                       |
                                              Josephine     =    Adolf Ernst
                                         (9/5/1836–20/9/1930)    (?–1/5/1898)
                                                       |
                                     ┌─────────────────┼─────────────────┐
                                  Pauline            Ludwig            Heinrich
                              (?–01/11/1940)   =    (lawyer)          (chemist)
                                                (?–11/1/1920)      (?–31/1/1921)
```

Figure 1   Jakob Ernst's first family and their descendants

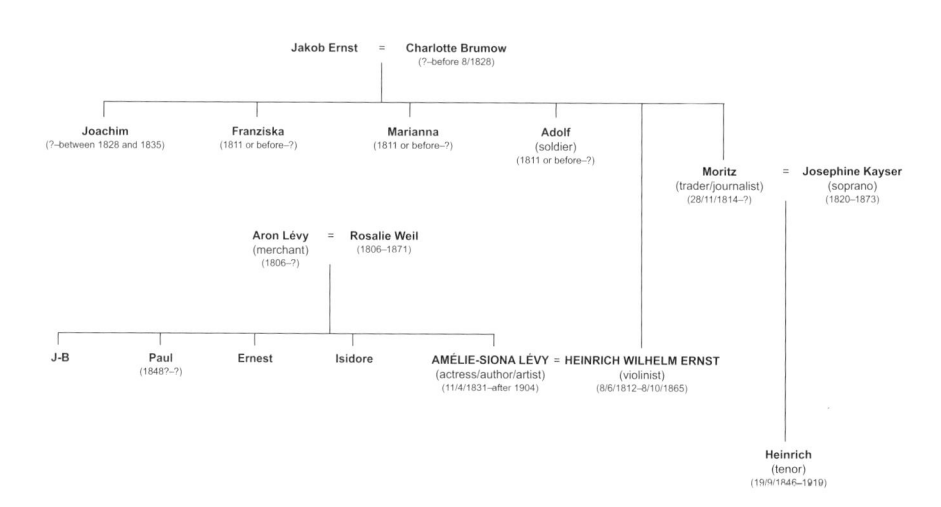

```
                     Jakob Ernst   =   Charlotte Brumow
                                       (?–before 8/1828)
                              |
     ┌────────────┬───────────┼──────────┬──────────────┐
  Joachim     Franziska    Marianna    Adolf         Moritz         =    Josephine Kayser
(?–between   (1811 or    (1811 or    (soldier)    (trader/journalist)         (soprano)
1828 and 1835) before–?)  before–?) (1811 or      (28/11/1814–?)            (1820–1873)
                                    before–?)

          Aron Lévy   =   Rosalie Weil
          (merchant)      (1806–1871)
          (1806–?)
                |
    ┌─────┬────┬────┬────────────────┐
   J-B  Paul Ernest Isidore    AMÉLIE-SIONA LÉVY  =  HEINRICH WILHELM ERNST
       (1848?–?)              (actress/author/artist)      (violinist)
                              (11/4/1831–after 1904)   (8/6/1812–8/10/1865)
                                                              |
                                                          Heinrich
                                                           (tenor)
                                                    (19/9/1846–1919)
```

Figure 2   Jakob Ernst's second family with that of Amélie-Siona Lévy

Chapter 2

Brünn: 1812–25

Moravia lies to the north of Austria, to the south of Poland, east of Bohemia and west of Hungary. In the early nineteenth century, it formed part of the Austrian Empire ruled over by the Habsburg Emperor Francis I (1792–1835).[1] He controlled vast territories in central Europe ranging from the Tyrol to Transylvania, from Bohemia to Montenegro, and these numbered amongst their peoples Germans, Czechs, Serbo-Croats, Romanians, Poles and Magyars. It was an unstable, heterogeneous mix. Perhaps the only common elements were that most of the aristocrats paid court to the Emperor in Vienna, the Empire was administered by a bureaucratic but efficient civil service, Catholicism was the dominant religion, and the language of administration was German. [HM:8–46]

Brünn – as Brno was then universally known – was the capital of Moravia, and at this time it had a population of about 30,000. It sits in a valley between two hills at a point where the rivers Svratka and Svitava meet, and the land is consequently rich and fertile, supporting sheep and cattle as well as cereal crops and fruit. Trade routes, which had met there since ancient times, initially encouraged the growth of markets, and later manufacturing and processing. By the early nineteenth century, income from trade and agriculture was supplemented by revenue from gun-making, brewing, distilling, milling, tanning and sugar refining. All this gave the town, according to one observer, 'a certain air of wealth'. [MP:114].

The most important industry in the town, however, was textile manufacture. In the mid-eighteenth century, the Empress Maria Theresa set up a government cloth factory in the town, and imported skilled foreign workers to operate it. After one false start, the factory was moved to the suburbs of Brünn in 1764, and had well over a hundred looms in operation by 1781. Lack of local skilled labour and inexperience in sales caused it to go bankrupt in 1789, but by then the immigration of foreign workers and the inflow of government money had stimulated local entrepreneurs to start their own more modest businesses, and many of these were hardy enough to survive. [ICEC:2–47] In addition, a number of factories manufacturing tools and machinery, originally set up to support the cloth industry, proved equally resilient, and ensured the town increasing prosperity as the nineteenth century advanced.[IMP:1. ICEC:176–86]

Culturally too, the city thrived. The Redulta, on the Vegetable Market, was one of the oldest theatres in central Europe. Its tradition dated back to the seventeenth century and the twelve-year-old Mozart performed there in 1767 when staying at the

---

1 Technically, the Emperor Francis, who lived from 1768 to 1835, ruled initially as Francis II, Emperor of the Holy Roman Empire (1792–1804); and then as Francis I, Emperor of Austria (1804–35).

Schrattenbach Palace. [BCG:8, 18] Opera performances had begun in the 1760s with performances of Czech plays with songs, such as the anonymous *The Enamoured Night-Watchman*, but within a short period major operas were being staged: Gluck's *Orfeo* in 1779, Mozart's operas after 1789, Beethoven's *Fidelio* in 1811, and Weber's *Der Freischütz* in 1822. Modern church music was not neglected either, and in 1824 there was a full-scale performance of Beethoven's *Missa Solemnis* at St Jakob. [G1:I:312; MGG1:II:189]

In spite of a rich cultural life and comparative prosperity, life was made difficult by a repressive government. Francis I and Metternich (the Minister for Foreign Affairs from 1809 to 1848) were horrified by the political ideas ushered in by the French Revolution, and made every effort to keep them out of their domains. The political climate rapidly ossified into a deeply reactionary conservatism. Travel into and out of their territories was made irksome and time-consuming by unusually rigorous interrogations and searches. The post was searched for incriminating books and letters, and a vast system of spies and informers (estimates vary between 6,000 and 10,000 in Vienna alone) ensured internal obedience to rules and regulations – including curfews – which controlled every aspect of public and private life. [MLBV:34–60] No citizens of Brünn could ever quite forget these circumstances if only because, wherever they went in the town, the skyline was dominated by the grim and forbidding Spielberg fortress. This was the Empire's harshest prison, and a place designed to appall and terrify the government's political opponents.

In the early nineteenth century, the Jews suffered worse repression than the Christians. A Jewish community was established in Brünn in the first half of the thirteenth century, but in 1451 the preacher John of Capistrano (known as 'God's Whip') stirred up local hatred against the Jews, and they were expelled from the city by royal edict in 1454. [ZOB:2. BCG:38] This was the beginning of prolonged state oppression. From then on, no Jew was allowed to live or even spend the night in Brünn (or four of the other so called Royal Cities), so that most of its Jewish inhabitants had to go and live in the Křenová district just outside the city walls. [EJ:IV:1384] This gave the authorities an opportunity to make their lives even more difficult. Jews had to pay a toll on entering the city; were only allowed to use the Jewish gate (which meant long queues); and had their access times strictly controlled. [ZOB:2]

By the middle of the eighteenth century, Jews were subject to a series of restrictions throughout Moravia. They could not set up their own schools or attend Christian schools or universities. They could not lease or work agricultural land, set up factories, work as artists or sculptors, or enter any trade or profession except brewing, distilling, tailoring, baking, and money-lending. They could not visit places of public entertainment, eat and stay at non-Jewish inns, or go out before noon on Sundays. At all times, they were obliged to wear distinguishing dress. [JBM:48–52]

In 1781, all of these regulations were reversed when Joseph II issued his Moravian Toleration Edict, but the regulations Joseph introduced or did not repeal were equally significant. The most important of the latter was the Familiant Law enacted by Charles VI in 1726. This originally restricted the number of Jewish families in Moravia to 5,106, although this was later raised it to 5,400. In consequence, only one son in a family was allowed to have children, which meant that only one son and daughter per family were allowed to marry. Families tended to be large, and for a variety of reasons children's survival rates were higher than in Christian families. Thus, unless they emigrated, the vast majority of the Jewish population was condemned to a life of lonely, involuntary celibacy. This created a great deal of tension within Jewish communities, and predictably led to bribery, corruption and prostitution. Some couples had religious marriages in secret, but the state considered these void, and any children illegitimate. [JBM:59]

Joseph did not allow the Jews to set up any printing works beyond those already existing in Brünn and Prague, and imported books were subject to special censorship. Tolls on Jews entering towns were reduced but not abolished. Jews were far more heavily taxed than other residents: they were subject to a 'family and food tax' which meant that they had to pay three times as much as Christians; from 1799, a Jewish class tax was added in Moravia, as well as a toleration tax for foreign Jews [JBM:56]; and in 1812, Brünn was made the beneficiary of a special tax on the Torah. [HJSB:5] Most importantly of all, Hebrew and Yiddish were banned. This effectively meant that all Moravian Jews had to speak and write German, and they were also required to give German names to their children, and adopt a German surname from a prescribed list. [JBM:48–52. ZOB:4]

The Congress of Vienna in 1814 eased some of the religious restrictions, but Jews were still weighed down with irksome regulations. Until 1848, for example, they had to carry a special passport even when travelling within the Empire; they had to identify themselves if the ticket collector asked if there were any Jews on the train; and they had to pay expensive guarantees if they wanted to move outside of the Monarchy. [ZOB:4]

In one respect enforced Germanization was beneficial to the Jews of Moravia: they were better integrated with the local population than the Jews of, for example, Bohemia, because all the Jews in that area were concentrated in the Prague Ghetto and spoke Yiddish. Except for the ban on Jews in the Royal Cities and a few other areas, the Jews of Moravia lived and worked with the ordinary populace. The obligation to speak and write German increased this integration and meant that they became part of a larger German-speaking culture, and this made success abroad much easier. In another respect, obliging the Jews to speak German and take German names was to have tragic consequences. In the second half of the nineteenth century, the rise of Czech nationalism meant that the Jews paradoxically became identified with oppressive rule from Vienna, and this made them vulnerable to increased abuse and persecution at home.

*   *   *

Ernst's grandfather, Franz Ernst, was a tailor from Neu Rausnitz (now Nového Rousinova), a Jewish village to the east of Brünn, where he fathered a son called Jakob in about 1754. Jakob Ernst, Ernst's father, continued to live in Neu Rausnitz, and sometime before 1787 he married Barbara (her maiden name is not known) who was born in the same village in about 1763. Clearly, Brünn's rapid expansion, combined with the greater toleration of Jews, was providing new business opportunities, and in 1800 they decided to move to the city. There they obtained a licence to brew and distil alcohol, as well as selling alcohol and coffee, at 58 Der Grosse Kröna (now called Křenová), and moved into the apartment above the café. [AMB. E:6–8. EOC:4]

In the early twentieth century the café was called 'Austria', and it could well have had the same name in Jakob Ernst's time. Its position, at the heart of the Jewish settlement, was well chosen. Der Grosse Kröna was the main road which heads east out of the city towards the important town of Olmütz. This was obviously good for business as was the fact that the café was close to the synagogue and one of the city's larger textile plants, the Kleine Kröna. The café was situated on the right-hand side of the street facing away from the town, about a hundred yards from the old city walls (now the Koliště ring road), on the corner of Der Grosse Kröna and Mittel Kröna (now Rumiště). [SP] The whole region is now completely built up and has the slightly insalubrious atmosphere of all areas around bus and railway stations, but at this period the wide street was lined with neat two-storey buildings. As you walked out of the town you passed numerous thriving Jewish businesses (there was certainly a baker and a pharmacy) and long before you passed the river Svitava, you were in wide, flat countryside.

By the time they moved to 58 Der Grosse Kröna, Jakob and Barbara had had four children: Katharina (b. 8 October 1788); Joseph (b. 10 August 1791); Samuel (b. 4 July 1796); and Johann (b. 22 May 1799). Barbara Ernst worked in the café as a cook, but on 23 September 1805 she suddenly died (she had not made a will) at the age of 42, and her husband was left with three dependent children. [AMB]

Her illness and death ushered in yet more difficulties. Within a month, Napoleon thrashed the Austrians at Ulm, and he entered the city without opposition on 20 November. Most of the French army camped to the east of the town (as far as Neu Rausnitz), and the inhabitants' worst fears must have been confirmed when troops began to loot and destroy houses at the far end of Der Grosse Kröna. [AZ:70] Jakob would have watched the French troops march past his café to take up their positions at Austerlitz, and then witnessed the return of the exhausted but victorious army several days later.

Within a short time, possibly before all the prisoners and wounded from the battle had left the town, Jakob remarried. He was now a man well into his fifties, and yet more children appeared at regular intervals. Allowing one year per child, his marriage must have been before 1808; if the previous birth rate of his children is a guide, then it was probably fairly soon after Barbara's death in 1805. His new wife was called Charlotte Brumow and she had been born in Leippa (now Česká Lípa) in Northern Bohemia. [RJBD] Like Brünn, Leippa was a textile town (it also has an Augustinian monastery and a castle) and it would not be surprising if she or her family emigrated when Brünn's expanding textile industry was drawing expertise from all parts of the Empire and beyond. Jakob Ernst's *Sperre-relation* shows that they had six more children, although their dates of birth are not recorded: Franziska, Marianna, Adolf, Joachim, Heinrich and Moritz. [AMB]

It's quite difficult to gauge the family's status and standard of living. Contemporary documents describe the inn as a *Garküchen*, literally a 'Jewish Kitchen'. These could often be impoverished, and rich Jews tended to avoid them and use the regular inns in the centres of towns. But because of the restrictions on Jews in Royal Cities this was much more problematic in Brünn, and Jakob Ernst's clientele may therefore have been rather wealthier and more cultured than was the norm in other places. In addition, Jews who owned brandy distilleries, as Jakob did, could grow quite rich. One contemporary account describes a distiller's daughter studying French and Italian, his son learning the violin, and his wife acquiring aristocratic airs. [JBM:104–5]

But the beginning of the nineteenth century was a difficult time economically. Napoleon returned after the battle of Wagram in 1809 and destroyed the outer fortifications of the Spielberg Castle, and in 1811 and 1816 the Austrian state went bankrupt. After the lifting of the continental blockade in 1815, a flood of cheap imported cloth from England undermined the competitiveness of Brünn's factories, and the introduction of more efficient looms led to an outbreak of rioting and machine-breaking in 1819. Consequently, one can well understand why Leone describes Ernst's family as 'not very well off'. [EOC:4]

Unfortunately the Café Austria no longer exists. Heller took a photograph of it in the early 1900s, and its position can still be identified by the two buildings on either side, but this end of Křenová was heavily bombed by the Allies in November 1944, and it is highly likely that the café was destroyed in the raid. In its place now stands 18 Křenová, an undistinguished block of Stalinist flats. Heller's photograph shows a substantial two-storey building in the Moravian eighteenth-century style, clean and symmetrical in appearance, with small windows in the roof and a certain amount of austere decoration on its second storey. (See Plate I.) It extends for at least four – and possibly six – windows along Der Grosse Kröna, and for nine windows down Mittel Kröna. It was large enough to be a concert venue in the fourth decade of the century, and the whole building enclosed a substantial courtyard. [SP]

Most nineteenth-century sources simply say that Ernst was born in 1814, and all modern reference books add that he was born on 6 May, but there are good reasons for thinking all of these dates are incorrect. The day and month are wrong because the bronze relief on Ernst's tomb in Nice – sculpted by his wife, who might reasonably be expected to know the day and month of his birthday – clearly says 'LE 8 JUIN 1814'. But the year is also incorrect because the one birth certificate that survives for any of Ernst's siblings shows that his younger brother Moritz was born on 28 November 1814. If the day and month on Ernst's tomb is correct, then this implies that Moritz had a gestation of only five months, and that is clearly impossible.

In what year therefore was he born? His English marriage certificate says he was 41 on 31 July 1854 which would imply that he was born between 1 August 1812 and 31 July 1813. If we couple this fact with the information on the grave, the two together would suggest that Ernst was born on 8 June 1813. However, there are difficulties with this proposal. First, Jewish birth certificates were issued in Brünn from February 1813, yet no certificate survives for Ernst. Second, on the marriage certificate, Ernst's wife, whose birth certificate does survive, reduces her own age by a year, and Ernst, as I remarked in Chapter 1, elevated his father's status. These minor fibs may imply that the couple did not consider it particularly important to supply full and accurate information for a certificate in a distant land, many years after the events referred to. [MC]

The obvious reason why Ernst reduced his age is that he was a prodigy, and the younger he claimed to be the more money he was likely to make. It hardly seems worthwhile to reduce your age by only a year (the fathers of Paganini and Clara Schumann reduced their children's ages by two) and the slim, pale and slightly-built Ernst could certainly have passed for 14 when he was 16. This pressure to be young, coupled with the absence of a birth certificate and unreliability of the marriage certificate, make me think that Ernst was actually born on 8 June 1812, and was therefore nearly two years older than is normally thought.

The only hint we get as to his parents' characters is Leone's remark that 'Ernst …. received from his father his earnest disposition and careful diligence, and from his mother, a Slav, his supple figure and love of music …' [EOC:20] Leone is right about Charlotte's Slavic origins (he is the only early source to mention this) and it therefore seems reasonable to believe him about the qualities Ernst inherited from his parents. Ernst's father and grandfather were amongst those forced to select a German surname, and 'Ernst', i.e. *serious* in German, would certainly seem appropriate to this family.

Jakob's *Sperre-relation* describes his second wife, Charlotte, as 'pre-deceased' in 1835, and there is also no mention of her in his will drawn up in August 1828. We can thus be fairly confident that she was already dead by that date. The only other document to mention her name is Moritz's birth certificate, and she is not referred to in any article about Ernst or any of his surviving letters. Ernst was an emotional, family-centred man, and one would expect him to be attached to his mother, especially if she died while he was a boy, and he inherited his musical ability from her. I suspect he says nothing about his mother because he never knew her, and that she died shortly after Moritz was born. Giving birth was clearly one of the most dangerous times in any woman's life in the early nineteenth century, and in Chapter 19 I shall consider some reasons why it may have been especially dangerous for her.

Katherina, Jakob's oldest child from his first marriage, married a brandy dealer called Popper before she was seventeen and continued to live in Brünn. [AMB] Her signature can be found on a legal document in 1817, but she is not mentioned in Jakob's will in 1828, and her name does not appear on the list of surviving children on Jakob's *Sperre-relation* in 1835. It seems likely that she died before 1828. Joseph, the eldest son, traded in wool, before becoming a wine merchant in the family's home territory of Neu Rausnitz.

I suspect that the child born on 4 July 1796, and referred to as Samuel on Barbara's *Sperre-relation*, later became known as Nathan. The name Samuel occurs on no other document, but a son called Nathan is mentioned on his father's will and *Sperre-relation* even though there is no record of his birth. His death certificate shows that Nathan, a 'midwife and wound-dresser in Lundenburg', died at 54 of 'hardening of the liver' in the family home in Der Grosse Kröna on 12 May 1849. This means he should have been born in 1794–95 when Jakob was married to Barbara, although this is apparently not mentioned on her *Sperre-relation*. If we allow for a little uncertainty about his age on the part of his family, then this makes it fairly likely that Samuel and Nathan are one and the same.

Johann was the half-brother most closely associated with Ernst so I shall discuss him further below. For the moment I shall merely note that Johann ran the family café after his father became infirm in 1828.

Marianna, Franziska and Adolph, the oldest of Ernst's immediate brothers and sisters, are described as 'of the age of majority' on Jacob's *Sperre-relation* of March 1835. The age of majority at this period was 24, so all must have been born between 1805 and March 1811. The entry about Adolph on the document is hard to decipher but it appears to read 'at Karl [?] Infantry Regiment at Wels [?] ...' In his will of 1828, Jakob also leaves money to a son called Joachim. This bequest is placed immediately below Adolph's on the list, and he is therefore likely to be the next oldest. However, he is not mentioned on the list of surviving children in 1835 and had probably died between the two dates. The same documents show that Franziska and Marianna were living at 58 Der Grosse Kröna in 1835. [AMB] In 1837, Ernst says in a letter, 'I wrote to ... dear sister Fanny in Pest', [EOC:6] probably implying that Franziska had moved permanently to Hungary – possibly after marriage.

Ernst's only sibling with any claim to fame is his younger brother Moritz. He emigrated to Hungary where he initially worked for a wholesaler named Conin in Aeratz, and then became a journalist. Later, he married the well-known singer Josephine Kayser who changed her name to Ernst-Kayser on marriage. Their son, also called Heinrich (no doubt in tribute to his famous and musical uncle), was born in Dresden in 1846 and died in Berlin in 1919. He became a highly successful singer, particularly associated with Bizet and Wagner, in the last quarter of the century.[2] [GSL:II:1049]

No information about Ernst's early childhood survives.[3] We must therefore imagine the small, pale boy playing in the fast-flowing but shallow Svitava river at the end of his street; watching the willow pollen blowing through the town; queuing to pass through the Jewish gate to get to the Vegetable Market (which also sold bread and meat in Ernst's time); causing his family anxiety by playing in the wide road outside the café; lying awake at night listening to ferocious summer thunder storms; being abused by older Christian boys; listening to vivid tales told by survivors from Austerlitz and Wagram; watching the house-martins in the Large Square; and trying to help in the café and having his hair ruffled by regulars.

He was certainly fascinated by music. Berlioz – later one of Ernst's best musical friends – tells us that he first came to love the violin at the age of nine through attending lessons given to his elder brothers (presumably Adolf and Joachim). [JD:27/1/52] His first teacher (and in all likelihood his brothers' too) was a baker called Sommer [EOC:4], and as one Johann Sommer witnessed the inventory of Barbara Ernst's will in October 1805, we can assume he was an old friend of the family, possibly a neighbour or business associate of Jakob's. [AMB] Ernst quickly showed remarkable talent and rapidly overtook his brothers.

---

2   Ernst appears to be no relation of the Bohemian violinist and composer Franz Anton (František Antonin) Ernst (1745-1805).

3   At the height of his fame, a number of fanciful stories circulated about Ernst's early career. One, recorded in Wurzbach, is that his grandfather, a famous violinist, had had to escape from the rubble of Seville (it is not explained why Seville was in ruins) and emigrated to Brünn. After hearing Paganini, Ernst took his grandfather's violin and, with the blessing of his grandmother, fled from the parental home to pursue his ambitions. [BLKO:IV:74] Distant knowledge of Franz Anton Ernst (see note 2) may have encouraged parts of this legend.

His progress was further enhanced by coming across a copy of Leopold Mozart's *Versuch einer grünlichen Violinschule* [*A Treatise on the Fundamental Principles of Violin Playing*] during his first year of study. [JD:27/1/52] This work, first published in 1756 and later issued in new and expanded editions in 1769–70 and 1787, established Leopold Mozart as one of the leading authorities on the violin, and contained one of the fullest and most complete account of violin playing then available. [GMV:112] Under its guidance, Ernst would have adopted a relatively modern bow grip, cultivated a judicious use of vibrato, and developed a deep respect of the classical Italian school of the eighteenth century. [GMV:84–6] Within a year or two of starting, Ernst's technique and musicianship were enough deeply to impress Leonhard, Brünn's leading violin teacher and a violinist well known in the area for his public concerts, who immediately took him on as a pupil. [EOC:4. E:9. JD:27/1/52]

There was no Jewish school in Brünn in the early nineteenth century, and Ernst, in accordance with the Toleration Edict, was sent to a Christian foundation. He was extremely lucky in that the local Christian school was run by the Augustinian Monastery of St Thomas, a remarkable institution that was a centre for advanced ideas in theology and science. [LJV:37. LJH:26. See Plate II.] Several of its most distinguished members were in residence when Ernst was a pupil. The priest, Philipp Nedele, ran into severe trouble with the authorities for publishing works that were thought to be fundamentally Protestant in outlook. In 1816, he was deprived of his income from these books, and in 1821, of his teaching duties. With all possible sources of income closed, he fell into debt, and died a broken man at the age of 47. [DML:30–36] The distinguished biologist and mathematician, A. Thaler, was also employed at the monastery, and grew Moravian plants in the experimental garden below the refectory windows. He died in 1843, and his work was inherited by Gregor Mendel, one of the greatest scientists of the nineteenth century, and the monastery's chief intellectual ornament. [GM:49]

This intense intellectual atmosphere was fostered by a theologian and philosopher from Olmütz, called F.C. Napp, who was appointed Abbot in 1824. Besides his scientific and theological interests, Napp was a passionate musician who played quartets regularly [LJV:36–8], and he thus took a deep personal interest in the monastery's music school. This school was founded and endowed by Countess Sibylla Polyxena of Montana (*née* Thurn-Wallesessin) in 1648, on the model of the Italian conservatoire or orphanage. All the boys wore a uniform of light blue with a white border (which made the citizens of Brünn nickname them 'Blue-boys') except on festive occasions when they wore long red coats with gold-edged collars.

Entry for musical children was by competitive examination – the standard was very high – and most boys entered between the ages of nine and twelve. Local musicians were brought in to teach them. [LJV:37. LJH:25] A probable chronology, therefore, is that Ernst was taught the violin by Sommer for about a year, after which he passed the audition for the monastery and was then taught by the more professional Leonhard from the ages of 10 to 13. His progress was certainly impressive because his first recorded public concert was on 24 March 1824 when he played two works by Mayseder at the National Theatre in Brünn [JP:E:9], and he performed again on 14 July 1825 just before he went to Vienna. [BMB:E:9] In a short biographical sketch printed by the *Morning Post* in 1843, Ernst apparently said that he first appeared in public at the age of 12. If he remembered the year, but was a little hazy about the exact date, this lends support to the idea he was born in 1812. [ME:22/7/1843:279]

The education on offer – both generally and musically – was exhausting and exhaustive. Jaroslav Vogel summarizes documents describing the boys' musical lives in the 1820s as follows:

> 'Blue-boys' were known throughout Brno. Their 'harmony' [wind-bands] welcomed ministers (Count Kolowrat) and other dignitaries (Count Žerotín). High state officials invited them to give 'Nocturnes' [evening concerts] and 'Academies' [daytime concerts]. They helped out in the theatre, in the orchestra, on the conductor's rostrum and on the stage. They accompanied burials of persons of rank with funeral marches. No church-choir could dispense with their services. A high standard was required for admission. For instance, Hoffmann from Zlín could play the trumpet, flute, violin, viola and organ at the time of his admission, while Matouš David from Skalice near Červený Kostelec could play the horn, trumpet, viola, flute, organ and double-bassoon.
>
> Boys were admitted between the ages of 9 and 12. (There were exceptions to this rule: Křížkovsy [Janáček's teacher], for instance, was admitted as a novice in 1843 long after he had completed his ordinary schooling.) The boys formed a band consisting of 2 oboes, 2 clarinets, 2 horns, 2 clarinos [trumpets], 2 bassoons and a double-bassoon. Where necessary, flutes, trombones and timpani were added. There were six violins. At a celebration in honour of the deputy director, the abbot Cyrill Frantisek Napp, Beethoven's symphony in C major [No.1] was performed by an orchestra of seventy 'men.' The most frequently played composers were Mozart, Cherubini, Rossini and Haydn. And you may wonder at the efficiency of the Blue-boys: according to one document, the largest-scale Mass in existence, Cherubini's *Coronation Mass* was learnt in the short period between 19th and 24th September, 1827. Beethoven's Mass, *Eroica* Symphony and 'Coriolan' Overture were performed in 1828.The overture to Weber's *Oberon* and a Mozart Quintet were played [at] sight. Mozart's *Don Giovanni*, Auber's *La Muette de Portici* and *Fra Diavolo* and Méhul's *Joseph and his Brethren* were produced in 1830. One of the ladies in Mozart's *Magic Flute* was sung by a Blue-boy. How much musical education was necessary to accomplish all this! Every day the pupils practised singing and playing the piano as well as their own instrument. There was training in quartet playing as well as other ensemble classes. Special teachers taught figured bass, counterpoint, violin, horn and piano. The charges were 30 *kreutzers* per hour. Tricks and dodges in handling wind instruments were passed from one boy to another. There is a long tradition of wind instrument playing in Bohemia and Moravia.
>
> The Blue-boys played at the most distinguished balls, and daily 'played the roast' at the refectory lunch; everyday at table and every Sunday in praise of God, in addition to all their other music-making. One's astonishment grows when one considers that every Blue-boy was either studying philosophy and logic, classics, grammar or a normal school course and that here also he was obliged to show satisfactory progress. In the 1830's a clarinet-playing student of philosophy composed several operas in collaboration with an oboist and a double-bassoonist. [LJV:36–7]

Ernst was a sufficiently good pianist to think at one stage of making it his main instrument; he was a fine improviser, and his major instrumental works were widely praised because of their expert orchestration. Much of this ability must be put down to the breadth and excellence of his early musical education. In addition to Ernst, the music school's most famous pupils were Leoš Janáček and Wilhelmina Neruda, later Lady Hallé, who owned Ernst's Stradivarius after his death.

For pupils, the regime was spartan. Boarders were woken at 5 am; from then until 6.45 there were prayers and study. At 7 am Mass was said. From then until lunch at noon, there was ordinary schooling. After lunch, there was a short walk followed by further study until singing practice at 6 pm. This continued until 7 pm when supper was served. A short free period was followed by prayers and bed. [LJV:38] Janáček, recalled feeling 'guarded but neglected', but said he never lost the iron discipline and capacity for hard work which the monastery instilled. [JLR:22]

Between six and thirteen pupils received free board, lodging and medical care, the others had to pay 100 florins a year. School fees, textbooks and more expensive extras had to be paid for by parents and guardians. It is not known whether Ernst's father paid for his education. He was reported to have had trouble finding the 30 kreutzers a week for his violin lessons so paying school fees is unlikely (unless of course that is the reason why he could not find the 30 kreutzers). [LJV:36–7] It is also not clear whether Ernst was a boarder. On the one hand, the monastery is within easy walking distance of Der Grosse Kröna, on the other, if board and lodging were free, his father may have been grateful that someone else now fed and cared for him. Given a poor but outstandingly talented boy, the rational arrangement would be to have him live at home and waive the fees for his tuition. This solution would have been additionally attractive given that, as a Jew, Ernst did not attend the prayers and masses early and late in the day.

Amely Heller tells us that the Ernst children were 'well brought up and distinguished by great family feeling and love for parents, children, brothers, and sisters'. [EOC:4] This is certainly borne out by the evidence. Ernst frequently brought his famous artistic friends, including Joachim, to stay with his family. Nathan was looked after by Johann in his last illness, and Ernst said he loved Nathan with all his heart. [BAL:I:117] In 1848, Ernst stayed at 58 Der Grosse Kröna for most of the year, and when he too became critically ill, he stayed there for several months in 1858.

It is notable that Leone does not say that Jakob had any musical interests, and Saphir reports that there was tension between Ernst and his father about the son's musical career. This is confirmed by Jakob's will: some money is left to Joseph and Nathan from his first marriage (even though they received money from his first wife's estate), and all the sons and daughters of his second, but Ernst is left nothing, not even something of sentimental value. Ernst is only included in the general injunction: 'As I leave behind sons, who are still minors, I summon them to come to the eldest son [in Brünn] Johann [who has been left the property at 58 Der [Grosse] Kröna].' Given the harsh commercial circumstances of Jakob's life, and his earnest, diligent character, it seems predictable that he and Ernst would not get on. However, despite the level of offence disinheritance implies, it was his elderly father who took him to the Conservatory in Vienna when he finished at the monastery in 1825.

Ernst's closest family relationship was with his youngest half-brother, Johann, who was thirteen years his senior. Johann married Caroline (1816–73) in about 1835, even though his eldest brother Joseph was already married. [NJC] This was possible because, in the years prior to 1848, the Familiant Law in Moravia was relaxed to allow a second son to marry, largely to stem massive Jewish emigration to Hungary. Nathan had first refusal but clearly indicated he had no wish to marry, and may have seen that a wife was necessary to help run the family business. Johann survived his wife by only a month, dying in Brünn on 18 May 1873, just before his seventy-fourth birthday. [NJC]

The only letters from Ernst to his family which survive are to Johann, and their joy, boastfulness and elan, suggest a genuine bond of sympathy. Johann visited Ernst on his travels, and he seems to have been an easygoing, agreeable fellow. Ernst's letters show that his brother was able to mix on familiar terms with members of royal households, had a sly sense of humour, was deeply responsive to music, wore opulent cravats, enjoyed cigars, and put too many seals on his letters. In later years, as these habits hint, he was clearly extravagant, and relied on his successful younger brother for much of his daily living expenses. Johann in his turn was clearly very proud of his brother. He lovingly saved his letters and reviews, and made the café a concert venue in the early 1830s, in celebration, no doubt, of his younger half-brother's fame and success.

It is not difficult, given Johann's winning character, to see why this bond between the brothers might have formed. If a boy comes to know his father when the father is already in his sixties and seventies, then it would not be surprising if the boy found him remote. This would be especially likely if the older man grew up in harsher circumstances, and shared none of the son's artistic outlook or interests. If, in addition, he had never known his musical mother, then it is foreseeable that a close bond would form with a genial music-loving half-brother who was constantly around the house and in his late teens and early twenties. He would seem to have a father's competence, with none of the father's responsibilities and distance.

Chapter 3

Vienna: 1825–28

After such rapid progress and such a degree of local success, it was natural that Ernst should begin to look beyond Brünn, and Leonhard approached his pupil's family, suggesting that he be sent to study at the Conservatoire founded by the Viennese Gesellschaft der Musikfreunde [Society of the Friends of Music].[1] [JD:17/1/52] Originally set up as a singing academy in 1817, the Conservatoire soon began to expand its range of teaching, and in 1819, Joseph Michael Böhm was able to announce in the *Wiener Musikzeitung* that he had been appointed as their first professor of violin. [JJ:17] By 1825, he was one of the most celebrated violin teachers in the Empire, and in the early months of that year his reputation as a performer was being enhanced by frequent and laudatory reviews of his quartet performances.

According to one obituary, Ernst was taken to see Böhm by his father. As I suggested in Chapter 2, I suspect Jakob's help was grudging; perhaps he was a little overawed and flattered by Leonhard and the grandees at the monastery. The obituary continues with a statement which confirms Ernst's extraordinary progress under his teachers in Brünn: 'Böhm, an amiable man, full of enthusiasm for his art, soon perceived how great a future was in store for the boy, and acknowledged that, though the latter might learn music from him, he was already nearly his equal in practical skill.' [NBMZ:MW:4/11/1865:690] Unfortunately no documents exist to tell us about Ernst's progress and experiences, but it is possible to deduce a certain amount from the character of his teachers and the main musical currents in Vienna at the time.

Böhm was born in Pesth in 1795, and studied with his father, the leader of the theatre orchestra. His lessons continued when he moved with his father to Poland in 1803, and four years later, when Pierre Rode met him on returning from Russia, the distinguished French violinist was impressed by the boy's talent and offered to give him lessons. Rode, who was a pupil of Viotti, was famous for the dexterity of his left hand and the flexibility and elegance of his bowing, and he clearly passed these virtues on to his pupil. [F:I:469–70] Joachim, recalling Böhm's playing, said: 'Based on an unfailing left hand and ideally smooth bowing, Böhm possessed an art of phrasing that enabled him to realize anything that he envisioned or felt.' [G1:VI:839]

---

1   Berlioz writes: 'Le premier professeur de la ville de Brünn le prit alors pour élève, et biantôt après conseilla à ses paren[t]s de l'envoyer au Conservatoire de Vienne.' [JD:27/1/52] This use of 'parents' may seem to throw doubt on my suggestion that Ernst's mother died in 1814. In fact, 'parents' in French can mean relatives as well as parents, so Berlioz's sentence neither confirms nor denies the hypothesis.

In 1815, Böhm moved to Vienna, where he made his debut in 1816, playing during an entr'acte at the Court Theatre, and his success encouraged him to settle in the capital. A few years later he embarked on an extended and successful tour of Italy, which included a performance at La Scala Milan, with the pianist Johann Peter Pixis. On his return, he was appointed to the Conservatoire (a post which he held until 1848), and discovered that the most celebrated quartet leader in Vienna – Ignaz Schuppanzigh, a close associate of Beethoven's – had departed for a tour of Russia. Böhm assumed the leader's position in Schuppanzigh's quartet (in which Holz played second violin, Weiss viola and Linke, cello) and took over the quartet performances held at the Erstekaffeehaus in the Prater-allee, held at 8 o'clock in the morning. The excellence of these performances led the *Musikzeitung* of 1821 to exclaim: 'This is the way that Beethoven's and Mozart's quartets should be played!' [JJ:18] During the 1820s in particular he enjoyed a very considerable reputation as a quartet player and soloist (where contemporaries were surprised to note that he played from memory) and in 1823–25 he toured as a virtuoso in Germany and France. From 1827 onwards, he seems to have largely withdrawn from the public platform, partly through nervousness, and confined himself to teaching and playing in the Court orchestra, a position he held from 1821 to 1867. He died in Vienna in 1876.

Böhm was an outstanding teacher, and part of his reason for his withdrawal from concert life must have been a realization that this was where his true talents lay. A glance at the list of his pupils – Ernst, Joachim, Reményi, Singer, Grün, Hellmesberger the elder, Ludwig Straus, Jacob Dont, amongst others – suggests that he, even more than Leopold Auer, deserves to be considered the greatest violin teacher in history. Joachim was Böhm's private pupil fifteen years after Ernst, but we can still get a good impression of Böhm's personality and method from Joachim's remarks to his biographer.

Although severe, earnest and matter of fact, Böhm was also kind and encouraging. He was particularly keen, as one would expect a pupil of Rode's to be, on bow control. To facilitate this, he made extensive use of works by Mayseder and Rode – particularly the latter's *Caprices*. He also laid special stress on the use of violin duets as a teaching method, a device which he felt improved intonation and ensemble playing. Often, nothing but duets would be played for months together, and one slightly younger contemporary of Ernst's – Grünwald – reports growing thoroughly tired of them. [JJ:21–2] Böhm was happy for advanced pupils to extend their technique by studying the most recent virtuoso compositions, but to prevent virtuosity becoming an end in itself he held evenings of quartet-playing at his own small house. Ernst played in these events, and Joachim later said that they were amongst his own fondest memories.

Böhm and his wife had no children, and they appear to have adopted a parental attitude – at once affectionate and chaffing – to his pupils, often young and far from home. Although not a musician, Frau Böhm would supervise the young Joachim's practice when her husband was out, shouting through from the other room, 'Peperl [Joachim's nickname], you know that wasn't good! It should sound better than that. You must practise that passage over and over again …' Or sometimes Böhm himself would come through the glass door saying, 'You little scoundrel! Will you play that properly?' [JJ:22–4] Joachim and Böhm always held one another in greatest affection, and a similarly strong bond existed between Böhm and Ernst. When in London in 1844, Joachim wrote to his old teacher: 'I am glad, for your sake, that you will see your dear Ernst this winter. Now that I have the honour of knowing him myself I can easily understand your affection for him; he really is the most charming person imaginable and certainly the greatest virtuoso.' [LJJ:1] Ernst evidently held Böhm in a similar regard since he did not dedicate a piece to him immediately, but saved one of his most splendid and durable compositions – his *Otello Fantasy* – for this purpose.

The Böhms were a tolerant couple. Frau Böhm was a strict Catholic, and would occasionally and good-naturedly complain about the strenuous time her confessor had given her for allowing a Jew to lodge with them: 'I say Peperl, I had such a sermon again today for housing a heathen like you; but never mind, practise like a good boy, and we will answer to God for the rest.' [JJ:23] Böhm appears to have been less pious but equally liberal. He had no qualms about teaching Jews, and many of his most famous pupils (including Ernst, Joachim and Grün) were of Jewish origin. He also tapped into one other hitherto unexploited source of violinistic talent: Böhm was the first Hungarian violinist of note, and it is striking that several of his pupils were not only of Hungarian origin (Joachim, Grün, and Reményi, for example) but also did much to popularize the Hungarian musical idiom. Ernst, Joachim and Reményi fall into this class. Reményi's Hungarian nationalism went far enough for him to change his name from Hoffmann, and take part in the fighting with Austria in 1848.

Shortly before Ernst's arrival in Vienna, Böhm's quartet had given the second performance of the first of Beethoven's late quartets – the one in E♭, op.127. Schuppanzigh had returned to Vienna and resumed leadership of his quartet in 1823, and they had given the premiere of the first new Beethoven quartet for fifteen years on 6 March 1825. It was a mere *succès d'estime*. Beethoven blamed Schuppanzigh and asked Böhm to lead another performance. This time, the work was much more successful, and the same group of performers went on to play it at two further concerts – on 23 March and 7 April. The latter was a benefit concert for Böhm himself. As at the concert on 23 March, the only item on the programme was op.127 played *twice* – a programming innovation designed to give the public a better understanding of such advanced and unfamiliar music. Within a month, therefore, Böhm had led five public performances of the work. The critic of the *Theater Zeitung* commented on Böhm's light touch, and said that the performances had significantly added to his fame. It is also highly likely that Böhm also gave the premiere of Beethoven's last quartet op.135 on 23 March 1828. Schuppanzigh was announced as leader, but he was ill at the end of March, and Böhm took over at least one other of his concerts. [DS:752]

Not only was Böhm involved with Beethoven, but he was a close associate of Schubert. In 1821, Schubert had been elected to the Gesellschaft der Musikfreunde [FS:76], and he was spending more and more time socializing with professional musicians. Böhm was one of a group of musicians who met him regularly at a tavern called the Oak Tree, where they drank, talked, and arranged musical engagements. [FS:295–6] As a result of this friendship, the Böhm quartet gave the premiere of the late G major quartet's first movement at the only benefit concert ever held for Schubert on 26 March 1828. Later in the programme, Böhm, Linke, and the pianist Karl Maria von Bocklet gave the first public performance of the E♭ piano trio op.100. [DS:753] After Schubert's death, the same players repeated the trio as part of a concert on 30 January 1829 to raise money for the composer's memorial. [DS:851]

Böhm's friendship with both Beethoven and Schubert was unusual since they had very few friends in common. Beethoven's milieu was aristocratic, while Schubert's friends tended to be middle-class young men employed by the Austrian bureaucracy. In addition, in 1825 they were far from being the most popular composers in Vienna. From 1814 onwards, family crises and illnesses severely affected Beethoven's creativity, and he was widely regarded as written out. In 1821, the *Allgemeine Musikalische Zeitung* asserted: 'Beethoven now occupies himself, as once did Papa Haydn, with the arrangement of Scottish folksongs; he is apparently quite incapable of greater accomplishments.' [BSQ:4] The few pieces he did write were regarded as difficult and incoherent, and ready explanations were found in his deafness and increasing eccentricity. Many of his aristocratic patrons had died or gone bankrupt by the 1820s, and the revolutionary message of freedom in the ninth symphony, or the religious emotions of the *Missa Solemnis* found little sympathy amongst the jaded, reactionary, and pleasure-loving Viennese. In 1820, a performance of the seventh symphony attracted fifty people. [BM:460]

If Beethoven had lost his audience, then Schubert had never really found it. He could not make his name known to the public as a virtuoso instrumentalist, and his work had not succeeded in the all-important area of the theatre. He was shy and retiring in public, and at the same time slightly awkward and tactless with authority. These traits, together with his youth, prevented him from holding any important official positions. Consequently, when he died in 1828, Schubert was known almost exclusively as a writer for domestic contexts, especially of dances and songs. It would be twenty years before his symphonies and chamber works became widely known, and it would take another century for the world to discover his piano sonatas.

Ernst's other violin teacher – Joseph Mayseder – was also known to Beethoven and Schubert. He was not a member of the Conservatoire, and he did not hold any other teaching position. He was therefore obliged to support himself through public performances and taking private pupils. These flocked to him and he was forced to turn many away. Unsurprisingly, Ernst managed to be accepted, but it does not appear that his study with Mayseder was intense or prolonged. One of Ernst's obituaries notes that he 'profited from the example and advice of Mayseder,' which suggests a briefer, more distant relationship than those he enjoyed with Böhm and Seyfried. [NMZ:MW:11/11/65:704] Mayseder, however, was the most experienced and successful instrumental performer amongst his teachers, and no doubt offered the kind of advice that would allow an advanced student to shine.

Mayseder had been born, the son of an impoverished painter, in October 1789. The first intimation that he might be a violinist was that, as a child, he frequently used to amuse himself by picking up two sticks and pretending he was playing the violin. After early lessons from Suche and Wranitzky, he caught the attention of Schuppanzigh under whose auspices he gave his first concert in 1800. He was the second violin in Schuppanzigh's quartet between 1804 and 1808. At the same time he seems to have led quartets himself at the home of the Hungarian Imperial Secretary, Nicholas Zmeskall von Domanovecz. These occasions allowed him to get to know Beethoven who was always deeply complimentary about his playing. As a consequence, Beethoven invited Mayseder to take part in one of his own concerts on 2 December 1808, and a manuscript letter still exists in which Beethoven thanks the young violinist for his services. In October 1814, already well known, he led the violin section in the first performance of Schubert's Mass in F at the church of Lichtenthal in Vienna. In 1816, he was made chamber virtuoso at St Stephen's Cathedral and at the Opera, and on 15 and probably 29 April 1825 he gave two double performances of the newly composed op.127 under Beethoven's direction. He became concertmaster to the Imperial Chapel, one of Vienna's most privileged positions, in 1835. Mayseder died in 1864. In his last moments, the dying man imitated playing a violin, just as he had when a child. Like Böhm, he seems to have been a man of simplicity and charm. In his house near the centre of the city, he enjoyed a happy family life, and his carefully exploited talent allowed him to live comfortably and amass a modest fortune. [R:MW:2/1/64:5]

His was a more public career than Böhm's, and as a violinist he seems to have had a slightly more forceful personality. Holz, Schuppanzigh's second violin, makes a revealing comment in one of Beethoven's conversation books. Discussing with the composer who should lead the E♭ quartet after Schuppanzigh's unsuccessful premiere, he writes: 'I believe that Mayseder would play it better – he leads the other three while Böhm lets them lead him.' [BSQ:229] He had a brilliantly piquant style, deft and graceful, with a particularly fine staccato. It was a manner of playing that the Viennese loved, and which contemporaries found particularly well suited to the works of Haydn and Mozart. Later, and unsurprisingly, Mendelssohn would also become one of his favourites. For some, however, his style lacked breadth and power, and more severe critics found it deficient in emotional charge. Hanslick wrote: '[The] beauty and purity of his tone, the sureness and elegance of his performance were fit to form a standard – one could only wish there were more warmth and energy of expression.' Weber was more pithy: 'A fine player, but he leaves one cold.' [CV:70]

In one other respect he resembles the mature Böhm – he did not want to travel or assert himself in other parts of Europe. 'It is much to be regretted,' writes his obiturist, 'that his bashfulness, or we ought almost to call it, his timidity, prevented his making any professional tours …' [R:MW:2/1/1864:5] Only once did he overcome his disinclination. This was when a pupil, Vincent Neuling, persuaded Mayseder to accompany him to Paris in 1820. Here he twice played in private before some of the leading French violinists and musicians, and more than justified his Viennese reputation. [R:MW:2/1/64:5]

Unlike Böhm, whose few pieces are not significant, Mayseder was highly regarded as a composer. Even though, for example, the Philharmonic Society in London only gave eight concerts a year, twenty-four performances of Mayseder's compositions are recorded between 1822 and 1849. [HPSL:569–70] Ernst played several of Mayseder's celebrated polonaises early on, and kept the Variations in E in his repertoire until the end of his career. Like Mayseder's playing, the pieces are charming, lyrical and lightweight: they treat the instruments idiomatically and are well constructed, but they lack the originality and force necessary to maintain their position in the repertoire.

Ernst's other teacher at the conservatoire was Ignaz Seyfried with whom he studied composition. Seyfried had been taught the piano by Mozart and Kozeluch and composition under Winter and Albrechtsberger (one of Beethoven's teachers). In 1792–93 he read for a philosophy degree in Prague with the intention of taking up law, but eventually opted for a musical career. This turned out well, and by 1797 he was a conductor in Schikaneder's Freihaus-Theater. (Schikaneder was the librettist of Mozart's *The Magic Flute*.) Four of Seyfried's scores appear amongst the twelve most frequently performed works at this venue, and later, when he worked at the Theater an der Wien, it is estimated that his music was heard there on 1,700 evenings. His first score *Der Friede* was given in May 1797 and his last in 1827 – although he continued to arrange and write occasional music for other theatres. In addition to his theatrical work, he composed symphonies, concertos, chamber music, and twenty mass settings; published several works of musical pedagogy, and wrote regularly for newspapers and music journals. As a teacher, his most famous pupils were Franz von Suppé, and Eduard Marxsen, teacher of Brahms.

Although very popular in its day, his music lacked the distinction to keep it in the regular repertoire, and he is now chiefly remembered for his friendship and collaboration with Beethoven whom he seems to have first met in 1800. [BIHC:35] Beethoven was a regular attender at the Theater an der Wien where he particularly enjoyed the works of Cherubini and Méhul [BIHC:40], and it is possible they first encountered one another there. By 1805 their relationship was sufficiently close and respectful for Beethoven to entrust Seyfried with the premiere of *Fidelio*. Although their intimacy seems to have ended around 1806, Seyfried later wrote a series of reminiscences of the composer, and was one of the eight eminent musicians (including Hummel and Kreutzer) selected to be pallbearers at Beethoven's funeral on 29 March 1827. Böhm, Schuppanzigh, Mayseder, Schubert and thirty-two others followed as torchbearers [BLD:85], while behind the torchbearers came a group of students from the Conservatoire. As all of Ernst's teachers were at the head of the procession, and he was one of their most outstandingly gifted students, it is probable that he followed them.

It is not difficult to imagine the effect that Vienna's musical atmosphere had on a young and intensely ambitious student. From taking up the violin under the guidance of a local baker in provincial Brünn a few years before, he was now at the very centre of musical culture. The atmosphere must have been heady. His teachers – who in some ways treated him as a friend, equal, and chamber music partner – were outstandingly talented in their own right, and on intimate terms with the greatest composers of the day – or any day. During the years when they taught Ernst, Böhm and Mayseder were meeting Schubert and Beethoven and giving early performances of some of their finest and most original last works.

The figure of Beethoven is particularly pervasive. Every one of Ernst's teachers was involved with the composer, and we know that Ernst was also partnered in quartets by Holz, Linke, Merk and others who gave early performances of the later chamber works. Ernst certainly venerated his memory for the rest of his life. Besides playing the violin sonatas regularly, and making the late quartets known throughout

Europe, he collected Beethoven memorabilia. In the Library of Congress there is a sheet of the corrected manuscript of Beethoven's piano sonata op.111 which was once owned by Ernst. More importantly, Ernst bought the Heilingenstadt Testament from Liszt in 1843, eventually presenting it to Jenny Lind and her husband Otto Goldschmidt in 1855 as a sign of his friendship and admiration.

Ernst's first public appearance in Vienna took place on 1 September 1825. [GCW:240. E:12] This was at the Karntnerthortheater during one of the Conservatoire's examination concerts. He must have made a good impression since on 30 October and 6 November he played again, and on at least one of these occasions played a set of variations by Mayseder. On 15 December he played a set of variations by Rode at the Gesellschaft der Musikfreunde, and in August 1826 he stunned the audience when, after only ten months under Böhm's tutelage, he played Mayseder's Variations in E at a final examination concert.[ADB:VI:325–7. E:11] After this performance, he was awarded the Conservatoire's first prize.[2]

Ernst's reputation must have spread very quickly because his name soon appears on the programmes of professional concerts that were unconnected with the Conservatoire. On 23 February 1827, Leon de Saint-Lubin, Kapellmeister of the Josephstadt Theatre, gave a concert in the smaller hall of the Redoutensaal, featuring Ernst, and two other young violinists. [AMZ:12/4/1826:Col.248. E:13] This is the first time that Ernst achieved some measure of international recognition since the concert was also reported in a British music magazine, *The Harmonicon*: 'On this occasion, besides the youth Aloys Schwartz, two others of nearly his age, of the name of Ernst and Wehle, displayed their talents on the violin; they all promise to become virtuosi of eminence in their profession, and display not only much power of bow, but also considerable taste and feeling.' [H:8/1826:171]

On 5 March, Ernst performed Mayseder's Rondeau for violin at a concert for the poor at the Apollo-Saal [AMZ:3/5/1826:Col.302. E:13], and on 6 April 1826 he gave a most successful performance of Lafont's sixth concerto at the hall of the Muikvereins. [AMZ:31/5/1826:Col.358–9. E:13] In the choice of this concerto, one sees the powerful French influence transmitted through his teachers. Lafont was probably the most celebrated French violinist of his day, the player who first replaced Rode in Russia, and later in the esteem of the French public.

Audiences continued to be impressed when, eight months later, Ernst played Böhm's concerto at a concert for the Gesellschaft der Musikfreunde on 10 December 1826, and probably a concerto by Rode at the Landhassal on 18 February 1827. [ADB:VI:325–7. GCW:240. E:13] At a concert in the autumn of 1827, he played the violin part in a performance in one of Mayseder's piano trios. This too was noticed by the *Harmonicon*:

> In a concert given by Professor Hackel, Mayseder's celebrated trio in B, was performed, in which Henry Ernst, a pupil of the Conservatory, executed the violin part with a brilliancy and force of expression, that called forth universal admiration. We understand that this young artist, who is only in his fourteenth year, is studying composition under

---

2   Ernst told Berlioz that he won the first prize after six months in Böhm's class. [JD:27/1/52] This seems like an understandable retrospective exaggeration.

Kapellmeister Seyfried, and affords the most promising hopes of future excellence. [H:1827:211]

Occasionally, Ernst would return to Brünn, and there are records of a concert there on 8 March 1828. [JP:88, 93–4. E:14] He was clearly establishing an impressive reputation, but – inevitably for such a young man – it was a reputation still largely confined to the Vienna area, and still largely shaped by his teachers' tastes and ambitions. But on 29 March 1828 any provinciality in his outlook was shattered: Paganini appeared at the Redoutensaal.

The Italian's name and reputation were not wholly new to the Viennese. For at least a decade, travellers from Italy had been reporting the existence of an extraordinary violinist who performed inconceivable wonders on his instrument. His reputation was sufficient to bring Kreutzer from Paris and Lipinski from Poland to hear him, and both Böhm and Mayseder had met him and heard him perform when they played in Italy. In addition, the Viennese could have gained some idea of his genius from his *Caprices* (the only virtuoso pieces he published in his lifetime) which Riccordi had issued in 1820, but their technical demands were so obviously absurd that they were dismissed as a publicity stunt. Consequently, nothing quite prepared the musical world of northern Europe for his impact: he struck like a planet.

Of all the breathless accounts written by astonished members of his first audiences, perhaps the best is that left by Jacques Rosenhain, a pianist and composer from Baden-Baden (and later a friend of Ernst's) who first heard Paganini in Frankfurt in 1830:

> I cannot describe to you the impression his playing made on me. I trembled in every part of my body as though I were standing in the presence of a despot; my senses were benumbed with astonishment, and I cried, laughed, and was in fact quite beside myself. Perspiration burst from my forehead as I heard and saw the most extraordinary difficulties overcome with consummate ease: runs in tenths from top to bottom, passages in thirds in the very highest positions, staccato – and what a staccato! No violinist could play legato passages more quickly and more clearly than he played staccato! Double-stopped harmonics such as no violinist has dreamt of, whole passages in harmonics, variations in which he played one note with the bow and the next pizzicato, all were rendered with the greatest ease and rapidity. Then he played some variations without accompaniment, in which, as a matter of fact, he accompanied himself, so that we were persuaded that a violin and a guitar were playing together.
>
> His appearance was awful! Imagine a lean lanky man, pale as a corpse, with sunken cheeks, unduly prominent cheek-bones, deep-set eyes, a thick beard which grew under his chin, small moustache, fingers like those of a skeleton, long unkempt black hair, and there you have Paganini! He looked precisely as though he had come from the grave. [P:316–17]

Legends swirled around him. He was a womanizer who had throttled his wives and mistresses in crises of thwarted passion, had dissected them like Leonardo in the interests of art, and had fashioned magical strings for his instrument from their intestines. He had spent years in prison because of his political opinions, or rotted in nameless dungeons where the ball and chain had permanently affected his walk.

His only company was his violin, and as the strings successively broke, he had to play exclusively on the lower ones until only the G string was left. This explained his extraordinary ability to play on that string alone. Like Faust, he had made a pact with the devil for his phenomenal skill, and like Cain or the archetypal Jew he was forced to wander forever.[3]

Paganini's feeling for showmanship was uncanny. He raised expectations and curiosity by regularly doubling prices. Rarely playing in the first item of a programme, he would allow an apparently interminable delay before his appearance, and frequently let his lingering shadow be thrown across the stage. There would be much stage business with gloves and handkerchiefs, and even his poor health managed to add to his dramatic impact. A doctor had advised him to protect himself from the limelight by wearing blue glasses, and these came to look like skeletal eye-sockets. After he had left Vienna and went to Prague, he had all his teeth removed, and this made his face even more shrunken and cadaverous, his lower jaw so shallow that he seemed to be biting the instrument.

The craze for virtuosity, Byronic Romanticism, and Italian music in Vienna ensured his success was immense. He was supposed to give six concerts but huge crowds and crushes eventually forced him to give fourteen. Despite the customary high prices (a five-gulder note became known as a 'Paganinerll' because this was the price of admission [VBC:97]) the concerts were attended by all classes of society, and people came away stunned by what they had heard and seen. At his opening concert he played his second concerto in B minor, the *Sonate Militaire* (on the G string), and a set of variations on a theme from *La Cenerentola*, to an audience consisting of Böhm, Saint-Lubin, Mayseder and the musical elite of Vienna. Many years later, when Mayseder was asked for his reaction, he replied: 'We never heard anything like it before ... nor shall we ever hear anything like it again. All of us wanted to smash our fiddles.' [PG:I:262] As Paganini specifically asked that violin students at the Conservatoire should be admitted free to all his public performances, it is difficult to imagine that Ernst did not attend this opening concert.

Caught up in the general enthusiasm, Schubert attended three of his concerts even though the publicity for his own benefit concert – at which Böhm played – was virtually obliterated by the furore surrounding Paganini. [PG:I:265–6] But Paganini's impact extended far beyond the educated musical elite, a fact made clear in one of the first Viennese reviews:

> Never has an artist caused such a terrific sensation within our walls as this God of the violin. Never has the public so gladly carried its shekels to a concert, and never in my memory has the fame of a virtuoso so spread to the lowest classes of the population. After his first two concerts, there was only one name on everybody's lips and it seemed as though the people had lost interest in politics, art, society, and even local gossip. There was only one thought, one topic of conversation – even amongst the lowest tradesmen – indeed, I believe the children almost momentarily forgot their toys. [PG:I:265]

---

3   I here follow de Courcy's original and indispensable paragraph on Paganini legends very closely. See PG:I:259.

When his health and engagements permitted, Paganini enjoyed playing with and attending concerts with some of Vienna's leading musicians. To his lawyer friend Germi he wrote on June 11: 'I've heard two new quartets of Beethoven played in my house by four of the best professors; I shall soon return the compliment by playing these works for them myself [he, like his contemporaries, thought of a quartet as a violin solo plus a trio accompaniment], but the music is very extravagant …' [PG: I:281] Unfortunately we do not know who these professors were. The Schuppanzigh quartet with Schuppanzigh playing first violin is the most likely, as he conducted some of Paganini's concerts, and Paganini heard him conduct Beethoven's seventh symphony, amongst other works, at one of his Ausgarten concert series on 1 May. Even if Böhm, Mayseder and Ernst were not playing, it is hard to imagine they were not in attendance.

The advent of Paganini stunned Ernst. Of course, the older man set an entirely new standard for violin-playing, but he also introduced an element that had been lacking in all of Ernst's teachers – world-conquering ambition. Seyfried, Böhm and Mayseder were all highly successful in the rather peculiar musical atmosphere of Vienna, but they showed no real desire to make a permanent mark in the wider world. Böhm was only thirty-three when Paganini arrived but the main effect was to reinforce his decision virtually to retire from concert life. Mayseder did not smash his violin, but continued to play in the refined, elegant style that delighted the Viennese before Paganini's visit, and continued to delight them afterwards. Neither made any attempt to assimilate what Paganini had done nor try to compete with him. It was Ernst – from a poor provincial background, sixteen, and beginning to feel the limitations of Viennese musical life – who felt compelled to assimilate and transcend the phenomenon he had witnessed.

Chapter 4

From Vienna to Paris: 1828–31

Ernst appeared at one of the four Conservatoire graduation concerts held at the Kartnerthortheater on 29 May 1828 [GMW:31. E:14], but this is his last recorded association with the institution, and two sources say that the Conservatoire decided to dismiss him for going home to Brünn and not returning on time. [ADB:325–7. NMZ:5/2/1841:45] The story is lent credence by Ernst's first surviving letter. This was written to 'Ritter von Seyfried' ('Ritter' indicates a minor order of nobility, roughly equivalent to a knighthood) while Ernst was in Brünn. Unlike his later letters, it is written in an extremely neat and elaborate hand:

> In the pleasant hope that this letter finds your honour in the best of health, I allow myself to bother you. I assure you that only the unexpected suddenness of my [departure?] could prevent me from taking leave of someone whom I esteem so highly and to whom I owe so much. What would music be to me if your honour by your wise guidance had not taught me to judge it, and had not communicated to me what is truly divine about it [?] And so I feel eternally obliged to you [.] I am always looking for opportunities to be able to repay you for only a part of the effort and eagerness which you so richly expended on my instruction. Finally I thank you devotedly for the sheet music which you kindly lent me (I hope my brother has already returned it to you.) And I wish you an early total recovery, for all of your relatives also for all beginning musicians who will be under your guidance. If your health allows, I would be flattered by your kind reply! I dare to beg …
> With respect and devotion, Heinrich Ernst [31 August 1828. Brünn. ON:51/138–1]

The letter also provides some clues as to why Ernst returned to Brünn. His sudden departure suggests an urgent family matter, and the surviving documents give a hint as to what this might have been. His father made his will on 13 August 1828, and it begins, 'As I have been feeling weaker and the hour of my death is uncertain, as is the custom I now report my wishes to my survivors.' [AMB] This implies that he has fallen suddenly and dangerously ill, and I would conjecture that it was this rapid decline in his father's health which caused Ernst to leave Vienna so quickly. The date of his letter to Seyfried – 31 August – would seem about right for Ernst to return to Brünn, see his father through the immediate danger, and then turn to matters left pending. His father does not seem to have regained his former heath because he formally passed his business on to his son Johann in 1829. [AMB] The fact that his father did not recover quickly, which may well have required Ernst to stay near him, lends plausibility to the story that Ernst – not usually given to flouting regulations – remained in Brünn longer than was officially permitted.

Ernst petitioned the governing committee as well as the honorary president of the Gesellsschaft, Beethoven's patron the Archduke Rudolf, to remain a student at the Conservatoire, but he also asked that the obligation to take regular lessons be waived because he needed to support himself by teaching. Pohl's account of the result is that the committee accepted him again as a pupil because a Jew could not be allowed to teach and practise in Vienna unless he was a student at the Conservatoire. [ADB:VI:326] Another source says that the Conservatoire refused to recognize him as a pupil, and also refused to give him a recommendation and graduation certificate because he had not studied for the required six years. [NMZ:5/2/41:45. E:14] As Pohl was the Conservatoire's official historian, I am inclined to accept his account; he could well have had access to papers which have now disappeared. The index to the records, however, does still exist, and shows that all the records relating to Ernst are from 1829. The date may well imply that they are to do with his appeal, and that he only returned to Vienna in the New Year having missed at least a term of teaching. [AGM]

At some point in his Viennese stay, Paganini heard Ernst play. [HWE:4] Ever since Paganini's awe-inspiring first appearance in Vienna, Ernst felt an intense desire to impress the older man, and he had systematically worked his way, note by note, through the latter's *Caprices*. Misunderstanding the word 'flautato' written at the head of number 9, in E, *La Chasse*, he had learnt the whole piece in double-stopped artificial harmonics, and played it this way to Paganini. The Italian could scarcely believe his ears, cried 'E un diavoletto!' ['He's a little devil!'], and prophesied the young man's future greatness. [JD:27/1/52. HWE:4]

This reaction must have confirmed Ernst's ambitions, and made him feel that Vienna had little more to teach him. It is striking that, even in 1827, the *Harmonicon* report of Hackel's concert only mentions Seyfried's composition lessons and does not mention either of his violin teachers. Perhaps Böhm, who thought when Ernst arrived that he rivalled his own practical skill, now felt that he had taught him all he could about music too. Certainly, Pohl recounts that Ernst learnt most from Böhm between the years 1825 and 1827.[1] [ADB:VI:326], and Moser, Joachim's biographer, reports Ernst as saying that he had learnt from Böhm 'all that can be learnt from a master.' [JJ:21] This is clearly a great compliment, but also implies that a further three years would not have been profitable. He had been giving concerts, and getting good reviews, in one of Europe's musical capitals for the last three years, and he may well have been beginning to find his status as a Jew and as a pupil irksome and restricting.

There were also some signs that Vienna was ceasing to be the musical centre it had been when he arrived. Beethoven and Schubert had both died, and there must have been a real sense of loss and flatness after Paganini had left the city and headed northwards. Vienna was about to enter an artistically fallow period, a period dominated not only by Rossini but by the two waltz kings, Joseph Lanner and Johann Strauss the elder. As Fanny Trollope, the novelist's mother, observed in 1836: 'Handel, Mozart and Haydn, and the like are banished from "ears polite", while Strauss and Lanner rule the hour. Nevertheless, there is not one to whom you can speak on the subject, but they will utter a very elegant phrase in honour of their very immortal composers.' [VBC:99]

---

1 Oddly, Pohl has Ernst studying at the Conservatoire from 1824 to 1828 in his history of the *Gesellschaft*. [DGM:134]

There was nothing to hold him at the Conservatoire either. That institution had got off to a shaky start in 1817, but lack of government subsidy and the comparative indifference of the Viennese to serious music ensured its next three decades were shaky too. As Berlioz wrote to a friend from Vienna in 1846:

> From the references in my first letter you will have formed no very brilliant impression of the Vienna Conservatoire. Despite all the ability of its director ... and the acknowledged talents of Joseph Fischoff [who taught piano], Böhm and one or two admirable teachers on its staff, it does not correspond in size and importance with what one would expect to find in a great musical centre like Vienna. A few years ago it was apparently in such decay that without the ingenuity and Herculean exertions of Dr Bacher, who dedicated himself to saving it ... it would by now be defunct. [BM:467]

There is little information about Ernst's activities before the spring of 1829. The letter to Seyfried at the end of August 1828, and reports of concerts in Brünn on 11 September and 24 October [JP:93–4], suggest he was helping his family, nursing his father, and making some money from teaching and the occasional public appearance. Later reviewers noted Ernst's capacity for hard work, and at this stage he must also have been practising systematically and furiously. Paganini had introduced, or reintroduced, any number of new and demanding techniques into mainstream violin playing: not only artificial harmonics and double harmonics, but *scordatura*, left-hand pizzicati, performances on one string, ricochet-spiccato bowing, fast chromatic passages in the highest reaches of the instrument, rapid jumps and leaps, huge left-hand stretches, vastly more difficult double-stopping, and so on. Each one of these requires extended practice to master when the music is in front of you and the technique widely understood. Ernst only had a printed text of the *Caprices*, which do not contain many of Paganini's more outlandish devices, and he had to work out for himself how these effects were achieved. One imagines there were tensions in the house above the café, between a profoundly sick elderly man, an overworked half-brother running the business, and a frequently absent sixteen-year-old, his mind wholly elsewhere, making shrieks and whistles upstairs.

One journal reports that, during this period, Ernst had to undergo surgery in Vienna. Worryingly, particularly for a violinist, he had developed a tumour on the fourth finger of his left hand, but after the operation the finger not only healed but grew as long as his third finger. [NMZ:5/2/41:45. E:14] The story is probably a naturalized version of the kind of tales told about Paganini, and sounds as if it was designed to explain the extraordinary left-hand stretches that Ernst's music requires. Kriehuber's 1846 portrait of Ernst shows quite clearly that his fourth finger is shorter than his third [see Plate VI], and there are no signs of scars or abnormalities on the sculptures of Ernst's left hand kept in the Nice Museum.

Ernst left Vienna in April 1829, but there is little agreement on what he did after that. There are three options:

1) D'Elvert says that Ernst first left Vienna in April 1829, and both D'Elvert and Pohl say that after visiting Munich and Paris he came back to Vienna. He then

visited Paris again in 1831 playing concerts in many German cities on the way. [ADB:326. GMM:90]
2) Leone claims that Ernst left Vienna in 1829 and slowly made his way to Paris. [EOC:5]
3) A well-informed obituary relates that '[in 1829] he set out on his first professional tour, exciting, especially at Munich, and afterwards at Frankfurt and Stuttgart, great interest by the early maturity of his talent. On his return to Vienna, an unhappy passion, it is said, occasioned even then those fits of melancholy to which he was subsequently often liable. In the year of 1831 or 1832 he went to Paris …' [NMZ:MW:11/11/704]

Contemporary reviews show that Ernst was in Paris in 1831, but otherwise the evidence gained from newspapers could fit any of these accounts, since they show he gave concerts in Munich and Stuttgart in late 1829. I am inclined to adopt Leone's suggestion of one German tour. This began in Munich. He then travelled through Augsburg, Stuttgart, Würtzberg, Dresden and Nuremberg, until he reached Frankfurt. From there, he proceeded up the Rhine to Strasbourg, via Mannheim, Heidelberg, Karlsruhe and Baden. He stayed long enough in Munich and Baden to travel to and from Paris or Vienna, so neither of these suggestions is impossible.

The story about his unhappy love affair is corroborated by Otto Ruppius, in his *Weltlichen Blätter* [*Worldly/Secular Writings*]. [OR:49–51] Ruppius, a German journalist, novelist, man of letters and minor composer, had to leave Germany in 1848 as a result of an article advocating the dissolution of the Prussian National Assembly, and settled in America. He returned home after an amnesty, and from 1862 until his death he worked as a journalist in Leipzig. His background, musical talents and interests mean that he could have heard the story from Ernst himself or from someone closely associated with him.

The scene Ruppius paints takes place in 'the lavishly furnished drawing-room of one of the largest houses in Vienna' in 1831. Two adolescents, a boy of seventeen and a girl of 'not more than fifteen', are gazing lovingly into one another's eyes, when the girl's father enters the room. The father asks the girl to leave so he can speak to the boy, whom he calls Wilhelm. He tells Wilhelm that he has noticed his interest in his daughter and has willingly given him access to the house because he regards the boy as enormously talented and upright. However, he also says that Wilhelm has not yet become the artist, and has not yet made the artistic reputation, which would allow the father to let him marry his daughter. If Wilhelm promises to achieve these heights, then the father will willingly let him marry his daughter, and furthermore he will 'not … persuade' his daughter to marry anyone else in the meantime. Wilhelm accepts the challenge, and the interview concludes when the father says:

> 'Very well! But then you must start from here tomorrow; I should almost think you had learned all there was to learn at our conservatoire.'
>
> 'I shall start for Paris to-morrow morning; it has long been my intention to go there. But, may I not – .'
>
> 'Come and see us to-night after you have finished your preparations; then you may say Good bye.' [OR:50]

Wilhelm goes to Paris and becomes a virtuoso that 'even Paganini honoured with regard', although he cannot compose a piece he feels is good enough to dedicate to his beloved. Two days before the expiration of seven years, when they have not been allowed to exchange letters, he races home, and enters her house through the open front door. There, to his horror, he sees the girl's body surrounded by flowers. He cannot attend her funeral because the shock, and the end of all his hopes, bring on a dangerous fever which lasts for two months. When he rises from his bed he is a changed and melancholy man who takes little interest in the outside world. All his sorrows are focused on his violin, and '[he] wrote a song of mourning for his bride – he penned the Elegy – whose deep pathos has rung the heart-strings of the whole civilized world – for the man we have been speaking about was Heinrich Wilhelm Ernst'. [OR:51]

This story receives further corroboration from two sources. The first is the printed edition of the *Elegy* itself which is subtitled 'sur la mort d'un object chéri', and is, unusually for Ernst, not dedicated to anyone. The second is Field Marshall von Moltke, architect of Prussia's military success in the Franco-Prussian war of 1870. He was friendly with Wilhelmj; and Wilhelmj's pupil, Dettmar Dressel, explains how the friendship came about:

> The friendship between the great violinist and the great soldier was founded on the latter's love of music. Above all other violin pieces von Moltke loved Ernst's *Élégie*, and on one occasion, passing through Wiesbaden, he called on Wilhelmj between the train of arrival and his train of departure, and begged him to play his beloved *Élégie*. When the violinist came to the double-stopping, the stern old soldier was in tears. The *Élégie* had its birth in a love-tragedy which concerned a member of von Moltke's family ... [UDS:98–9]

He then goes on to give an abbreviated version of the story related above. Wilhelmj clearly endorsed the story because he had Ruppius's account translated and reprinted on the back of his own edition of the *Elegy*. Unfortunately, prolonged enquiries have not yet revealed the girl's identity.

The dates of the story, however, require some adjustment. The first sentence of the story is: ''Twas in 1831.' If my conjecture about Ernst's birth-date is correct, then he was seventeen not in 1831 but in 1829. This date would fit the facts gleaned from histories and reference works much better. The girl's father's comment, 'I should almost think you had learned all there was to be learned at our Conservatoire' would make little sense in the early months of 1831. Ernst could have had no thought of staying on or returning to the Conservatoire since he had already left at least two years before, whereas in early 1829, he was petitioning to be readmitted. In addition, the father's concern that his prospective son-in-law was an untried youth would have been justified in 1829, whereas by 1831 Ernst had already challenged Paganini in Germany and played in many very successful concerts. This, of course, makes a return to the Conservatoire additionally unlikely. The interview described is therefore most likely to have taken place in the first four months of 1829.

The date and place from which Ernst returned to discover his misfortune is also disputed between the obituary and Ruppius. The obituary implies this occurred when he returned from his German tour in 1830 or 1831; Ruppius says it happened when he returned from Paris seven years after leaving Vienna, which would be between 1836 and 1838.

I am inclined to endorse Ruppius's account of the place from which he returned, but I believe the obituary comes closer to the date. As I pointed out above, Ernst could easily have returned to Vienna for a period of more than two months when he was either in Munich or Baden. The difficulty with his returning from either of these places is that both were low points on his tour, and his achievements would be unlikely to impress a future father-in-law: in Munich he had done little beyond arranging one concert; in Baden he was depressed and short of funds. The difficulty with the date Ruppius suggests is that seven years without contact seems an implausibly long time to wait for a fiancée, even in an age given to extended courtships. Moreover, by 1836–38, Ernst had a flourishing career and was quite a well-known figure in Parisian circles. If an event as romantic and tragic as the one Ruppius describes had occurred around these dates it would have been reported in the contemporary music press. But no such account appears to exist.

My intuition is that Ernst did return to Vienna from Paris to find his fiancée dead, but between April 1831 and April 1832 – a year when no documentation has survived to suggest what Ernst was doing. This idea allows him to have a plausible motive (he could show his prospective father-in-law that had become a serious rival to Paganini, and was established in Paris) and it also preserves the idea that a 'return from Paris' and '1831' are significant elements in the story. It is also worth noting that 1831 was a particularly deadly period for young people in Vienna. In addition to the normal ravages of typhus, dysentery and tuberculosis, cholera stuck Vienna in June 1831 and raged until the end of the year. [FCPW:46–7] Of the large number who died from all causes, nearly half were less than twenty years old. [VLR:149]

One fact that supports a date of 1836–38 is the first mentions of the *Elegy* in the press. It is first mentioned as being played by Panofka – another ex-student of Mayseder's – in a review on 15 January 1838; and it was advertised as a newly published work in *La France Musicale* on 21 January 1838. But it is quite possible that the *Elegy* was composed and published long after the events which inspired it, and it is also possible that it was an adaption, or even merely a retitling, of an existing work. Between 1830 and 1838, Ernst frequently played a piece which is just entitled *Adagio* and this could easily be an early version of the *Elegy*.

To return to firmer ground and an earlier period, we know that Ernst left Vienna in April 1829 and made his way to Munich. Here he stayed for seven or eight months and diligently practised the violin and piano. According to Leone, there was a possibility of his being offered a position at the Royal Chapel, but at a chance meeting with Paganini – who was on a tour of southern Germany – the older violinist encouraged him to turn the offer down and aim for something higher. It was at this point that Ernst determined to head immediately for Paris. With Vienna in decline, the French capital was now the main centre for composers, singers and virtuosi. [HWE:4]

This city was also Paganini's goal, but the Italian must have been surprised and irritated when Ernst took his advice to aim for something higher by following in his footsteps, attending every possible concert, imitating his manner, trying to transcribe his compositions, and playing concerts soon after his own. This looks like absurd hubris on Ernst's part: how could he possibly make any money or establish any sort of reputation having placed himself in Paganini's shadow? I suspect, however, that Ernst's intention was simply to learn as much as possible from the Italian, and that playing concerts soon after the *Maestro* was the only way he could support himself. Probably Ernst's most annoying habit was renting rooms next door to Paganini. In London in the 1850s, Joachim asked Ernst's reasons for doing this, and the conversation eventually found its way into print seventy years later:

> **Joachim:** Tell me, dear friend, what did you really aim to achieve by renting a room next to Paganini's? You heard him play many times in public!
> **Ernst:** Yes, at least twenty times; but it meant a lot to me to observe him practising. I didn't get my money's worth though: he played the violin a good deal, but mostly very quietly and often using a mute; for the most part he was preparing pieces for his next concert but at best he would practise some *Caprices* which he wanted to play as encores.
> **Joachim:** Did he play faultlessly?
> **Ernst:** Yes, absolutely, although at home it was much less astonishing than on stage. He must have practised enormously when young, because when a passage didn't come off as he wanted, it emerged as though fired from a pistol when repeated. His iron will-power helped him. So did his hand which, although not large, was supple and flexible, and the fingers came down like bell-clappers on the strings. [GV:429]

Paganini played in Munich on 20, 21 and 26 November [CPL:42], so the meeting must have occurred around these dates. Probably in the same month, Ernst gave a concert in Munich when he played, amongst other works, Böhm's concerto and some of his own compositions. The concert was a success and receives high praise in the *Allgemeine Musikalische Zeitung*. [27/1/1830:Col.59]

When Paganini set off for Augsburg and Stuttgart, Ernst followed. In the latter town, Ernst played shortly after Paganini who gave concerts there on 3, 5 and 7 December 1829, and both men's concerts were reported in a review written in the middle of February 1830 but published two months later. Ernst's concert was given at the Redoutensaal, and he played the first movement of Rode's concerto in B minor, variations on a theme by Rossini, an adagio composed by himself, one of Mayseder's polonaises, and a set of variations by Lipinski, probably his *Variations de Bravoure* op.22. The review includes the first lengthy and detailed analysis of his playing:

> Herr Ernst, still a young man, possesses all the qualities which, combined with his evident capacity for hard, disciplined work, could place him perhaps in a few years amongst the very best performers. He has tremendous skill in passages, jumps, double-stops etc, alongside a powerful pure tone and nimble bowing; also, his playing in the Adagio, although not beyond criticism, is nevertheless not to be despised. But it is regrettable that Herr Ernst finds himself on the wrong artistic path, in that he performs as an imitator and tries to play 'à la Paganini.' Herr Ernst, with his unmistakable skills, his feeling for beauty, and his obvious career as an artist, should follow in his own artistic path in his own way, and strive to become great according to his own lights. Each to his own! [AMZ:28/4/1830: Col.270]

But this sage advice was premature for a young man besotted with Paganini and all he represented. It would take another ten years and their encounter in Marseilles before Ernst could finally throw off the influence of the Italian wizard.

The variations on a theme by Rossini are almost certainly one of Ernst's first published compositions – the *Variations brilliantes sur un Thème de Rossini* op.4. These variations are based on the theme from the cabaletta *Sorte secondami* to be found in the introduction to Rossini's opera, *Zelmira*. [EOC:28] They were issued by Hoffmeister in Leipzig in 1834 [E:225], and there is also an undated French edition by Launier in Paris. [CPM]

The German edition is dedicated to the King of France and mentions that Ernst played it at the court; the French edition has no dedication, but says that Ernst is 'le premier violon du Prince Electoral de Hesse' and played the variations at this court. The Hesse referred to is Hesse-Kassel, which at the time was ruled by Wilhelm II, and the Electoral Prince was his son Freidrich Wilhelm. It is very unlikely that Ernst's appointment was official or long lasting; perhaps it was merely an honorary position. Spohr had been appointed director of music to Wilhelm II in 1822. He was deeply interested in fellow violin virtuosi, and, had a violinist as talented as Ernst visited Kassel in 1830, Spohr would certainly have mentioned it in his *Autobiography* – even if only to express his disappointment at missing him. In fact, that work makes clear that they did not encounter one another until 1846. [SA:II:280]

The variations consist of an introduction, theme and five variations – in thirds, tenths, double-harmonics, and the whole arsenal of virtuoso effects – and the entire composition is skilful, graceful, and brilliant. It is therefore something of a mystery why Ernst played it so infrequently and why it received so few republications. The problem may lie in its length. Although it uses one of Ernst's standard forms (introduction, theme and variations), it is very much longer than all his other pieces in this format: the introduction alone has 45 bars and the last variation 80, and he may have felt that it tried the patience of his audience.

After Stuttgart, Paganini returned briefly to Frankfurt before playing a concert in Würtzburg on 19 February 1830. This was also the site of Ernst's next concert, but he, unlike Paganini, had to undergo the indignity of being auditioned by Professor Franz Joseph Frölich, the composer and pedagogue, before being given permission to play. [EOC:5]

At this point Ernst and Paganini parted company. Paganini returned to Frankfurt and gave at least nine concerts. Ernst headed east, first to Dresden then to Nuremberg. This was probably because the competition with Paganini was proving too fierce. Leone tells us that Ernst's 'appearances before the public won much applause but little money', and that 'Paganini, the giant meteor in the musical sky, overshadowed everything else at the time'. [EOC:5] If this was Ernst's reason, then his plan was not a success. At Nuremberg, where Paganini had played more than three months before, Ernst became so depressed that he locked himself in his room for five days and refused to see anyone. However, this open acknowledgement of his failure may have been beneficial. He seems to have taken courage and decided to make the competition with Paganini even more intense than it was before.

He set off for Frankfurt – the centre of Paganini's tours in Germany – and decided to play one of Paganini's most demanding and famous showpieces. Ernst's eavesdropping was more fruitful than the exchange with Joachim implied, because by this method he was able to note down at least two of Paganini's major compositions. One of these was Paganini's set of solo variations on *Nel cor piu non mi sento*, a true compendium of every one of his bravura tricks and innovations. Shortly after Paganini played in Frankfurt, Ernst performed the *Nel cor* variations in public perfectly; a feat that dazzled and amazed an audience which included Paganini himself. Oddly, the review in the *Allgemeine Musikalische Zeitung* does not mention this achievement. Instead, it continues to regret Ernst's imitation of Paganini, and makes clear that this was not the first time Paganini had kept an eye on his rival:

> A still very young violin virtuoso, her Heinrich Wilhelm Ernst from Vienna, who has already been praised in these pages, has also earned much applause here. Paganini himself, who is still staying amongst us and composes something new from time to time, showed his appreciation again. The young man's compositions also earned praise. His Adagio was exquisitely beautiful, not so, however, his playing in the manner of Paganini, whose presence probably made it awkward for him. [AMZ:5/1830:Col.329]

A few days later, Ernst went to see Paganini in his room and found him holding his guitar while composing. Paganini promptly hid his manuscripts under the bed cover and said: 'Non mi fido dei vostri orrechi, ma nemeno più dei vostri occhi!' ['I must guard myself not only against your ears but also against your eyes!']. [EOC:5][2] Despite his wariness, Paganini did not take much interest in Ernst because he regarded him as a mere imitator, and not someone from whom anything significant could be learned. [EOC:5]

Paganini's friend, the violinist and *Kapellmeister* in Frankfurt, Carl Guhr, was also transcribing the Italian's works. He was to become famous for his series of articles on 'Paganini's Art of Playing the Violin' which was later published as a book. This contains a transcription of the *Nel cor* variations (together with the slight *Duet for One Violin*) which Guhr reported hearing 'some twenty or thirty times'. [PAPV:v–vi] Guhr's book became celebrated as the first cool-headed analysis of Paganini's technique, and also because its transcription of *Nel cor* was the only one of Paganini's concert showpieces available in print before 1851; it was therefore obligatory reading for any aspiring virtuoso. Samuel Wolf [EOC:30] suggests that Ernst may have assisted Guhr in his transcription but this is unlikely given that the preface to the book is dated 1829. [PAPV:v–vi] It is even more unlikely that Guhr assisted Ernst: a valued friendship with Paganini would be unlikely to survive helping his fiercest rival transcribe one of master's most innovative works.

Paganini played at Frankfurt on 7 February, 1 and 11 March, and 26 April 1830. [CPL:43] The young Robert Schumann heard him for the first time on Easter Sunday, 11 April, and like everyone else, was awed and astounded. Shortly afterwards, he met Ernst in the same town. According to the composer's friend Eduard Röller, Ernst had a

---

2   Paganini is also reported to have said of Ernst, 'Il faut se méfiez de vous' ['One should be wary of you']. [CV:92] Whether this is simply a paraphrase of his longer remark in the text, or whether he said it on another occasion, I am unsure.

strong and decisive influence on Schumann, and from then on Schumann assiduously sought out the violinist's company. [SPP:532–3] Although Schumann was practising the piano in an attempt to become a virtuoso, he was also unenthusiastically studying law at Heidelberg, and was undecided as to whether to take up music as a career. Ernst, besides being the astonishing Paganini's most ardent disciple, was already beginning to enjoy the kind of success Schumann badly wanted, and his friendship, example and advice substantially strengthened Schumann's resolve to follow music as a career. [S:33] Schumann later heard Ernst play in Heidelberg, an experience he recalled with pleasure ten years later:

> Ernst ... made his first tour up the Rhine in 1830 at the same time as Paganini. His remarkable execution though openly displaying much of Paganini's manner already created a sensation. In the arrogance of youth, he always gave concerts in those cities where Paganini had played but a short time before him. I joyfully remember one of those concerts in the Rhine cities, to which he, like an Apollo, attracted all the Heidelberg Society of the Muses. His name was generally known. [SMM:163]

Paganini spent May and June 1830 touring in north Germany, and spent the rest of the year staying in Frankfurt with only very occasional outings to play in other towns – Ems, for example, on 24 July, and Baden on 1 August. The reason for this uncharacteristic inactivity was because his plans to visit Paris had had to be postponed owing to the revolution which broke out there on 28 July. This sparked off revolutionary instability throughout Europe, and at the end of 1830 there was a Polish rising against Russian occupation, and a revolution in Brussels.

By the time Schumann heard Ernst in Heidelberg, the violinist had travelled from Frankfurt to Mannheim, and he would go on to give concerts in Karlsruhe and Baden. Consequently, in spite of what Schumann implies, Ernst's tour up the Rhine from April to June 1830 did not offer a direct challenge to Paganini in the way that his earlier performances had done in southern Germany.

Ernst stayed for nine months in Baden almost certainly because, like Paganini, his plans to visit Paris had been upset by the 1830 revolution. This was a difficult time for musicians. Any hint of revolution caused concerts to be cancelled and people to stay at home, and the German states were severely worried by the possibility of unrest. Even in comparatively liberal Baden, there was an upsurge of radical feeling which made musical positions scarcer and concerts less remunerative. Consequently, Ernst continued to suffer from money problems and sank into a depression. This so exhausted him that he put his violin aside for a time and thought of transferring to the piano. [EOC:5]

In Baden, Schumann was in Ernst's company for at least the third time (indeed, he seems to have followed the violinist up the Rhine from Frankfurt), and on Thursday 5 August 1830 there is a most intriguing entry in Schumann's diary. It is highly compressed and impressionistic, but it gives an evocative account of an evening with Ernst and his friends:

> The beautiful girl – the shameless young people with her – then we walked to the spa hall – I smart in a hat – I gambled away two kroner – beer and an air of great happiness – the secretary of Ernst – the Elector of Hesse won a lot – then to Ernst – his amiability

– very lively conversation – very intimate with his nauseating secretary – cigars and embarrassment – with Ernst in the spa – haunting glances,

Then he leads me to the theatre – terrible heat and steam – *The Hunter of Iffland* really bad – my coarseness in response to Ernst's question – a walk and departure from him – unbearable heat – to bed and exhausted sleep. [STB:290]

This usefully confirms a link with the Electoral Prince of Hesse, who would soon be affected by the atmosphere of political unrest. A little over a month after this evening with Ernst, revolution broke out on the streets of Kassel. As a result, Wilhelm II went into voluntary exile, and his son – Ernst's gambling partner – was appointed co-regent. He turned out to be every bit as reactionary as his father, and made life particularly difficult – usually by refusing permission for absences and concerts – for the liberal-minded Spohr. [SA:II:203, 243, 301]

The passage also makes clear that Ernst had a male secretary. Leone tells us, writing of events in 1837, that Ernst's secretary was a 'friend by the name of Frank who had travelled with him up to now', [EOC:6] and we know from later letters and Berlioz's *Memoirs* that his real name was Frankowski. [BM:304] Accordingly, it seems likely that Frankowski had accompanied Ernst on this German tour, and that they had met when the violinist was a student in Vienna.

The most pressing question raised by the passage from Schumann, however is: what exactly is going on? In what way is Ernst intimate (*lebhaftes*) with his secretary? In what way is Ernst's secretary nauseating (*ekelhaften*)? What was the embarrassment (*Verlegenheit*)? Who gave and who received the haunting (*verfolgende*) glances? What prompted Schumann's coarseness (*Grobheit*) in response to Ernst's question? What was Ernst's question? And does the odd break in the text between paragraph one (which ends on a comma) and paragraph two suggest censorship or erasure?

One explanation that makes sense of all these remarks is that Ernst seems to be sexually involved with his openly gay secretary, and that later in the evening, after lingering looks in Schumann's direction, the eighteen-year-old violinist makes a pass at the twenty-year-old student. Schumann rebuffs him coarsely – although apparently without great surprise or later reflection. This would be in accordance with what we know of Schumann's sexuality. There is no evidence to suppose he had homosexual experiences (although of course this suggestion has been made) but his diary shows that he was overwhelmingly and exclusively susceptible to beautiful girls. [S:12]

Was Ernst sexually attracted to men as well as women? There is only one hint in the Ernst literature, and that comes from an article published in an American journal called the *Musical Courier*. In the issue for 9 September 1908, there is an article on Ernst and de Bériot, written by an acquaintance of Joachim (who knew Ernst well) called Aurthur M. Abell. Discussing the onset of Ernst's final illness and death, Abell notes his constant travelling and then writes: '[His] end [was] prematurely brought on by his erratic, unnatural mode of life and excesses of all kinds.' [FVP:5]

Ernst drank, smoked and gambled, but he shared these vices with most other nineteenth-century musicians and they are hardly worthy of special comment. Similarly, a life of travel hardly merits being described as erratic, unnatural and excessive. But the word 'unnatural' at this time was frequently used to hint at and condemn homosexuality, and this may well be what Abell is implying. In addition to the love affair mentioned earlier, there are many signs in the letters that Ernst was attracted to young women, but the only accounts we have of him showing physical affection in the early part of his life are when he showed affection to men: he publicly kissed the young Reinecke, and embraced Hallé and Berlioz on separate occasions. Ernst was a spontaneous, tactile, emotional and demonstrative man; the manners of the early nineteenth century, and its attitudes to male friendship, are quite different from ours; and most of his close colleagues were men. It is nonetheless striking that no report of similar physical contact with women has come down to us.

Ernst and Frankowski were certainly close. On at least one occasion Ernst started a letter to the publisher Schlésinger, let Frankowski write the middle section, and then finished the letter himself. [BN] A letter to Dantan, quoted in the next chapter, has them sitting at windows admiring the *danceuses* and other pretty sights, and Ernst says that after one concert he fell 'unconscious into the arms of my friend'. [EOC:7] A sexual relationship is not out of the question; no other nineteenth-century performer – Paganini, Liszt, Bull – was so intimate with his secretary or employed him for so long. Frankowski only left Ernst's employment when the violinist married in July 1854, which means that Frankowski had had one employer for twenty-five years.

It is possible that Ernst was bisexual, and it is possible that he made an advance on Schumann; it is certain that Ernst in Baden repeated the advice he had given Schumann in Frankfurt, and this appears to have influenced Schumann's decision to give up the law, and return to Leipzig to study with Frederik Wieck. [S:38] This is the first of several occasions when Ernst's advice set a musician on the path to fame.

By the early months of 1831, the political climate in France had begun to settle, and Ernst's depression begun to clear. His name was generally known in Germany and he now felt ready for Paris. Paganini had set off in February, and Ernst, as usual, followed in his footsteps.

Chapter 5

Paris: 1831–36

Paganini arrived in Paris on 24 February, and gave concerts throughout March and April creating the usual immense sensation. Ernst arrived in April, and probably caught the last concerts of the series. He was well used to arriving in towns where people talked of nothing but Paganini, and his talent, charm and networking abilities continued to serve him well. Within eight days, he met a countess whose introduction allowed him to play at the Athénée Musicale. He had virtually no time for rehearsal, and the instrument available to him was poor, but nonetheless his debut was successful enough for another appearance to be arranged, during a benefit concert for Madame Schroeder-Devrient, at the Théâtre des Italiens. [JD:27/1/52. D:330–42. E:21]

This was a considerable coup. Madame Schroeder-Devrient was one of the era's best known singers, and the Théâtre des Italiens was one of the most prestigious venues in Paris: there was intense competition for boxes (duels had been fought over them) and the lobby was always filled with the most refined and fashionable society. Ernst, however, was largely unknown to the Parisian public, and when he walked on stage he was greeted by a barrage of hissing so hostile that he came close to fainting. Appalled by this insulting behaviour, and seeing its effect on the nervy, volatile artist, the orchestra rose en masse to applaud his entrance, and he recovered himself sufficiently to play to the best of his ability. [JD:27/1/52] Even so, Ernst had noted the partiality and aggression of the average Parisian audience, and vowed not to expose himself to it again until he felt fully prepared. Accordingly, in the words of Leone, '[he] retired into solitude, far from all influences, and lived only for his studies. With untiring zeal and restless energy he practised on the violin, finally determined not to appear again in Paris until he felt himself mature enough for that city.' [EOC:5].

He found lodgings with the Lippman family at 374 rue St Denis. The apartment was central but noisy, as the street, now the boulevard de Sebastopol, was full of small shops, and the main north–south route through Paris. Always attracted to borderlands, Ernst had taken lodgings on a road which usefully abutted four *arrondissements*: the Fourth was the centre for the newspaper industry; the Fifth held the less fashionable theatres and pleasure gardens; the Sixth swarmed at night with musicians, dancers, and storytellers; while the Seventh still contained fine aristocratic houses from the time – long past – when it was considered a fashionable area. [PWFC:27–8]

Ernst was soon joined in his lodgings by a young violinist whom he had recently met, who would later make a great name for himself in the world, the Norwegian Ole Bull. Bull had arrived in Paris on 19 August 1831. He had acquired a very considerable reputation in Norway as a violin virtuoso, but had recently failed to become a student of Spohr at Kassel. Disappointed, he returned to Norway, but a chance encounter with the folk-fiddler Torgeir Augundson established his abiding interest in his national music, and when he set off for Paris two months later he carried a Hardanger fiddle as well as two fine Italian violins in his luggage. [OB:16–19]

It is not known how the two violinists met, but Ernst evidently liked Bull, and within a few weeks they were established in the apartment on terms of friendly rivalry. On 16 September, Bull wrote excitedly to his mother:

> Ernst [has been] a pupil at the Vienna conservatory, and composition pupil of the famous Ritter von Seyfried who in turn was a pupil of the immortal Mozart and finally a pupil of the great Paganini. He plays and composes entirely in [Paganini's] manner with double-stopped harmonics, pizzicato, spiccato etc. Before my acquaintanceship with him, I had secured a copy of Paganini's Violin Method book by Guhr from Frankfurt in which I had studied the double-stop harmonics, pizzicato, Paganini-style flying staccato, and his famous variations on *Nel cor più non mi sento*, and … *Duet for One Violin*. We play Paganini's *Caprices* together, he also plays variations on his own compositions, while I tortured out some bizarre dances on the Hardanger fiddle. [OB:22. MKM:15]

At this stage, Bull's taste in repertoire seemed slightly more conservative: 'I play things by Spohr, on which I have more practice, while he plays things by Lipinski[1] and by Ernst himself ... so much is certain, that as far as my skill is concerned, I have nothing to fear from the virtuosos of Paris.' [OB:21]

Despite Bull's characteristic self-confidence, it would seem that as violinists they were evenly matched, and both would go on to become two of the most important violinists of the post-Paganini generation. Understandably, Bull was chiefly impressed by Ernst's musical education and his place in a musical tradition. As a violinist, Bull had been soundly trained in Bergen by J.H. Poulson and M. Ludholm, pupils of Viotti and Baillot respectively, but Bergen was a backwater, he lacked direct contact with leading musicians of the era, and his training in music theory was patchy at best. Realizing this, Ernst offered to give him a three-month course in harmony and counterpoint free of charge, but Bull declined, fearing he might lose some of his individuality. [OB:21] Although one can sympathize with this worry (and possibly a desire not to feel patronized by a younger man) Bull's refusal was ill-judged. Everyone acknowledged that Bull could write a haunting melody, but his compositions were repeatedly criticized for defective form, harmony and counterpoint. This lack of technical competence is one of the reasons for the sudden decline of Bull's reputation in the 1850s. It also explains why Bull published very few of his compositions, so that many are now lost.

Ernst's talent and agreeable personality allowed him to make friends and establish important musical contacts quickly. Seeing his friend was short of money and prospects, he tried to help Bull by introducing him to his own circle, but the Norwegian was not an easy character to assist. He was undeniably lively and charming, but also exceedingly proud of his physical strength, overbearing, self-advertising, egotistical, and touchy. Consequently, all Ernst's attempts to secure permanent posts

---

1 Although there are no records of Ernst giving any public performances of Lipinski's music after he came to live in Paris, he clearly continued to practise the older man's music: Berlioz wrote to Ernst: 'The beauties of [Lipinski's] concertos have long been fixed in your infallible memory.' [BM:370]

and engagements for Bull foundered. Time did not mellow him, and even the most decorous occasions could lead to trouble. As his second wife recalled:

> Ole Bull used to relate an amusing story of his early acquaintance with Ernst in Paris in 1836. He had been engaged by the princess Damerond to arrange and take part in some quartette music at one of her soirees, and he had secured the aid of Ernst and the brothers Boucher. As the musicians descended the stairs some white Polish dogs followed them, snarling and barking, to the salon. Ernst, who had on silk stockings and low shoes, began to retreat, thus encouraging one of the little brutes to bite him. The cur then rushed at Ole Bull, who deliberately lifted it on his toe and sent it among the lights of the great chandelier. The attendant found on picking it up that the fall had killed it. The princess, raised on a sort of dais at the end of the apartment, had seen her pet's mishap, and in her agitation sent a messenger to request that the musicians leave immediately. Ole Bull expressed his willingness to comply with the gracious request as soon as the compensation of the artists he had engaged should be handed to him. Her feelings were somewhat mollified at this suggestion, but as three of the quartet had already left, there was no other course but to pay him the twenty five louis d'or, which the four friends spent in a supper at the Palais-Royal. [OBM:142–3]

Years have turned it into an amusing story, and Bull's companions clearly smiled on his actions immediately after the event, but it is impossible to imagine Ernst behaving in a similar fashion.

For the rest of 1831, Bull lived far beyond his means, spent vast quantities of money on a new violin, suits, and supper parties, and picked up a bad gambling habit. By the beginning of 1832, he had run into serious financial difficulties. He parted from Ernst and moved into a cheap boarding house largely patronized by German musicians. This was dangerous as well as uncomfortable because the cholera which had wrought havoc in Vienna had now reached Paris. Luckily, in April 1832 he received an invitation to play at the home of the Count of Montebello, an invitation which resulted in his meeting Ernst and Chopin at breakfast. [LOB:22] There they planned a concert that would revive his fortunes. Under the auspices of the Count, this was held on 18 April 1832, and all three artists performed. Despite the cholera epidemic, the concert was well attended and successful. Bull's share of the profit – 1,400 francs – was probably immediately claimed by his creditors, but the concert marked the end of his lowest period. He was taken in by a Madame Villemot who, thinking he resembled her dead son, nursed him through a serious illness and paid off his remaining debts. As he recovered, Bull became attracted by the dark and fragile beauty of her fourteen-year-old daughter Félice. He fell in love, and by the time they married four years later, he had made a European reputation. [LOB:23]

After Bull's concert, Ernst allowed himself to appear twice in the summer of 1832. On 24 June, he performed at a matinée given at Dietz's Nouvelle Salle de Concert, where he played, amongst other things, in Maurer's *Concertante* for four violins; and on 15 July he appeared at a concert organized by the singer Richelmi in the same hall. [RM: 30/6/1832:174–5. E:22] At both concerts he received several rounds of applause, but a number of critics still felt his youth and inexperience showed: his playing was not always elegant, his intonation was fallible, and he tended to rush difficult passages. The report on the second concert in the *Revue musicale* is typical:

> M. Ernst plays the violin and did not have to prove his talent; however, he has a great deal to do before his playing becomes irreproachable. His most incontestable quality is energy; but he lacks elegance and he is not always secure in difficult passages. M. Ernst was applauded many times; but, we repeat, he is young and must do a great deal of work … [RM:21/7/32:199–200. E:22]

To someone used to receiving glowing reviews, such reasoned and temperate criticism must have been even more sobering than the mindlessly hissing audience at the Théâtre des Italiens. But whatever the state of Ernst's confidence, he was invited to play alongside Chopin, Liszt, Hiller and the cellist Franchomme at concert in the Wauxhall d'Eté on 23 March 1833, and such an opportunity was too good to turn down. [FCPW: 68–9, 194]. He was advertised as playing an unidentified 'violin solo', but since the Wauxhall was an outlying pleasure garden, 'more appropriate for a ball or a fencing match than a concert', no critics ventured out to review the concert, and it is thus impossible to tell either what Ernst played or how well he played it. [RM:30/6/32]

He may still have felt that his public re-emergence had been premature, because after the concert he withdrew to Switzerland for several months. [D:330–45. FM:13/6/52:198. RGM:25/7/52:199] Following more intense practice, he gave a concert in Geneva in early October, assisted by the veteran Irish pianist John Field, whose acquaintance he had made in Paris earlier in the year. Field's biographer feels that 'the participation of such a celebrated assisting artist must have done much to promote the sale of tickets for Ernst's concert, and it is a characteristic example of Field's readiness to help a young artist whose talent he admired.' [LMJF:86–7]

Ernst probably left at the end of October because a surviving album leaf is inscribed: 'Souvenir à M. Wolf par ton ami, H.W. Ernst, Geneve 28th October 1833.' [MGB] This 'M. Wolf' is likely to be Pierre-Etienne Wolf, one of Liszt's pupils, who became one of the first professors of piano when the Geneva conservatoire opened its doors in 1835. 'Souvenir' suggests Ernst is leaving, and probably implies that he was back in Paris by November 1833. Musically, Geneva was quiet and out of the way. It must have been a useful venue for Ernst to try out his newly acquired and hard-won skills before performing again in front of the Parisian critics.

He was not quite ready for the critics and public concerts yet. On 12 January 1834, the *Gazette musicale* announced that Ernst would shortly play some of his new compositions. [GMP:12/1/34. E:23] The next month, Ernst gave a private performance 'before some artists' of his new and recently published *Introduction et Variations brilliantes en forme de Fantaisie sur le Quatuor fav. de Ludovic*, op.6. Although the piece was largely designed to display his virtuosity, his playing was said to bring out the melodic line and have a powerful emotional impact. [GMP:23/2/34. E:23] In spite of this praise, Ernst may still not have been entirely pleased with his performance because no more is heard of him until the end of the year.

It is probable that Ernst spent some of this time in Switzerland composing the three *Rondinos* op.5 for violin and piano (or second violin). Dedicated to le Comte de

Montendre, and based on themes by Carafa (*Nathalie*), Meyerbeer (*Robert le Diable*) and Halvéy (*La Tentation*), these are straightforward, melodious, pieces requiring no great technique. They were clearly designed for a ready sale rather than Ernst's own use, and although they carry an earlier opus number than the *Ludovic Fantasy*, Schlésinger's plate numbers indicate that they were published shortly after.

Ernst was supposed to have played a solo at Berlioz's concert on 23 November, but the audience wanted to hear the *March to the Scaffold* from the *Fantastic Symphony* so Ernst graciously bowed out. [YL:191] The concert was still important to Ernst because he heard the first performance of *Harold in Italy* with Chrétian Urhan as the viola soloist. [BSG:41–2] Ernst would later perform either the whole or parts of it several times with Berlioz conducting, and the piece helped to confirm and cement their friendship.

On 23 December, Ernst gave a Soirée Musicale at F. Stoepel's salons. [GMP:14/12/34; E:23] Franz Stoepel was an unstable music teacher who owned a drab schoolroom at 6 rue Monsigny. Once a month, Stoepel's pupils used the room to give recitals, for the rest of the time it was available to hire. [FCPW:88–90] The room was not large, and the ticket price was low (five francs) so Ernst cannot have made a great deal of money, but it may fairly be said that this was the event that marked the true beginning of his Parisian reputation. He performed an unidentified *Andante* of his own, one of Mayseder's *Polonaises*, a *Duo sur des motives du Pré aux Clercs*, composed and played with the pianist Charles Schunke, and finally his new *Ludovic Fantasy*. The fantasy won thunderous applause and the press notices more than justified his years of isolated study. The critic of the *Gazette musicale* wrote:

> In the concert on 23rd December, it was above all M. Ernst who shone because of his rare talent on the violin. To an extraordinary facility on his instrument, he added so noble and individual an execution, so delicate and penetrating an expressiveness, that we do not hesitate to place him next to the greatest artists of the present day. As a composer, we have also seen him make an excellent start ... [GMP: 28/12/34:427. E:24]

While another critic commented:

> [Ernst's] playing ... seemed to us entirely free of the pretensions and charlatanism which Paganini's imitators introduced into the modern school. He combines with an exceptional lightness and mastery of his instrument such a noble and personal execution, such a tender and sweeping expression, and such sincere feeling that we do not hesitate to place him at the side of the greatest artists of our day. [EOC:5–6]

After months of intense self criticism, the influence of Paganini was just beginning to abate, and his own more emotional but still vigorous style was starting to develop.

On 25 December, Christmas Day, Ernst and Schunke repeated their success with the duo on *Le Pré aux Clercs* at the Opéra-comique, and Ernst played in another soirée at Stoepel's. This time, Liszt and Chopin played compositions for four hands by Liszt and Moscheles, and Liszt accompanied Ernst at sight – and perfectly – in several solos. [GMP:28/12/34:427. E:24]

Compared with musicians of a similar stature, Chopin gave very few concerts, but this is the third time Ernst shared the platform with him, and in all they would appear together seven times at concerts in Paris. This is all the more remarkable because Chopin was extremely fastidious about other musicians and, like many middle-class Poles of the time, held a low opinion of Jews. [CF:65, 137, 150] The first record which places Ernst and Chopin together is Bull's account of meeting them for breakfast at the Count of Montebello's. They may have met before this, but it could not have been long before because Chopin had only arrived in Paris in September 1831. The two musicians evidently liked and admired one another, and communication was facilitated by the fact that they both spoke French and had a number of friends and acquaintances in common. Chopin had twice visited Vienna and knew many of the performers there, and on 4 April 1831 he had appeared at the Redoutensaal on the same programme as Joseph Böhm. [FCPW:43]

Ernst became known as 'the Chopin of the violin' and there are a number of reasons for this. There were certain physical and emotional similarities since both were small, slightly-built men with a striking pallor, who were both prey to frequent bouts of illness, depression and melancholy. Musically, both were profoundly influenced by the *Bel Canto* style of contemporary Italian opera. They were particularly impressed by the work of Rossini, Donizetti and Bellini, with its emphasis on long-drawn lines of melody sweetened by added thirds, sixths and tenths, and given additional plangency by chromatic colouring in the simple accompaniment. Like Paganini, Chopin translated and developed this inheritance in instrumental terms, and it is striking that nearly every form Ernst used had already been utilized by Chopin (who was much the stronger creative personality): sets of variations, jointly composed fantasias on operatic melodies, the nocturne, polonaise, rondo, étude, concerto, romance, *Andante spianato*, bolero, and so on.

Both Liszt and Ernst were profoundly influenced by Paganini, and had a similar attitude to audiences. Berlioz observed in the 1850s: 'Chopin …was strictly a virtuoso of the elegant salon, the intimate gathering. For Ernst, vast halls, crowded theatres, the great pulsating public, hold no terrors. On the contrary, he loves them and like Liszt, is never more potent than when there is an audience of two thousand to subdue.' [BM:538] Ernst and Liszt would later be linked by their generous donations to charity, and a joke (that unfortunately does not translate well) intended to deter any virtuoso thinking of travelling to St Petersburg: 'Pianists much watch out for Liszt [List = trick, cunning] and the violinists must be E(a)rn(e)stly on guard.' [EOC:14]

There does not seem to be much mutual influence on their compositions, and this is hardly surprising. Ernst at this stage had written very little, and Liszt had hardly come into his own as a composer. But according to Schumann, it was Liszt's transcription of Paganini's 24th *Caprice* that inspired Ernst to write his *Carnival of Venice* [SMM:363], and Ernst could well have been led to write his virtuoso versions of Schubert's *Erlking* and of the sixteenth-century dance *La Romanesca* by the success of Liszt's earlier transcriptions. The real impact of Ernst as a composer on Liszt would have to wait until after the 1848 revolution.

In 1835, Ernst had every intention of building on this success the previous year. At a performance in Pleyel's salon on 13 February, where he played an *air varié*, his playing was described as elegant and secure, but some of the old complaints about his lack of individuality resurfaced. [RM:22/2/35:61. E:24] These were conclusively answered by another performance at the hôtel Lafitte, when he and the Irish pianist George Osborne played an *Andantino* and the *Ludovic Fantasy* on the same stage as some of the greatest singers of the era – Rubini, Lablache, Santini, Grisi and Stoltz. Playing in such company raised Ernst's profile with the general public, and his performance was received with warmth and appreciation. [GMP:22/2/35:84. E:25]

Saturday performances at the Opéra-comique were followed by another appearance with Chopin and Liszt at the Théâtre des Italiens in a concert designed to raise money for Polish exiles. [FCPW:97–100] Ernst was now becoming a familiar feature of the best concerts in Paris, and the critic for the *Gazette musicale* could observe the marked improvement in his technique: 'M. Ernst, in a violin solo of his own composition, gave new evidence of the steady progress of his talent. He seems to have acquired more skill in his rapid trills and greater assurance in his upper notes since the last time he appeared in public.' [FCPW:226] After such a good review, it is not surprising that Liszt asked Ernst to appear at a concert organized for his pupil Hermann Cohen at the Salle Chantereine on 23 April. [YL:195]

Several sources claim that Ernst became de Bériot's pupil, but there is no documentary evidence to support this suggestion. One of Ernst's reasons for coming to Paris was to hear and emulate the capital's leading violinists, and since the older French school (Baillot, Kreutzer, Rode, Haberneck and Lafont) was beginning to give way to the newer Franco-Belgian school (de Bériot, Artôt, Hauman and Vieuxtemps) he was deeply interested in the leader of the new school. He certainly would have attended de Bériot's concerts and admired his extremely neat, finished execution, and enjoyed the refined prettiness of his melodies and arrangements. If your playing had been criticized for lack of elegance, then de Bériot was clearly the man to study. But it is also worth remembering that Bull described Ernst as a 'pupil of the great Paganini' (and perhaps this was Ernst's own description of himself at the time) because Ernst listened to Paganini assiduously, and spoke and played to him on a number of occasions. If this was enough to count as being someone's pupil, then it seems reasonable to suppose that Ernst's reputation as a pupil of de Bériot rests on a similar foundation.

It is likely that the *Andante* and *Andantino* mentioned above are early versions of Ernst's *Two Nocturnes* (in A and E major) op.8 (although these are not quite the tempo indications in the published work) and that the *air varié* is an early version of his *Thème Allemand Varié* op.9. The *Nocturnes* are two of Ernst's most Chopinesque compositions. The first is straightforward and tuneful (it would eventually became the introduction to his *Carnival of Venice* op.18), and the second is a more elaborate exercise in double-stops and *filoritua*. They were both dedicated to Mr Andrew Fountaine, a rich Englishman who would later play an important role in Ernst's career. The *Thème Allemand varié* is a brilliant and effective little piece: an introduction and set of five variations based on the theme that Beethoven used in his *Andante Favori*. [EOC: 28, 60]

At this point, Ernst decided to look for success beyond Paris, and set out on a tour of the provinces. This had barely begun when news of his father's death reached him in Bordeaux in late April. He stayed on to appear at a soirée, and played so movingly, according to one account, that the audience sat in stunned silence at the end of his performance. When they had recovered themselves enough to applaud he had disappeared. [NMZ:5/2/41:45–6. E:25] The next day he was on the way back to Paris, and from there he made his way directly to Brünn. Jakob's death, on 27 March, was not unexpected since he was 81 and had been in poor health for seven years. Although Ernst's relations with his father had not always been easy, he evidently felt sufficient tenderness and respect to say his farewells.

He was not, however, prepared to let his new-found success evaporate. Having overseen the elaborate bureaucratic formalities which, in the Austrian Empire, death set in motion, he returned to France in August. He gave a number of concerts in Angers [RM:16/8/35:262. E:25] and the following month he was warmly applauded at Nante, where he appeared with the famous soprano Mme Cinti-Damoreau, one of Chopin's favourite singers. [RM:13/9/35:285. E:25]

In the early months of 1836, the *Gazette musicale* reported that Ernst and Schunke had appeared in Paris again: 'M. Ernst, the young violinist of such capable and powerful abilities, also garnered his share of the honours in a duo on the theme from *Oberon* composed and performed by him [with M. Shunke at the piano] as well as variations for violin alone.' [RGM:14/2/36: FCPW:227] The set of solo variations has not been identified, and unfortunately no copy of the fantasy, which Schunke and Ernst published in 1837, has survived.

By the time Ernst came to play with Osborne again, in the huge hall of the Salle Chanteraine in April 1836, they had jointly composed the *Brilliant Variations on the Favourite Air: I tuoi frequenti palpiti*. This was played at the end of the concert after a performance of a salon piece by Ernst (possibly one of the two *Nocturnes*). The applause was prodigious and the concert was warmly reviewed by Berlioz in the *Gazette musicale de Paris*. The delighted composer said that Ernst's extraordinary talent was approaching closer and closer to perfection, and that the slight stiffness, particularly in difficult passages, which some critics had noticed in earlier performances, had been altogether banished. [RGM:10/4/36:111. E:26]

On 1 April 1836, Ernst played at a concert given by a young composer called Despréaux at the Théâtre du Palais-Royal, and in August he moved on to Orléans where he had been invited to distribute prizes to the pupils at the Institute musical. He had already given several concerts there, and mention of them at the ceremony brought bursts of applause. [RGM: 2/10/36:351. E:26] In September, he showed the first signs of a serious intention to perform in England. He travelled to London, not to play, but simply to make contacts, observe the musical scene, and find his way around. There he met the pianist and composer Moscheles, one of the directors of the Philharmonic, and booked himself in for two concerts once he had finished his tour of southern France. [EOC:7–8]

He played in Rouen and Le Harvre in early November 1836 [RGM:18/12/36:449. E:27] and on the 19th of the month we find him in Lyon, writing to his friend the sculptor Jean Pierre Dantan. Dantan had developed a new and popular kind of caricature sculpture, and would eventually portray Liszt, Rossini, Berlioz, Paganini, Chopin, Ernst and many other leading musicians. The beginning of the letter is obscure, but it would appear to imply that Dantan is having second thoughts about a love affair, and that Ernst may at one stage have been romantically involved with the same woman: 'Cut the whole thing short. That's the best advice I can give you, because it's based on facts and not on appearances. When you want a fuller explanation I can give it to you, although it would be painful for me ...' [IC:265]

He soon moves on, as he often does, to giving an account of his own musical successes:

> Yesterday, I gave my first concert here. It was so successful that the director of the concert immediately contracted me for five concerts on the same attractive terms. I have been all the more pleased at this outcome for the fact that I was preceded here by two great violinists, Hauman and Bull. These five concerts will keep me here for two weeks and I don't know what will happen after. Frankowski and I are living here in a nice fashion. We don't have time to get bored, what with rehearsals, concerts, a few old acquaintances we ran into, some new ones, the theatre, the danceuses and some pretty sights we see from our windows – all this makes the time pass very pleasantly. H.W. Ernst, [Hotel du Parc, No.45. IC:265]

Secretaries had to deal with accommodation, travel and concert arrangements, and if they were musical, accompanying, copying and arranging. Frankowski certainly had musical talent because, in the opening section of the letter quoted above, Ernst reports that Frankowski is relishing the extraordinary popularity of a waltz he has just composed [IC:265], and Berlioz would later thank Frankowski for some shrewd critical advice: 'M. Frankoski [*sic*], Ernst's secretary, drew my attention in Vienna to the weak and much too abrupt ending of the Queen Mab scherzo [from his symphony, *Romeo and Juliet*], and I wrote the present coda in its place.' [BM:304]

Chapter 6

Paganini and Marseilles: 1837

By late November or early December, Ernst and Frankowski must have heard that Paganini was returning from Italy to give concerts in the south of France, and they hurried to Marseilles. Initially, Ernst had no thought of performing himself, but after a four-year gap, he wanted to attend Paganini's concerts and, if possible, observe his practice again.

Since 1834, Paganini's career had been in decline. Unsuccessful tours of the Low Countries and then England had been followed by legal wrangles with the singer Charlotte Watson and her father. On returning to Paris, he had been subjected to vicious attacks in the press over his alleged refusal to play at a charity concert, and, chagrined at this treatment, he went home to Italy after six years abroad. Successful concerts followed, and in November 1835 he was appointed to the governing board of the court orchestra in Parma. Under his guidance, the orchestra improved markedly, but demoted players complained to jealous court officials, and in July 1836 Paganini resigned rather than be drawn into petty squabbles and intrigues.

He decided to resume his career as a travelling virtuoso, and arranged concerts in Nice in December 1836 and at Marseilles in January 1837. Illness, intrigue and administration had made him neglect his violin, but the renewed stimulation of eager audiences made him feel optimistic. As he wrote to Germi on December 23 1836: 'My violin is still a little out of humour with me but after six or eight concerts, which I shall give at Marseilles, it will go perfectly. I have more courage than strength, but I'm glad to say I've taken up my instrument again and have presented myself before the public, because such a shock has had no little effect upon my health.' [PG: II:240]

The 'six or eight concerts' in Marseilles dwindled to two, and those were much less successful than he had hoped, partly because of declining health and partly through fierce competition from Ernst. The latter wrote a long and detailed account of the matter to his brother Johann on 15 April 1837. The letter is written from Avignon, four months after Ernst had met Paganini again, and six weeks after the Italian's departure:

> Dearest Brother Johann and all my Sisters, For some time it seems that a real fate rules over us, and I neither receive letters from you nor you from me. I cannot explain it other than the frequent accidents that happen to the mail coaches this winter are to blame for this, for several letters which I sent in the interior of France have not reached their destination. Four months ago I wrote to you from Lyon and to dear sister Fanny in Pest with the comment that you would receive a bust of me in bronze by Dantan, the most famous sculptor in Paris. This bust was actually sent without my receiving notice of its

arrival. Just yesterday I received the letter that you wrote to Dr Roth,[1] and how great was my astonishment to learn that you complain about a silence of seven months on my part; it pained me immensely because I could easily imagine the uneasiness which you must feel. However, I am comforted by this, that you are too convinced of my brotherly love for you to believe for even one moment that negligence was the reason for my silence.

My tour this year was up to now not very profitable financially: in Lyon special circumstances were responsible, and in Marseilles there was the meeting with Paganini, that Colossus. But he has not harmed me, and from my report you will learn that I could be happy over this meeting: I knew that Paganini was to come to Marseilles and went there only to hear him again after four years. When I arrived it was said that he could not be coming yet. I made use of this opportunity to announce a concert. The public knew that he was to come, and in expectation they wanted to save their money for him. Nevertheless, there were very many people in the audience since there are many concert subscribers. I received a storm of applause and was called back twice. Paganini had already arrived, but the day of his concert had not been decided. I profited from this situation and, encouraged by this acclaim, advertised a grand concert which was much better attended than the first. There was even more applause, and I was recalled twice and this on a Friday.

The following Sunday, Paganini was to perform. People in general were saying, 'What more can Paganini do?' The public was in a state of highest expectation, and Paganini did not meet the demand – he did not receive as much applause as I, and it was generally said that he does not speak to the heart as I do. He advertised a second concert, saying in the newspapers to the public, 'You may prefer Ernst, go and hear Paganini on Sunday when he will play the Moses variations on the fourth string, and you will weep.' People came again with the highest expectations and again were unsatisfied. After that opinions were divided, but in general it was said that I play with more feeling and that he conquerors more difficulties.

I must tell you that Paganini is no longer the same man, that he has lost much. After his second concert the carnival was approaching, which I let go past and then gave my third concert after Paganini in which I played the same Moses variations on the G-string, his own composition in order to show that I can play everything that he plays, since this was proclaimed his most difficult piece. I had memorized this piece and also written an orchestral accompaniment. This time the house was crammed full; a large part of the subscribers had renounced their rights and paid for their tickets. My share of the receipts amounted to 1500 francs, and as much went to the director plus the expenses, so that 3000 francs was taken in, which is unheard of for Marseilles. I cannot describe to you my anxiety as I stepped before the public this time. However, I was received so enthusiastically that I was immediately set at ease. This concert was a great triumph for me; to be received thus after Paganini is a great honour; at the end I fell unconscious into the arms of my friend. [EOC:6–7]

As soon as Paganini arrived in Nice, Ernst returned to his old trick of spying on him. Paganini was staying at the Hotel Beauvau [PG:II:241], and through a relative of Frankowski's – an old sergeant's widow – Ernst arranged to rent the room next door. Here he hid for a day and a half, listening to his practice and taking down his compositions by ear. He was especially successful with the *Moses* variations

---

1 Dr Roth was a good friend of Ernst and Heller, but I have been able to find out very little about him beyond the fact that he was a homeopathic doctor who briefly attended Chopin in the last months of his life.

on the G string which, as he mentions above, he played at his final concert. By a similar subterfuge, Ernst also managed to gain access to all Paganini's rehearsals, from which, as always, the public was excluded. [EOC:6]

Ernst, in part, ascribes his triumph to Paganini's decline, a factor on which he expanded in conversation with Joachim in the 1850s:

> When I met [Paganini] again years later in the south of France, his confidence on the fingerboard was much decreased, so that I, without being conceited, played some of his showpieces just as well if not better than himself. I was successful at this, partly because I didn't use his grotesque playing position [he liked to thrust out his right leg], which occasionally worked against him. [GV:429]

What Ernst does not mention is that Paganini boosted the fortunes of his rival by seriously mishandling his public relations.

A certain amount of hostility was latent in the town. There were two active musical organizations: the Concerts Thubaneau, a private society founded in 1805 which had been farsighted enough to perform Beethoven's symphonies before the Paris Conservatoire; and the younger, more efficient Société Philharmonic, founded in 1835, and made up largely of musicians drawn from the theatre. Paganini had close links with the latter, and this upset some members of the older organization.

Staying alongside Paganini and Ernst that winter in Marseilles, was a French violinist called Alexander Boucher, with whom Ernst had played in Paris the year before. Boucher was a considerable technician but also a considerable self-publicist and charlatan. The French could still be swept away by ungovernable nostalgia for the glory days of Napoleon, and Boucher, as it happens, bore a remarkable similarity to the Emperor. He therefore liked to begin his performances by imitating several famous Napoleonic stances and gestures – placing his hand in his jacket, removing his hat, and taking snuff in the imperial manner – while the crowd, beside itself with patriotic ardor, exploded in shouts, cheers and applause. [VC:89–90]

He soon saw an opportunity to exploit the tension and wrong-foot Paganini, whose refusal to play at a charity concert in Paris had recently caused a scandal in the press. The catalyst occurred on New Year's Eve, the day after Ernst's first concert, when fire broke out in the shop of a cabinet maker at 28, rue de Rome. Largely owing to late discovery, intense cold and inadequate fire-fighting equipment, the fire took hold quickly and wiped out an entire block, leaving many families destitute and homeless. On hearing the news, Boucher invited Paganini, along with Ernst and himself, to take part in a benefit concert for the fire victims in which 'Italy, France and Germany [sic] would be worthily represented.' [PG:II:240] Paganini, who disliked the implied element of competition, especially in his weakened state, declined the offer, whereupon Boucher let it be known that the scheme had collapsed because of Paganini's refusal. Several members of the Thubaneau orchestra then wrote open letters to the press, endorsing Boucher's account of the matter and deploring Paganini's behaviour.

Their campaign met with some success. One local paper commented: 'It is certain that Paganini will leave Marseilles without lending his name to a charitable undertaking. His great renown is not enough. He is duty bound to show a charitable side, to demonstrate beyond a doubt that he is a friend of the wretched and unfortunate.' [PG:II:241] Paganini's decision to cancel his own concert, planned for 22 January, because of ill health did little to assuage local opinion.

He had also managed to alienate the members of the Philharmonic Society by restricting his performances in Marseilles to Sunday matinées as subscribers to the Society were entitled to free entry in the evenings. He therefore wanted to play in the afternoon, and Sunday was the only day he could guarantee that most people would not be working. This, as can be imagined, exacerbated his already considerable reputation for meanness and lack of charity. He had now set both of the town's musical organizations against him.

When Ernst announced his third concert for 3 March, he made a point of granting free admission to the 800 members of the Philharmonic Society. The gesture was much appreciated: 'In a spontaneous feeling of admiration for Ernst,' one local paper wrote, 'a number of the subscribers had refused to avail themselves of this privilege and had bought their tickets.' [PG:II:242] In these circumstances, it is hardly surprising that he was rapturously received. Just in case anybody did not notice the contrast with Paganini, Arsene Truc, solo trombone of the Thubaneau orchestra, wrote a vitriolic attack on the Italian, pointing out the reason why he had only played at matinées.

Having cancelled his last concert, the disillusioned and embattled Paganini retired to his hotel room. He was only too aware that the decline in his playing was due to failing health but was remarkably open and unapologetic about his treatment of the Philharmonic Society. He writes to Germi:

> If my physical forces were not inferior to my spirit, I should have been more satisfied with my playing at the three concerts in Nice and also at the two I gave in the large theatre here in the daytime so as to exclude the 800 subscribers who would have been entitled to free entry in the evening. After announcing that my second [concert] was my last, I'm not giving any more here because I've firmly decided, before taking up my instrument again, to improve my health with the aid of a famous German doctor who promises me complete recovery. I can't leave Marseilles for another twenty days since I have to have a light treatment at the neck of the bladder ... [PG:II:242]

He passed the time in his room playing Beethoven quartets with members of the Rossi and Ronstand quartets, who also happened to be staying in the same hotel, before departing for Nice again on 25 February. He immediately became bed-ridden, and described to Germi his ghastly range of symptoms: 'rheumatism, ...orchitis [my left testicle had swollen to the size of a large pear or small pumpkin], ... fever, hemorrhage, tenesmus, and finally flu with catarrhal cough.' [PG:II:244]

In contrast to Paganini, Ernst was flushed with success and enjoying local hospitality and popularity to the full. He writes to Dantan from Marseilles on 23 March 1837:

> My Dear Friend, I thank you for your kind letter which I would have answered sooner if my time hadn't been taken up completely by continual dinners, luncheons, all kinds of parties, resulting from my coming departure. Even as I write this letter my room is full of

friends. You shouldn't be surprised, therefore, if the style of this letter, written in the midst of a horrible din, is a little disorganized.

I am sorry to be leaving Marseilles; in no other city have I found such friendliness towards me – as well as an appreciation of my modest talent. Here they have a club – they are the most likeable chaps in the whole world. As of this moment, your busts have not yet arrived, and this upsets me because during my stay here, I could have used a few dozen more. The ones which did arrive are already reserved.

You must have received the small package; if not it should arrive shortly. My last concert was a complete success. My performance of Paganini's sonata on the G-string had an overwhelming effect. All the newspapers in the town were full of news of this concert whose receipts got all the way up to 3000 francs. If you can find, among your connections, a way to spread the news around in a few newspapers, I would be eternally grateful to you. Anyone else but me would have taken greater advantage of such a gloriously successful encounter with the great man. On Easter Monday they are preparing a big concert for me at Aix (seven leagues from Marseilles). The elite of Marseilles will go with me to Aix in order to fill out the audience, with the result that the really fashionable set, both men and women, will be attending the concert, the last one I am giving in Provence. We are in a hurry to get to Paris so that I can get from there to London which is where I really want to go. They are saying that Paganini is off to America and that he is already at Le Havre, but I know he's sick in Nice from where I receive news every day. [IC:266]

Ernst's intelligence from Nice was remarkably accurate. Paganini had been attracted by the Watsons' offer to organize an American tour and had even gone so far as to purchase his transatlantic passage. But his continued ill health in Nice made him cancel his ticket, a fact which he mentions to Germi in a letter of 16 March – a mere week before Ernst's letter to Dantan. [IC:266]

Being a virtuoso in the nineteenth century, to a greater extent than now, involved being responsive to local mores. You had to charm the audience you interacted with, woo the critics, send complimentary tickets to just the right people, cultivate local worthies, keep tabs on your rivals, smooth the feelings of local musicians, and be aware of institutions and rivalries. The episode in Marseilles shows just how good Ernst was at these tasks. He seems to have absorbed the nature of local musical politics effortlessly, and went to remarkable lengths to secure the necessary intelligence about his rival. He then manages to respond in the most tactful and effective manner, getting both musical organizations on his side, but without any hint of the opportunism which people ascribed to Boucher. With the entire town delighting in his presence, he then takes great care to market images of himself, frets about their availability, and uses contacts to insert helpful stories in the Parisian press.

Ernst left Marseilles towards the end of March. Initially, he planned to spend a year in Italy, but, like Paganini, he fell ill in Nice and the plan had to be abandoned. Instead he continued to tour in southern France. He wrote to his family from Avignon:

> I am sorry you did not receive my letter from Marseilles, since I sent you many of the most splendid reviews. Now I still have some others which I shall not delay in sending. I shall also not hesitate to write to Marseilles in order to get the same ones, and then send these duplicates on to you. Marseilles and some excursions from there to Toulon, Draguignan,

and Nice (in the latter Paganini was also there before me) took me three months, and I hope that news of my splendidly reviewed concerts in the capital of southern France will be advantageous for me in all the other cities in the same part of France. If my receipts turn out as I hope, I shall soon be with you. From Marseilles I went to Aix and feel already the favourable influence of the Marseilles reviews; tomorrow I give a concert here and go from here to Nîmes, Montpellier, Toulouse, and several other cities. I hope to write to you a good deal more from these cities, not only about myself, because these cities offer very many curiosities, dating from the old Romans, and many monuments are to be found there.

Up to now I have told you about my public triumph in Marseilles; if I wanted to tell you about my cordial reception, I would not be able to stop at all. My portrait was painted there and is a good likeness: from Paris I shall send you several by the cabinet-courier. They were sold in Marseilles like bread, just as the bust was, which Dantan sent there. One of these was set up in a theatre box, and when the public noticed it, I was applauded with real enthusiasm. I have asked M.D. Roth again to send the bust when convenient, and you can count on receiving it. The Leon[e]s are saying that they have been without a letter from me for an eternity; I don't know what I am to think. Write to Monsieur H.W. Ernst, general delivery Toulouse, France, département de la haute Garonne.

My health is fairly good; however, I have to take care of myself and dare not work too hard; my contest with Paganini has tired me very much.

If you have not received my letter from Lyon, then you don't know that I was in London for some weeks in September, but only to orientate myself there. I saw Moscheles and was received by him with friendliness and consideration; he booked me for two concerts (since he is one of the directors of the Philharmonic Society), and when I have successfully finished my tour of southern France, I shall be in London by the middle or end of May, since this month, June, and [the first] half of July constitute the only good season for music in London. [Nothing seems to have come of this plan.] If not, then I hope to turn my steps at once to Germany. God grant me good fortune, for I have too much ambition to return to my fatherland with my financial expectations only half fulfilled.

Farewell, may God be with you. Think of your devoted brother,
H.W. Ernst.
From London I went to Rouen and Le Havre, from which latter city I am enclosing a newspaper. [EOC:7–8]

No later than October, Ernst was back in Paris. He made a welcome appearance at several salons, and played a number of times to the Royal family at the palace. [RGM:15/10/37:449; 29/10/37:473. EUZ:14] On 10 November and 8 December, he was invited to play at the Opéra. This was a singular honour: amongst violinists, only Paganini and Bull had performed in the enormous building. Ernst's talent was widely acknowledged, but one reviewer still thought he modelled himself too closely on Paganini and attempted to use too much power. [RGM:5/11/37:481; 12/11/37:490] Perhaps his recent encounter and the size of the auditorium explain both criticisms. [RGM:10/12/37:543; 17/12/37:557. E:35–6]

At the Opéra, he may well have given the first performance of his *Concertino* in D, op.12, dedicated to his friend and mentor Habeneck, and the most substantial work he had yet written. Although the violin writing is of Paganinian brilliance, the basic form and outline of the movement is clearly influenced by Böhm's D major concerto which Ernst had played in the late 1820s and early '30s. This may explain why the main theme of the first movement is a little stiff and formulaic, although the second theme has Schubertian life and warmth. The second movement in F♯ minor is a most melancholy Italian aria with some fine interplay between the violin, horn and solo cello, and melodic writing in octaves that foreshadows the concerto op.23. The opening of the finale is like a waltz-chorus from a comic opera, while the sinuous and charming second theme, in E major, can raise a smile with its unexpected modulations.

This was also the year in which he composed the *Carnival of Venice*, a piece which grew so popular it eventually became a millstone round his neck. [MW:27/7/43:252] The published work consists of an introduction (the *Nocturne* in A), the main theme, 'Cara mamma mia' and twenty-five burlesque variations – although he had a repertoire of more than a hundred, and was always improvising new ones. These make extensive use of what he later termed 'Paganinian difficulties' and include some genuine technical innovations, including the following ingenious mingling of *arco* and *pizzicato*:

Example 6.1   Ernst, *The Carnival of Venice*, op.18, bars 243–248

Paganini had already composed a piece of this name, using the same theme, in the late 1820s. This work remained unpublished until the 1850s, and Ernst's failure to publish his own version immediately later caused confusion and professional problems.

From the point of view of his playing, the end of 1836 and the first few months of 1837 was one of the defining periods in Ernst's career. He had placed himself in direct competition with Paganini before and largely suffered from the comparison, even to the point of considering giving up the violin. But in this period, he once again played in the same place over the same weeks and emerged triumphant.

PART II
Early Tours

.

Chapter 7

Holland, Germany and the Austrian Empire: 1837–40

Ernst was coming to be known as a composer as well as violinist. On 18 December 1837, Vieuxtemps played a set of his variations in Berlin [AMZ:17/1/38:Col.49]; on 21 January 1838, *La France Musicale* recommended his *Elegy* [FM:21/1/38:5]; and on 15 January, his friend Heinrich Panofka played the same piece to enormous acclaim at an aristocratic salon. Delighted with his performance, Ernst promised to play a piece of Panofka's at one of his own concerts. The German pianist Charles Hallé, soon to be a close friend of Ernst's, appeared on the same programme, and this is their first recorded association. [RGM:14/1/38:16]

The *Elégie sur le mort d'un object chéri: Chant pour violon* op.10, consists of a genuinely melancholy, long-spun C minor melody over a simple arpeggiated accompaniment. Towards the end, the melody turns itself into ecstatic double-stops in C major, and these eventually subside into a calm, pianissimo repose. Early editions use Ernst's own fingering, and from these one can see how he used *portamenti* to increase the emotional impact of his playing (Ex. 7.1):

Example 7.1   Ernst, *Elegy*, op.10, bars 14–16

The sudden and unexpected use of the seventh-position on the G string in the theme's first statement introduces a heart-stopping density of tone (Ex. 7.2), and the melody's reprise on the A string, in high positions, reduces it to a ghostly wail (Ex. 7.3):

Example 7.2   Ernst, *Elegy*, op.10, bars 1–5

Example 7.3   Ernst, *Elegy*, op.10, bars 31–32

Several later editions preface the work with an introduction by Spohr (originally part of the adagio from his sixth violin concerto) and this was the version that was usually played – by Joachim and Wilhemj, for example – in the second half of the nineteenth century.

Although not harmonically adventurous, and with an occasionally tricky violin part, the *Elegy* became one of the nineteenth-century's best loved pieces, largely, one imagines, because its basic outline fits Victorian ideas on eschatology like a glove. The British Library contains 24 editions published between 1844 and 1912 and these include transcriptions for concertina, flute, organ, viola, piano, cello, and voice. There are many further arrangements, including some by distinguished musicians (Busoni, for example, transcribed it for clarinet and string quartet). But even these commercial arrangements could not always fit demand, and a recent country house sale in England showed that one Victorian amateur loved the piece so much she produced manuscript arrangements for no less than six different instrumental combinations. The extent of its fame is further demonstrated by the role it plays in Tolstoy's short novel *The Kreutzer Sonata*. After the ill-fated protagonists play the *Kreutzer*, it is the Russian *audience* which insists that Ernst's *Elegy* be played, and it is recalling this piece rather than the *Kreutzer* that convinces the narrator that his wife (the pianist) and the violinist are having an affair.[1] [KS:123, 127] Such a successful piece naturally set a trend for writing elegies, and Panofka, Bazzini and Vieuxtemps all followed suit.

After two concerts in Lille [RGM:21/1/38:29], Ernst performed Osborne's piano trio with the composer and the cellist Franchome at the Salle Chantereine in Paris on 1 March. The work received mixed reviews, but the *Elegy*, and one of Mayseder's compositions were well received. [NMZ:30/3/38:104. RGM:4/3/38:104] The real sensation, however, was created by Ernst giving the first performance of his *Fantasie brilliante sur le marche et la Romance d'Otello*. Although he looked subdued before he played, he showed dash, vigour and dexterity in the virtuoso passage-work, and wonderful sensitivity in the cantilenas. Dropping his head, he became completely lost in his own performance and seemed astonished to hear the audience's applause at the end. [RGM:4/3/38. FM:4/3/38:3–4. E:39]

The *Otello Fantasy*, based on the march from act 1 and Desdemona's aria from act 3 of Rossini's *Otello* (1816), is one of Ernst's finest pieces. Rather than following the usual scheme of writing a set of variations on one operatic aria, Ernst follows the procedure, made popular by Liszt and Thalberg, of writing a more integrated and symphonic form of fantasy based on several themes from an opera. Ernst develops a unique and satisfying structure (introduction, march, two variations, romanza, third variation, finale) and he makes his arrangement all the more effective by having the violin play quietly for long periods. The overall effect is that, with the exception of

---

1 The narrator describes the instant when he becomes convinced of the couple's guilt as follows: 'It was at that moment that I called to mind their faces as I saw them that memorable Sunday evening when, after they had played the *Kreutzer Sonata*, they played some little piece, I forget by whom, I only remember it was passionate to excess.' [KS:127] As only the *Elegy* and some 'lighter pieces' were played after the sonata [KS:123], the *Elegy* is the one piece that fits the narrator's description.

the soloist's first statement of the march, four-square outbursts from the orchestra are answered with delicate spiccato bowing, harmonics, and filigree brilliance from the violin.

A number of Thalberg's fantasies (for example the *Moses Fantasy* of 1837) begin with a theme of his own composition, and Ernst extends this device. The lyrical introductory section is entirely his own, and he brings the theme back before the finale as a way of unifying his work. In addition, the finale, while distantly related to Roderigo's aria in act 2, scene 9 ('Fra tante smanie et tante …') and a rhythmic idea from bar 91 of the overture, is again entirely his own work. When Liszt began to write this kind of fantasy, he used the title 'Reminiscences' rather than 'Variations on …' and the new title indicates we are supposed to be hearing an opera through an individual consciousness. Similarly, we can think of Thalberg's and Ernst's use of their own themes, as well as the selection they have made from the opera's melodies, as ways of indicating that the current piece is a personal and subjective response to a work of art. The effect of Ernst's hesitant, reflective melody reappearing is similar to that of Musorgsky's recurrent promenade theme as he walks with us through Hartmann's pictures.

The *Otello Fantasy* is the first important multi-themed fantasy for violin and orchestra, and it is one of only three works, alongside Wieniawski's *Faust Fantasy* and Sarasate's *Carmen Fantasy*, to hold any place in the repertoire. Both these latter works were written later in the century (c.1860 and 1883 respectively) and neither can boast the formal innovations of Ernst's composition.

Two days after appearing at the Salle Chantereine, Ernst performed at the concert hall of Henri Pape, 19 rue des Bons Enfans, in a concert given by that eccentric but imposing genius, Charles Valentin Alkan. Although only 25, Alkan had already acquired a formidable reputation as a pianist, and was becoming known as a composer of strange and ferociously difficult piano music that had come to the attention of Schumann and Liszt. [CVA:24–5] The highlight of this concert was a performance of Alkan's two-piano eight-hand arrangement of Beethoven's seventh symphony played by Alkan himself, two of his neighbours from the square d'Orléans – Chopin and Zimmerman – and Chopin's pupil Adolf Gutmann. [PWFC:24] Unsurprisingly, in spite of the performers' excellence, the arrangement was found to be a travesty of the original. Other pieces were better received: 'A trio for violin, piano and cello by Mayseder,' wrote the *Revue et Gazette musicale*, 'opened the concert in an admirable fashion. It was performed with verve and excellent coordination by M. Ernst, the beneficiary [Alkan], and M. Batta.' [11/3/38. FCPW:229]

In August 1838, Ernst was wildly applauded in Bordeaux and Pau, where he met two other violinists already making considerable names for themselves – Ghys and Hauman. [RGM:19/8/38:327] Hauman would later become one of Ernst's serious rivals, and Ernst would later fall out with both violinists in a dispute about authorship, but in the summer of 1838 all was sweetness and light. To hear the three virtuosi play Viotti together, it was said, was to be ravished by the emotional power of music. [FM:23/9/38. E:40]

Ernst gave further concerts in Lille, Nancy and Rouen where he created the by now expected sensation, and in November he was back in Paris. Here he played some of his new pieces, including the *Otello Fantasy*, at public concerts, and he often performed with the Hungarian pianist Stephen Heller – who was to become one of his closest friends and collaborators – in the homes of the Marquis de Custine and Count Appony. [FM: 25/11/38. NMZ:28/12/38:210. E:40]

Ernst began a tour of Holland in late November 1838, and sent a number of letters to his publisher Maurice Schlésinger, who also owned the influential *Revue et Gazette musicale*. Ernst is naturally keen to emphasize the scale of his own success, and chivvies his publisher about not snapping up his most popular works:

> I would never have believed that I would drive so many people in Holland crazy with my violin. From all sides, offers are streaming in. In 14 days I've now played officially approximately 7 times, of which 4 can be counted as totally on may account. My 2 concerts in the French theatre in Amsterdam brought in 5500 francs; the second was even fuller than the first and on the evening before the concert you couldn't get a ticket. I have to give 6 more concerts between now and the 23rd. Monday in Rotterdam, Tuesday in Delft, Friday in Amsterdam, Tuesday 22nd in Leyden, Wednesday in Harlem and Friday in Amsterdam again. Dear Schlesinger, why are you hesitating with my *Otello* [*Fantasy*]? I've already played it to enormous applause everywhere and it's always being requested. My *Elegy* is in massive demand, why have you been so stupid as not to buy it, or more like it, not to take it as a gift [?] By the way[,] I don't believe Lemoine [another Parisian publisher] has to profit from it because he has been tricked in Germany. There are an awful lot of violin amateurs, at least a far greater number than in the provinces of France. You will get through Scott of Antwerp a portrait, which is a good likeness of me. Do you want to pay for it to be made into a lithograph [?] I think you'll find a good demand here, since they are being asked for in general and there has even been a lithograph made of the one done in Lille, admittedly a very bad one.
>
> … My health is not so good, little sleep, constant travelling and rehearsing and playing are probably the cause of it. If you are writing, address it to me at the Hotel Maréchal de Turenne. I have set up home here and make many trips from it. I will give another one or two concerts here due to general demand, despite the fact that I've already given two concerts and played once at the Dilligenzia.
>
> Are you still in favour of my études? I'd be pleased my dear Maurice to recall the lovely gift of Madame Schlésinger. I really meant to write directly, but talking almost always in German, I feel the little French I know is disappearing and I'm increasingly thinking that I would be incapable of expressing in this language all the feelings I have for her. Please be my interpreter, my dear Maurice, and tell her (in French) that I'm madly in love with her. Live well and think of me. Best wishes to all your family. Yours, Ernst.
>
> Ps. I want to make some of the études from opera motifs, tell me which ones belong to you. <u>The idea remains between ourselves alone</u>. [13 Jan 1839. The Hague. BN]

Ernst was not the only one casting passionate glances in the direction of Madame Elisa Schlésinger. The fourteen-year-old Gustave Flaubert had met her in Trouville in 1836 and had fallen hopelessly in love, even though she displayed a mysterious and impenetrable reserve. In fact, she was secretive because she had a terrible secret which Flaubert was never to learn: Schlésinger had bought her from her previous husband. Born Élisa Foucault, she had married a Lieutenant Émile-Jacques Judée in 1829 when she was nineteen. He was being prosecuted for embezzlement, and in order to raise enough money to avoid arrest, Judée had sold her to Schlésinger. The publisher was unable to marry her until Judée died, and her first child, a daughter, was illegitimate. [SE:8] Even in promiscuous Paris, this was a story worth hiding.

Ernst's next letter is largely concerned with his own success, but it does establish the date of one of his compositions: *Variations de Bravoure sur l'air National Hollandais* op.18. This work, based on the song *Wien Neerlandsch Bloed Door d'Aadren Vloert* and associated with the Dutch war of independence [EOC:28], was clearly written for this tour:

> My success here in this country continues to be fabulous. I can barely get out of the carriage or the concert halls. The smallest towns of 3,000 to 4,000 inhabitants compete amongst themselves to see which one will enjoy me first, and some Parisian concerts are not perhaps so profitable as some of these small town offers. On Thursday 21st I am giving a big concert in the wonderful Odeon Hall, after that I've already played 5 times to a full house in the French Theatre, in which Vrugt, Madame Marinoni, Madame Fink-Lohr and Mlle. Buys (a *gorgeous* girl with a big voice and lots of feeling and talent) will all sing. The last one I will perhaps recommend to you, because she intends to go to Paris. On top of this[,] the majority of the orchestra from the Hague are coming to this concert. Forty men, led by the court orchestra leader Lübeck. The King himself has given permission for this. I'm going to play for the first time in this concert my caprice on the Dutch folksong. I believe that the concert will be a great success. The tickets are going for an unusual price here – 4 guilders, which is over 8 francs [–] and yesterday over 400 tickets had already been bought. Orders are coming in from 10–14 miles away. I hope to be in Paris in the spring and am already looking forward to telling you rogues (I'm including Panofka in this especially) orally the details of my artistic excursions.
>
> My best wishes to Mme.Schlésinger and a thousand compliments to your family.
>
> If you have instructions for [me] here, do not spare me. Your devoted friend, Ernst. Hotel de pays bas [19 February 1839. Amsterdam. BN]

Having discovered they were so profitable, Ernst continued to give concerts in the small towns in Brabant, Gueldre and Overysel. In Ziwolle, at the third of his concerts, the hall was so full that there was scarcely room for the musicians, and Ernst had to play in the midst of the crowd. His tour continued via Deventer, Doesburg, Gorcum, Bois-le-duc, Breda, Nymwegne, and on 26 April he gave a second concert in Arnhem – his fiftieth in Holland. After giving 67 concerts in Holland (including eleven in Amsterdam and five in the Hague) he returned to Paris. [RGM:25/4/39:140; 16/5/39:164. FM:19/12/39:309. E:41]

He did not stay long. In June, he was in Orléans from where he sent his publisher the news. The second half of the letter reads:

> From Heller (to whom I've sent three perhaps worthless nocturnes) I haven't had a word of an answer. Lecture him a little. What do you say to J— n's lovely articles? Out of sight, out of mind is the saying to which these conform on a daily basis. My études are progressing. I'm working the violin a lot. My health is good and I hope to begin my new journey with strength and progress. Do not forget me in the meantime in your correspondence for Berlin and all Germany. [16 July 1839. BN]

The 'three perhaps worthless nocturnes' are probably early versions of pieces that would that would eventually be included in Ernst and Heller's joint *Pensées*

Fugitives. The 'J—n' mentioned in the letter is the Parisian music critic Jules Janin, who had presumably not mentioned Ernst in his recent reviews.

The études, already mentioned in the first letter to Schlésinger, are rather more puzzling as there is no sign that they were ever published. It is possible that some of their material was used in the *Polyphonic Studies* twenty-five years later, but none of theses are based on 'motifs from operas'. (The last of the *Polyphonic Studies* is based on the Irish folksong *The Last Rose of Summer* that became well known through its use in Flotow's *Martha*, but that opera was not performed until 1847.)

I suspect that the only surviving remnant of these early études is a manuscript entitled 'Trio pour un Violone' kept in the museum in Carpentras, France. [BIC] It is a short study in combining accompaniment and melody, bowed and plucked notes, based on Bellini's tune *Tu-vedrai*, and the dedication says, 'à Monsiuer Laurent [a joint friend of Heller and Ernst] par son devoué, H.W. Ernst, 30 Avril 1837'. The date would seem about right if Ernst had completed twelve such études by 1839. The manuscript remained unpublished, and the tune would eventually form the basis of Ernst's *Introduction, Caprices et Finale sur un Thème de l'Opéra Il Pirate de Bellini*. None of the music of the manuscript is used in Ernst's larger concert piece, probably because the manuscript's arrangement of the tune would be insufficiently powerful to tell in a large space.

If this study remained unpublished, it seems reasonable to suppose the others remained unpublished as well. Schlésinger does not appear to have embraced the idea of a set of studies enthusiastically, and probably felt that such difficult solo pieces would have a very limited sale. At this period, Ernst had not composed much concert material, and Schlésinger may well have suggested that would do far better to recycle the pieces he had written as works for violin and orchestra.

There was some thought that Ernst would make a tour to St Petersburg, and it was hoped that he would play in Hamburg on the way. [IGT:11/10/39:164. E:41] However, as the earlier note to Schlésinger shows, he had already decided on a tour of Germany. After playing the *Elegy* and *Otello Fantasy* at the salons of M. Pape on 8 September [RGM:15/9/39:373] he bade farewell to Berlioz. Ernst said, 'You will receive letters from me,' to which Berlioz replied, 'You need not write to me, for Europe will write letters about you.' [EOC:11]

Ernst's first appearance in Germany was in Hanover where he had been invited by the composer and court *Kapellmeister*, Heinrich Marschner. Delighted by his performances, the King of Hanover, Ernest Augustus, presented him with a valuable ring [RGM:2/2/40:84], and Ernst reciprocated by dedicating his newly completed *Pirate Fantasy* to the King. It is written using uneven *scordatura* (the G string is raised to B♭, the rest of the strings are tuned up a semitone), the only time he used the device. After a long, lyrical introduction, the soloist plays the theme *Tu-vedrai* from Bellini's opera, and this is followed by four variations and a finale. Although extremely effective, and occasionally employing very high positions on the D string, it is not so taxing a piece as the *Otello Fantasy*. Ernst eventually published it in 1844 as op.19, and played it until the end of his career.

In December he played in Hamburg and Braunschweig [AMZ:25/12/39; NMZ: 4/1/40:Col.45], and in early January of 1840 he arrived in Leipzig. Here, on 13 January, he made his debut at the Gewandhaus. [NMZ:24/1/40:30]

Nearly five years before, Mendelssohn had been made music director in Leipzig, and he had made every effort to improve the already fine Gewandhaus orchestra. There were about forty musicians whose unanimity of ensemble had much improved since Mendelssohn had started to conduct them (using a baton – by no means a regular practice at the time), and Ferdinand David had been appointed leader. With David conducting the orchestra, Ernst played Mayseder's E major variations, and his own *Concertino* and *Otello Fantasy*.

Although far from full, the concert was a resounding success. David must have been much relieved because the previous concert on 9 January had been nerve-racking. The violin soloist, Carl Stör from Weimar, had disappeared after his first solo, necessitating the performance of two unrehearsed Beethoven overtures in the second half. [TM:387] In the audience on the 13th was Robert Schumann, reacquainting himself with Ernst's playing after ten years. He was no longer the dilettantish law student whom Ernst had encouraged while travelling up the Rhine, but a well-established composer and the widely respected editor of the *Neue Zeitschrift für Musik*. His genial notice read as follows:

> Berlioz's prophecy that Ernst would one day be talked of as was Paganini, begins to be fulfilled. I have heard nearly all the great violinists, from Lipinski down to Prume. Every one found enthusiastic support from the public. Some were constant to Lipinski; his imposing personality impressed at once, and it was only necessary to hear a couple of his grand tones to judge him. Others began to rave at once about Vieuxtemps, most genial of young masters, who already stands so high, that we can scarcely look forward to his future without secret fear. Ole Bull found many opponents, though he presented us with an enigma of deep meaning, difficult to unriddle; while de Beriot, Prume, David, Molique, C.Müller all found their own especial admirers, as well as their shield-bearers among the critics. But Ernst like Paganini, is able to satisfy, to win all parties whenever he pleases; for he, of a varied individuality, has made himself familiar with all styles and all schools. He even approaches Paganini in his gift for improvisation – most fascinating of virtuoso gifts – and this quality may have been influenced by his early and frequent intercourse with Paganini …
>
> Not much was heard of him after … [his tour up the Rhine in 1830]; he had gone to Paris, where one must spend a considerable time before one can be heard. He improved more and more through persevering study; Paganini gradually ceased to influence him; and of late years his name has again appeared, placed on an equality with the best artists in Paris. His old desire to see his fatherland, and especially his home, again, and to display his greatly increased proficiency there, reawakened within him. Having travelled through Holland during the past winter, giving sixty to seventy concerts there in a few months, he went straight to Germany after a short stay in Paris; a genuine artist, secure in his art, he disdained to announce his visits beforehand. Through the inducements of Marschner, he first appeared in Hannover, and then in many concerts at Hamburg and in neighbouring cities. And thus, almost unprepared, and unaware of his coming, we heard him here. The hall was not over full, but the applause was so rapturous, that the usual public seemed to have doubled its numbers. The most brilliant point of the evening was his performance of Mayseder's variations, which he interwove enchantingly with his own, and closed with such a cadenza as we had never heard except from Paganini, when, overflowing with artistic boldness, he let loose all the sorceries of his bow. This feat met with applause that far exceeded the usual bounds of North German enthusiasm; and if wreaths had been prepared beforehand, they would have been showered by the score upon the master. But

this will yet be his fate, though one of the most modest and self-effacing of men, he would doubtless escape it if he could. We shall hear him again next Monday. The railway has borne him away for a few days to the neighbouring capital. And then, if he plays the 'Carnival of Venice,' we shall have something to report of him, to whom, it seems, the famous Italian magician, on departing from the artistic world, bequeathed the secret of his power, that masters make comparisons, youths become emulous, and all the world enjoy. [NMZ:24/1/40:30; 31/1/40:40. SMM:162-4]

The 'neighbouring capital' to which Ernst travelled was Dresden, and he gave his first concert there at the Hôtel de Pologne on 24 January, playing the *Concertino*, *Otello Fantasy* and *Carnival of Venice*. Here he would have met Lipinski, who, growing weary of the stress and insecurity of the touring virtuoso's life, had taken up the position of concertmaster in 1836 at a salary of 1,200 thalers a year. In contrast to Leipzig, the emphasis in Dresden was on opera rather than concerts or church music. Indeed, the most likely reason for Ernst playing in a hotel was that Dresden had no hall suitable for orchestral concerts until the Hoftheater, built by Gottfried Semper, opened in 1841. [DL:143]

Unlike Schumann, some critics found Ernst inferior in certain respects to Vieuxtemps and Lipinski, but all acknowledged him as one of the greatest of living violinists, notable for his control of nuance and portamento, the taste of his embellishments, his silvery harmonics, his evenness in all compasses of the instrument and the general smoothness of his playing. His stage manner and bow-control were elegant, although his body sometimes twisted in difficult passages. Overall, his playing was found characteristic of the Parisian and Belgian school in that the tone was soft, warm and tranquil but lacking in fullness and power.

He was ill whilst in Dresden, but was well enough to return to Leipzig in time for his second concert on 27 January when he played the *Otello Fantasy*, *Pirate Fantasy*, the *Elegy*, and – as Schumann had hoped – the *Carnival of Venice*. This time reverberations from the previous concert ensured the Gewandhaus was packed. Passages in the *Carnival* were found so droll and bizarre that the audience laughed out loud, and the applause at the end of pieces was thunderous and prolonged. [AMZ:22/1/40:Col.117. NMZ:7/2/40:48. E:43]

As Mendelssohn relates to his brother, Ernst also took part in several performances of chamber music:

> I have been living a stirring life all through this winter. ... Last Saturday week, the first Quartett Soirée took place, where pianoforte music was introduced; so I played Mozart's sonata in A major, with David, and the B♭ major trio of Beethoven. On Sunday evening Ernst played four quartets at Hiller's; one of them was the E minor of Beethoven, and mine in E flat major. Early on Monday the rehearsal took place, and in the evening concert, where I accompanied him in his *Élégie*, and in three songs besides ... [7 February 1840. LFMB:198-9]

The quartet performances and rehearsals cemented a lifelong friendship with Ferdinand David. Hiller recalls:

> That winter [1840 in Leipzig] was remarkable for the appearances of some of the most brilliant players. First of all, Ernst, then at the summit of his talent, and enchanting the whole

world. Mendelssohn was very fond of him. Ernst told me one day, almost with emotion, how at the time of his first concerts in the Königstadter in Berlin, he was very much pressed one morning in Mendelssohn's presence to put his *Elégie* down in the programme again, though he had played it I don't know how many times. When Mendelssohn also began urging him to do it, Ernst answered in fun: 'If you will accompany me I will;' and Mendelssohn in fact made his appearance on the Königstadter stage, accompanied the *Elégie* and disappeared. It was not only their beloved violins which united David and Ernst, but also the beloved game of whist. I certainly believe that neither of them ever played the violin so late into the night as they did whist. It was harmless enough, and good and bad jokes played just as great a part in it as the game. [FHM:524]

David had studied with Spohr, and when only thirteen went on tour with his pianist sister, Louise, before taking up positions at Königstadt and Dorpat. In 1836, he married and moved to Leipzig. Here, he achieved eminence through assisting others: teaching, editing, leading the orchestra and advising Mendelssohn in the composition of his violin concerto. His career presents a strong contrast to Ernst's, and in many ways serves as a template for Joachim's later in the century.

On 28 January 1840, Ernst set out for Dresden again, missing an important concert in Leipzig on 8 February when David gave some of the first modern performances of Bach's unaccompanied works for solo violin. [TM:389] On 30 January, Ernst gave his second concert in Dresden, and, delighted by his playing, the King of Saxony invited him to perform at the palace on 1 February. As a mark of esteem and favour, the Queen presented him with a particularly beautiful diamond ring – he was beginning to acquire a collection – a few days later. [NMZ:7/2/40:48; 18/2/40:60]

By February, Ernst was in Vienna, and from there he returned to Brünn for the first time since 1835, although he had not played there since 1828. [NMZ:5/2/41:5–6] A European celebrity, loaded down with presents from royal courts, and honorary diplomas from musical organizations, he played at the Redoutensaal in Brünn twice in late February to wildly enthusiastic crowds. In the first concert, they broke into applause after eight bars of the *Otello Fantasy*, and would not let him leave until he had played the *Carnival* twice, the second time introducing many new and extraordinary variations. [EOC:19] On 5 March, one journalist found awed words to describe the second coming:

> So we have finally seen him, the tall, the slender, ghostly pale man with hair black as night, mysterious, visionary eyes, and unrestrained yet quite modest bearing, the most celebrated son of Moravia. We have listened to his tones, his languishing *Élégie*, trickling down from his bow like tears, and felt his sounds fall into the chambers of our excited hearts so that all our feelings melted together into his. Thus we have heard him, this master without equal, who a dozen years ago left his home ground as an unnoticed tiny boy, in order to sprout, develop and mature in distant lands. Ernst was born in Brünn, a Moravian! Who here did not glow with the purest fire of pride? [EOC:19]

At the second concert, his reception was said to have outshone Liszt's, and his local popularity became even greater when it was learned that he had already donated 400 gulders for local poor-relief, and 500 florins to the inhabitants of Baja, Hungary, to help them recover from a disastrous fire. Ernst's charitable nature was a subject of widespread and appreciative comment. [EOC:9] Leone wrote in 1847:

With the exception of Liszt, no other modern artist accomplished so much for charitable institutions and noble purposes as he. How often in the course of his filled-to-capacity concerts did Ernst hasten to some distant city and sacrifice with joyful generosity his own interests for the benefit of the suffering! How often did he make trips of several days on his own in order to take part in some concert for charity! Thus he travelled from Posen to Breslau especially to play there for the poor; thus from Pressburg to Vienna … [He] practises Good, like everything he does without any ostentation, in a deeply felt but quiet manner. He regards his divine talent as a noble vehicle for benefiting his fellow man. [EOC:9]

After the second concert he left for Vienna.[2] From there he sent a letter to Schlésinger via Herr Pollack, a painter and relative, on about 28 February. As we might expect of a man who bought his wife, the publisher and his circle were slightly louche, and there is a hint of this at the letter's close:

My journey in Germany was a real triumphant procession for me, and especially here and in Brünn I have been received brilliantly. Here I have already given a concert in the Redoutensaal, witnessed by Herr Pollack [*sic*] who will tell you about it. In Brünn they performed some night-music on my arrival in which 80 active members took part and a self-composed cantata was performed. Then I gave two concerts to overflowing houses. On Sunday 1st March I am giving my second concert here and already a large number of the tickets have gone. My *Concertino* and *Elégie* have made the greatest impression amongst the pieces played so far. Now it is the turn of *Il Pirate*.

Adieu, if you require anything of me, I am at your service. A thousand greetings to Panofka. I hope he has become wiser. Sigmund Hoffmann is here now and sends his best wishes to you all, as does Herr Frankowski.

Adieu, your devoted friend. Don't shag too much![3] [BN]

Ernst had further triumphs in Brünn on the 8 and 22 April, and gave his farewell concert on 5 September. [JDN:26/3/40:103. E:45–6]

That winter in Vienna, de Bériot, Liszt and Madame Pleyel had already made a great impression, but, as can be imagined, there was considerable interest in hearing Ernst. Eleven years before, he had left many friends and admirers in the city who were now eager to hear him again, and their interest was being fanned by reports

---

2 Ernst did not arrive in Vienna until 1840, but he is shown in Josef Danhauser's painting *Die Schachpartie* [*The Chess Match*], which was finished in Vienna in 1839. He stands on the far right, leaning against a classical statue, holding white gloves in his right hand. The portrait is not a good likeness, and I assume it was either done from memory or on the basis of portraits which already existed. He does not appear in early sketches for the picture, and I take it was added in anticipation of his arrival in 1840. Ernst may also be represented as a seated figure in Danhauser's *Die Brautschau* [*Looking for a Wife*]. See JDGZ:69–75, 86–7, 132.

3 At the end of this letter, Ernst has drawn a picture of two birds. Peter Ward Jones, who kindly transcribed these letters, writes as follows: 'The one thing which eludes me is the significance of the birds at the end of the letter of 3 March 1840. They clearly stand for a noun which then gets turned into an imperative verb with the addition of the following "n" and "Sie". The most obvious word is "Vögel", but the verb it then forms is "Vögeln", a vulgarism meaning "to shag", so the sentence would mean, "Don't shag too much!".' [Letter to author, 23/7/2003]

filtering out of Brünn and the German cities. Consequently, even his first rehearsals were packed with violinists and music lovers who were stunned by what they heard. The immensely difficult *Concertino* caused a considerable impression (and no doubt the waltz finale seemed like a tribute to the city of his youth) but it was the *Carnival* which here, like everywhere else, proved the most popular. The orchestral parts are written in B♭, and the solo violinist usually tuned all his strings up by a semitone so he could play in the easier and more sonorous key of A. For some reason in Vienna, Ernst decided to play the solo part in B♭ without retuning his violin, thereby having to overcome virtually insurmountable difficulties. [EOC:9]

Although the audience was keen to hear him perform, Ernst's first concert at the Redoutensaal was not particularly well attended because the price for admission was as high as it had been at Liszt's concert eight days before. Nonetheless, the success was so startling that the next two concerts were filled to capacity, as were his next two at the marginally cheaper Karthnerthortheater. So many people wanted to hear him that one of his concerts was given in the large hall of the Redoutensaal, where three thousand people could enjoy the performance of his most popular showpieces. Altogether, including charity performances, he performed seventeen times in Vienna [NMZ:15/5/40:160. GMP:9/4/40:260. E:47], and there was great general satisfaction that at last a German-speaking violinist was making a noise in the world. [DH:30/3/40:258]

His triumphs in Vienna consolidated his European reputation, and made at least one of his admired models seem dated. As one of his obiturists puts it:

> His most brilliant period began in 1840. Bériot was then in Vienna, achieving a tremendous success with his endless 'airs variés', and his 'Tremelo' on a theme from Beethoven (his Kreutzer Sonata), when Ernst appeared, played the 'Otello Fantasia,' the 'Élégie,' and the 'Carnival de Venise,' and with these compositions excited among the Viennese a degree of enthusiasm that spread far beyond the limits of the monarchy. His journey resembled a series of triumphs, bringing in pecuniary profit as well as fame. Ernst, who possessed a thoroughly good heart, did not save, and, on one occasion, sacrificed a very large sum to preserve from ruin a person closely connected with him. [NBMZ:MW: 4/11/1865:690]

The last sentence refers to the appalling occasion when Ernst had to pay off a debt of 12,000 gulders which his half–brother Johann had run up at the Hotel Lamm in Vienna. [EUZ:56] (Jakob Ernst had valued his house, his café, his licence, his distillery, and all his other possessions at 40,000 gulders in 1828. [AMB]) One imagines the genial and bibulous Johann, freshly arrived from Brünn and in the first flush of his brother's heady success: telling all who will listen about Ernst's triumphs and the part he himself played in them, buying rounds of drinks, giving out cigars, dining splendidly, refurbishing his wardrobe, attending dazzling concerts, and being introduced to celebrities he has only read about. Several weeks on, there would be the horrified realization of how much he had spent, a shamefaced confession to his brother, the extraction of promises, and finally a subdued return to his wife and the café in Brünn. From now on, Ernst makes a point of telling his brother exactly how much he earns, the purpose being, no doubt, to indicate that he is not rich and his funds are not bottomless.

Johann was not the only individual on this tour to whom he offered help of life-changing importance. Shortly before Ernst arrived in Vienna, the ten-year-old Joseph Joachim had come to the same city. The Joachim family had moved to Pesth when Joseph was three, where the boy was taught by Serwaczynski. He was one of Pesth's leading violinists, but a peculiarity of his teaching was to concentrate exclusively on left-hand technique and pay no attention to bowing at all. Perhaps because of this deficiency, Joachim was then sent to Vienna to study first with Miska Hauser and later with George Hellmesberger the elder. In 1840, Hellmesbeger had watched his new pupil take part in a performance of Maurer's *Concertante* for four violins and decided, although the audience loved the performance, that Joachim's bowing was so stiff that nothing could be done with him. The boy's parents happened to be visiting him in Vienna at the time, and all three were mortified by Hellmesberger's pronouncement. The father in particular decided that any hope of a musical career was illusory, and resolved to take his son back to Pesth and begin training him for another profession.

At this point, Ernst announced his concerts, and Joachim persuaded his parents to let him stay long enough in Vienna to hear a violinist that the whole musical world was talking about. The impact Ernst made on Joachim was overwhelming, and his uncle, Nathan Figdor, obtained his parents' permission to take him to Ernst in a final attempt to save the boy's career. Ernst recognized Joachim's exceptional talent at once, and sent a message to his parents saying that they should have no anxieties over the boy's musical future. He advised them to place Joachim under his own old master, Joseph Böhm, who would soon make his bowing free and flexible. The parents felt they should listen to someone of Ernst's reputation, sent the boy to Böhm, who conscientiously ensured the acquisition of a peerless technique. At the time, Ernst can have had little idea how close his relationship with Joachim would become, or how his intervention would change the course of nineteenth-century music; even less can he have realized how, at the very height of his success, he was grooming his own musical supplanter. [JJ:19–21]

Months after he left Vienna, Ernst's spectacular concert-series was still a subject for excited discussion. In remembrance of his visit, Johann Strauss the elder wrote his waltz *Erinnerung an Ernst oder: Der Carneval in Venig* (*Memories of Ernst or: The Carnival of Venice*), whose introduction conjures up the opening of Ernst's *Otello Fantasy*, and whose main section is based on the theme Ernst so famously varied. It received its first performance on the 25 November 1840 in the Hiezinger Theater, the evening of the Katharinen-Ball, and was published by Haslinger in May of the next year.

From Vienna, Ernst returned to Brünn, (where he must have heard the melancholy tidings of Paganini's death on 27 May) and then set out to Pesth and Pressburg. In the latter town, 'with many a vociferous *Eljen!* [Hail!]' he was asked to play the *Rákóczy March*. [EOC:9] It turned out he did not know the piece, and he therefore got the orchestra to play it. On the spur of the moment, he then executed a brilliant set of improvised variations that were greeted with tremendous enthusiasm. The gesture was not without political significance. Hungary was part of the Austrian Empire and entirely under the thumb of Vienna. For 150 years, its culture had been derided, its language banned, and now a tide of nationalism was sweeping through the nation. Because of its capacity to inflame nationalistic feeling, the *Rákóczy March* was officially proscribed, and when Liszt had played it as an encore in Pressburg six months before, the reaction was not only patriotic hysteria but a report to Metternich's secret police. [FLVY:320-21] Since Ernst did not know the march, it is a moot point whether he understood its significance.

After these triumphs, Ernst began a long slow journey back to Paris playing in Linz, Salzburg (where he performed at a concert to raise money for a Mozart memorial), Munich, Augsburg, Stuttgart and Karlsruhe. [RGM:1/11/42:517] After performing in Strasbourg (where he played in a concert to relieve victims of a recent flood), he returned to Paris in December 1840, having spent fifteen months on tour. [E:49–50]

Chapter 8

Paris and Vieuxtemps: 1841

At the beginning of 1841, Ernst was afflicted by nervous headaches caused by the fatigue of endless travel, rehearsal, concerts and entertaining. But early in the New Year, he took a short trip to Orléans and returned to Paris by the end of January. For the next few months we are able to catch a glimpse of the private man. This is because some of his activities are recorded in the Paris diary of Anton Schindler, the biographer of Beethoven, who was in the capital to collect material for his essay 'Beethoven in Paris'.

Schindler first met Ernst on 29 January 1841:

> At 5 o'clock, I went to Panofka's, who's still unwell. There I met Heinrich Heine, the violinist Ernst and Rosenhain. Heine was ill-humoured as he has been for a long time, yet he was very funny and sarcastic. Herr Ernst had only arrived from Orléans that morning. About half-past nine, Rosenhain called on me, and I went with him to a party at Erard's, where there were about 400 people. [AS:38]

Heine had come to Paris in May 1831 mainly because of his interest in Saint-Simonism. Although *Gedichte* (1822) and *Buch der Lieder* (1827) had made him famous in Germany, he had never found satisfactory employment, largely because he wanted a highly paid job which left him all his time to write. Consequently, he was not wealthy and existed on a small income from his books, a very modest annuity from his fabulously wealthy uncle Salomon, secret payments from the French government, and writing articles for the *Allgemeine Zeitung*. Heine was rather less generous about Schindler than Schindler was about him, and he responded to their meeting by writing a devastating description of Beethoven's biographer in his report of the 1841 musical season.

Because he was aiming to write an essay about Beethoven's reception in Paris, Schindler spent his months there attending every concert he could manage. The standard of Viennese musicians caused him some embarrassment:

> 1st February ... At about 10 o'clock, I went from there to Madame Schlésinger's, rue Grammont, No.17, carriage entrance. The company was 100 strong. Herr Hallé played the piano, a young woman with no voice at all sang. ... The violinist Goldberg from Vienna performed a solo fantasy and prostituted himself. Such spiritless, talentless and tuneless fare is best suited to the Viennese bourgeoisie, but this was done in a circle where Jules Janin and many other artists and scholars were to be found. [This] betrays in the highest degree the poverty of spirit and complacency from which the German artists who live here seem to suffer regularly, and is greatly to be regretted. What I've noticed up to now, or so it seems is that Rosenhain, Panofka and Ernst are laudable exceptions. They have common-sense and look beyond their instrument. [AS:39]

Having met Ernst, Schindler arranged to call. 'Wednesday 10th February. I called after 11 o'clock on Herr Ernst, who lives at no.6, rue neuve des Mathurins, which is furnished in a princely fashion. If Herr Ernst were a great composer instead of a violinist, he would not be able to afford it.'[AS:47]

The new address shows Ernst's prosperity even more clearly than his furnishings. Situated in the First Arrondissement (which enclosed an area from the Arc de Triomphe to the east end of the Louvre), the rue neuve des Mathurins ran west into the rue chausée d'antin, which itself ran down to the boulevard des Capucines. Aristocracy, money and leisure were the predominant tone of the arrondissement; the clangour of traffic, the cheap rooms, shouts, and small shops of the rue St Denis were a world away. [PWFC:7–11]

Schindler's visit was evidently a success, and he returned to the rue neuve des Mathurins on the 20 Febuary. This time there was music, and Schindler gives a thoughtful estimate of Ernst's playing:

> In the evening I was at Ernst's house, and played on request several movements from Beethoven's sonatas, and Herr Ernst then played us his *Carnival* which was remarkable, a piece full of the most outrageous difficulty, but also full of feeling, which would be very difficult for another to play after him. He also played his *Elégie* and a fantasy on motifs from *Otello*. Ernst is a great violinist with imagination and feeling, but lately he suffers from the unnatural mannerism of sliding up and down, and frequently does not observe the note values correctly. I can never get used to this way of imitating the voice on the violin, which is typical of violinists these days, and I'm always pained if I see a really great talent stick with this style – Panofka plays his *Cantabile* in just such a manner. Paganini was the first to exhibit this mannerism, but his genius made more skilful use of it than his imitators or copiers do. [AS:51]

Schindler, a conservative and a stickler, clearly found Ernst's use of *rubato* and *portamento* offensive, although many others admired the emotionality of the effect. Boris Schwatz supposes that Ernst's style was the result of his having acquired the Viennese *maniera languida*. [GMV:205] This is unlikely. Schindler explicitly says that Ernst's expressive devices derive from Paganini, and one suspects that Schindler is comparing both violinists with the best Viennese violinists of his youth (Clement, Schuppanzigh, Mayseder) who were, presumably, free of such mannerisms.

Less than a fortnight later, on 2 March, there was an evening of more serious music: 'In the evening I was at a quartet with Ernst and Dr Roth, where 2 Haydn and 2 Beethoven quartets were performed, the latter in F and E minor.' [AS:61] These are the first two of Beethoven's Razhumovsky Quartets op.59; both, particularly the slow movement of the second, would become Ernst's specialities.

On Tuesday 16 March, Schindler and Ernst planned a trip to Versailles together, but it had to be called off because Ernst was ill. On Thursday 18 March, however, there was a supper party. Schindler gives an expansive description:

> The evening was great fun. Herr Ernst asked me to be his guest for dinner, Dr Roth, Heller and both Franks were also to be there; it was said we were going to a restaurant (rue de la Victoire) where not many people go, and which is meant to be very good. Ernst had already ordered for all of us. Upon entering the courtyard, the house seemed to me to be a noble palace rather than a restaurant. We went up to the first floor. In the anteroom sat

a lady with oysters, as in every restaurant, and that deceived me so that I didn't think anything was going on, as the gentlemen were acting as if they were in any public place, and there was also a waiter with a white apron. In the middle of one room there was a round table with 9 place settings and at the side, two small tables with 2 settings each. We sat down at the large table and Herr Heller complained that he was really hungry and that he should be served immediately, and Herr Ernst had no patience left either. Whilst two gentlemen came into the room and sat at the small table, no notice was taken of them – Herr Ernst merely noticed that one of them could understand a little German. Later both of them joined us at our table and we all ate together. For some particular reason, Ernst asked me to criticise every dish, he seemed to want to do that too and did. Soon one of the strangers was named as the painter of a picture which had caught my eye that afternoon in the Louvre. But I still didn't know who the other gentleman was, and I wasn't bothered, however much I noticed his worthy manner and lively mood. But when the champagne was flowing, Ernst and Co. couldn't keep it up any longer, and admitted that the whole thing was a joke, that we weren't in a restaurant but instead in Monsieur Froberville's house (the 2nd gentleman) who was a great admirer of Beethoven, whose works he studied, [and who] wanted to entertain me in his home. Everything then became very jolly, as especially Herr Ernst was very funny. After dinner Herr Ernst played us his *Carnival* and the variations on 'Nel cor più non mi sento' by Paganini, an extraordinarily accurate imitation, and Herr Frank (jun) played some preludes and songs without words by Mendelssohn splendidly and by heart. After 9 o'clock I left with Dr Roth, the others stayed. [AS:73]

This joke is characteristic of Ernst's humour. A false identity is ironically projected on to a place or person and he settles back, apart from a few gentle promptings, to watch the misunderstandings which result. The incident shows Ernst's characteristic powers of sympathy and discernment. Schindler was a notoriously stiff and touchy man, and yet Ernst perceived there was a strain of humour in him that might forgive or even enjoy a joke against himself. Ernst's little ruse (which clearly needed some preparation) pulled off the difficult trick of simultaneously amusing his friends and humanizing Schindler.

But there were more serious matters afoot. The beginning of the year had seen the triumphant Paris debut of the Belgian violinist Henri Vieuxtemps. Ernst missed the concert because he was in Orléans, but on his return he discovered that Vieuxtemps' immense powers were the topic of heated discussion. A rival in Paganini's class had arrived on his doorstep.

A child prodigy, Vieuxtemps had been taken up by de Bériot, who first brought him to Paris in 1829. When de Bériot left Belgium to marry the soprano Maria Malibran in 1830, Vieuxtemps was largely left to teach himself before going on a tour of Germany. Here, in 1833, he met Guhr and Spohr, and heard *Fidelio* for the first time. On arriving for an extended stay in Vienna, he was persuaded by the group of musicians who had gathered around Beethoven, to perform the master's violin concerto. This had acquired a reputation as ungrateful for the soloist and lacking in brilliance, and had consequently languished since Clement had premiered the work in 1806. Vieuxtemps learnt the concerto in fifteen days and his performance was a triumph. After visits to Leipzig, London, Pesth and Vienna, he departed for an extended tour of Russia. By the time he returned, he had completed his first violin concerto in E (actually the second to be composed) which had a spectacular premiere in Brussels. He now felt ready to tackle Paris as a mature artist, and on arriving in the capital he practised for eight hours a day in preparation for his debut.

The concert took place on 12 January 1841, and besides the usual fantasies and sets of variations, Vieuxtemps played his new concerto. As a virtuoso, he was placed in the front rank. Berlioz wrote in his review:

> M. Vieuxtemps is a prodigious violinist in the strict sense of the word. He does things that I have never heard from any other; his staccato is brilliant, delicate, radiant, dazzling; his double-stopped singing rings extremely true; he braves dangers that are frightening to the listener, but that move him not in the least, sure as he is of emerging from them safe and sound; his fourth-string sings with a voice full of beauty. [V:24]

But it was as a composer that he astonished. Admittedly, there were some members of the audience who found the concerto too long and elaborate, and Schindler thought the piece a series of butt-jointed episodes, but leading musicians in the audience – including Chopin, Wagner and Berlioz – realized they had heard something important. In his review, Berlioz, the master orchestrator, is particularly admiring of the concerto's orchestration:

> His Concerto in E is a very beautiful work, producing a splendid effect generally, inundated with ravishing details both in the orchestra and in the solo part, and instrumented in the manner of a great master. Not a single member of the orchestra, however obscure, has been forgotten in the score; he gives each one something pertinent and piquant to say; … Vieuxtemps combines his eminent merits as virtuoso with those, no less great, of composer. [V:68]

At the end of the long orchestral exposition of the E major concerto, there is a pause before the entry of the soloist, and here the audience bust into applause before Vieuxtemps had played a note – no better tribute to his purely compositional skills could be imagined. [VMW:66] When the performance had finished, the white-haired Baillot, leader of the French violin school and the only other violinist to give a performance of Beethoven's concerto since the composer's death, mounted the stage and embraced the soloist.

Amongst Vieuxtemps's most ardent supporters was the young Wagner. They had met when Wagner was director of music at the theatre in Riga and Vieuxtemps was on tour. Since then, Wagner and his wife had had to make a dramatic escape from Riga to avoid their creditors, and after a storm-lashed journey to London, slowly made their way to Paris. The two and a half years he spent there were amongst the most miserable of Wagner's life. He was patronized by the German expatriate community; no plan to stage his operas came to fruition; and a performance of the *Christoph Colombe Overture* at a concert organized by Schlésinger was a disaster. Hack-work for the publisher helped alleviate some of his financial problems, but he still had to spend some time in a debtors' prison.

One of the few bright spots in these miserable years was the friendship he re-formed with Vieuxtemps. The violinist, on arriving in Paris, took lodgings opposite Wagner's, and in this way they became reacquainted. Vieuxtemps played to Wagner when he was ill ('I fell into a lovely sleep; delicious dreams came over me'), and attended his soirées. Many years later, Wagner recalled: 'The young musician, who was having an immense success in Paris at the time, entertained me and my friends a whole evening with his playing, which lent my drawing-room a quite unusual brilliance.' [V:24] Wagner, of course, attended Vieuxtemps's debut at the Conservatoire, and was deeply impressed by the concerto:

> So one man has dared to restore his art from that dignity from which it had so shamefully debased; to place himself before the jaded ears of the crowd with a noble, sterling piece of music, purely and chastely conceived, performed with life and freshness, – a composition for which he claims the exclusive attention of his audience, and to which he manifestly welds his art of virtuoso with a single eye to lifting his work to an ideal understanding. [LRW:I:318]

The extraordinary success of Vieuxtemps and his composition caused difficulty for Ernst. On 20 March, he was due to play his *Concertino* at the sixth concert of the Paris Conservatoire with Habeneck, the work's dedicatee, conducting. Schindler attended two rehearsals and refrained from comment. At the concert, however, he expressed doubts about both the work and Ernst's performance of it:

> Sunday 21st March The *Concertino* by Ernst (F-sharp minor), as I feared, I didn't like it. [Only the slow movement is in this key; the rest is in D major] It is so full of difficulties that every passage is risky and Herr Ernst is really unsuccessful in some of them. On top of that, all these difficulties are in the highest range where the notes have ceased to have any meaning. Neither is Herr Ernst free from scratching. [Beethoven's] 9th Symphony was the greatest success feasible. [AS:76]

Wagner sat in the same audience. Unlike Schindler on this occasion, he admired Ernst's playing, but felt that, compared with the immensity of Vieuxtemps's concerto, the *Concertino* seemed thin fare:

> Already [Vieuxtemps's] influence has made itself clearly felt, as indeed it should, in the concerto at the Conservatoire, that citadel of true and genuine music. It was there that Vieuxtemps' first appearance was rapturously received, and it was here that the next man to follow him learned exactly what he needed to do if he wanted to preserve his reputation. This man was the violinist Heinrich Ernst, who is an excellent player in his way. At the Conservatoire there were no complaints about his virtuosity, but the same audience that had just heard Vieuxtemps' concerto could not refrain from showing its displeasure with Ernst's Concertino, thereby giving this otherwise popular virtuoso a much needed lesson. [WWP:126]

On the other hand, Ernst may have been the beneficiary of equally biased reporting. Heine considered the Belgian virtuoso wildly overrated:

> Vieuxtemps is regarded as one of the lions of the musical season. Whether there is a real king of beasts under the shaggy coat of this lion, or only a little ass, I will not take it on me to decide. To tell the honest truth, I cannot agree with the extravagant laudations which are lavished on him, for he does not seem to me as if he had climbed so very high on the ladder of art. Vieuxtemps is about at the middle of the ladder on whose summit we once beheld Paganini, and on whose very lowest rung is our admirable Sina [a mediocre

violinist from Vienna], … and the owner of an autograph of Beethoven. But it may be that M. Vieuxtemps is much nearer to M.Sina than he is to Nicolo Paganini. [HS:337–8]

Despite this criticism it is clear that Vieuxtemps had a number of achievements to his credit that Ernst could not match. He had won a considerable reputation not only in Europe but in Russia. He had given a pioneering performance of Beethoven's concerto that indicated the way violin-playing would progress in the second half of the century: the virtuoso would no longer be self-sufficient, he would be the servant of the great composers. He had also written the first truly symphonic violin concerto of the nineteenth century. It is this richly orchestrated and dramatic work, rather than the transparent and lyrical Beethoven and Mendelssohn concertos, which is the true origin of the great line of Romantic concertos which stretches from the Bruch of 1869 to the Walton of 1938–39.

Heine took the opportunity to review the Franco-Belgian school of violinists who now dominated Paris and virtually replaced the older generation of French violinists:

> Vieuxtemps is the son of Belgium, and in fact the most remarkable violinists seem to come from the Low Countries. … The most distinguished of this national paternity is beyond question Bériot, husband of the late Malibran, and many a time I cannot but entertain the thought that the soul of his departed wife sang in the sweet tones of his violin. It is only Ernst the Bohemian [*sic*], so rich in poetry, who can draw sounds from his instrument so sweet while bleeding.
>
> Artôt is a fellow countryman of Bériot; he is also as distinguished a violinist, but one whose playing never suggests a soul; a well-dressed, neatly turned fellow – un garçon fait a tour et tiré à quatre épingles – whose execution is as smooth and brilliant as a japanned table-top. Hauman, the brother of the Belgian pirate-printer, carries on with his violin the business of his brother; what he plays are clearly counterfeits of the most distinguished fiddlers, the texts being margined here and there with superfluous original notes, and enlarged with brilliant typographical errors. [HS:338–9]

Heine is not a wholly reliable witness. Quite apart from his tendency to force reality into preconceived patterns he had very little musical training. He learnt the violin for a few months as a child, but persuaded his teacher to do most of the playing to give his family the impression he was making progress. His opinion of de Bériot is eccentric. Few others describe his playing as emotional, and Heine's judgement may be coloured by the tragic death of de Bériot's young wife in 1836. Most critics found de Bériot's playing neat, elegant, charming, exquisitely finished, but a little chilly. Ernst was a much more emotional player and had infinitely more to offer in terms of bravura and virtuoso display. As the obituary quoted in the last chapter makes clear, the joint appearance of the two violinists in 1840 firmly placed de Bériot and his salon trifles in a previous era.

The name of Theodore Hauman has disappeared from all modern books about violinists and music encyclopaedias, but he had quite a distinguished career. Aged twenty-one, he had appeared at a Philharmonic concert in London in 1829 where his playing was criticized for 'a sort of jerking squeak in his high notes that was somewhat anti-musical, and was one of the consequences of his too frequent use of extra shifts'. [DV:179] But he, like Ernst withdrew from public performance in order to slave over his technique, and Castil-Blaze gave him a much more positive review in Paris in 1833: 'M. Hauman [is] one of our most distinguished virtuosos. ... This young violinist executes the most difficult passages with absolute perfection fit for the ears of Paganini himself [who was actually in the audience].' [FCPW:221] On the basis of such reviews, Hauman had a successful touring career, and was eventually appointed leader of the orchestra in Brussels. Unlike Artôt and de Bériot, he was not primarily a pretty player, but famous for the power of his sound and the *pathétique* character of his interpretations, although his performances could be uneven, and he used too much *rubato*, and too many shifts. In some respects, as Heine's review indicates, his characteristics seemed to be exaggerations of Ernst's.

Ernst's musical superiority to Artôt receives independent and more reliable support. In his autobiography, Hallé tells the following story:

> My circumstances were gradually improving, thanks to the number of my pupils increasing constantly, so that I was able to move into better quarters, in the Rue d'Amsterdam, where I first began to have a few evenings at home, reunions of friends such as Berlioz, Heller, Ernst, Batta (the accomplished and refined violoncellist), Artôt, known as 'le bel Artôt', Delsarte, the marvellous tenor ... and several others. One evening Artôt proposed that we should play the Kreuzter Sonata, and we did so. Now Artôt, most elegant violinist and most successful performer though he was, was entirely out of his element in such music, which was so painfully evident that when he had left us rather early, Ernst sprang up and said, 'Come, Hallé, let us play the Kreuzer!' he played it magnificently, and I have never better understood than on that evening how much depends upon the power of interpretation; how the want of it can deprive the finest work of its charm and interest. [LLCH:56–7]

On 2 April, Ernst spent the afternoon with Chopin and Schindler, and on the 26 April Ernst and Chopin appeared together at the Salle Pleyel. There can have been no discussion of the concert on the 2nd, because it was organized at little more than a week's notice. Liszt had recently returned from a tour and given several concerts, and there was much animated discussion amongst Chopin's friends about Liszt's triumphs. They pressed Chopin – who had not appeared in public since the spring of 1838 – to give a concert himself, but he was profoundly reluctant: 'the crowd intimidates me' he once confided to Liszt, 'and I feel suffocated by its eager breath, paralysed by its inquisitive stare, silenced by its alien faces.' [CF:88] However, his friends, his need for money, and possibly some envy for Liszt, prevailed. As soon as the fatal 'yes' was uttered, George Sand (his lover) set to work with immense efficiency. Within days, three-quarters of the tickets were sold, and the supporting artists were arranged: '[Chopin] has thrown himself into the arms, I mean the feet, of Mme [Cinti-]Damoreau,' wrote a delighted Sand to Pauline Viardot, and 'M. Ernst will scrape his splendid violin.' [SCFC:193] [See Plate IV]

The concert proved to be immensely fashionable, brilliant and successful. Liszt wrote:

> At eight o'clock in the evening, the Salons of M. Pleyel were splendidly illuminated. At the foot of a staircase covered with carpets and perfumed with flowers, numerous

carriages continuously deposited the most elegant women, the most famous artists, the richest financiers, the most illustrious aristocrats, a whole elite of society, a whole aristocracy of birth, fortune, talent, and beauty ... [FCPW:232]

On previous public appearances, Chopin had only played a couple of his own pieces. At this concert he performed four Mazurkas, the A major 'Military' Polonaise, the second Ballade, and the Scherzo in C♯ minor. Overcoming his nerves, he played brilliantly, giving the audience numerous encores which were greeted with furious applause and foot-stamping.

Reviews were ecstatic. *Le Ménestral* said that 'heart and genius alone speak, and in these respects his talent has nothing to learn'. *La France Musicale* said that his school and manner and manner of piano-playing were unique and 'should not and cannot be compared to anyone'. Heine proclaimed Chopin, 'the Raphael of the pianoforte'. [CZ:194] All at once, it seemed, he had joined the great masters. Chopin was delighted with this success and the 6,000 francs it brought, and felt that, at some distant date, he might give more concerts. Only the behaviour of Liszt caused some irritation. He had rushed onto the stage at the end of the concert and caught the exhausted Chopin in his arms, and he had asked the editor of the *Revue et Gazette musicale* to allow him, rather than its regular critic, to review the concert. Chopin felt that, by both these actions, he seemed to be arrogating some of the triumph for himself. Acknowledging that Liszt had proclaimed Chopin king of the evening, the latter wrote acidly, '"King" yes, but within *his* empire.' [CF:93]

Although Chopin had decided not to emulate Liszt by appearing on stage alone, the format of his concert had moved in the direction of Liszt's recitals. Chopin was clearly the main attraction and the function of the other two artists was simply to add a little variety and allow the pianist time to gather breath: Cinti-Damoreau sang just two songs, and Ernst played only his *Elegy*. Despite this, the historic importance of the occasion, and the genius of the protagonist, Ernst secured good reviews. 'After all the bravos cast at the feet of the king of the evening's entertainment,' wrote Liszt, 'M. Ernst proved expert in obtaining some well merited ones for himself also. He played an elegy in an expansive and grandiose style with intense feeling and a purity worthy of the masters, which made a vivid impression on the audience.' [FCPW:233] The critic of *La France Musicale*, Léon Escudier, was more struck still. He seems almost concerned by the emotionality of Ernst's performance:

> M. Ernst played his *Elégie*. He too [like Chopin] is an artist who can move and charm you without twisting his face into horrible contortions. Melody pours out of him effortlessly. Perhaps he allowed himself to be a little overcome with melancholy on this occasion, but at least he has an original clear-cut style. If you want to hear a violin weep, listen to Ernst. He wrings such heart-rending, passionate sounds from his instrument that you fear any minute the violin will literally shatter in his hands. It would be difficult to achieve any greater expression of sorrow, suffering or despair. [FCPW:236]

The rest of the spring and summer must have seemed anticlimactic. Ernst devoted a good deal of time to finishing some new works: the *Morceaux de salon: Deux Romance*, op.15, dedicated to the cellist Franchomme (and playable on his instrument); and the *Boléro*, op.16, a piquant piece with a lyrical middle section, dedicated to Panofka. [FM: 31/10/41:379; 7/11/41:379] However, there was also time for some domestic music-making. At a concert held at his home on Friday 6 August, Ernst played his new *Bolero*, a rondo and the *Elegy*; the pianist Charles Mayer from St Petersburg played a concerto and some études; and Panofka played first violin (and Ernst second) in a performance of an *Andante* from a Beethoven string quartet. [RGM:8/8/41:376. E:53]

One of his few expeditions nearly had serious consequences. Returning from a concert in Baden given with Meyer later in August, the coach in which he was travelling fell into a gully ten feet deep and was totally destroyed. Fortunately Ernst escaped with only some bruising to the head, but he must have recalled that the famous violinist Charles Lafont had been killed in just such an accident exactly two years before. [LBM: 22/8/41; 19/9/41]

Chapter 9

Germany, Poland and Paris: 1841–42

On 30 October 1841, Ernst left Paris to begin a second major concert tour. [FM:31/10/41:379; 7/11/41:389] The five concerts he gave in Prague in November were the heady triumphs he had come to expect, and the last of these raised 8,000 francs for the poor. From there he went to Dresden, and was in Berlin by the beginning of December where his concerts began the season. The town contained a galaxy of musical talent: Sivori and Liszt played that winter, the latter arousing enormous enthusiasm, and Meyerbeer and the critic Rellstab were amongst Ernst's audiences. [AWMZ: 25/11/41: Col.592. RGM:28/11/41:535. E:53–4]

The critics particularly enjoyed Ernst's polyphonic playing, his staccato, consecutive trills, harmonics and pizzicati. His tone was pure but not large, especially in passage-work, and in this respect at least, de Bériot, Prume and Sivori surpassed him. But there was no doubting the effect of his elegance and melancholy, and when it came to playing expressive melodies on the violin he excelled everyone. [RGM:19/12/1841. E:55]

Another positive aspect of his stay in Berlin was the strengthening of his friendship with Mendelssohn and his family. The King of Prussia, Frederick Wilhelm IV, had assumed the throne in June 1840, and wished to turn Berlin into a centre for the Arts. To this end, he invited Mendelssohn to become the Royal *Kapellmeister* at a generous salary of 3,000 thalers a year. After some misgivings, the composer accepted and his appointment was confirmed in October 1841. Initially, his prospects looked good, but he was faced with constant bureaucratic obstruction and, despite being made General Music Director in 1842, he resigned in 1844.

On 1 December 1841, before disillusion set in, Ernst wrote two inscriptions in the Mendelssohns' autograph books. In Mendelssohn's wife's, he writes out the theme from the final section of his *Otello Fantasy* and comments cryptically beneath it: 'You can show the writer of this nothing more pleasant than if you forget the composer and just remember the quite humble joy.' [GB] The choice of the fantasy's last section is important because it contains one of Mendelssohn's favourite musical moments. This is the bar immediately before the piece goes into 12/8 time when the soloist leaps up to a high C♯. When Mendelssohn first accompanied Ernst in the fantasy in 1842, the section so delighted him that he made Ernst play it three times. Two years later, in the autumn of 1844, Joachim was scheduled to play the piece in the Gewandhaus. Mendelssohn, who was conducting the orchestra, was immensely struck by the way the boy played the same passage. After the rehearsal, he turned to Joachim and said: 'Listen you little Devil. If I should ever write a concerto for your violin, I'll make sure that Ernst's bravura, which you've reminded me of today, will find a place in it.' Mendelssohn was true to his word, and in the finale of the violin concerto, the leap from the E to the C♯ can be found 42 bars from the end of the last movement. [GMV:520]

In Mendelssohn's own book, Ernst copies out several bars of an *Andante* in B major, and remarks: 'To the joyful memory of your unfruitful friend and deepest admirer, H.W. Ernst.' [GB] The word 'unfruitful' refers to the fact that, as yet, Ernst had not composed as much as he would have liked. It was clearly a fact which weighed on him, and he would return to it later in the year.

In spite of the critics' notices and his friendship with the Mendelssohns, his stay in Berlin was not an unalloyed pleasure. The two harshest critics he had encountered to date, Schindler and Wagner, were both German, and there is some evidence to suggest that Ernst, like Mendelssohn, found Berlin hard going. ('Berlin –,' Mendelssohn once commented in a letter, 'one of the sourest apples one can bite, and yet it must be bitten.' [TM:387]). On 18 December 1841 Ernst wrote to Jules Janin (perhaps to ensure that he was in mind if not in sight) describing his experiences and explaining why he preferred Paris – a sentiment that cannot have been uncongenial to the French critic. The original letter cannot be traced, but the following full paraphrase comes from an autograph-dealer's catalogue:

> Ernst reports on his vagabond life which began under favourable auspices. He gave five concerts in Prague and four in Berlin, two of which were at the Royal Opera. His audience in the first two Berlin concerts was to 'the elite of society' but the larger crowds came to the two last concerts. 'Berlin is for Germany what Paris is for Europe, it's the supreme tribunal of criticism' with the difference that in Paris one can throw off all restraint, while in Berlin audiences are cold and guard themselves against showing enthusiasm vis-à-vis international celebrities. With a great effort he managed to bring about a miracle: he aroused the public to a point that it was said to be the greatest manifestation of enthusiasm since Paganini's appearance. He was recalled and felt he had to ask the audience's 'pardon for having played well, such is the effect these socially inhibited scenes produce on me.' But he is leaving Berlin without regret. Despite its size, Berlin 'is a small village which resembles its inhabitants in its stiff and cold appearance. Paris is a great city, and Berlin is a vast city.' He passed some pleasant evenings with Mendelssohn and his family and they played Beethoven and Mendelssohn. Ernst is going to Breslau, Warsaw, and St Petersburg. He would like to make Paris his home; it has a magnetic attraction for him. The further he moves away the more he feels drawn to it. [BC]

Between 9 and 23 December, Ernst gave five concerts in Berlin including one held in the mansion of Count Redern, where Liszt, Ernst, Ganz and Richter played an unpublished quartet by Prince Louis Ferdinand of Prussia. [RGM:30/1/42:47] In early January, he travelled to Breslau where the enthusiasm he generated verged on hysteria. [RGM:16/1/42:24; 30/1/42:48] Two newspaper reports covering his fifth and sixth concerts give some idea of the kind of response he was becoming used to:

> Since Paganini no artists has made such a sensation here as Ernst; indeed the response of the public to this unrivalled artist is truly unparalleled. After his fourth concert, Ernst was supposed to leave our city, but a fifth concert was arranged for our theatre. The announcement for this had scarcely appeared when an hour later all the boxes and reserved seats were taken, and this at 10 o'clock when nearly 1000 persons who called and demanded such seats had to be turned away. The tumult and stormy demand for these

reserved seats was so indescribably strong that only with the greatest effort could the frantic crowd be warded off from the ticket office. The incident did not terminate without many an injury. At 4 o'clock in the afternoon the theatre was surrounded by a surging crowd, and by the next hour there were no more tickets for the pit to be had, and many a distinguished theatre-goer had to make do this time with a seat in the highest gallery, an unheard of event in the annals of the theatre here! The playhouse, filled to suffocation, received the celebrated artist with jubilation, and after every one of his splendid performances a passionate bravo sounded from a thousand voices! The unparalleled success of this fifth concert induced Herr Ernst to postpone for the second time his departure from here, to the joy of his admirers, and to come to an agreement with the theatre management for three more concerts which will take place on the 17th, 18th and 20th of this month. With these, Herr Ernst will have given no fewer than eight concerts! [EOC:12]

On 22 January 1842, the same critic could report that the enthusiasm showed no sign of abating:

Ernst seems not only to have charmed but also to have enchanted the people of Breslau. Within three weeks this artist has performed in public 11 times, twice for charity and the rest for his own benefit. Nevertheless, the desire to hear him was still by no means satisfied! Such a success has no precedent here, and it borders really on the phenomenal when I tell you that last week on five successive days gave his five last concerts in a theatre filled each time to capacity! The ticket sales for his concerts developed each time into a real fight between 2000 to 3000 people who struggled from early morning on to occupy their place in the queue at the box office. Already at 8am it was hard pressed, at 9 violently stormy, at 10 all tickets taken, and after 10 one saw many hundreds of bitter faces going away as a result of a failure to obtain tickets. This ticket scramble was repeated each time an Ernst concert was announced, and in the heat of battle many a one lost his hat, a sleeve, or half his coat. In short, Ernst's stay in Breslau is an event, the like of which has not occurred in the artistic world, and no artist before him has ever made such a colossal impression on the public as a whole, as he has. The celebrated artist departed from here immediately after the last concert (on 21st this month) by way of Kalisch to Warsaw, where he is already patiently awaited. [EOC:12–13]

His reception in Warsaw, where he played four concerts, and Posen, where he played five concerts in ten days, was equally ecstatic. [EOC:10] At this point, however, Ernst decided to cancel, for the second time, his proposed journey to St Petersburg, because the strain of incessant travelling and concert-giving was proving too much for his increasingly fragile health. [RGM:13/3/42:110. E:57] In addition, he knew that three violinists – Sivori, Artôt and Hauman – were already giving concerts in St Petersburg and this could only reduce his own impact and takings. Ernst appears to have returned to Berlin in March, where he briefly crossed paths with Hauman who was returning to Paris because his wife had fallen gravely ill. [RGM:24/4/42:183. E:57]

Ernst's own illness did not prevent him from giving eight highly successful concerts in Berlin, in which he premiered a number of new compositions. At the sixth, he played his *Nocturne et Rondo Gracioso*, which had been published in 1841 by Litolff in Braunschweig and Ewer in London as *Deux Morceaux de Salon: Adagio Sentimentale et Rondo Grazioso*, op.13. They are dedicated to Adolphe Schönstein and Sigmund Hoffman de Hofmansthal. The *Adagio* is particularly operatic and intense, and makes passionate use of high positions and octave writing. The other major work, the *Polonaise*, eventually published as op.17, was premiered at either the seventh or eighth of these Berlin concerts. [RGM:1/5/42:197] Although Ernst performed this piece rarely, it is a particularly splendid composition. It has all the élan and bravura of Wieniawski's polonaises but coupled with more memorable thematic material.

Ernst also re-established contact with the Mendelssohns. It was in one of Ernst's early concerts that Mendelssohn agreed to appear as his accompanist [EOC:13], and Mendelssohn, Meyerbeer and several other celebrities attended an evening of quartets at the violinist's Berlin residence. Ernst and Mendelssohn then collaborated in two important recitals of chamber music in the Hall of the Royal Singspielakademie on 16 and 21 April, the first of which was attended by the King and Queen. [EOC:13]

As well as all his usual musical duties, Mendelssohn was deeply involved in the Berlin premiere of his incidental music to *Antigone*, and Ernst's unplanned arrival left him exhausted. On 20 April, before all his commitments with Ernst had ended, he wrote to Ferdinand David:

> Last week nearly killed me; on the previous Wednesday, Thursday and Friday it was *Antigone*, on Friday there was another concert by the King, on Saturday it was Ernst's soirée with my trio, in between there were rehearsals and meetings without end, in the morning it's Ernst's soirée once again with Beethoven's A Major sonata for piano and violin, on Saturday a concert by the King again in Potsdam, on Monday another concert and on Wednesday, Thursday and Friday the *Antigone* once more. [FMBB:183]

In addition to all this activity, he was also trying to help organize the Lower Rhine Festival later in the year. At first he hoped that Ernst might participate, writing to David on 26 March that 'Ernst told me recently that he is going to visit the Rhine and maybe is even willing to go as far as Düsseldorf and be present at the Music Festival.' [FMBB: 178] But Ernst's enthusiasm appears to have cooled, and by 7 April, Mendelssohn reports with some disappointment to David that '[Ernst] does not seem to be very enthusiastic about the music festival, he hardly said a word about it and I don't think he will come …' [FMBB:181] Perhaps, after his own concert series, he was feeling as exhausted as Mendelssohn.

In early May, Ernst gave many concerts in Leipzig. On the 2nd, Mendelssohn once more appeared on stage with him to play his D minor piano trio. The concert was attended by Clara Schumann, who made a sceptical comment in the diary she kept with her husband: 'On Monday May 2nd Ernst, whom I had not yet heard, gave a concert. I liked him very much, but did not feel myself enraptured – unfortunately he played only his own compositions [when playing solos], which although they are pretty as concert pieces, become intolerable when [played] one after another.' [SMD:149] This is the first indication that advanced German musical opinion was beginning to have problems with Ernst's concert repertoire. But when she heard him in 'classical music' two days later, her opinion was no longer equivocal: 'Wednesday 4th … Ernst ate at noon at [our house], and after the meal played the A [major] Sonata by Beethoven with me, very beautifully.' [SMD:150]

On 11 May, he gave a concert to help raise money for the small village of Dennstedt where 26 houses had been destroyed by fire, and then on the 12th he performed in Weimar to raise money for the city of Hamburg, where a much larger conflagration on 5–8 May had destroyed a third of the city, killed 51 and made 20,000 homeless. [AMZ:22/6/42:Col.505–6. RGM:29/5/42:231] The public and their rulers were deeply grateful. The King and Queen of Prussia presented him with a particularly valuable snuff-box, and the citizens of Leipzig arranged for a choir to sing him a farewell serenade at his last concert. [AMZ:22/6/42:Col.505–6. RGM:15/5/42:216]

It was at one of these Leipzig concerts that he gave the first performance of his transcription for violin alone of Schubert's *ErlKönig*, one of the most demanding pieces ever written for the instrument, and one of the most frequently played of Ernst's pieces today. [AWMZ:7/5/42:Col.228. E:59]

The main difficulty Ernst faced in his transcription was that there are six voices or strands in Schubert's original: the hammering octave triplets in the accompanist's right hand representing the horse's hooves; the doom-laden rising figures in the accompanist's left hand; and the four different characters which the singer has to impersonate – the narrator, boy, father, and Erlking himself. Ernst succeeds admirably, even if his solution requires transcendent virtuosity. The accompaniment is adhered to throughout (except where Schubert's original demands it pause); the narrator's voice is placed in the middle of the instrument; the voice of the boy, especially when severely frightened towards the end of the piece, goes much higher; and the father is often on the G string below the accompaniment. The Erlking himself is represented on his first appearance by eerie harmonics, and his accompaniment is varied for each reappearance – staccato arpeggiated triplets on the first, legato arpeggiated triplets on the second, and tremolo on the third. The use of double-stops in the middle of a melody, where the top note is a harmonic and the other note is stopped in the conventional fashion (a device also found in the *Last Rose of Summer* variations) is one of Ernst's most tricky technical innovations (Ex. 9.1). [TW:28]

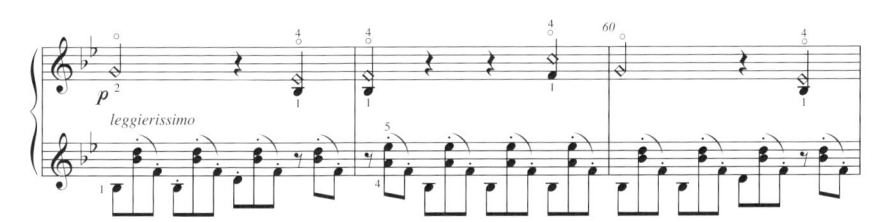

Example 9.1   Ernst, *Le Roi des Aulnes: Grand Caprice*, op.26, bars 58–60

As a whole, the transcription is more successful than Liszt's. His octave doublings, widely spread chords, and use of the right hand's fifth finger to take successive notes of the melody, mean that the transcription is more sonorous than the song, and has to be taken at a slower tempo. The overall effect is rich and well-upholstered but there is a definite loss in urgency and dramatic impact. Ernst's transcription, on the other hand, has to be taken quickly (otherwise the melodic notes would not give the impression of being sustained) and the unavoidable distress of the player – who often has to play widely spread chords or harmonics against a relentless accompaniment – mirrors and enhances the distress of the characters he is portraying. Some scratchiness and mistuning is inevitable, but truth gains by beauty's loss.

Unfortunately Ernst was ill again in Leipzig and had to postpone his departure until 23 May. On that day he left to play concerts in Dessau, Halle and Düsseldorf, before returning to Paris for rest and recuperation. [EOC:13]

It was probably during this stay that Ernst acquired the Stradivarius he played for the rest of his life. It is a beautiful instrument with a particularly striking one-piece back. The Hills, writing in the early 1900s, remark: 'We recall a violin of special tonal merit made in 1709 – ... formerly Ernst's. ... The ripe, woody and yet sparkling quality, its perfect responsiveness and equality on all the strings, and the ever-swelling sonority, all contribute to delight the cultivated listener.' [ASLW:160–61] At present, it is owned by Dénes Zsigmondy, and can be heard, for example, on his complete recording of the Mozart violin and piano sonatas. The sound is not glossy or forceful, and the instrument's most striking characteristics are responsiveness, and the way its tone is preserved at even the lowest volumes.

It is not clear which violin or violins Ernst played on before he acquired this one. There are rumours of an Amati, and he may have owned another Stradivarius, the 1726 'Plotenyi'. [COZ] What is clear, is that the occasional complaints about the smallness of Ernst's sound disappear after the acquisition of his new instrument. From now on, he could produce the sound which Joachim described as being like molten gold [FVP:5], 'rich and grandiose with a touch in it of that vibratory Italian quality, characterizing players of the Southern school, as distinguished from the more solid – perhaps less expressive – countrymen and followers of Spohr.' [A:21/10/65:541] A review by Henri Blanchard in late September notices the improvement in his tone, but misidentifies its cause:

> Not long ago, there was an element of the elegiac and melancholy in Ernst's style; he made the ladies dream, and moaned and sang on his violin by turns. He has since sensed the necessity of capturing the esteem of the male sex, and has made progress. He now has more spirit, more audacity; his bow is now more firmly attached to the string; his sound is better nourished, rounder, more powerful, it even colours his Paganinian tricks and gives to his talent a life, an animated expression, that it did not have before. [RGM: 25/9/42]

Ernst did not buy the violin for himself. It was purchased and given to him, apparently from a choice of forty fine violins, by Andrew Fountaine of Narford Hall, Norfolk. [MW:18/4/44:134] Ernst had been on friendly terms with him since the early 1830s and Fountaine had been the dedicatee of his *Two Nocturnes* op.8. He was born on 16 September 1808, the son of Andrew and Hannah Green Fountaine, and matriculated from St Mary Hall, Oxford, on 10 June 1826. [AO] Throughout the 1830s and '40s he seems to have enjoyed the life of an English milord, travelling, collecting, gambling, entertaining, and spending a good deal of time in Paris.

His wealth and taste soon allowed him to become one of the leading English collectors of violins. His first recorded purchase was the 'Emperor' or 'Kubelick' Stradivarius in 1833; he presented Ernst with his Stradivarius in 1842, and then purchased the Stradivarius still called 'The Fountaine' in 1844. At various points in his life he owned one Amati, six Stradivarius, and three Guarnerius violins, together with a Stradivarius cello (the 'Hausmann'). Several of these were sold in 1872, just prior to his death, although one or two instruments may have been kept in the family. [COZ]

Ernst did not allow his new instrument to distract him from composition. He and Heller had now been working on their joint collection of pieces for violin and piano – the *Pensées fugitives* – for three years, and one of the major tasks of the summer of 1842 was to finish the collection and sell it to a publisher. Heller was utterly opposed to virtuosity for its own sake, and consequently found himself at odds with the prevailing taste in Paris. Although an excellent pianist, he had not once appeared in public since arriving in 1837 which meant his name was not widely known and there was not a ready market for his compositions. To overcome this problem, Ernst agreed to collaborate with him. [MW:19/1/50:34] Attaching his famous name would not only ensure a much larger sale, but would allow a much higher fee to be negotiated from publishers. Heller was therefore delighted when lucrative offers from publishers duly poured in. As he wrote to his friend Eugène de Froberville on 1 August: 'Our 12 pieces have been sold in Leipzick to the publisher Kistner (the unfortunate publisher of my Sonata [op.9]) for sale in only Germany for 2000 francs. Schlésinger wished to buy them for France; and I am at the moment engaged in negotiations with MM. Wessel and Cocks of London.' [LMRP:105]

Ernst evidently enjoyed this collaboration, and while the mood was upon him, arranged one of Heller's solo studies – op.16, no.15 – for violin and piano. Again, an early edition shows Ernst's fingering and his almost Kreisler-like interest in tonal colour (Ex. 9.2):

Example 9.2   Ernst, *Feuillet D'Album*, bars 1–6

Having played this successfully at a concert of his own in early August [RGM: 14/8/42:339], he opened negotiations with publishers. Despite being one of Ernst's closest friends, Heller could not quite suppress a note of rueful envy at Ernst's negotiating power. As he wrote to Froberville:

> As you will have seen in the news columns of the *Gaz[ette] Musicale*, Ernst has transcribed my *Feuillet d'Album* from my 24 Etudes, and he plays it admirably. He played it the day before yesterday at Madame d'Agoult's with great success. But what amused me is that he sold this arrangement for 100 francs to Schésinger here, and for 200 francs to his brother [Heinrich Schlesinger] in Berlin, who was staying for some weeks in Paris. That was exactly the price that Schlésinger gave me for all 24 Etudes and for the copyright in both countries. Admire, dear friend, the effect of a great reputation! M. Maurice [Schlésinger] also wants to acquire the French copyright of our dozen pieces. But Ernst finds the offer of 500 francs too mean. Then he asked for 3 duos on operatic themes for 600 francs for all three; Ernst rejected this too for the same reason. His brother in Berlin offered us 1000 francs for 2 duos on Richard-Coeur-de-Dandy and on *The Huguenots*, which we'll put together shortly. [LMRP:110]

In fact, the two musicians did not write any duos on operatic themes until their fantasy on *Dom Sébastien* in 1844.

The *Pensées fugitves* – which in England appeared as *Les Gages d'amitié* – were published later in 1842. Some of the basic ideas certainly came from Ernst. The three nocturnes he sent Heller from Holland were probably initial outlines for some of the pieces; and the scrap of paper on which Ernst bade farewell to Pierre Wolf in Switzerland in October 1833 contains a sketch of what would become No.5, *Agitato*, of the *Pensées Fugitves*, a full four years before he met Heller. I suspect, however, that Heller, established in one place and with no concert appearances to distract him, did the majority of the work. The final pieces are certainly more characteristic of Heller than Ernst. Each piece has a poetic title and epigraph designed to indicate a mood, devices which Ernst did not otherwise use, and while the violin part is plain and understated, the piano part is deft, fluid and sophisticated – quite unlike the piano parts Ernst had been writing up to this time. The *Pensées fugitives* proved popular and retained their appeal until the beginning of the First World War. Brahms, for example, played them on a number of occasions, including one performance at a benefit concert for Ernst in 1863. Ultimately, their lack of melodic distinction made them slip from the repertoire, but a group of two or three – which is how Ernst tended to present them at the end of his concerts – could still bring a touch of welcome novelty to a modern violin recital.

Chapter 10

The Low Countries, Germany and Scandinavia: 1842–43

Emboldened by his new violin, Ernst set off for a tour of Belgium, Holland and Germany in the late autumn of 1842. He was already on friendly terms and had appeared on stage with three great composers – Mendelssohn, Chopin and Liszt – and the early stages of this tour were notable because he gave a concert with Berlioz. This was the first time Ernst had performed with him or played one of his works.

In the early 1840s, Berlioz entered a fallow period and wrote nothing of importance for five years. He was depressed about the general state of French music, few of his works were being performed in Paris, and he had been turned down for several positions. Yet he heard several reports of his music succeeding abroad, and read of the ecstatic reception that Ernst was achieving in Germany, Austria and the Low Countries. Hitherto, Berlioz had not released the scores of his major symphonies because he wanted to ensure adequate performances, now he decided it was time to direct concerts of his own music in other countries, and he chose to undertake a short expedition to Brussels.

He had been invited there by Snel, the director of the Société Royale de la Grande Harmonie, to perform the *Symphonie funèbre et triomphale* as part of the celebrations commemorating the revolution of 1830. Harriet Smithson, Berlioz's wife, now beset with ill-health and alcoholism and a mere ruin of her former self, had always been violently opposed to his travelling abroad because she was compulsively jealous and lived in continual fear of his taking a mistress. Partly because of her behaviour this eventually became true, and Berlioz took up with a singer of French and Spanish extraction called Marie Recio. When he left for Brussels, Berlioz had had to smuggle his music out of the house, depute his friend Auguste Morel to keep an eye on Harriet, and make sure that Marie's name did not appear in the newspapers.

The first concert was to take place at the Salle Cluyesander in the rue de la Madelaine, and it was lent prestige by Ernst agreeing to play the solo part in the *Pilgrims' March* from *Harold in Italy* – Berlioz had to borrow a viola for the purpose – as well as his own *Elegy* and *Otello Fantasy*. [CGB:III:14] As this concert was Berlioz's first attempt to perform his music abroad, he was obviously anxious for success, but in the event the results were slightly equivocal. The orchestra, made up of military bandsmen and students, tried its best, but the Salle Cluyesander proved too reverberant for complex music, and Marie's voice was found a little thin. Critical opinion about Berlioz's music was deeply divided: the orchestral musicians were appreciative, but the influential head of the conservatoire, Fétis, did his best to subvert the occasion by pronouncing Berlioz's music to be 'hideously ugly' and 'mad'. The one complete success (although Fétis remained intransigent) was Ernst's performance of the *Pilgrims' March* from *Harold*, and Berlioz later presented the King, Leopold I, with the manuscript. [BSG:255–65]

Liszt asked Ernst for news of Berlioz's concert, and on 4 October he replied: 'In the rehearsal, after several repetitions, [his music] seized the musicians, and some passages provoked surges of enthusiasm. He was not equally fortunate during the concert itself; where the execution was anything but irreproachable.' [BAL:I:52]

Berlioz set off for Germany on 12 October. Ernst had urged him to avoid the smaller towns (most of which lacked decent orchestras) but he was not always able to follow this advice. [BM:365] Problems with the two music societies in Brussels, made Ernst decide to accept an invitation from The Hague. [BAL:I:52] While in the area, he gave concerts in Amsterdam (where he played with the King's cellist, Jacques Franco-Mendès) and Rotterdam. [BAL:I:52. RGM:6/11/42:439] Writing to his brother from Cologne on 6 November 1842, Ernst his more concerned with his own triumphs than Berlioz's difficulties in Brussels:

> Dearest Brother! Your dear letter I received promptly and with much pleasure in Brussels. I was pleased to know of your good health; my health is good too, insofar as I can judge it in my present active life with my almost perpetually agitated mind and physical condition, but I can rely on it. I wrote to you, my dear Johann, that I would arrange a concert in Brussels and that Berlioz would take part. This was indeed the case and with the most excellent and brilliant success. It was the first time I had appeared in Brussels, the home of Bériot and Vieuxtemps. I myself attach much importance to its success. However, I did not consider it a favourable time to travel through Belgium and went again to Holland where I spent six weeks in all. I gave three concerts in Amsterdam. At the rehearsal I was received with enthusiasm by the orchestra. On the evening of the concert they all went truly quite mad. The enthusiasm and the applause of the public, when it had mounted to its climax, competed with the fanfare of trumpets and drums which the orchestra let resound at my reception.
>
> In the Hague just then were the festivities for the marriage of Princess Sophie with the heir of the Duke of Weimar. So I was invited to play at a court concert on October 12th and treated most excellently by the entire Royal family. The King conversed with me for a very long time, and I used the opportunity to ask him for the theatre for a concert that I wanted to give for the benefit of those widowed and orphaned by the unfortunate shipwreck at Schewennigen at that time. He immediately gave the order to grant my wish and had me given a very beautiful diamond ring. The Crown Prince was so delighted that he at once engaged me in person for a Soirée at his home on October 25th. The concert for the Schewennigen victims took place on October 19th and it was crowned with the most splendid success. The entire court was in attendance, and the King was always the first to give the signal for the outbreak of applause. The public was in an unusually enthusiastic mood. At the end they shouted, *da capo*; since I was very over-exerted, I allowed the hubbub and uproar to continue for several minutes so that the court which had waited had already left the box when I came out again. But they appeared in the box again after I had again begun to play. They were greeted by the audience as if the latter wanted to thank the court for the attention given to me. It was a splendid, joyous evening.
>
> On the 25th I played at the home of the Prince of Oranien when the King and Queen were also present. The King and Queen thanked me in the most flattering terms for the concert in the theatre and for the enjoyment I had provided for them. From the Mayor I received the enclosed letter [which made me a freeman of the city]. The Prince of Oranien sent me via his secretary a really splendid gold snuff-box, upon which his monogram

and the Royal crown in diamonds are to be seen. It is the finest present I ever received. In the box is: *pour M. Ernst*. The Prince seemed in general to be extremely well disposed towards me, for he invited me last Tuesday informally, to his home. Unfortunately I was away in Leyden playing in the student concert there. That is to say, I found out that they had the greatest desire to hear me, but on account of the paltry honorarium they were barely in a position to offer, they did not dare to invite me. I therefore wrote to them that I would play for them with pleasure, but that I would make a single condition that the honorarium be disposed among the Arminia [student association] members. The acclaim was unending, and at the close the chairman, after a speech presented me with a diploma making me an honorary member and a ring as a souvenir.

You see, dear Johann, that I am not lacking in honours. In confidence I can tell you that it was even spoken of that King would confer a decoration on me. Since I am not counting on it, I beg you to keep the strictest silence about it, because it is ridiculous if one talks of such things and then they do not materialize. Likewise I know from a reliable source that the Order of the Falcon is intended for me in Weimar; whether it will come to that God knows. To me, as surely as I sit here, it is a matter of indifference. However it may be, as you can surely see, I am being singled out for distinction everywhere.

In the Hague I have entrusted to the adjutant of the Crown Prince of Weimar, Count von Beust, the manuscript of the *Erlkönig* for the Grand Duchess of Weimar, who has requested it for herself, and I am awaiting an answer. It is even likely that I will go on to Weimar, for from here I intend to go by way of Frankfurt to Berlin and then to Warsaw, then to St Petersburg. In Frankfurt two concerts are already settled, and hopefully these will lead to several more. Here, I am playing tomorrow in the theatre.

Now I have but one thing more to tell you. I have firmly decided from now on to give you the plain truth about the proceeds of my concerts, so that you will not be surprised later as you were earlier about my pecuniary circumstances. Thus I can tell you that up to now, since my last departure from Paris I have lost money, if I naturally do not count the presents. I hope that the amount of my cash will increase in Frankfurt so that I can afford the high cost of living in Petersburg without worry! [EOC:14–15]

Sixteen days later he writes again:

My Dear Brother, The day before yesterday to my very great joy I received your nice letter and was very pleased with the assurance you gave me of your welfare as well as that of our family. Recently I have again been none too satisfied with my health; however, I am so accustomed to this kind of contingency I am not upset by it, but long very very much to be in a position where I do not have to seek to force myself into an excited state, but would be able to give myself up to the immediate care that is needed. For instance, I was very unwell yesterday afflicted with fever and headache, but my third concert had been announced, and it was necessary to strain every nerve in order to justify the brilliant success that was obtained in the two earlier concerts. I succeeded, thank heaven, and everyone wondered how I could play better than ever in my condition. I was called back five times on this evening. The *ErlKönig* which I played for the first time [here] aroused general astonishment. [22 November 1842. EOC:10–11]

He goes into more detail about the reception of his *Erlking* transcription in a letter to Schlésinger on 28 October 1842:

Yesterday for the first time [in this country] I played the *ErlKönig* transcribed by me for the violin and the effect it aroused was beyond my expectation and it was especially nice to see how the musicians in the orchestra paid astonished attention. I hope that in Germany, where this ballad is better known than here, it will be a great sensation. How are our twelve pieces going? [Presumably the French edition of the *Pensées fugitives*.] Are you really active with them [?] I would like to play them everywhere and have not got a copy and don't want to play them before they have been published. [BN]

His letter to his brother continues:

My first concert I gave on the 16th, one day after Liszt and Rubini [the famous tenor] had given a very brilliant and lucrative one. Mine was poorly attended, but the impression I made was enormous compared to theirs. It was generally said that no instrumental artist since Paganini had been so enthusiastically received. Although not a single paper had time to speak about it before the second concert which took place on the 18th, all the boxes for this one were taken the day before, and the receipts were already doubled. Yesterday there was again the same financial result as for the second concert. To be sure it is not outstanding (you know approximately the receipts for Germany) but it is a beginning and the income grows. In three evenings I took for my half about 1700 francs, and I am playing on Friday for the fourth time. Consider, all this comes to me naturally, without sensation-seeking, without charlatanism. What would it be if I understood that type of business? But it is not in my nature; I don't offend anyone when I only benefit myself and do no harm. I desire no more than that.

Have you heard about an article that was in the *Journal des débats* for November 1st? Frank has written it out and here is a copy I made: 'Ernst travels at this moment in Holland where his marvellous talent which we were hardly aware of in Paris excites the most animated and justified enthusiasm. I can say without exaggeration that he is the true Paganini of his time. I have heard him with a rapture equal to my surprise two months ago in Brussels. I shall not describe all the bold and new effects he obtained on his violin, but as to his *Otello-Fantasy*, he literally sang the famous romance from Saule. For heart rending and impassioned expression, for poetic singing, he leaves the celebrated cantatrices far behind. It was truly sublime. It was inspiration with extended wings soaring to the seventh heaven of art.' This was the finest that was ever said about me – and by such a man as Berlioz!

Since being here I have received through the Saxon ambassador baron von Fr. Asch a diamond ring with a very flattering note from the grand Duchess of Weimar as a token of her satisfaction and gratitude for the dedication of the *ErlKönig*.

I don't know yet, dear brother, at what time I shall come through Berlin, but it might be just in the middle of December; at any rate I shall let you know about this closer to the time. You can imagine that I would be happy as a child to embrace you there. In any case I do not intend to stay for very long in Berlin, I don't know yet whether I shall ever play there in public, for I do not want to lose any time in getting to Russia.

I believe that I shall be able to play here in the theatre twice more before the end of November; then I intend to stop a few days in Weimar and Leipzig. Now you know everything that has happened to me recently, and from now on you shall have such news, if only briefly but often, so that you can be kept informed about the more important steps of mine. Your faithful brother, Heinrich. [22 November 1842. EOC:11]

Berlioz's high opinion of Ernst was clearly reciprocated. In a letter to the composer Johann Friedrich Kittl, Ernst writes of Berlioz, 'He's a great man, and he truly merits all progressive people having a lively interest in him.' [NHB] While in Braunschweig on 23 December 1843, Ernst wrote at greater length in the autograph book of Wolfgang Griepenkerl, one of Berlioz's earliest and most ardent advocates in Germany. On the page opposite Ernst's remarks, Berlioz had written several bars from his *King Lear Overture*. In his own entry, Ernst places himself, as well as Griepenkerl, amongst Berlioz's inner circle:

> I'm writing on the same page as Berlioz, to make sure that you won't forget me. Besides, the sympathy which we feel for a great man may already be fixing me in your memory. Geniuses, who advance across their eras with giant strides like Berlioz, always create a crowd of followers, but simply for themselves, a group of hand-picked favourites with creative and receptive powers. We congratulate ourselves delightedly on belonging to this small band of brothers. I am pleased that this was the first group that bound us together, because I recognise in it the best chance for the continuation of your good will and friendship for me. [SL]

In many ways Ernst and Berlioz were complementary personalities. Both were ardent, impulsive men, and both were addicted to travel. 'Of all musicians,' wrote Berlioz, 'Liszt, Ernst and I are, I believe, the three greatest vagabonds that 'restlessness and the desire to see things' ever drove to leave their own countries and wander the earth.' [BM:465] But here the similarities cease. Much of Ernst's music and writing is vague and emotional; Berlioz's work is always glittering and concrete. Ernst was not an intellectual; Berlioz was intensely literary. Ernst was ingenious; Berlioz was fiercely original. Ernst was a masterly instrumentalist and good at languages; Berlioz was neither. Berlioz fought to change the taste of the musical world; Ernst accepted it as he found it. Ernst's humour was benign and ironic; Berlioz's humour could be hard-edged, grotesque and sardonic. Ernst found intense happiness in marriage; Berlioz was not wholly happy in either of his. To a certain extent, it was the attraction of opposites.

From Rotterdam, Ernst intended to travel to Weimar and Leipzig. [BAL:I:53] On the way, he gave six concerts in Frankfurt in early December [RGM:18/12/42], together with an additional soirée for the Mozart memorial. He told Liszt that he had enjoyed several pleasant hours with the Arnim family, and passed on Berlioz's 'best wishes above a pedal of double admiration.' [BAL:I:25–6]

After Frankfurt, Ernst passed through Kassel, where the great German violinist and composer Loius Spohr was still director of music, and continued to enjoy a difficult relationship with his employer. 'Ernst has passed through without stopping,' wrote Spohr in a letter of January 1843, 'I very much regret not having heard him, although I cannot blame him for passing by Kassel, since the prince and his police vie with one another in putting as many difficulties as possible in the way of foreign artists. This is in many respects a horrible resting place.' [LS:273–4] Spohr would eventually hear Ernst in Carlsbad where he complimented his younger colleague highly on his playing of the *Rondo Papegeno* – in spite of its extensive use of ricochet spiccato bowing, a device Spohr disliked.[1] [HWE: 20]

---

1 In his *Violin School* of 1832, Spohr allows the use of multiple spiccato notes taken with one bow stroke, but these must be taken at a fairly slow tempo and controlled by the wrist. [SVS:127–8] He disapproved of Paganini's thrown stroke where a large number of very rapid notes are taken by allowing the bow to bounce, as quickly as possible, of its own accord.

A little over a month after the letter containing Berlioz's praise, Ernst writes to his brother again, but this time from Hanover:

> My Dear Brother, Yesterday I received your letter with much joy and learned from it that you are all well. How very well I am remembered here you cannot at all imagine, dear Johann. The M's have prepared the finest apartment in the hotel; every day I get fresh flowers from the wife and all the attention. You too, dear brother, are remembered very well here. All, but all, have enquired after you in the most friendly way. The Wenzels, Dr M. (who lately told me how you came to him and sounded him out about me and finally identified yourself as my brother), and the Bohrers spoke with hearty thanks for your reception and are seeking in every possible way to give you tit for tat. The charming Captain von Hoenemann, the King's aide-de-camp, with whom we have breakfasted and who remembered that tears were in your eyes when I played the *Elégie* for him the same morning, and the Chamberlain von Busch who brought you to the court concert, inquired after you especially kindly and charged me to give you the most friendly greetings. Here I also visit Dr Mensching with the long coat. He wears spurs, but I have not as yet seen him ride. He is now a lawyer. He is a fine and quite clever man, very happy when I told him that you sent him greetings. The Bohrers and Wenzels thank you for your greetings and return them most heartily. When I visited them, a concert in the theatre had already been arranged for Tuesday, December 20th, under my earlier conditions. It was packed full, many coming in groups from surrounding areas, and from Celle alone (where we stayed overnight) there came to our hotel a caravan of 28 people who urgently begged me to give a concert for them; this has been arranged for tomorrow, the 29th.
>
> The acclaim I received here was indescribable. The King was at the concert and immediately upon my arrival when he had found out about it, he decided on a court concert for December 22nd, in which I was received in the most excellent manner. The entire evening I thought of you, of your shoes, of our white neck-cloths. Frank and I laughed heartily and only regretted that you were not here again. The King spoke with me several times, reminded me of my stay here three years ago and [how] delighted he was with me at that time. He said to me in a jocular way: 'Last year in Berlin you tricked us all. You were to come to the King and instead sent us an inferior Belgian.' (Between us, that was Hauman.) Thereupon, I explained to the King that I had been invited by Count Redern in an impolite way, so that my artist's pride did not permit me to accept this invitation. After the court concert, the King expressed a wish to hear me again, and decided upon the second concert in the theatre, yesterday, the 27th. Imagine my joyful surprise when on Monday, through His Eminence Count Platten, I received by order of the King, the gold medal of honour with the ribbon, for Art and Science. I expressed my thanks for it at once and requested permission from the King to be allowed to give the concert already announced for the poor. 'Whatever Ernst does is all right by me,' his answer is supposed to have been, and the approval note read: 'The concert for the benefit of the poor by H.W. Ernst is approved by the highest authority.' The house was as full as it could possibly be, and countless people could not find seats. The receipts came to 550 thalers, the most that can be taken in at the usual prices. The enthusiasm of the audience reached its climax, and after I played the *Erlkönig* a laurel wreath with a poem was thrown to me, and at the same moment it rained poems all over the theatre. After the concert the King had me called to his box, as did the Crown Prince, and both conversed with me in the most friendly and

---

Consequently, the device is not discussed in his chapter on bowing. [SVS: 118–31] Joachim was inclined to endorse Spohr's prejudice until Mendelssohn said to him: 'Why not [use it] if it sounds good and if it is appropriate for that particular spot?' [GMV:263]

kindly manner. Tomorrow I give a concert in Celle and come back here again on Friday to play once more on Monday in the performance for a pension fund. I am especially inclined to do something here because the King, to whom I am surely a stranger, was the first to do me honour in such a way.

On Tuesday, January 3rd, I travel to Bremen where I have a concert on the 5th and in Oldenburg on the 6th. From all these cities invitations have come to me. From Bremen I go to Hamburg by way of Kiel to Copenhagen and Sweden. Perhaps I may change my plans in Hamburg and still go to Russia, combining the two trips. Here I am very often in the house of the Minister Frau von Schultz and am received as well as possible. She intends to write me a letter to the King of Sweden and one to the Queen of Denmark. This evening I am invited to a great ball at her house; the King and Crown Prince are also supposed to come.

Now I have written to tell you everything new and pleasant, dear Johann. Share it with our dear brothers and sisters and give them a thousand greetings. A thousand greetings to to dear Caroline and the children, to Joseph and his wife and niece Philippine. Don't leave me out with anyone. Now farewell and write to me again very soon at the music shop of Mr August Cranz or general delivery. Don't put so many seals on your letter. Keep well and healthy.

I forgot to tell you that the music director of the King's bodyguard has arranged the *Elégie* for military band, and that this was played for me to my very great satisfaction early today for the second time in the officers' mess. The Crown Prince was supposed to come but was prevented by other matters. Several days ago I was invited by the Officers Corps to dinner. Farewell, Your Heinrich. [28 December 1842. EOC:16–17]

Ernst gave concerts in Celle, Oldenburg, and Bremen, followed by five sensational concerts in Hamburg, [E:67–8] but, as he tells his brother, his travel plans for Scandinavia were interrupted by the arrival of an unexpected message:

Dearest Brother, You will perhaps be surprised to get a letter from me from Hanover; I shall therefore hasten at once to give you an explanation about this which will certainly please you very much. I was in Hamburg (where I also received your letter), having already performed my concerts which were five in number, and ready to go to Copenhagen by way of Kiel, when I received, through the Hanoverian minister there, an invitation from the King of Hanover to come back here, in order to take part in the court concerts on the occasion of the wedding festivities of the Crown Prince. I accepted this invitation and arrived here on the 15th of last month. Unfortunately, however, since that time I have not been well and, with the exception of the court concert, when I made an unusual effort, I was unable to put a foot out of the door. The doctor promises me that I will again be able to travel by the middle of next week. The court concert went extremely well, and as listeners I had the King of Hanover, the Crown Prince and his new bride, the Princess of Altenburg, the King of Prussia, the Princes Carl and Wilhelm of Prussia, and the Duke and Duchess of Altenburg, the Prince of Wurttemberg, the Duke of Dessau, the Duke of Nassau, the Duke of Braunschweig, and others. The King of Hanover also spoke immediately after the first pieces and thanked me for coming back from Hamburg. There upon all the royal personages spoke to me because I already knew the majority of them personally. The next day I received the most beautiful golden snuff-box with the monogram of the King and the crown of diamonds. They say it cost 100 louis d'or. Three days ago the King named me the Royal Hanoverian Concertmaster with the wish that I spend a month here every winter in order to play at the court concerts, to which I readily agreed. I left it to the King to decide the honorarium.

In Hamburg it went very well for me. I was received with rejoicing, due in part to the gratitude for my contribution, delivered at the time, to the unfortunate city (because of the great fire.) A group of young people gave me a serenade. As soon as I can get away from here I shall hasten to Copenhagen, where I have the most promising prospects, and I hope finally to be able to lay the foundation there for a modest capital sum. Up to now I am still only swimming on the surface, to be sure without danger of drowning, but yet not catching sight of any land.

The Duke of Braunschweig has also given me a pressing invitation to come to Braunschweig between the eighth and tenth of this month; however, because of not being well and my other engagements I have not been able to give a definite answer.

In Hamburg there is Fischof, a dear, good boy. He expects a permit from his brother for cigars and has promised to remit 500 for you, if I should find something excellent. I have already seen to this and will do so again when I return to Hamburg, but I can assure you that up to now I have nowhere seen such good cigars as in the large selection in Vienna in Godfroy's. It would please me if I could find something really superfine for you.

Now stay well and healthy. Write to me, general delivery, in Copenhagen. A thousand greetings to dear Caroline, Joseph, and the children. [EOC:8–9]

The position as Hanoverian Concertmaster was the first and last fixed position of any substance which Ernst accepted, and a note in the King's own hand, awarding the title, is still in the Hanoverian archive:

We, Ernst Augustus etc, hereby recognise that we have granted the violin virtuoso Heinrich Ernst from Brünn the title of our Concertmaster, with obligation, accepted by him, to be present here for 4 to 6 weeks in the winter months and to take part in our court concerts then. It is also stated that the aforementioned should be respected by all as our Concertmaster. Certificate issued Hanover 27th February 1843. [NHH]

The honorarium was fixed at 1,500 thalers. [SMW:14/3/43:77. RGM:15/1/43:26. E:67] When it is recalled that someone as distinguished as Mendelssohn only received 3,000 for an entire year of exhausting work, and that a virtuoso as celebrated as Lipinski received 1,200 for the same period, we see how lavish were Ernst's terms.

The King of Hanover, Ernest Augustus, was an Englishman – the fifth son of George III and Queen Caroline. He had attended the University of Göttingen, and when Victoria ascended to the throne of England in 1837, Ernest, hitherto the Duke of Cumberland, became King of Hanover. The reasons for this were that George I had been King of Hanover before he became King of England, and Hanover had been ruled by an emissary of the English crown through the reigns of the next three Georges and William IV. When Victoria came to the throne, however, because the Salic law prevailed in Hanover, no woman could inherit the throne, and Ernest, the next in line to the English throne, became King of the German territory.

Tall and muscular, his appearance was made additionally forbidding by a shrunken left eye – partly caused by a cannonball's shockwaves at the battle of Tournai in 1794. [WE:28–35] Nonetheless, he could be jocular and charming and he was genuinely fond of music. As a child he learnt to play the flute (he was so shortsighted that this was the only instrument he could play while reading the music at the same time) and he passed on his taste to his son, Crown Prince George, who spent many hours improvising at the keyboard. [WE:24] The King was the first of a number of awkward, forthright Englishmen that Ernst charmed, although at this point the violinist had little idea of what kind of man he was dealing with. His trip to England the following year would enlighten him.

Saying farewell to the King, Ernst headed for Kiel, but two concerts which he gave on the way, in the Schauspielhaus in Darmstadt, proved disappointing. Not many people attended the first, and the second was nearly empty. Presumably the interruption to his travel plans had meant that publicity was poor, but, whatever the cause, the citizens of Darmstadt were taken to task by the critic of the *Signale für Musikalische Welt* who reminded them that, of living violinists, Ernst was much the best. [SMW:21/3/43:93]

Unusually, there is an eyewitness account of Ernst's stay in Kiel and Copenhagen. It was written by the German pianist and composer Carl Reinecke some fifty years after the events took place:

> Ernst, though he was only twenty-nine when first I crossed his path, had then already been for some time the most famous violinist of his day. To that generation he was almost what Sarasate is in this, with this difference: that, while a host of rivals has sprung up in a moment round Sarasate, no one at that time, except Vieuxtemps and Ole Bull, had ever enjoyed a reputation equal to that of Ernst. Spohr and Paganini were gone from the field of action, the star of Joachim and the Milanollos [two girl prodigies] was only just rising, while Bazzini, Lafont [who had actually died in 1839], and Sivori did not enjoy, at least in Germany, so distinguished a reputation as Ernst.
>
> It was therefore no wonder that on my arrival at Kiel, on the way from Altona to Copenhagen, early in the year 1843, I went straight to the concert in the Concert Hall (Harmonie), in order to hear for myself Ernst's performance, of which until then I had only read in the concert notices.
>
> Ernst was a virtuoso in the truest sense of the word, and he made no secret of his desire to work upon the multitude by his dazzlingly brilliant performance, a desire which was shared in those days by almost all performers.
>
> At that time one could still hear Clara Wieck play variations by Herz, or fantasias by Thalberg, and Joachim, then thirteen years old, liked to play Ernst's *Otello-Fantasy*. But Ernst not only overcame with grace and ease difficulties which would have made most people's hair stand on end, but also ennobled them, as Liszt did, by the spirit with which he surmounted them; while, on the other hand, he could bring out the melody with heart-stirring fervour, and when necessary with a wondrous glow. It may well be believed that he stirred the public to enthusiastic applause, in which I joined with all the ardour of youth.
>
> But my heart sank and my courage failed when I looked from this great artist in the fulness of his power, in the radiance of his fame, applauded by all the world, to my humble self, on the way to Copenhagen to ask his Majesty King Christian VIII, for a stipend to enable me to continue my studies.
>
> And even while I was reflecting on the differences in our situations, there came up to me a very elegant cavalier, who asked if were indeed, as he thought, the pianist Reinecke from Altona? Of course I assented, and he thereupon brought me a message from the Duchess of Glücksburg, who was at the concert, to the effect that I should play something, as she wished to hear me. In vain I stammered that I knew not how I came to have the honour of being known to her Highness; in vain I referred to my travelling costume, and to the fact that I was quite unknown to the giver of the concert. The courtier

replied that the Countess Plessen had told the Duchess of my arrival in Kiel, that it was not impossible to play the piano even in travelling costume, and finally that he himself would present me to Herr Ernst. What could I do, when the formalities were over, but sit down at the piano and play?

To play Mendelssohn's Concerto in G minor right through was a very remarkable fancy on my part, but in the hurry of the moment I could not think of anything else. At all events, it brought me friendly words from Ernst, and (what pleased me even more) an invitation to visit him next morning. The early hours of the next day sped all too slowly with me, for I could scarcely wait for the time when I might with propriety pay my visit. But at last I stood in Ernst's rooms, and was bidden welcome with friendly words, and after a short time Ernst asked me to play with him. He showed me copies, just arrived from Leipzig, and still almost damp from the press, of the twelve 'Pensées Fugitives' by Stephen Heller and Ernst, which were later much played as excellent drawing-room pieces, and which even now are not forgotten. [It is more likely that these were the French edition of the pieces.] As I had always been accustomed by my father to play at sight, I was able to play these twelve not very easy pieces with him to his satisfaction, and, as several visitors appeared during the morning the pieces had to be repeated many times. Finally, Ernst took up Beethoven's *Kreutzer* Sonata, and when we had finished it he said, 'Yesterday you played at my concert; now you must give a concert, and I will play at yours.' Of course I gratefully acquiesced, and in a few days (it was Friday, April 7th, 1843) I gave my concert at which Ernst played his renowned 'Elégie' and as duets with me one of the above-mentioned 'Pensées Fugitives' and the *Kreutzer* Sonata.

I found it hard to part from the man who had shown me so much kindness and so great an honour, but I knew I should see him again in Copenhagen in a few days. There, of course, I had recommendations to the Court, but for the rest the outlook was uncertain enough, for, besides Ernst, there were in Copenhagen, Ole Bull and the once famous pianist Theodor Döhler, the same Döhler of whose well-known Nocturne in D-flat major, Robert Schumann said that it was as sweet and as cold as the ice which was handed round at the time.

These three noted virtuosi of course took up all the attention of the public in the by no means large capital, to such an extent that no one could take any interest in me.

Ernst gave his first concert in the Court Theatre, and had an enormous success, so that he had to arrange another concert in a day or two, and when I visited him at the Hôtel d'Angleterre on the morning after the first concert, he received me with 'I'm so glad you have come, for I have a request to make: next Saturday I give my second concert at the Royal Theatre, but one number is wanting in the programme, and I wanted to ask you to play a solo.' The kind hearted artist knew that I should scarcely find an opportunity for making myself heard in public in Copenhagen unless he stretched out his helping hand, and so he chose this way of fulfilling a wish which I should never have dared to express. As may be imagined, I did not wait to be asked twice.

The evening of the 22nd arrived, and with all the confidence of youth I marched on to the platform, and seated myself, at the grand piano, of course receiving no sign of welcome from the public. I played as well as I could an Allegro of my own, accompanied by the orchestra. Scarcely had I struck the last chord when Ernst rushed out of the artists' room, and embraced and kissed me, thereby, of course, giving rise to a reception such as I had certainly not deserved. It may easily be understood that such kindness as this could never be forgotten.

I was present on one occasion when Ernst and Ole Bull serenaded Theodor Döhler on his birthday, April 22nd, 1843; the slim and slender Ernst was mounted on the giant shoulders of Ole Bull, and scraping away with his bow at the violin held under the chin of his noble steed. It was a picture worthy of Oberländer. Once he challenged Döhler and me to play the overture to *Euryanthe*; when we got to the famous *pianissimo* passage in the middle of the overture we suddenly felt our heads weighed down by something. Ernst had stolen behind us, and placed upon our heads, as symbols of the mutes (*sordini*) which at this point are placed on the violin bridges, two cheese-covers which he had softly stolen from the luncheon table.

He was always ready for that sort of joke, and once, when I expressed to him my astonishment that in spite of the unheard of admiration which was continually offered him, he should have preserved such an incredible modesty, he said 'My dear fellow, what is a virtuoso, a mere artist who practises his art? We performers have every opportunity for being modest. None but a creative artist can have the consciousness of having composed something beautiful. And what have I written? A few concert pieces, and the 'Elégie,' that is all.' (The F[♯] minor Concerto was not then in existence.) On occasion, however, he was capable of showing the true artistic pride. Once, when he received an invitation to supper, accompanied by the request that he bring his violin, he answered, 'I will come with pleasure myself, but my violin never takes supper.' [HFPV:54–5]

Before Ernst arrived in Copenhagen in April, Bull had already given two concerts at low prices in the enormous Royal Riding School. Ernst performed in the Hoftheater der Christiansburg at three times Bull's admission price, but still managed to gain 800 thir for himself. Sadly, relations with Bull became much less amicable because the Norwegian, in characteristic fashion, claimed that Ernst's secretary, Frankowski, was plotting against him. [OBM:143–4] Ernst and Döhler gave eight concerts at the theatre altogether and then two concerts for the less well-off at the Riding School so an additional 7,000 people could hear them. They also planned to give up to six soirées of chamber music in the foyer of the Hôtel d'Angleterre, but after the third of these, news arrived that Döhler's father had died. The rest of the concerts were cancelled so that Döhler could return to Paris. [RGM:21/5/43:181. AMZ:5/8/43: Col.500–502. E:70]

It was now time to head for London. Pausing briefly in Kiel on 13 June 1843, Ernst sketched the theme for a second elegy and give it as a souvenir to his 'dear friend and travelling companion', Anton Melbye. There is no sign it was ever completed or published. [BC]

Chapter 11

England, Sivori, and King Ernest: 1843

On 23 June, Ernst arrived in London. [MW:29/6/43:223] The next day, the English pianist and composer Wiliam Sterndale Bennett held a soirée at his home in Charlotte Street to entertain Spohr, Dreyschock, Filtsch, Hallé and other lions of the musical season. They were soon joined by Ernst and Moscheles who arrived together. This was to be Ernst's entrée into English musical society. [LSB:150–51]

A few days after this soirée, another party was nearly the cause of Ernst's undoing. As Hallé recounts:

> The directors of the Philharmonic Society had decided upon feting Ernst on his arrival and arranged a party at Richmond in his honour, which took the shape of an early dinner. The day was very fine, the company, including the principal critics, very numerous, and the dinner sumptuous. Ernst had to respond to many civilities, to empty his glass at the separate request of each of the 'convivies', so often that at last I saw that he was overcome, and feared that he might roll under the table. It was at this critical moment that somebody proposed Ernst should play something. The proposal was cheered vociferously, and as Ernst's violin did not dine out, some one was dispatched into the village to try to find one. He soon returned with a violin, the price of which, with the bow, was marked fifteen shillings. This was handed to Ernst, and he gave the very first proof of his talent to a select English audience by playing his arrangement of Schubert's 'Erl-King', for violin alone, an impossible piece, which in his best days he could not play satisfactorily. Upon this wretched instrument and in more than half-tipsy condition, it was excruciating, and I gave him up for lost; but, whether it was that his listeners were in the same state as he, or that the extraordinary sounds they heard bewildered them, his triumph was complete! What is more, after his great and legitimate success, at a concert given on July 18th in aid of the German Hospital, his first public appearance in London, I heard it said with conviction, 'Ah but his playing in Richmond was even finer!' The party was further enlivened by poor half-blind George Macfarren running straight into the Thames and having to be fished out, fortunately without any hurt to him. [LLCH:81–2]

Ernst's health was poor and he had arrived late in the season. Initially, he had no intention of playing in public, but he was persuaded to perform at two charity concerts. The first, on the 15 July, was a concert for the French poor to be held in private rooms in Brook Street. Here he played his *Elegy* and the *Carnival of Venice*. The latter had to be repeated three times, and on each occasion Ernst substituted new variations. The critic of the *Morning Post* was deeply impressed:

> The melancholy expression on the face of Ernst is the type of his style. It is the intensity of his passion, the overwhelming sentiment which he draws from his instrument, and in the highly wrought out-pourings from his strings, as if his very soul were discoursing most eloquent music, that Ernst is not only without a rival, but has never been approached by

any violinist within our recollection, and we number in our reminiscences Paganini, Spohr, Ole Bull, De Bériot, Lipinsky, Molique, Haumann, Artôt, Panofka, Sivori, Blagrove, Mori, and a host of other illustrious names. ... The volume of tone drawn out by Ernst is absolutely prodigious. It is like the viola in its breadth, but united with the most elaborate and finished violin execution. In double and triple stops, staccato, arpeggio, and pizzicato passages, Ernst yields to no player. In harmonics we think Sivori has more truth of tone. [ME: 22/7/43:279–80]

The second concert on the 18 July, was as a grander affair for the benefit of Dr Freund's German Hospital, held in the Hanover Square Rooms. In the Royal Box was Ernst's employer, King Ernest of Hanover. He was widely disliked in England, and had recently been the cause of much public gossip. In 1837, before the death of William IV, he was second in line to the throne, and there were rumours that he was plotting to assassinate Princess Victoria. Consequently, there was widespread relief when he left for his German kingdom. It was not until Victoria had three children, and there were four obstacles between him and the English throne, that he was invited back to England for the christening of Princess Alice in April 1843. This explains his attendance at Ernst's English debut. He came to England eagerly but not without resentment since he nursed a number of grievances against the English crown. He believed he had not been given the kind of influential position he deserved; he maintained that the English monarchy had purloined valuable jewellery truly belonging to Hanover; and he felt that Victoria had married an inconsequential German princeling – Albert of Saxe-Coburg-Gotha – who now claimed precedence over him. [WE:232–8]

He arrived too late for the christening, but in time for the wedding of his brother's daughter. From the first, his behaviour was boorish and absurd. As the Queen was about to lead the congregation out, Ernest claimed his right as a sovereign to stand next to her in the place reserved for Albert – in Ernest's view a 'paper' non-king. The Queen resisted; Ernest refused to move. Albert pushed him and Ernest, 72 and stiff with rheumatism, nearly fell over. He had to be escorted out, fuming, by the Lord Chamberlain. Ernest clearly felt all was not lost, and made a second attempt to assert himself at the signing of the register. He placed his elbow on the register and invited Victoria to sign, his intention being to sign immediately below. She outwitted him by going round to the other side of the table and asking that the register be passed across. She and Albert then signed before Ernest could reach the other side. [WE:235–8] He was disappointed, although the only person surprised, when Victoria asked him to dine only once. When he took his seat in the Hanover Square Rooms, one can imagine a certain amount of tepid applause and ironic cheering.

The concert on 18 July was Ernst's first official public appearance, and he therefore played a more ambitious programme than at the concert for the French poor: Spohr's eighth concerto, Mayseder's Variations in E, and his own *Otello Fantasy* and *Carnival*. The critic of the *Musical World* thought that he showed some initial nervousness, but that 'his success was, beyond all description, triumphant. M. Ernst proved himself ... the most accomplished living violinist'. Ernst's performance of the Spohr concerto was:

[the] most entirely inspired and superb performance we ever heard from any living violinist whatever. The most exquisite poetry of the reading, the masterly boldness of the execution, and the immense variety of expression, were together unprecedented in our remembrance. A more complete triumph could not have been desired by the warmest admirers of M.Ernst;– the applause was tumultuous. [MW: 20/7/43:239]

But it was the critic of the *Musical Examiner* who really let himself go. He gives the impression of a man so drunk with delight that he is incapable of organizing or editing his thoughts, and writes in a prose which is at once woozy, repetitious, profuse, deliriously incoherent, full of esoteric references, and altogether careless about whether it communicates or not. The first page is entirely devoted to the Orpheus myth:

> Orpheus, we repeat, built a city – that is to say we are told he built a city, though most likely the said city was after all nothing more than a castle, and that castle, a castle in Spain, or a castle in the air, as the case may be … Orpheus, once more, built – that is to say caused to be built, for he did not build himself … Orpheus, to conclude, Orpheus – Orpheus – Orpheus, what? [ME:22/7/43:277]

His conclusion, if such writing can be said to have conclusions, is that the soul of Orpheus was, by metempsychosis, transferred to Ernst. Ernst and Orpheus *are one*:

> Yes, reader, sure are we that Ernst and Orpheus are one and the same person, for, except Orpheus, no mortal or immortal could have produced such strains as did Ernst on Tuesday morning, in the Hanover Square Rooms, before a critical and multitudinous assembly, open mouthed with wonder; and, except Ernst, we rigidly hold that no mortal or immortal could compete with Orpheus. Ernst, then, is Orpheus. … [Like] Orpheus, [he] has built an edifice, or, in other words, has raised in the minds of those who listened to him, a temple of fame, which shall endure as long as fame shall be desirable, and honour be a boon. … It was veritably the most kingly performance we ever heard from an earthly violinist. … [He] evinced resources unsurpassed by Paganini himself, and drew down an enthusiasm of approval which made the building shake. *Quel coup d'archet!* What a sweeping and majestic stroke of the bow – as though power were his offspring, and he drew his arm around it. *Quelle profondeur, quelle pureté de son!* As though tone were his creature, and he dallied with it. And then, what thrilling pathos – what a weeping, wailing, heart-rending, passionful complaint, was the prayer, from his hands! As though the violin were a human being, from which the bow, uttering a tale of sadness, drew tears and lamentations. Finally with what quaint humour – what tantalizing grotesquerie – what endless wit in his delineation of the *Carnaval*! [ME:22/7/43:278]

The young critic whom Ernst had thus bedazzled and befuddled, was a good conquest to have made, since he was J.W. Davison, soon to be the most powerful music journalist in England. When he reviewed Ernst's debut, he was editor and almost sole writer of the waspish *Musical Examiner*, and the more established *Musical World*'s critic for new compositions. Within a year, the editor of *The Musical World* died, and Davison took over his position. The paper was unrivalled amongst English music journals for its readership and coverage of London concerts, and between 1844 and his death in 1885, Davison wrote a good deal of the copy.

But it was his position on *The Times* that gave Davison his influence in the world at large. *The Times* was by far the most authoritative and widely read European newspaper (the philosopher Schopenhauer, for example, read it every morning) and Davison was asked to become its music critic in 1846 on the death of Thomas Alsager, its city editor and occasional contributor of musical notices. By the time of his retirement in the mid-1870s, Davison had contributed literally millions of words, and established a platform of unrivalled readership and authority. 'Just reflect how colossal and universal is the paper of which I am speaking,' wrote a rueful Wagner in 1869 about the drubbing he received at its hands in 1855. [FMW:65] And before the debut of a singer friend, Théophile Gautier wrote Davison a note whose nine words bear ample witness to the critic's power: 'Faites sa fortune avec trois lignes, je te prie.' [TMM:75]

Davison's power was social as well as literary. He was the acknowledged leader of the London music critics, including Bennett of the *Musical World* and *Telegraph*, Glover of the *Morning Post*, and Ryan of the *Standard*. Bennett wrote:

> Few, perhaps none, of the critics who have risen since, ... can form any adequate idea of the power exercised by that remarkable man. It is often said that in respect of music he held the London press in the hollow of his hand ... Over his colleagues ... Davison's influence was commanding. Where he led they followed more or less closely ... submitting to guidance, the secret of which lay not only in superior knowledge and literary skill but also, to a remarkable extent, in personal charm. [TMM:101]

Ernst and Davison became mutually admiring acquaintances and eventually intimate friends (addressing one another as 'tu' after 1845). Davison, being a staunch atheist, anti-royalist and lover of the ethereal, revered the memory of Shelley, and it is a sign of Davison's intimacy with Ernst that he took the violinist on a pilgrimage to Shelley's hallowed ground at Marlow. [FMW:47]

On the other hand, Ernst's relationship with the Italian violinist Camilo Sivori, who had come to England several weeks before, was not prospering. Three years younger than Ernst, Sivori was initially taught by Paganini's old teacher Giacomo Costa, and then, in early 1824, he had lessons from Paganini himself. He had the distinction of being Paganini's only important pupil, although in later years he acknowledged that Paganini was probably the world's worst teacher – impatient, rude, and bitterly sarcastic. [G1:XVI:357] Emerging largely unscathed, Sivori became professor of violin at the Genoa Conservatoire, and after giving a series of concerts in 1839, in the cities of Northern Italy, he went to seeing the dying Paganini in Nice. Paganini sold him the Vuillaume copy of his Guarneri (sending the money to Vuillaume), and Sivori began on the extensive series of tours that would take up the next twenty years of his life. In 1841 he played in all the major musical centres of Europe, from Brussels to St Petersburg; in 1842 he played in Genoa, and then wintered in Paris where he was awarded a gold medal of honour.

At the beginning of 1843, he arrived in England for the beginning of the season, and in a series of four grand concerts created a considerable impression. The *Illustrated London News*, for example, wrote of his farewell concert:

He played four times, at each time surpassing himself, for he is a creature of enthusiasm, and he kindles into higher rapture when he is warmly and judiciously applauded. ... Each of these pieces received applause to the echo, particularly [a G-string fantasia on themes from the 'Somnambula'] than which nothing could be more soul-moving and expressive ... Sivori stands the first in the world as a violinist, and even 'fills up the pause' that Paganini made. [ILN:5/8/43:90]

In character, he was simple and genial. '[He] was a small, thin man, with a narrow, oval face, ordinary features, small, dark, kindly eyes, and a deprecatory smile,' wrote Alice Mangold. 'There was a simplicity and gaiety about [him], the holiday humour of a child out of school, which infected his companions.' [AMDM: 275–9] Hallé certainly found him sympathetic, until the name of Ernst was mentioned:

I was charmed to meet Sivori in London [in 1843], having made his acquaintance in the previous year, and fully recognised his claims to distinction, in spite of the pompous title 'only pupil of Paganini,' which he assumed. I was often with him and glad of his society, when a few weeks later Ernst arrived. He was fresh from a triumphant tour through Holland and Belgium, and his coming was expected with great curiosity. Ernst was an older friend of mine than Sivori, as a musician he was far his superior, our tastes were more similar, and I naturally continued those friendly relations with him which had so long been my wont. I did not mean to neglect Sivori, but found to my surprise and sorrow that he looked upon my conduct with Ernst as upon the worst of betrayals. He had fully expected that I should *cut* Ernst, whom he considered his rival, and could not understand how I could dream of being friends with both sides. I had indeed dreamed of bringing them together, which would have been a pleasure to Ernst; but when I hinted at this, the ire of Sivori knew no bounds, and I had to make a selection between the two, much against my will, but of course in favour of my old friend. Ernst achieved a great success and a well deserved one, for his talent was at its very height and his passionate playing was most impressive. [LLCH:80–81]

There was much controversy in England about who was the greater violinist. The *Musical World* decided to conclude the discussion with a magisterial summary:

It is singular that the short stay of Herr Ernst in London should have excited so much interest as to have given rise to two distinct parties in the world of music – the Ernstists and Sivorists – and it is curious to remark, that the latter comprise nearly all the violin-players – we mean persons limited to the performance and comprehension of that instrument – and that the former consists of nearly all such persons as have studied and known music, in its wide and general developments, persons who have spent their lives, in the analyzation and admiration of great works, rather than the solution of mechanical intricacies and the practice of individualities.

The Sivorists allege that the head of the opposite faction is uncertain in his intonation, unfinished in his execution, and, withal, so given to a morbid melancholy feeling as to be incapable of joyous expression. The admirers of this much-vituperated hero are thus forced upon recrimination, and adduce the performance of last Monday in testimony to his rival's fallibility, asserting that he played many passages very far from quite in tune (for instance much of the variation in triplets on the air from Somnambula, and a great deal of the minor variation in the same piece, which, however, he played with considerably more precision on its repetition, for it was on account of its peculiar difficulty, encored); and that he missed many of his tours de force, exemplified in the failure of harmonics and the like; and that, wanting the pure passion of an artist, either quick or morbid, he proved himself incapable of any expression, either glad or grievous. For our own part, we despise this petty principle of picking out the failings of a great man – either in execution or imagination – and prefer to mention only his peculiar excellences, as fit themes of admiration and for precedent.

On the whole, then, we should say, that Ernst is remarkable for his full rich tone, especially on the lower strings, while the tone of Sivori is, perhaps, sweeter and more even throughout the whole compass of the instrument; that Ernst is remarkable for vigour and energy of style, and for grandeur of conception, while Sivori is to be more noticed for completeness and delicacy, and prettiness of thought; that Ernst, in his performances, seems to open the extremest depths of passion, and to expose the acute, strong, and impulsive workings of a musician's heart, while Sivori evinces only the superficial gallantries of art, and captivates rather than commands our feelings, by the fascination of his graceful deportment; in short, to express all in a few words, we should say ... Sivori is a *fine player*, Ernst is a *great one*. [MW:10/8/43:268–9]

The hostility between Ernst and Sivori was not just occasioned by their rival styles or different national schools. It had its origins in a dispute which arose before Ernst's journey to England. This was brought about by Sivori's practice, a practice he shared with several other leading virtuosi including Hauman, of playing of Ernst's *Carnival of Venice* without acknowledging the composer. Letters from several friends informed Ernst of this, and he wrote to Sivori asking if the reports were true. Receiving no reply, he then sent an open letter to the editor of the *Revue et gazette musicale* from Copenhagen on 20 April 1843, asking Sivori and Hauman publicly if they were playing his variations under Paganini's name. [RGM:30/4/43:151. E:74–6][1] Again, no response to his request was forthcoming.

Sivori was using the *Carnival* to spearhead his very successful tour of England, [LM:II:111] and one motive for Ernst's trip to England in 1843, which was at a very inauspicious time from the performance point of view, was to hear exactly what Sivori was playing. By the time Ernst wrote his next letter, from London, he had listened to Sivori's performance and could be more confident of his own cause. As he wrote from Long's Hotel in Old Bond Street to the editor of the *Musical Examiner* on 28 June:

> I can now speak with more certainty I have had an opportunity during the short time I have been in London, of convincing myself that with regard to M. Sivori, not only is the assertion of these letters [well] founded, but he even makes no scruple of playing the *Andante* which precedes the *Carnival*, without naming me as the author. The *Andante* has, nevertheless, been published [for] several years at M. Lemoine's, in Paris – with accompaniment for piano alone – and I am not aware how M. Sivori has procured the quartet accompaniment, which is still my property, and differs considerably from that for the piano. Anyone may convince himself of this, by asking for the first book of Ernst's *Morceaux de Salon*. I shall abstain from qualifying the behaviour of M. Sivori, and think his proceeding, with regard to my *Andante* may also serve as a guide for the *Carnival of Venice*.

---

1 Ghys was also performing a version of the *Carnival of Venice* very similar to Ernst's which he claimed he heard Paganini play in 1827. See HWE:13–16.

> I conclude my letter by declaring positively that M. Sivori plays, although imperfectly, the greater part of my variations which I composed, like Paganini, under the name of the *Carnival of Venice* ... . [ME:1/7/43:256–7]

The still silent Sivori's response, when he next played the *Carnival* in his third English concert, was simply to omit the *Andante*, but by this stage the dispute was becoming something of a national scandal. Ernst's letter was republished in *Atlas*, *Morning Post*, *Britannia*, the *Court Journal*, and several other papers, and even the all-powerful *Times* began to interest itself. Fearing that the anger of critics might spread to his audience, Sivori decided to reply in the *Morning Post* before his fourth and last concert on 31 July. He conceded on the *Andante*, but the main body of the *Carnival* was too valuable a piece to attribute to his rival. The *Post* did not publish the letter but, after summarizing the dispute thus far, paraphrased it as follows:

> Signor Sivori states that Paganini was the first to compose variations on the air 'Cara, Mamma mia,' and that Ernst and Sivori only played the subject in public after Paganini's death. As the only pupil of that great violinist, Sivori executed that as well as the other pieces of his master, and it is very natural that a resemblance should be found in burlesque variations on such a simple motif. In respect of the *andante*, M. Sivori received it in manuscript, and was quite unaware that it had been published in Paris with the name of Herr Ernst. From the moment the latter claimed it Signor Sivori ceased to play it, and substituted an *andante* of his own. Signor Sivori expresses his regret that such an unimportant subject should have given rise to such a discussion in the public journals. He is one of the greatest admirers of the distinguished talents of Herr Ernst, and disavows positively any intention of depriving him of the credit for his own composition. [MW:27/6/43:251]

Ernst immediately wrote a response to this, but before it could be published he had an interview with Sivori on the morning of Wednesday 26 July. The two violinists came to an accommodation, and Ernst then sent another letter to the *Musical Examiner* requesting that his earlier letter be suppressed. On the same day he wrote: 'I met M. Sivori this morning and we talked about the Carnival. After that he sent a declaration to the *Morning Post*. I am so impatient to finish an unpleasant discussion between two artists and I have declared myself content. Please let me withdraw the letter which I sent to you yesterday to answer [the] few lines which which M. Sivori inserted in the *Morning Post* on July 24th ...'

The *Musical Examiner* suppressed Ernst's first letter, but the *Musical World* was not in the least satisfied with the argument's apparent conclusion. Saying that it could not eulogize Ernst's leniency 'which smacks to us somewhat of indecision', it weighed into Sivori on its own account, drawing at several points, no doubt, on Ernst's suppressed letter. Davison – he is undoubtedly the writer – points out that there is a world of difference between a composition being *in the style of* Paganini and being *by* Paganini; and that it would have been more honourable conduct, not to withdraw Ernst's *Andante* once the authorship was known, but to play it with the author's name published in the programme. But it is when he turns to maters of empirical fact that he scores two palpable hits. The first is:

> Sivori asserts that himself and M. Ernst did not play the variations on *Cara mama mia* till after the death of Paganini. To which we reply – that Paganini died in the month of May

1840, and that M. Ernst had been in the habit of playing the variations alluded to for *more than six years*, consequently *three years before the death of Paganini*; whereas signor Sivori first played them about *eighteen months ago*, at his concerts in Italy.

The second is more devastating still:

> With regard to Signor Sivori's declaration that he was not aware of the *Andante* being the composition of M. Ernst ... how happens the following item to have found its way into the advertisement (No.6) of the *Revue et Gazette Musicale de Paris*, Fevr. 5, 1843, of the first concert given by M. Sivori, in the *Salle de Herz*:–
> "IX *Carnaval de Venise de Paganini, avec introduction, par Ernst*" And in the *Journal des Debats*, and the *France Musicale*, of the same period:–
> "*Andante de* ERNST," &c. &c. &c.?
> We are compelled to conclude that the second assertion of M. Sivori is nothing less than a gross *misrepresentation*. We need hardly say that the advertisement of a concert can only have been sent to the journals *by the concert giver*. But the fact is, the *Andante* was already published in Paris, and was too well known as the composition of M. Ernst to allow of the suppression of the fact. [MW:27/7/43:252]

On the same day, the *Morning Post* outlined the terms of the accommodation that had been reached between the two violinists:

> We have receive two communications from Herr Ernst and Signor Sivori, stating that the question between these two distinguished artists, as to the authorship of the Carnival of Venice ... has been amicably arranged – Signor Sivori admitting, after an interview with Ernst, the undoubted claims of the latter to be the composer. Signor Sivori, in justice to Herr Ernst, requests us to publish this fact, whilst the latter, on his part, expresses his satisfaction at the explanation of M. Sivori. [ME:29/7/43:291]

Noticing this report, Davison, in the *Musical Examiner*, made some tart remarks about the convoluted reasoning of Sivori's first letter to the *Post*, and his backtracking in the second. [ME:29/7/43:291]

By this stage, it was completely clear that Sivori was in the wrong, both for playing the piece without acknowledgement, and then for lying about his practice. He had lost a public relations war with Ernst just as decisively as his teacher had lost a similar battle six years before. Ernst looked noble, honest, forbearing; Sivori looked jealous, calculating and dishonest.

At this point Ernst left for France, and Sivori took the opportunity to backtrack. A new letter concedes that the *Andante* and 'three or four variations' are by Ernst, but he then adds a postscript that again tries, in the guise of homage, to confuse style and authorship:

> I pray you Sir, have the goodness also to declare, that after I was attacked (even with some want of courtesy) by M. Ernst about a subject to which I never attached any importance that ... I shall invariably announce the composition as *Souvenir de Paganini* for it was really after having heard him play that both Mons. Ernst and myself sought, not only to imitate his manner, but even to play variations wholly his, as everyone [who] heard them played by Paganini can easily perceive. [ME:5/8/43:296–7]

Ernst was rightly incensed and wrote from Boulogne on 7 August: 'I was surprised to read that M. Sivori, having given me an explanation, with which, out of a feeling of regard to his position I declared myself satisfied, has the want of delicacy to contradict almost every thing he had previously stated, and to venture on other false assertions – and all this after my departure.' He then asked the editor to print his suppressed letter which detailed the depths of Sivori's dishonesty. The editor was compelled to say that he had mislaid it. [ME:12/8/43:304]

The weaker Sivori's position became, the greater his compulsion to write to newspapers. After his letter to the *Examiner*, he attempted to justify himself in more shameless terms in a letter sent to *The Times*, the *Courier de L'Europe*, and the *Morning Post*. The last of these refused to publish the letter, remarking:

> We shall best serve the reputation of Paganin's pupil by the non-publication of his last letter. He has admitted that he played Ernst's *Andante* and *variations* without acknowledgement, and Ernst, with creditable forbearance, withdrew a statement as to the surreptitious manner in which his composition has been obtained, which would have compromised Signor Sivori seriously. Now that Ernst has left the country, Sivori comes forward with a miserable quibble unworthy of a great artist and an honest man, to the effect that Paganini was a type and that Ernst has only imitated him – *"argal"* Sivori had the right to steal the writings of the latter, and perform them as *"Souveniers de Paganini."* Sivori must be assured that the musical public of this country will not admit of such dishonest practices. [ME: 26/8/43:313]

This gives a clear hint as to how Sivori obtained the quartet parts for the *Carnival*; and the telling allusion to the sophistries of *Hamlet*'s gravediggers is neatly done.

In spite of unanimous press support, Ernst felt it necessary to reply, and the dispute rumbled on through August and September, with Ernst growing more intemperate and Sivori more obfuscatory. The dispute ended initially with Sivori's last letter of 4 September. It is a farrago of woozy abstractions ('Emulation is a noble struggle, the only one I understand, the only one I think worthy of men who respect themselves... in all I have said or written, I have ever rendered the sincerest homage to *truth* ...' [ME:2/12/43:347]) As Goethe once observed, everyone agrees at the level of generalities. The dispute finally ended when Ernst, tired of unacknowledged performances and pirate editions, decided to publish his variations under his own name. The first edition is prefaced by a note:

> Notice to the public, – when I composed these variations on a theme which had already been varied by Paganini I had no intention of publishing them [as] it was my wish to introduce a piece whose form and character would permit the introduction of that part of the Paganinian difficulties, which, if introduced in a composition of any other kind, appeared to be ill-placed and indicated a want of taste and originality. However, the different and inexact arrangements of those which have lately illegally published, as well as the by no means delicate proceedings of certain artists who have played this piece in public without affixing my name, have induced me to consent to its appearance. I declare at the same time, that the present edition of my variations on the Carnival of Venice is the first which has been published with my consent. H.W. Ernst

On 29 July, Ernst and Hallé gave a concert in the Salles des Concerts in Boulogne and then headed for Paris. Ernst, whose health had improved, intended to stay for a few months. He had his violin repaired and then played at a concert for the Société des Musiciens on 15 September. [BN] In October, he returned to Hanover to take up his duties as concertmaster, and gave a number of performances at court, culminating in a truly magnificent concert on 26 October.

Heine much regretted Ernst's absence from Paris, and wrote several paragraphs about the violinist in his account of the 1843 season. The poet begins his discussion with a preamble about unevenness of performance, and this, like Clara Schumann's remarks about the deficiencies of Ernst's repertoire, is the first extended discussion of a difficulty that would eventually cause Ernst serious problems:

> The matadors of this year's season were Sivori and Dreyschock. The first is a fiddler, and I place him as such above the latter, the terrible piano-thumper. Among violinists, skill is not entirely the result of mechanical fingering and mere technicality, as with the pianists. The violin is an instrument which has almost human caprices, and which is, so to speak, in sympathetic relation to the disposition of the artist. The least discomfort, the slightest mental trouble, a breath of feeling, manifests itself in a prompt and direct echo, which may well come from this, that the violin is pressed so closely to the breast and catches the beating of our hearts. This is, however, only the case with artists who really have hearts which beat in their bosoms, and above all souls. The more sober and heartless the violinist, the more uniform will his execution be, and he can count upon the obedience of his fiddle at any hour in any place. But this valued certainty is only the result of a limited mind, and it is just the greatest masters whose [playing] is often dependent on external and internal influences. I have never heard any one play better, or at times worse, than Paganini, and I can say the same thing in favour of Ernst. This latter, Ernst, who is perhaps the greatest violinist of our time, [is] like Paganini in his faults as in his genius. His absence this winter caused many regrets among all friends of music who know how to value high art. Signor Sivori was very flat compensation, but yet we heard him with great pleasure. [HS:379–80]

It would be comforting to believe that Heine's explanation of Ernst's unevenness was correct. The true explanation is both more prosaic and more terrible. Paganini, when Heine heard him, was suffering from the chronic disease which would eventually kill him and, although neither Heine nor Ernst had any intimation of this in 1843, the same was true of Ernst.

Soon after writing his account of the season, Heine set off on his first journey to Germany for twelve years, during which he planned to meet Ernst in Braunschweig. Heine's friend Detmold was in Hanover, and the poet wrote to him from Hamburg asking for information: 'Is Ernst still in Hanover? How long is he staying there for? Does he not even want to come to Braunschweig? Tell me this and ask him whether he is going directly to Petersburg.' [9 November 1843. HB:II:482–3] Detmold replied that he had spoken to Ernst, and that the violinist's travel plans depended on the Duke of Braunschweig's movements. Heine was delayed by flu, but he wrote to Detmold again on 7 December: 'If Ernst is still in Hanover, which I doubt, [Ernst's contract was for a maximum of six weeks' residence] would you be kind enough to tell him that I shall arrive there the day after tomorrow?' [HB:II:492–3]

But Ernst would never be in Hanover in an official capacity again. After the court concert on 26 October, a dispute arose between him and the King, and the absence of comment in the above exchange of letters suggests that the incident occurred after the first week in December. The King apparently asked to see Ernst, and then kept him waiting in an antechamber for two hours. When the King eventually appeared, he said that he was going hunting for the rest of the day and that Ernst must arrange another time. An impolite invitation from Count Redern had made Ernst cancel a series of concerts in Berlin the previous year, and now his artist's pride was incensed by Ernest's treatment. He handed back his official contract to the King, and left Hanover on 15 December. [E:73–4]

In itself, the cause for Ernst's offence does not seem major, and I suspect that relations had already begun to sour. Although the King's visit to England was not the disaster it could have been, many members of the establishment treating him as a lovable old rogue past creating serious mischief, he must have felt some pain to see the attention and adulation his concertmaster was receiving. Perhaps this was the cause of friction. Some have felt that anti-Semitism lay at the root of the problem, pointing to the fact that Joachim would later resign from his position at Hanover because of the treatment of his Jewish colleague Jakob Grün. [EOC:30] The King certainly objected to the presence of influential Jews at the English Court [WE:237], but there is no reason to suppose that he particularly objected to Jews who only held artistic appointments. The real reason, I suspect, was that Ernst was coming to know something of the King's character. The latter's reception in England must have indicated that something was amiss, and I imagine that Davison filled Ernst in on some of the more unsavoury aspects of the his royal patron's past.

The King's absurd behaviour at Royal engagements was merely the tip of the iceberg. Ernst's English friends would soon have told him of dark and disturbing rumours which had been circulating for years, and which modern scholarship has shown to be well founded. The first was that, when young, Ernest had had an incestuous relationship with his sister Sophia. She had borne him a son, Thomas Garth, who, when grown up, tried to blackmail the Royal family by threatening to publicize his paternity. He was tricked out of the documents proving his origins and then spent a number of years in a debtors' prison. Eventually, he was quietly pensioned off. [WE:11–39, 239–46]

If committing incest with his sister was not bad enough, there were more scandalous stories concerning Ernest's sometime valet, Joseph Sellis. One night in 1810, the alarm was raised in Ernest's suite in Kensington Palace, and the future King was discovered with sabre wounds to the head. A trail of blood led to the room of his valet, Sellis, who lay on the bed with his throat cut. Ernest avowed that he had been attacked by his servant as he slept, and that Sellis was later discovered to have committed suicide. Several aspects of this story did not ring true, the most obvious one being that Sellis was a quiet, devoted family man who was very attached to his employer and had absolutely no motive to attack him. It emerged, however, that Sellis had a deep dislike for one of Ernest's other servants, Cornelius Neale, who he felt had some kind of power over Ernest. Rumours began to circulate that what had actually occurred was that Sellis had discovered Ernest and Neale having sex. Fearing exposure, they chased Sellis to his room where Neale held him and Ernest cut his throat. What they had not foreseen was the four-foot jet of blood from the carotid artery which drenched Ernest's upper body. To explain this, Neale wounded Ernest's head with a sabre, to suggest that he had been attacked while sleeping. Ernst recovered from his surprisingly superficial wounds with gratifying swiftness. No difficult questions were asked at the inquest, several important witnesses – including Ernest – were not called, and a verdict of suicide on Sellis's part was pushed through without opposition. [WE:50–72, 206–224]

On arrival in Hanover, Ernest set about making himself hated again. He revoked the constitution put in place by his predecessor, his brother Adolphus who acted as viceroy, because he thought it would make him 'a mere cipher'. [WE:233] Seven professors at the University of Göttingen rebelled, including the famous brothers Grimm, and became seen as liberal martyrs throughout Germany when Ernest had them all dismissed and three of them exiled. [WE:233–4] He then made the elected assembly declare allegiance to him under the old illiberal constitution plus a few minor modifications. '*All* has gone off most *admirably*,' he reported to some old friends, and ascribed his success to thirty-nine years' experience dealing with radicals and malcontents in the English Parliament. [WE:234]

One can imagine the relish with which Davison would have conveyed this information. Ernst must have realized that if he did not want to be reviled by liberal Europe, and if, in particular, he wanted to build on his success in England, then he could not be associated with such a figure. According to a newspaper article, the meeting between Ernst and Heine in Braunschweig took place as planned (this is supported by Ernst's entry in Griepenkerl's autograph book in Braunschweig which is dated 23 December 1843), and it is hard to believe that the wittiest and more virulent critic of oppressive German regimes did not entirely endorse and applaud Ernst's decision.

When the wily Liszt had visited Hanover a year or two before, he surmised rather more quickly than Ernst what kind of character he was dealing with. As he wrote in 1860:

> Twenty years ago, Fräulin von Schulz was a maid of honour in Hanover, where, if I am not mistaken, her father had a junior minister's portfolio. During my very brief stay there the whole family took a liking to me, especially Fräulin von Schultz ... Ernst the violinist was much loved in that house, and perhaps had a notion of creating for me a position similar to the one he was occupying, *Concertmeister* with a large salary. The little differences I had with the late King – who is said to have preferred to put up with certain vulgarities corresponding to his own, than with a way of life in which he scented some kind of independent opinion, intolerable to sovereigns of his kidney – made things impossible for me in Hanover. Besides, it never entered my head to seek anything there whatever. It was in early 1844, before the Belloni [Liszt's secretary's] concerts in Paris, those little difficulties took place. [FLSL:525–6]

Liszt must be wrong about these incidents occurring in 1844 since Ernst had already stalked away from his position by then. It must have been in 1843 or late 1842. We can be less sure what those 'certain vulgarities' were. Ernest's crimes give such a rich selection to choose from.

Chapter 12

Mendelssohn, Joachim and the Philharmonic: 1844

Again, health problems prevented Ernst reaching Russia and, after meeting Heine in Braunschweig, he went back to Paris. [RGM:5/11/43:381] On 9 January 1844 he was well enough to appear in a triumphant concert in Orléans, [FM:4/2/44:39; RGM:25/2/44:54], but Liszt's mistress, Marie D'Agoult, clearly felt pessimistic about his Parisian prospects. Her remarks to Liszt suggest that, after his row with Ernest Augustus, the normally urbane and well presented Ernst was suffering from the agitated state of mind which often accompanied his physical illness: 'Ernst is here. He wants to give some concerts, but he's proud and badly dressed. I've a feeling that he no longer knows anyone here and will not succeed.' [CLMD:II:320] In fact, Ernst did manage to arrange a concert on 28 February at the Salle Herz [FM:21/1/44:22] but he was so ill it had to be postponed three times, and rumours began to circulate of his death. [ME:6/4/44:512] In spite of serious debility, he found strength enough to compose a fantasia on tunes from *Dom Sébastien* with Stephen Heller [FM:31/3/44:102. RGM:7/4/44:126], and to see his *Pirate Fantasy* through the press. [FM:4/1/44:15. E:82–3]

Heine, in his account of the Paris season in 1844, was left to lament Ernst's absence from the stage, and to fall into one of those charming poetic reveries that even the absence of Ernst's playing seemed to occasion:

> Ernst has been here, but, from caprice, he would give no concert; he prefers to play only among friends and to true connoisseurs. Few artists are so loved and esteemed here as Ernst. He deserves it. He is the true successor of Paganini; he inherited the enchanted violin with which the Genoese could move rocks, yea even logs and clods of men. Paganini, who now leads us up to sunny heights, and anon with the touch of his bow shows us the terrible abyss, had of course far more daemonic power, but his lights and shadows were sometimes too striking, his contrasts too cutting, and his grandest sounds of nature must often be regarded as artistic mistakes. Ernst is more harmonious, the softer tints are more predominant in his playing; and yet he has a fondness for the fantastic, even for the *baroque* and the odd, if not even for the scurrilous; and many of his compositions remind me of the fairy-tale comedies of Gozzi, or the wildest masques, or of the 'Carnival of Venice.' The piece of music so well known by this name, and which was pirated in the most shameless manner by Sivori, is a charming capriccio by Ernst. The lover of the fantastic can be, when he chooses, purely poetic, and I have heard of late a nocturne by him which seemed to be dissolved in beauty. One seemed in hearing to be rapt away into a beautiful Italian night, the Cyprus trees standing in silent charm, white statues shimmering in the clear moonlight, and bubbling fountains lulling us to dream! Ernst, as is well known, has resigned his office at Hanover, and is no longer Royal Hanoverian

Concert-Master. In fact, it was not a suitable place for him. He is much better fitted to lead the *musique de chambre* at the court of some fairy queen – as, for instance, the fair Morgana; for there he would find an audience which would best understand him, and among them would be many a form of the fabled days of yore of those who felt the deepest charm of art, such as King Arthur, Dietrich of Berne, Ogier the Dane, and the lords who live in song. And, oh! What ladies would applaud him there! The blonde Hanover ladies may be fair, but they are only awkward peasant maids compared with the fairy Melior, Lady Abunda, lovely Mélusine, Queen Guineveve, and many like them, who dwell with Queen Morgana at her court in the famed fairy isle of Avalon! Yes, there I trust to meet with Ernst again, for there he promised me a place at court. [HS:426–8]

This is a nice example of Ernst reception. Solid, unpleasant facts are softened into wistful fantasies. Illness becomes 'caprice', a row with Ernest Augustus is overlooked, and then reality is left behind altogether. However, there may well be some truth in the idea that, after resigning his post, Ernst came to realize that the role of *Kapellmeister* did not suit him: institutional membership, administrative responsibilities, organizing other people, being tied down to a schedule – these were all things which interfered with his improvised, self-sufficient, 'vagabond' life-style. And his two attempts to hold regular posts, even posts with as few prescribed duties as those at Hesse and Hanover, were short-lived.

By the end of March, his illness seems to have abated, and he travelled first to London and then on to Manchester for two concerts on 8 and 9 April. These were a tremendous success, and Davison reprinted a selection of reviews in the *Musical World* to advertise Ernst's forthcoming London appearances. Some of these provide insights into his tone and technique:

His tones struck us as being at times very clear and silvery, then vocal-like and singing; at other times soft and velvety (an awkward comparison we know no other word that will convey the idea); while his wailing tones were much like the pathos of Paganini's in his finest pieces. His harmonics had some very unusual and extremely difficult intervals, and were exceedingly well stopped. Applause burst forth at the end of a very brilliant passage, in which there was an ascending run of these harmonics, touched in with a most delicate hand. [*Manchester Guardian*: MW:18/4/44:134]

What shall I say of him and his violin playing?'... [To] my taste, he is the finest player I ever heard; I say this with a perfectly vivid memory of many times hearing Paganini; also of once hearing De Beriot at our festival in 1836, and more recently Sivori; I think Ernst excels them all, not so much in any one particular as in general *effect*. ... [The] fire of his genius burns as brightly but more steadily, and he has a *gentlemanly* way of introducing all the immense difficulties which his predecessors mastered. [*Manchester Times*: MW:11/4/44:129]

All this prepared the way for Ernst's spectacular debut on 14 April at the second concert of the Philharmonic Society, where he played on a splendid Guanerius lent to him by Andrew Fountaine:

Herr Ernst may be said, by the triumph of Monday night, to have raised himself at once, in the estimation of the severest audience in Europe, to the highest rank among living violinists. The passionate and many emotioned scena of Spohr found in him a true and zealous interpreter. No vocalist ever sang with more impressive energy, more touching pathos, more varied feeling, more finished execution. The violin, in the hands of Herr Ernst, is a human voice capable of infinite expression. It sings, it declaims, it laughs, it weeps, and whatever it says goes directly to the heart of the hearer. The recitatives were perfect eloquence – the *andante* was thrillingly pathetic – the majestic *Allegro* was a torrent of energy and passion. The whole *concerto* was received with marks of approval as they were vehement and incessant. ... This must be termed the debut of Herr Ernst before a London audience, and triumphantly has he gone through the dreaded ordeal. ... [MW:18/4/44:133–4]

Ernst also played a *Romance* accompanied by Davison, and the concert was enjoyed, amongst others, by Mendelssohn, Moscheles, the pianist Leopold de Meyer, Offenbach (then known as a virtuoso cellist rather than a composer of operettas) and the thirteen-year-old Joseph Joachim.

Engagements followed on 19 and 24 April at the Dublin Philharmonic, and at a concert of chamber music organized by Davison and Macfarren on the 26th. [MW:18/4/44:139. RGM:28/4/44:154] After the tensions of his resignation from Hanover, and his illness in Paris, Ernst at last felt he could write something optimistic to his brother.

> Dearest Brother, I must beg your pardon this time for being silent so long. This was caused by the constant uncertainty of my plans, and because I had only unpleasantness to share with you. In Paris I had to give up my announced concert because of sickness, and when I was better again, I had to leave in order to fulfil some already contracted arrangements. My first appearance in England was in Manchester in two enormous concerts. The most decisive one, however, was here for the second Philharmonic concert. This is the first music society in London. My success was in the extreme, and since that time I have already received several engagements here as well as in the provinces. There is no talk in this country of one's own concerts because music has become a commodity here in the hands of speculators. A concert here often involves 36 men, the best players that can be engaged. The artist himself, especially a foreigner, cannot be involved in the arrangements, and if one gives a concert it is more for the renown than the proceeds. Sivori, who last year made a very great sensation here, had his concert quite poorly attended this year. Nonetheless, I have decided to give a concert with Moscheles on the first of June.
>
> I do not intend to tire you with all these details, as one must be here to have an idea of these goings-on. I will put up with what I can, and in all likelihood I shall make a fair profit. The big newspapers have all spoken of me with the greatest enthusiasm. I have already played here in Covent Garden for a charitable cause, and as elsewhere the Carnival had to be repeated. In another concert in the evening I had to repeat the Elegie. In short, every appearance is a triumph. In Dublin I was engaged by the Philharmonic Society. Tomorrow I will play here for the Società Armonica. On the 8th I play in Liverpool; the 17th, 20th, 30th, here again. On June 1st I have my own concert, and on 4th and 6th I am again engaged for the Gentleman's Concert in Manchester. Here the proceeds must amount to a fair sum. I hope that still more engagements will come. The frequent trips that I have to take are, thank Heaven, not so tiring since they can all be made by rail. The arrangements are really excellent.
>
> Sivori is also here; however, my presence has caused his stock to go down significantly, although he still has an important following. He has made himself popular only by means of lies and charlatanism, in that he spread a rumour in a leaflet that he is the only pupil of Paganini, and that he also has Paganini's violin. The English are very

naïve in this respect, and let themselves be willingly taken in by such things. However, one cannot deny him a great talent *d'animation*.

    Little Joachim is here too, creating a sensation. He is really extraordinary and to be placed far above the Milanollos with regard to execution and musicianship. I love him very much and see him often. [5 May 1844. EOC:18]

Joachim had flourished under Böhm's tuition, and at the end of his course, his teacher advised him to head for Paris where Ernst had inaugurated his dazzling career. But Joachim's aunt, Fanny Figdor, who had been instrumental in taking him to Vienna, now recommended that he study in Leipzig where she herself now lived. (She had recently married a merchant called Hermann Wittgenstein, and two of their grandchildren would become famous in the twentieth century: the one-armed pianist Paul and the philosopher Ludwig.)

Despite Böhm's initial opposition, Joachim followed his aunt's advice and entered the Leipzig Conservatoire. Here he took violin lessons from David – with whom the boy studied the works of Bach, Paganini, Spohr and Ernst – and composition with Moritz Hauptmann. The strongest influence, however, was Mendelssohn who played chamber music with Joachim every Sunday, and emphasized how important it was not to change a single note in the works of serious composers, considering such tampering 'inartistic even barbarous'. [GMV:263] Mendelssohn was greatly taken with Joachim's playing and general musical ability, and as conductor of the Gewandhaus orchestra, he encouraged the twelve-year-old to play a solo. Joachim appeared on 16 November 1843, and paid tribute to two of his early mentors by selecting Ernst's *Otello Fantasy* – a work which is dedicated to Böhm and which Joachim had studied under him. The performance was received with enormous enthusiasm, and it was during one of the rehearsals that Mendelssohn said Ernst's high C♯ would find a place in his own violin concerto.

In the following March, Joachim travelled to London with several letters of recommendation from Mendelssohn. Billed as 'The Hungarian Boy' (as a counterpart to the posters advertising Balfe's opera *The Bohemian Girl*, premiered the previous year and now all the rage), he played two works he had already performed in Leipzig, Spohr's *Gesangsszene* and the *Otello Fantasy*. His success was immense, and some critics even preferred his performance of the Spohr to Ernst's.

Joachim also led performances of Beethoven's Quintet in C and the late B♭ quartet at private gatherings organized by the English violinist and impresario, John Ella. [MSAH:250–51] The morning after the B♭ quartet, Mendelssohn (who had arrived to conduct the Philharmonic on 8 May [TM:472]) called to thank Ella for supporting his protégé, and Ella suggested Mendelssohn play his own D minor trio at the next concert. Mendelssohn wrote in reply: 'I shall be most happy to play my trio on Tuesday next, and if Ernst will accompany it (as he has often done [in Berlin]) I anticipate a *great* treat from it.' [MSAH:251]

Ernst readily consented, and Ella's later account shows that the impresario recalled the event as one of his finest moments. To understand one of the pleasantries in his anecdote, one needs to know that, to prevent excessive speculation, Parliament had passed a law in 1844 separating the monetary department of the Bank of England from the banking department, and pegging the issue of notes to the Bank's reserves of silver and gold. [EBR:26]

> Had the art of photography in 1844 been popular, as at the present time [1878], we might have had a pictorial souvenir of this performance of Mendelssohn, and Joachim at his side [turning the pages], with Ernst and Hausmann at the violin and cello. In the first Allegro, Ernst failing to turn his page in time for the *rentrée* of the violin, Mendelssohn improvised an elegant rhythm of four additional bars of music, which elicited bravos from all present. A bank director humorously accused Mendelssohn of 'putting more notes into circulation than allowed by printed authority.' The composer, with joyous spirit, laughed heartily at the success of his improvisation, and Thalberg had his joke upon Ernst 'Voltando, non subito'. It has never been our duty to record a greater musical treat,' said the *Morning Post*, 'than the effect of the Trio in D Minor, and the Elégie for the violin, performed by their respective composers – Mendelssohn and Ernst.' The programme also included Beethoven's Quartet in E minor, to which Mendelssohn listened with intense delight. [MSAH:252]

Ella mentions that this quartet was a particular favourite of Ernst's and that the audience were moved by the intensity of expression Ernst put into the opening bars of the slow movement, where Beethoven indeed requests: 'Si tratta questo pezzo molto di sentimento.' [MSAH:216–17]

Joachim himself takes up the next phase of the story in a letter to Ferdinand David. Although Joachim's admiration for Ernst shines through, he has a number of criticisms that reveal his training and background. Unlike Clara Schumann, he does not criticize Ernst's repertoire, but he does disapprove of alterations made to acknowledged classics:

> I have played in public here several times already, and on the 27th I am playing at the 5th Philharmonic concert, which has given rise to many difficulties. I have no choice but to give the Beethoven Concerto (as Ernst played the *Gesangsszene* at the second concert). I find the Philharmonic concerts are not worthy of their reputation, for after hearing the Beethoven symphonies in Leipzig, their performance here is not very edifying. Even the tempos in my opinion (which is probably mistaken) are quite wrong. Ernst did not play the *Gesangsszene* correctly; he modernised the cadenza (although he used the same harmonies), put in some very difficult passages, left out the beautiful modulation in the Allegro (in F) entirely, made modern conclusions to every one of the solos in the Allegro, and played the staccato passage in thirds so that he had to take it rather slower. I consider Ernst to be a *very great* violinist, and he seems to me to be incomparably greater than Sivori as virtuoso, artist and man. The latter plays the most astonishingly difficult things, but he is often out of tune, and is altogether a great charlatan. There is a superfluity of foreign violinists here. Ernst, Sivori, Pott (who is to play in the next and 4th Philharmon.), Gulomy (of whom one hears nothing at all), and Rossy, sixteen years old, who brings good recommendations from Rossini and is said to play badly, so people tell me who ought to know. [May 1844. LJJ:2–3]

Although he had no choice but to play the Beethoven concerto, his performance – from memory and under Mendelssohn's baton – was rapturously received, and he was immediately invited to play for the Queen and Prince Albert at Windsor Castle.

The foundation for sixty years of musical and social success in England had been laid.

Ernst, too, was evangelizing on behalf of Beethoven's neglected works, in his case the late C♯ minor quartet which he played at a concert organized by Davison and Macfarren. An article in the *The Times* explains that, because of their strangeness and difficulty, Beethoven's late quartets initially had no public performances in England. When at last the English violinist Blagrove attempted to put them on at the 'Antient Concerts' they were pronounced a bore, and Blagrove gave up the attempt to makes the works more widely known. The article continues:

> Last night affords a hope, however, that they have fallen into better hands. Ernst has an energy and determination about him, without which, such a task as this can have no chance of being delivered as it was intended to be; Goffrie is an excellent second violin, steady and true; Hill, the best tenor player in England; and Hausmann, the violoncello, a thorough artist in every respect. ... The success of the performance was indisputable, but, as in all works of great refinement, the feeling is sure to increase at every repetition. ... The quartet was played with great care, and in a very effective manner, considering the extreme difficulties it presents – difficulties which require continual study to overcome. [MW: 23/5/44:174]]

As Ernst's letter to his brother shows, he played in Liverpool, Dublin, the Society Armonica in London, and at a concert in Covent Garden. The last, on 26 April, was in aid of distressed needlewomen, and the *Musical World* took the aristocracy severely to task for their poor attendance. [MW:2/5/44:152] By the end of April, he felt confident enough to organize a joint concert with Moscheles to be held at Hanover Square Gardens on 1 June. Both the concert-givers would play, and along with the usual vocal numbers, Mendelssohn would conduct his overture to *A Midsummer Night's Dream*, and take part, with Thalberg and Moscheles, in a performance of a concerto for three pianos by Bach. [MW:23/5/44:176; 13/6/44:198] From the musical point of view, the concert is now largely remembered because of the extraordinary hail of octaves with which Mendelssohn ended his improvised cadenza to the Bach (Mendelssohn clearly did not regard this as inauthentic). [GP:218–20] But something traumatic occurred in the first half whose details will be important when I come to discuss Ernst's illness in Chapter 19:

> After a good performance by the band of the wonderful overture of Mendelssohn, and the air of Herr Staudigl, Ernst came on to play his concerto, and was enthusiastically received. He looked pale and ill; and we had a foreboding that all was not right. However, Ernst achieved the *allegro* and *adagio*, with beautiful finish, though with less than his accustomed energy – but he had hardly delivered the subject of the rondo, when he stopped suddenly, waved his bow to the leader, and staggered out of the orchestra. We entered the *salles d'artistes* just in time to see him fall prostrate on the floor, and listen to the screams, which told plainly of the dreadful severity of the attack. Ernst is so much loved, as well as admired, by every one who has the pleasure of knowing him, that the room was soon filled to inconvenience with artists and amateurs, painfully anxious to know the circumstances of the case. After being insensible for nearly half and hour – with the assistance of Dr Babbington, and two other medical gentlemen, whom Mendelssohn and Benedict summoned from among the auditory – Ernst was finally restored to

consciousness, and gradually the influence of the attack wore off, leaving, happily, no result but that of exceeding weakness. In spite of the remonstrances of all around him, Ernst insisted on performing his part of the programme, and accordingly, after several pieces had been gone through, entered the orchestra with Benedict, amidst the general and enthusiastic plaudits of the room. He sang through his plaintive and beautiful Elegie, with such touching pathos as to move many to tears. In spite of unavoidable feebleness of tone, the consequence of what had occurred, we never recollect Ernst to have played more exquisitely; – but after this, nature could do no more, and he was compelled, in spite of himself, to leave the remainder of his pieces unperformed, and to proceed home with a friend. [MW:13/6/44:198]

Ernst's complete understanding of public relations (as well as his generosity) are nowhere better shown than in how he turned his apparent disaster to account. On 13 June, he wrote to the musical agent and publisher Beale in Regent Street:

Sir, The unfortunate accident which befell me on the 1st June, a the concert given by M. Moscheles and myself, makes me doubly a debtor to the public who were present: first, because I was not able to fulfil the promise that was contained in the bills, and then, as it appears to me, an essential duty to prove to them, all my true and lively gratitude for the interest and kindness that were shown to me on that occasion.

The only way that occurs to me of partly acknowledging this consideration – and I do not hesitate for a single instant in doing so – is sending you the sum of seventy-four pounds, my share of the above named concert, which I beg you to forward to the Royal Society of Musicians.

If I have not made this arrangement sooner, it is because the accounts were only settled yesterday. I particularly desire that the sum be not regarded as coming from me, but as a voluntary gift of the public who were present at the concert; and I hope you will approve of the arrangement I have made.

H.W. Ernst [38, Great Marlborough Street. MW:20/6/44:204]

The *Musical World* said it could only endorse the German opinion that Ernst 'is not merely a great artist, but ... a noble, upright, and generous man'. [MW:20/6/44:204] The *Athenaeum* felt his name should be written in 'the golden book for artists for acts of munificence. ... So noble an act of generosity, so delicately administered, should not be forgotten.' [MW:4/7/44:224] It was not. When Ernst next returned to England in the spring of 1849, it was this donation – worth about £6,000 in today's money – which all the newspapers recalled to their readers, and it helped set the seal on his English reputation. The fact that Ernst went on to play in two massive concerts in Manchester on 4 and 6 June shows how quickly he could recover from such an apparently life-threatening attack.

His relationship with Sivori remained at a low ebb. The general consensus amongst German and French musicians – that Sivori was a charlatan and a liar – is not in general deserved. He may have used the facts that he was Paganini's only important pupil and owned one of his master's violins in his publicity material, but both of these claims, contrary to the assertions of Heine and Ernst, are true. However, Ernst was correct in saying that Sivori's tour to England in 1844 was less successful than the one the previous year, and this was largely because his reputation had still not recovered from the *Carnival of Venice* affair. The *Musical World*, an ardent supporter of the Ernst-Joachim faction, weighed into Sivori's performance at the third meeting of the Philharmonic Society with some gusto:

> Though his *general intonation* is admirable, he plays as many *mere notes* out of tune as any *great* violinist we can bring to mind. ... The other faults of Signor Sivori are the unparalleled thinness – nay poorness – of his tone, and a remarkable absence of all traces of passion or sentiment. ... [In] the *harmonics* he is uncertain, unsteady, and ineffective. His double stopping is sometimes good, sometimes bad. He has a (very convenient) habit of taking all the *bravura* passages very considerably slower than the *tempo* of the movement ... [MW:2/5/44:149]

Sivori, however, had built up a considerable reputation in Paris while Ernst was absent in the seasons of 1843 and 1844, and a letter from a London correspondent for *La France Musicale* takes a view of the dispute which is far less sympathetic to Ernst – both in terms of who was responsible for the animosity and who was the better violinist:

> Ernst has declared himself Sivori's irreconcilable enemy. ... I have heard the two rival violinists: Ernst is elegant and poetic but very unequal; Sivori has perfect tone and prodigious facility in the most hazardous difficulties. Next came young Joachim, a German who excited a great deal of sympathetic interest, and plays the music of Ernst as well, if not better, than Ernst himself. [FM:14/7/44:221]

The continuing difficulties between Ernst and Sivori began to manifest themselves publicly once again, this time in the concert hall rather than the letters columns. The occasion was the sixth Philharmonic concert when Ernst was invited to play in Mauer's *Concertante* for four violins:

> There was some trouble about this *concertante*, which was originally to be played by Ernst, Sivori, Blagrove, and Joachim. Prince Albert, it was said, desired to hear it interpreted by those artists. When Ernst was applied to he declined becoming one of the party. His reason we do not pretend to call in question – but if, as we imagine, he objected to become one in a raree-show for the gratification of Prince Albert and the subscribers of the Philharmonic Society, we applaud his independence and respect his refusal. However, it appears that Dr Mendelssohn was persuaded to use his influence with Ernst, and that Ernst, to oblige Dr Mendelssohn, consented to play in the quartet, on the condition that he should be violino primo – a station due, not only to his commanding talent, but to his name, which was celebrated all over Germany before any of the others was heard of. To this, we understand, we understand, Dr Mendelssohn consented – but Sivori, not agreeing, proposed that the four should draw lots for positions. When this was communicated to Ernst he at once declined any part in the affair. Any one who feels like an artist, and would disdain to toss up, head or tail, with the first comer, for his reputation, will easily comprehend, that one with every feeling of a great artist in his breast (one, in fact, like Ernst) should refuse, with disdain, any participation in so un-artist-like a transaction. Thus the anticipated show-lion-quatuor was, for the instant, unhinged.
>
> However, one Sainton, a violinist – who had performed at the *Opéra Comique* in Paris, and at one or two meetings at the residence of a Mr Ella – was applied to and consented to supply the vacant place of Ernst, and so the quatuor was again *en train*. At the rehearsal, however, when the four violinists were called upon, little Joachim, a good

artist and true, seeing that Ernst was not present, was not to be persuaded by any argument to ascend the orchestra. He declared, and properly so, that he had only acceded to make one of the quartet on the understanding that Ernst was to lead it – and that although he would play anywhere or anything under the auspices of the great violinist, he would by no means place himself under the same control with any one else. Nothing could be more straightforward than this, and the little violinist was as firm as a rock – not to be shaken.

At last the directors were compelled to ask Mr Willy to play; and Mr Willy, with his usual good nature, consented. So that on Monday we had the advantage of hearing two first-rate English violinists (Blagrove and Willy), one first-rate Italian and one first-rate Frenchman (Sivori and Sainton), perform before an English audience, one of the most supreme pieces of rubbish that was ever penned to flatter popular prejudice or tickle uncultivated ears. The performers, we need scarcely say, were as faultless as the composition performed was destitute of any kind of merit. [MW:13/6/44:197]

Davison's suggestion that Ernst behaved as he did was because he did not want to be at the beck and call of Prince Albert is disingenuous, and shows Davison's profound dislike for Royalty. It is quite evident that the reason for Ernst's behaviour was his contempt for Sivori, as is shown by his reluctant consent to appear on the condition that he play a more prominent part than his Italian rival.

After his debut at the Philharmonic, Ernst's most important concert in England this season was held in the Hanover Square Rooms on 5 July. This may have been organized at quite short notice (it is not mentioned in Ernst's letter of 5 May) to compensate for his failures at the joint concert on the 1 June. A reviewer describes Ernst as 'evidently in health and spirits' and he seems to have played excellently. The Bach triple concerto (with Döhler replacing Thalberg) was repeated, and Ernst led a performance of Mendelssohn's E minor quartet and played the *Kreutzer Sonata* with Moscheles. The reviews could not have been more enthusiastic. From amongst his own pieces, Ernst selected the *Ludovic* and *Pirate* fantasies, and gave the official English premiere of the *Erlking* transcription. It shows remarkable courage to play this piece immediately after a performance of the song by two of the greatest performers of the age – Mendelssohn and Charlotte Dolby – and the notices give the lie to Hallé's remark that even on his best days Ernst could never play it properly:

The greatest curiosity prevailed about the simple method of *mechanism* which Ernst might employ. Ere he had achieved twenty bars, anxiety was changed into pleasure, and all uncertainty vanished before the evident facility with which the violinist accomplished difficulties which by many had been pronounced insuperable. The admirable manner in which the characteristic accompaniment, of twelve quavers in a bar, was sustained throughout, created the utmost surprise: and the effect of the song of the Erl King, rendered by harmonics, to a distinct arpeggio accompaniment, added delight to astonishment. In short, the whole affair was accomplished without a blemish, and the burst of applause at the conclusion plainly testified to the triumph which Ernst had achieved. Perhaps this may, without exaggeration, be pronounced the most complete and difficult feat that was ever performed on the violin. [MW:11/7/44:228]

Before leaving London, he repaid the favour to Döhler by playing Beethoven's C minor sonata and the *Elegy* at the pianist's third concert. And at another of Ella's gatherings, led performances of Beethoven's quartet in C minor op.18, and the first of the Rasumovsky quartets op.59.

On 20 June, he set off for Paris by way of Southampton and Le Havre. [ME: 10/8/44:730] He didn't stay long, and was soon engaged on a tour to Aix-la-Chappelle, Cologne, Elberfeld, Düsseldorf, and Crefeld. [ME:12/10/44:829–30. RGM:1/9/44:298] From Mayence, he wrote to Davison on 6 October. After giving a list of all the friends he had run into, he writes: 'I am tolerably industrious now – I am about a *Fantasia* on Irish airs, which will soon be finished.' [ME:12/10/44: 829–30] This would eventually form the basis of one of his most famous pieces.

On 24 October he gave a concert in Weimar, and on the 26th he arrived in Leipzig. [SMW:10/44:341] Here he played a series of concerts in the Gewandhaus which unusually included a good deal of chamber music. In the last of these, on 25 November, Joachim got his chance to erase two unhappy memories of Maurer's *Concertante*, when he performed it with Ernst, Bazzini and David. [AMZ:20/11/44: Col.786–90] Dörffel writes in his *Geschichte der Gewandhaus Konzerte*:

> When it came to the cadenza, Ernst and Bazzini laid out their highest trumps, Ernst taking the lead, but Joachim, who was playing the third part, so entirely put them in the shade, that Ernst unintentionally burst out with a loud 'Bravo!' and David, who was the fourth player, left his cadenza out altogether. The event was quite unique of its kind. A general wish being expressed for the repetition of this performance, the four artists repeated the concerto at a subscription concert on 12th December, the piece again creating a great sensation. [JJ:62]

The first performance of the Maurer was followed by a private soirée at the home of the music publisher Dr Härtel when Mendelssohn's Octet was played with the same quartet of violinists in a different order (David, Ernst, Bazzini, Joachim). The company on this occasion was particularly distinguished and included Mendelssohn, Robert and Clara Schumann, Moscheles and the singer Livia Frege. [HFPV:55]

The year ended with Ernst being presented with a medal made from the melted bronze of the cathedral bell in Hamburg. It was a gift from the citizens to thank him for the concert he gave for Hamburg's poor, after the fire, in 1842. [AMZ18/12/44: Col.870. SMW:12/44:388. E:96]

Chapter 13

New Repertoire: 1845–46

There is not much to report of Ernst's performances in 1845 and early 1846, so let me just list Ernst's travels, giving the dates of known concerts in round brackets:

Dresden: Two concerts (the second on 27 January). [SMW:3/45:38]
Prague: Five concerts, March (the last on 15 March). [EUZ:39–40]
Vienna: (13, 22, 27 April). [AWMZ:15/4/45:176,180; 22/4/45:192; 26/4/45:198–9. SMW:4/45:123,133,142]
Brünn: (30 April). [EUZ:37–8]
Vienna: Two or three concerts (the last on 4 May). [EUZ:39. SMW:5/45:150. MW:15/5/45:150. RGM:4/5/45:143]
Graz: At least three concerts (including 6 and 13 May). [SMW:5/45:155. AWMZ:27/5/45:252]
Pressburg: (27 May). [AWMZ:31/5/45:260]
Pesth: Eighteen concerts in Pesth and surrounding area. (29, 31 May; 2, 4, 7 10, 14 June). He was still in there on 31 August. [AWMZ:5/6/45:268; 26/6/45:303–4. SMW:8/45:254, 275. EUZ:40–42. CEAM:no.749]
Olmütz: (18, 20 September). [SMW:8/45:275. AWMZ:25/9/45:459; 11/10/45:487. EUZ:38]
Vienna: Arrived 7 October. He stayed for about five weeks apart from two concerts elsewhere – one in Brünn in mid-October, and one in Pressburg on 15 October. [RGM:2/11/45:363]
Lemberg: (16, 20, 23 November). [AMZ:31/12/45:Col.503. SMW:9/45:309. EUZ:42–3] He left Lemberg on 29 November, planning to arrive in Vienna by 12 December, giving concerts in Tarnow and Krakow on the way. [AMZ:31/12/45:Col.503; SMW:9/45:309. EUZ:42–3. E:98–107]
Vienna: (11 January 1846) A performance of *Harold in Italy* conducted by Berlioz [BSG:337]
Brünn: (16 January). [AWMZ:27/1/46:48]
Vienna: 15, 17 21, 25 March. Joint appearances with Liszt. [FLUP:93, 96–101. FLPD:162]

Overall, this was a hugely successful period for Ernst: he frequently had to return to the stage fifteen or twenty times; when the *Carnival of Venice* was performed, he often had to repeat it with new variations, and when it was not programmed, audiences refused to leave, stamping their feet and shouting, until it was played; extra concerts had to be planned at short notice to meet popular demand, and critics were ecstatic. Yet there is no disguising the fact that what causes difficulty for the biographer was also causing difficulty for Ernst. He was playing the same limited number of pieces in many places he had played before, and there were few signs that his career, either as a performer or composer, was developing. Amongst the educated there were signs of familiarity and sometimes boredom. Critics in Pressburg said that his playing was so wonderful and the audiences so excited that description was no longer necessary [AMZ:11/10/45:487]; and in Pesth, the seats in the stalls and orchestra sold well, but the first class boxes remained completely empty. [AWMZ:5/6/45:268; SMW:6/45:189; RGM:15/6/45:199]

Ernst was clearly aware that his limited repertoire was causing problems and he made efforts to extend it. He performed one or two of his less familiar compositions – the E major *Nocturne*, the *Variations on a Dutch Air* – and he took the unusual step of including a piece by a living rival – Bazzini's *Allegro de Concert* – in his programmes. Bazzini may well have introduced him to the work in Leipzig. Ernst had become friendly with the Italian virtuoso, and Puccini – Bazzini's pupil – would later describe the two violinists' friendship as 'intimate'. [TGC:129]

Above all, he began to compose again himself. The first fruit of his new labour was a piece initially called *Rondo Scherzo* and later – because of the little five-note panpipe figure which recurs throughout – the *Rondo Papageno*. It is one of Ernst's most scintillating compositions, and begins with a theme closely related to the rondo melody from Paganini's first violin concerto. There is a particularly delightful syncopated secondary theme, and throughout the piece, the orchestra offers quirky interjections of the Papageno motif, beginning on the second beat of the bar, which greatly enhance the comic effect.

The work's final section is a *moto perpetuo* in staccato triplets, which makes severe demands on the soloist's ability to play very fast high notes with firmness and delicacy. This passage may have been at the back of Saint-Saëns's mind when he composed the final pages of his *Introduction and Rondo Capricioso*. The whole piece was certainly at the forefront of Bazzini's mind when he composed and dedicated *Le Ronde des Lutins* to Ernst in 1850. This pays conscious tribute to the *Rondo Papageno*, not only in its title and breathtaking virtuosity, but in the very similar melodic outline of its main theme – although Bazzini's version, of course, is in the minor. Bazzini's gesture may well have been prompted, not only by their meeting in Leipzig, but also by the way Ernst championed the *Concert Allegro* throughout Europe.

One rondo, however lively and agreeable, was not going to solve his repertoire problem, and in the first four months of 1846 – and probably October and early November of 1845 – he largely retired from concert life to concentrate on composition. The first work from this period is *Airs hongrois Variés*. I suspect this was inspired by Ernst's recent and protracted sojourn in Pesth, where he no doubt stayed with his sister Franziska and her family. Hungarian national feeling was reaching boiling point, and anyone who wrote a piece incorporating national airs was virtually assured of an overwhelming reception – as Berlioz was to discover with his *Hungarian March* in February 1846. [BM:474–6]

Like the rondo, *Hungarian Airs* is written in the key of A major – the easiest and most resonant key on the violin – and added brilliancy is given to the orchestral part by again assigning an important role to the piccolo. The first melody displays and contrasts the violin's capacity for coquettish airy elegance on the highest string with earthy truculence on the lowest. This is followed by an impressively difficult variation – full of fast tenths, artificial harmonics, rapid cadenzas, and scales set against held notes – which introduces the second melody – *Andante con molt'espressione* in F major. The melody is ideally suited to showing off Ernst's expressive rubato. When the first eight-bar phrase is repeated, it is decorated with semiquavers and even faster notes – almost a variation before the variation – as in Ernst's earlier treatment of Desdemona's aria from *Otello*. The tempo increases for the variation proper which is played in artificial harmonics on the G string. Rapid trills and daring leaps outlining diminished seventh and dominant chords prepare the way for a cadenza (not supplied by Ernst) and the energetic last melody.

As in several earlier works, Ernst actually composed rather more of the piece than one might expect from the title: the first two themes are genuine Hungarian folk melodies but the last is Ernst's original composition. [MW:21/4/49:242] Indeed, one can recognize some of his technical fingerprints from the *Rondo Papergeno* – the rapid upward run in staccato thirds, for example, and the rising double-stopped E major arpeggio followed by a high downward run in thirds. Four variations and *ritonelli* follow: an exercise in spiccato sixths alternating with the open E string; a variation in turns, grace notes and rapid scales; and the two following devices which appear to be Ernst's innovations:

Example 13.1   Ernst, *Hungarian Airs*, op.22, bars 57–59

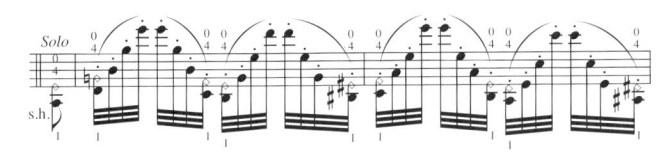

Example 13.2   Ernst, *Hungarian Airs*, op.22, bars 68–70

The latter figuration – one of Ernst's most ingenious technical ideas – leads into a *più mosso* finale. The soloist continues his arpeggios, but they now require even greater stretches and are bowed across the beat, and a flute picks out a lively new melody which is later taken up by the bassoon and the strings. An A major arpeggio – sent dazzlingly high – introduces the final chords.

The piece has had its influence. At the age of 20, Elgar heard Wilhelmj play *Hungarian Airs* at a recital in Gloucester Cathedral. 'From his account of the affair,' wrote the violinist W.H. Reed, 'Wilhelmj must have had a colossal tone; and his attack on the opening tenth on the G string must have been hair-raising. It excited Elgar to such an extent that he never forgot it; and when he showed me how it was done I felt thankful he was content to perform upon an imaginary violin and not mine; for the movement he made would have cut an ordinary violin in half.' [ECL:73–4]

Wilhelmj's recital fired Elgar's ambition, and he decided to go to London for some serious violin lessons with Adolf Pollitzer, professor of violin at the Royal Academy of Music. Pollitzer had received advice and encouragement from Ernst, and had originally come to England at the Moravian's suggestion. He had played with Ernst a number of times in the 1850s at the Musical Union and the New Philharmonic, and edited several of his pieces. Elgar was thus inducted into the tradition of Ernst's virtuosity, and wrote a number of short display pieces under its influence, notably *La Capricieuse* for violin and piano, and the five difficult *Etudes Characteristiques* op.24 for violin solo which are dedicated to Pollitzer.

Elgar's love of the virtuoso violin and its full panoply of effects is most evident in the violin concerto of 1910, but in both Elgar's mature works for violin – the concerto, and the sonata of 1918 – there is one very obvious imprint of *Hungarian Airs*. The G string leap from the low A to the C♯ a tenth above, which so impressed the young composer (Ex. 13.3), can be found in slightly altered form at climactic moments of both Elgar compositions. In the violin sonata, the leap occurs at figure 12 of Novello's edition (Ex. 13.4). It is now transposed into the minor, but the two following notes are also the same:

Example 13.3   Ernst, *Hungarian Airs*, op.22, bar 13

Example 13.4   Elgar, Violin Sonata in E minor, op.82, first movement, bars 170–172

In the concerto, it is now in the major, but transposed down a semitone to A♭ and C (Ex. 13.5).

Example 13.5   Elgar, Violin Concerto in B minor, op.61, second movement, bars 93–94

Hungarian Airs was one of Wieniawski's favourite pieces, Kreisler played it at his American debut, and it remained in print until the 1960s. In spite of these endorsements, it is not one of Ernst's most impressive creations. The themes themselves are pretty but short and square in outline, and the piece itself is essentially three sets of variations played in sequence. There is no attempt, as there is in the *Otello Fantasy*, to unify or integrate the themes and variations in a more symphonic manner. Slight nationalistic colouring in the themes cannot disguise the fact that *Hungarian Airs* is essentially old-fashioned drawing-room music which relies on the contrast of pretty episodes. Technically, it is much more demanding than Sarasate's *Zigeunerweisen*, but the passionate melancholy and dazzling excitement of that piece make *Hungarian Airs* look stiff and pallid.

Altogether more significant is the next work to be composed, the one movement violin concerto in F♯ minor. I suspect the main spur for writing this was Vieuxtemps. Ernst's light and frothy *Concertino* had been wholly eclipsed by the weight and seriousness of Vieuxtemps's first concerto when they had been played at the Paris Conservatoire, and the Belgian virtuoso had now completed three. Ernst needed a work that could stand comparison with these, particularly as he wished to go to Russia where Vieuxtemps would soon take up residence.

A genuine one-movement concerto (unlike a work with three linked movements, for example, the Mendelssohn violin concerto) now strikes us as anomalous, but the form was popular throughout the nineteenth century. De Bériot's first concerto is in one movement, as are Lipinski's third and fourth. In addition, there were several popular works with names like *Concert Allegro* and *Konzertstück* – Bazzini's *Concert Allegro*, and Mayseder's *Grosses Konzertstück* come immediately to mind. Mass audiences in the nineteenth century did not, for the most part, enjoy extended instrumental works, and long programmes with multiple performers favoured works of no more than fifteen or twenty minutes. Consequently, even three-movement concertos tended to be broken in two: the first movement in the first half, and the final movements in the second, as frequently happened in early performances of Mendelssohn and Paganini concertos. A one-movement work clearly avoids such awkwardness.

To signal the seriousness of his intent, Ernst not only took several months off from touring but withdrew from Vienna to the centre of German academic composition – Leipzig. There were other reasons why the place was propitious. Mendelssohn had listened to the premiere of his own violin concerto there the previous year, and Ernst could also seek advice from Ferdinand David, the eventual dedicatee of both concertos. As he worked, he was visited by Reinecke, who gives a vivid impression of the effort that Ernst put into this composition: 'I saw [Ernst] again in Leipzig in 1849 [*sic*], but he had grown much more serious. It was there, in the Hôtel de Bavière of those days, that he wrote his F[♯] minor Concerto, which is not only his most important work, but also a work important in itself. There he sat, in spite of the bright daylight, working with curtained windows and by candlelight, and there was something fantastic about his whole appearance.' [HFPV:55] Good as he is on atmosphere, Reinecke is certainly wrong about the date. The most likely time is between 16 January and 15 March 1846.

The new seriousness Reineke discovered in Ernst, and the intensity of the darkened hotel room, colour the whole work. Although fantastically difficult from the technical point of view, it could not be further removed from the loose structure, catchy tunes, passage-work, triangles, and bass drums of the period's virtuoso froth. The concerto is carefully structured and extremely compressed, yet at the same time gives an impression of being free and improvisatory. It is also one of the most gloomy, dark-coloured, and emotionally over-heated concertos in the repertoire, and points away from the concertos of Paganini, towards Joachim's *Hungarian Concerto*, the Brahms D minor piano concerto, and the Sibelius violin concerto; indeed, I shall argue that on the two latter works it had some direct influence. It could thus not be further removed from the one-movement concertos and concert allegros that went before it.

Efraim Zimballist once commented, 'Ernst invented a new form in this concerto,' [EOC:29] and the form needs to be looked at carefully. In the orchestral exposition there are two groups of themes. The first seven are severe in character (Exx. 13.6–13.12):

Example 13.6   Ernst, Concerto, op.23, bars 1–9

Example 13.7   Ernst, Concerto, op.23, bars 9–11

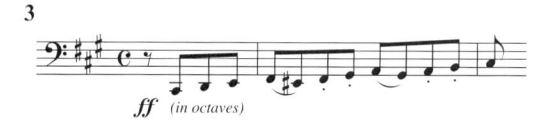

Example 13.8   Ernst, Concerto, op.23, bars 11–13

Example 13.9   Ernst, Concerto, op.23, bars 13–15

Example 13.10   Ernst, Concerto, op.23, bars 24–26

New Repertoire: 1845–46

Example 13.11   Ernst, Concerto, op.23, bars 30–32

Example 13.12   Ernst Concerto, op.23, bars 55–57

These are largely in the minor, they tend to be short (2, 3 and 4 are only a couple of bars long); they tend to appear out of their original sequence later in the concerto; and they frequently occur in combination and counterpoint. Indeed, the opening bars of 1 and 5 are often used as motifs throughout the work, and tie the various sections together. Of these severe themes, 1 and 2 are much the most important.

They are followed by a group of more lyrical themes (Exx. 13.13–13.17):

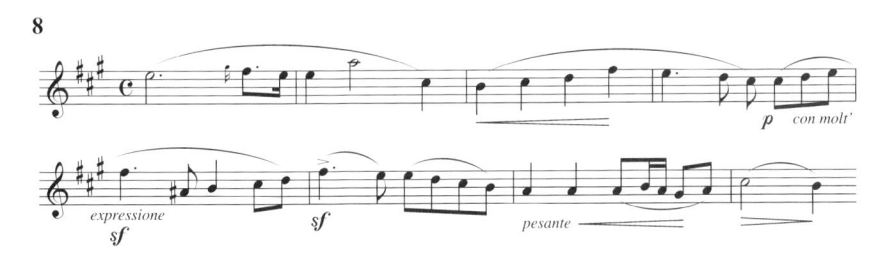

Example 13.13   Ernst, Concerto, op.23, bars 58–65

Example 13.14   Ernst, Concerto, op.23, bars 65–73

Example 13.15   Ernst, Concerto, op.23, bars 73–80

Example 13.16   Ernst, Concerto, op.23, bars 93–95

Example 13.17   Ernst, Concerto, op.23, bars 96–102

These tend to be longer, quieter, largely in the major, and frequently appear in their original sequence. Of this group, 8 and 9 are clearly the most important. There are thus four main themes altogether.

The next 370 bars or so – from the end of the exposition to the end of the piece – add very little in terms of melody. There is the soloist's downward plunge at bar 105 (theme 13); the new semiquaver figure in the bass (bars 238–240) which starts life as a vigorous accompaniment to 1 (theme 14); and finally the orchestral violins' impassioned semiquaver figure at bars 245–255, which the soloist will later take up just before the piece's major climax at bars 442–452 (theme 15).

However, the two-part grouping suggested above, disguises how interrelated all the themes are. Theme 8, the first main theme of the second group, is simply an extended version of 1, except it is now in the major and has a new ending influenced by 6; 2 picks up the final rhythm of 1; 5 follows the pattern of 3, acts as a bass to 7 and provides a new ending for 3 (bars 50–54); 11 and 12 are transformations of 9. In addition, is 3 simply the second half of 2? Or is 4 the second half of 3? It is quite clear that, even in this orchestral exposition, Ernst is transforming and developing his themes.

An early Viennese reviewer suggested that the concerto falls into the three sections of a normal concerto – F# minor first movement (bars 1–288), D major second movement (bars 289–365), and F# major finale (bars 366–467). [HWE:17–18] But all these sections use similar material, and all of them contain passages which are both rapid and lyrical. There is thus no reason to treat sections in one key signature as important structural units.

It is more fruitful to look upon the whole piece as an example of altered sonata form, with the orchestral exposition acting as the sonata exposition, and the rest of the piece until bar 411 acting as the development section. However, as in Chopin's B♭ minor and B minor piano sonatas, there is no straightforward recapitulation, and, as in the piano concertos of Hummel and Chopin, the function of the cadenza is taken by a brilliant coda.

More than most works in sonata form, this concerto is a dialectic between the severe first subjects and the lyrical second subjects, a dialectic which the second group of themes triumphantly wins. Themes 2 and 8 play a special role in the work. Sections dominated by the severe themes sometimes appropriate the lyrical theme 8, which is a major-keyed and more extended version of 1. Sections dominated by the lyrical themes sometimes borrow theme 2, which is the most song-like tune in the severe group.

After the soloist enters, the severe themes dominate until bar 171, when the lyrical themes take over until bar 237. The severe group reassert themselves through bars 237–288. Theme 2, the severe group's most lyrical melody, dominates the beginning of the D major section (bars 289–310), but its place is gradually supplanted by the lyrical group proper (bars 310–312, 337–343). The two groups tussle in the tutti (bars 343–366) but the lyrical group emerges victorious, and dominates the F# major section at bars 366–403. In bars 403–430, the severe group tries to reassert itself, but it no longer has the energy. Instead of a full recapitulation of 1, we are given a passage of recitative. Here the soloist plays only the opening phrase of the theme at a much reduced speed, and is answered by the horn. The solo violin tries this again and receives the same dreamy answer. The third time, like a dying swan, the soloist ascends to a high C# on the D string before outlining a dominant chord in F# major. His rapid figuration then implies the return of the lyrical group (the same figuration originally appeared as an accompaniment to 9) and the same theme is asserted triumphantly and ecstatically in the concerto's final pages (bars 430–467).

Technically, the concerto presents tremendous problems to the player; not until the Sibelius and Elgar concertos would there be any work to touch it. Ernst denies himself the usual virtuoso tricks – harmonics, left-hand pizzicato, and so forth – in this more classical format, but the technical difficulties are still ferocious: long runs in slurred legato thirds; very high, quiet broken tenths; G string passages ascending up to the B more than two octaves above the open string; very high thirds and double-stopping at rapid tempos; and extremely high positions across all the strings. These last difficulties are particularly clear in the following bars (Ex. 13.18):

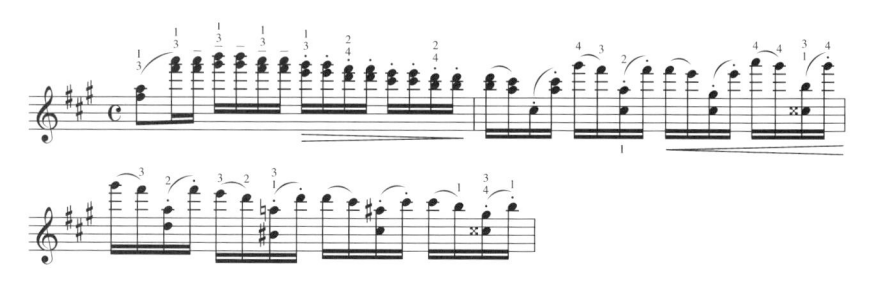

Example 13.18   Ernst, Concerto, op.23, bars 437–439

One notable feature of this concerto, and one which gives it some of its hollow melancholy intensity, is its emphasis on the barer, harsher intervals – the fourth, fifth, and octave. (In this, of course, it is quite unlike the *Bel Canto* tradition drawn on by Paganini, which tends to emphasize the third and sixth.) Partly as a consequence of this, the soloist has to play melodically for long passages in octaves soon after his entry; and the fierce octave passage-work, and the final appearance of theme 9, in octaves and F♯ major, is altogether unprecedented.

Like Ernst's two previous works, the concerto has three sharps in its key signature, but here the key makes for much greater technical difficulty: the most closely related major keys to F♯ minor are F♯ and C♯ major, and the number of accidentals makes both awkward to play on most instruments, including the violin. The work is also finely orchestrated. He denies himself the use of the piccolo, but the writing for woodwind (particularly bassoon) is idiomatic, expressive, and melodic.

The concerto has always had its admirers. Amongst the first was Berlioz who felt that Ernst, unlike Beethoven or Chopin, had achieved the right balance between virtuoso display and orchestral interest. Reviewing a performance by Ernst in January 1852, he wrote:

> The concerto in F♯ minor ... is a magisterial work from the point of view of both symphonic writing and violin technique. It presents immense difficulties ... [but they] are always expressive difficulties and not merely designed to create astonishment. ... [The] last passage in octaves, when the forceful sonority of the two strings goes on increasing as the solo approaches the orchestral explosion, produced on the audience the kind of frisson that can be brought about only by things which are truly new, bold to the point of recklessness, and performed with stupefying facility. ...

In Chopin's compositions all the interest is concentrated in the piano part; the orchestra's role in this concerto is confined to a frigid and practically superfluous accompaniment. Ernst's are the very opposite. The works he has written for his own instrument and orchestra are conspicuous examples of qualities once thought mutually exclusive – brilliant technical display and sustained symphonic interest. Beethoven was the first to find a successful solution to the problem of how to give the solo instrument full scope without reducing the orchestra to a minor role. Beethoven himself, it can be argued, was inclined to let the orchestra overpower the soloist; whereas the plan adopted by Ernst, Vieuxtemps, Liszt and one or two others seems to me to strike the right balance exactly. [JD:27/1/52. BM:537–8]

Sixty years later, Auer praises it as an aid to advanced technique, but also dwells at greater length on its lyrical beauty:

[The concerto] makes the very highest demands on the technique of both hands ... and supplies one of the most important factors in the higher development of violin left-hand technique. ... The cantabile portion of this concerto is extremely rich, elaborate and beautiful, and decidedly heightens the value of the composition. It would be unjust to regard the work as one which aims only at external effect; in part, to be sure, it represents no more than technical violinistic 'apparatus,' mechanical scaffolding; but its major portion, owing to its genuine musical content, and the manner in which its themes – in the orchestra as well as in the violin solo part – have been developed, gives it a place among the more distinguished works of its kind written for the instrument. [VMW:88]

The work would make its mark on music later in the century. Brahms's first important professional engagement was a short concert tour with the violinist Reményi from April to July 1853. It was while playing in Hanover with Reményi that Brahms met Joachim, who, deeply impressed by the young composer, recommended him to Liszt and Schumann. The meeting with Schumann, of course, resulted in the article which proclaimed Brahms the new hope of German music, and set him on the road to fame and immortality.

The associations with Ernst here are rich and complex. Reményi, like Ernst, was a pupil of Böhm; he performed Ernst's concerto on many occasions; and he also played Ernst's *Elegy* while on tour with Brahms. Joachim played a good deal of Ernst's music (he particularly liked the *Otello* fantasy and the concerto), recommended it to his pupils, and admired Ernst as a man, mentor and violinist. [MCF:31. VPAT:6] Over the next seven years, Brahms and Joachim became very close, and regularly played together. It therefore seems highly likely that they played some of Joachim's favourite pieces, including Ernst's concerto. This would explain why theme 5 of Ernst's concerto (first published in 1850–51) is virtually quoted in the first double bar of Brahms's D major orchestral serenade (written 1857–58) (Exx. 13.19 and 13.20).

Example 13.19   Ernst, Concerto, op.23, bars 24–25

Example 13.20   Brahms, Serenade no.1 in D major, op.11, first movement, bars 200–202

This motif turns into the main new material for the opening of the first movement's development section.

There are two less obvious but more important connections with Brahms's music. The first is the similarity between the solo violin's entry in Ernst's concerto (Ex. 13.21) and the piano's entry in Brahms's first piano concerto (composed 1854–58) (Ex. 13.22). Neither is a virtuoso flourish. In both, the orchestra dies down to *pp* and introduces a new rocking figure in the bass. The soloist enters very quietly with a ruminative theme (often in sixths) which moves in stepwise tones and semitones towards the end of bars, circling around one note:

Example 13.21   Ernst, Concerto, op.23, bars 100–104

Example 13.22   Brahms, Piano Concerto no.1 in D minor, op.15, first movement, bars 91–96

New Repertoire: 1845–46

The second analogy with Brahms is between Ernst's theme 14 – a crochet tied to the first of a group of descending semiquavers in scale patterns (Ex. 13.23) – and a very similar figure, also used for whipping up excitement, in Brahms's violin concerto (Ex. 13.24):

Example 13.23 Ernst, Concerto, op.23, bars 323–324

Example 13.24 Brahms, Violin Concerto in D major, op.77, first movement, bars 491–492

Like Elgar, Sibelius originally hoped to be a virtuoso violinist, and from early on, Ernst formed part of his musical landscape. As a boy, one of his most stimulating musical environments was his uncle Pehr's home in Turku. Here, writes his biographer, '[his] uncle with his long pipe and beard would tell him about [Heinrich] Wilhelm Ernst and all the other great violinists he had heard in Stockholm and St Petersburg, and took him to concerts in the town.' [SB:I:19] Sibelius went on to make an assiduous study of the virtuoso literature, and a letter to his uncle in September 1889 shows that Ernst formed part of his repertoire: 'The last two weeks I have been at Walter Konow's and played the violin there so that everyone became captivated by violin music, including the Colonel who even wanted to hear Ernst's *Élégie* several times.' [HL:107] The *Elegy* seems to have been particularly popular with elderly military men.

Ernst's concerto was widely played in the 1890s. It was in the repertoire of Sauret, Wilhelmj, Nachez, and Lotto, but one of its most distinguished advocates was Willy Burmester. [HPSL:444] From the beginning of his work on his own concerto, Sibelius hoped Burmester would give the first performance, and was in contact with him throughout the compositional process. Jukka Tiilikainen has shown how Burmester's predilection for Bach influenced the first version of Sibelius's concerto [GVC:79–80]; and Burmester's performances of Ernst's concerto also influenced the work. The bleakness Ernst achieved with his emphasis on the barer intervals – the fourth, fifth and octave – finds an echo in Sibelius's concerto, as does Ernst's device of having the soloist play in octaves for extended passages. We find the same use of long, upward-moving scales in thirds, but perhaps most significant similarity is the octave passages at the end of Ernst's concerto (Ex. 13.25) and at the end of the Sibelius concerto's first movement (Ex. 13.26).

Example 13.25   Ernst, Concerto, op.23, bars 438–441

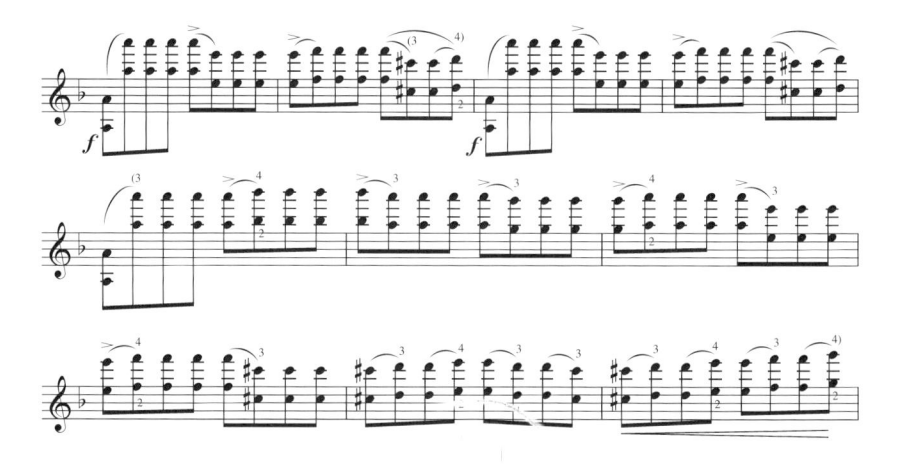

Example 13.26   Sibelius, Violin Concerto in D minor, op.47, first movement, bars 447–456

In November 1845, the *Signale für die Musikalische Welt* [SMW:373] announced that Ernst would soon publish a new violin concerto, but it was probably not finished until the beginning of March 1846, and it did not receive its premiere until 19 April. This was in the large hall of Vienna's Redoutensaal, where Ernst was accompanied by the Hofoperntheater orchestra under Hellmesberger.[1] The contrast between Ernst's concerto and the average virtuoso work was well understood by some of its first reviewers. The following notice appeared in a Viennese paper shortly after its second performance in the city, and the reviewer is more inclined to see analogies with Mozart and late Beethoven than with Paganini and Sivori.

---

1   Even though Joachim heard the concerto played by many virtuosi later in the century, he always favoured Ernst's interpretation: 'Even if Ferdinand Laub, for example, can play the passages in the F-sharp minor concerto more cleanly – because he has greater finger strength – I still preferred Ernst's interpretation which was more elegant and (when he was in the mood) far more characteristic, because he knew how to shape a phrase with more plasticity.' [GV:519. GMV:206]

H.W. Ernst's Concert, 19th October 1846

Concerto Pathétique composed and played by H.W. Ernst

The title Ernst has given this work is no empty name, unlike thousands and thousands of 'Reveries,' 'Inquietudes,' 'Coquettes,' 'Campenellas,' composed by the modern virtuoso clique. No, Ernst has offered us here a real tone-poem, full of deep passion and ardour for that high moral idea we call pathos. There is nothing morbid or affected here. On the contrary, a true and healthy inspiration, a thorough intelligence and clear passion, speak unmistakably from every feature of this concerto. In this work, our Ernst, who has long been sympathetic to us as a deeply spiritual virtuoso, has now ensured himself an important place amongst artists in the full meaning of the word. ...

Among many other beauties, all of which show an excellent knowledge of harmony and instrumentation, the Dolce in D major is especially worthy of notice, as this shows touches of Mozart as well as Ernst's own personality.

But has not Ernst, in the solo marked 'Modo di recitative,' and in the concluding stretto in F-sharp major, poetically overextended himself? Have not many of his contemporaries done this as well? I leave the question here unresolved. But this much is certain: these two passages could not have been written without a mighty inspiration, and Ernst seems here to transcend the merely human. In these sections, Ernst comes close, I believe, and very significantly, to the ideal of free fantasy that only one person to date has ever fully realized (in the introduction to the finale in his mighty op.106) [Beethoven's *Hammerklavier Sonata*].

Although people might wish to question this statement, I remain firmly convinced that the finale of the Ernst concerto is a masterpiece of its kind, that the concerto itself is the work of a beautiful poetic soul, that it demands the attention and respect of critics, and that it will not be long before we hear it in public again. [HWE:17–19]

On 19 April, Ernst also gave the premiere of *Hungarian Airs*, and played the *Pirate Fantasy* and Beethoven's Romance in F. The *Pirate Fantasy* looks back to his Paris days of Chopin and Italian opera, but there are hints of two new directions in the other pieces. The first is the nationalism of *Hungarian Airs*. The second is a move in the direction of the Viennese classics: a dense and serious concerto (which critics compared with Mozart and Beethoven), and a work by Beethoven himself. It is also worth observing that one of the concerto's themes (3) is taken from the first movement of Mozart's piano concerto in D minor K.466 (bars 109–110, for example), and even the light *Rondo Papageno* suggests Mozart in its title and one of its motifs – although the fact that this was the second title may suggest any thought of Mozart was *post hoc*.

We can find hints of both new directions in Kriehuber's famous print, *Ein Matinée bei Liszt*, which could have been drawn in the last week of February 1846 and was released to the public in early April. [*Wiener Zeitung*: 10/4/46. PHB:339] According to one contemporary journalist, this shows Liszt improving on Ernst's *Elegy*, which the violinist has just played. [*Allgemeine Theaterzeitung*: 9/4/46. PHB:339] Liszt sits in front of his own *Ungarische Nationalmelodien* and Beethoven's sonata in A♭ op.26. Ernst holds his Stradivarius on his knee (its one-piece back is clearly visible), and, perhaps to suggest his technical interests, he is the only member of the group to be looking at the pianist's hands. [See Plate VIII.]

Kriehuber drew Ernst three times. The artist caught him looking youthful and alert in his first portrait from 1840, and his third portrait from June 1846 is not so very different, although the hair has receded a little and his face is slightly darker and more serious. [See Plates V and VI.] But on this visit, Ernst also sat for the other leading Viennese portraitist, Prinzhofer, and his work, while less perfect in finish, has greater emotional impact. [See Plate VII.] Here, Ernst hunches forward slightly, his arms crossed, and he looks altogether more troubled and melancholy; the first signs of exhaustion and illness are beginning to show.

Ernst gave his final concert in Vienna on 4 May and had made his way to Carlsbad by August. The concert at the spa in Carlsbad was important, because this was the occasion when Spohr at last heard Ernst. His wife writes:

> The concert of so celebrated a virtuoso [as Ernst] was quite an event for Carlsbad, and afforded us much pleasure. Besides the song scene of Spohr, he played several of his own things, some of which were very beautiful, curious compositions replete with all manner of difficulties and wonderful artistic resorts for display, and which he executed with great precision and ease; but although he played Spohr's concerto with much care and great expression, yet we have not only heard it played by Spohr himself, but by his talented pupil Jean Bott, much more correctly. The overcrowded house presented a curious spectacle, for not only was the space allotted to spectators, but the whole stage as well also, occupied by the public, which sat round disposed in a large semicircle. [SA:II:280]

Clearly, Spohr raised an eyebrow at Ernst's recomposition of the *Gesangsszene*, just as Joachim had two years earlier, but there were evidently no hard feelings. One of Spohr's admirers had sent him two large herring:

> [And though] Spohr had always been used to receive a great variety of presents, and frequently of the strangest kind, as tokens of esteem and admiration, yet he had never before received one of so surprising and comical a kind, at which Ernst, who happened to be present at the moment [Spohr] received them, laughed very heartily, and then without much speculation or care as to who the anonymous donor might be, ate with much relish the delicious fish, as a change from the scant prescriptive supper permitted to the bath patients. [SA:II:280–81]

The remainder of 1846 was spent on tour, making the most of his new repertoire, and adding Beethoven's Romance in G. His known concerts are:

Ischl: 31 August [NZM:30/9/46:110]
Graz: 19 and 20 September [AWMZ:1/10/46:475–6]
Linz: Two concerts, October [AWMZ:10/11/46:546]
Vienna: 19, 27 and 31 October [AWMZ:27/10/46; 29/10/46:523; 3/11/46:530. SMW:11/46:375]
Hanover: November. He travelled there and back via Leipzig [EUZ:43]
Dresden: 17 November [SMW:11/46:381]
Berlin: At least four concerts (the first on 10 December, the last on 4 January 1847) [SMW:11/46:381. RGM:5/12/46:391. AMZ:27/1/47:Col.56–7. E:109–12]

The majority of these concerts were triumphant, but the tour was not entirely successful. At Linz, the hall was not full (possibly because of raised prices) and the sensation was less than it had been in 1840; and in Vienna, newspapers criticized him for pandering to the public by always playing the *Carnival* at the end of every concert. [AWMZ:10/11/46:546] In Vienna and Dresden, technical failings were more notable: his intonation was criticized in his opening concerts, although this tended to improve in later appearances. [SMW:10/46:381. E:111] Similarly, in Berlin sharp-eared critics noted that a few harmonics did not sound, some octaves were out of tune, and a number of difficult passages were not clear enough [SMW:2/47:79], although, once again, his accuracy increased as the concert series progressed. [E:108–13]

Physical debility should have made Ernst rest and recoup. Instead, spurred on rather than depressed by three or four abortive attempts, he decided to head for Russia, the most arduous of all the normal touring routes.

Chapter 14

Russia and Revolution: 1847–49

At the beginning of 1847, Ernst finally set off for St Petersburg. On the way he gave four concerts in Königsberg, three at Mittau, four at Riga (on 15, 18, 23 and 26 January), and two at Dorpat. [RGM:14/3/47:92. NMZ:12/3/47:86. E:113] It was probably to the last of these towns that Berlioz sent the following letter on 28 January:

> My Dear Ernst, I received the letter that Franko[w]ski was kind enough to send me from Koenigsberg just as I was about to put an article in the *Débats* which mentions your name in connection with young Pixis who recently dared to play your *Carnival of Venice*.
> Soon, I must write another article where I'll describe your great journey to Berlin, Koenigsberg and St Petersburg; it's only a matter of finding the time to write the piece and finding a day when the journal has space to print it. The two chambers [of Parliament] fill everything, and these wretched politics, God damn them, are doing us, and everything to do with the arts, an immense amount of harm. In every case, this situation causes at least a temporary hold up.
> Now, you'll be pleased to know that we are going to meet one another at St Petersburg. Like you, I'm making this great journey, planned many times and abandoned many times. I wrote to Count Wielhorski, to General Lwoff and to M. Gévéonof to warn them of my arrival and to find three days for my concerts during Lent.
> Be good enough, when you've got your own affairs sorted out, to cast a glance over mine and talk to these gentlemen about them. … [VN:346. See also CGB:III:404–5]

At this point, Berlioz can have had very little idea of just how serious the musical consequences of the growing political crisis in France – the immediate precursor of the 1848 revolution – were going to be.

Ernst's journey did not proceed as planned. On 20 March, the St Petersburg correspondent of *Der Spiegel* reported:

> H.W. Ernst, the famous violin virtuoso, has been taken ill with rheumatism and chickenpox in Dorpat, and for the time being has had to postpone the winter journey to St Petersburg. On can say that the entire city literally competes in giving evidence of sympathy for the gifted artist. In Petersburg they are looking forward to his arrival with the greatest suspense. [EOC:20]

The journey by iron sledge to St Petersburg took four days and nights, and it froze and traumatized even the most robust passengers. [BM:517–19] For Ernst, there were additional problems to contend with on arrival. In the spring of 1846, Count Wielhorski, one of the two brothers at the centre of musical life in St Petersburg, had approached Vieuxtemps and offered him the triple position of court violinist, soloist in the Imperial Theatre, and teacher of music classes in St Petersburg (there was as yet no conservatoire) for six years. Thinking the terms sounded magnificent, he took up his posts in September 1846. Vieuxtemps was already a familiar figure in Russia, and when he started to give concerts, critics immediately recognized that his playing was even more impressive. Consequently, when Ernst arrived, shattered by travel and illness, Vieuxtemps had had nearly six months to gain more friends and further his reputation. This caused some difficulties at Ernst's first concert in St Petersburg on 22 February. As *Der Spiegel* reported in its summary of the Lent concerts:

> Ernst, the famous violin virtuoso, for many months vainly expected here (Petersburg), succeeded gradually in awakening the public from its musical lethargy, to interest it actively, and finally to kindle its enthusiasm. Ernst had here to contend not only with a great music and concert boredom, but also with a solid opposition which turned against the Romantic, the elegiac, the humoristic in favour of a great, rightly celebrated artist of the same weapon. Since, as everyone knows, Ernst is not everyday equally well equipped, just as heaven does not make the same beautiful weather every day, thus the admirers of the famous Vieuxtemps who is engaged here, found reason to protest when Ernst in his first concert, in the first numbers of the programme, did not play as people expected according to his European reputation. And these expectations were stretched to a fabulous height. Although Ernst then played the closing pieces of this first concert splendidly and with great applause, yet the whole of the first evening could only be called a two-thirds success. [EOC:20]

There were other difficulties at this first appearance. Unfamiliar with the country, exhausted and ill, Ernst misjudged the admission price for his concerts, and 25 silver roubles for a box, and 8 for the first row in the orchestra, proved too much. The hall was thus only half full, and he was forced to reduce the prices for his next concert on 26 February. From this point onwards, matters progressed more satisfactorily. His concerts on 5 and 29 March, and 13 April, were considered some of the most brilliant of the season, and he also gave well-received performances at concerts by the pianists Damcke (14 March), and Promberger.

Dostoevsky attended Ernst's third and fifth concerts, and gives a vivid account of just how exhausting the St Petersburg musical season could be:

> However sweetly the prima donna Borsi and the tenors Guasco and Salvi may sing their rondos, cavatinas etc., we dragged ourselves to the opera just as though we were dragging a cartload of firewood; we were tired out, we were utterly exhausted, and if we did fling bouquets on the stage at the end of the scene, we did so simply because the opera was drawing to an end. Then there was the famous violinist Heinrich Wilhelm Ernst ... It was with an effort that the whole of St Petersburg came to his third concert. Today [13 April] we are saying good bye to him. We do not know if there will be any bouquets ... But having heard our marvellous artist describe on his violin the other night what a southern fancy-dress ball is really like, I was completely satisfied with his description and did not go to our highly respectable northern fancy-dress balls. [DOW:6]

On 13 April, Berlioz sat in the same audience as Dostoevsky, and the closing minutes of the concert remained etched on his memory. The thought of Ernst often sanctions a flood of reminiscence and fantasy in other writers. For Berlioz, this particular memory – which seemed to come into his mind whenever he recalled Ernst in later years – became an emblem, not only of true glamour, happiness and success, but of the romantic, evocative mystery of music itself:

> It was an unforgettable moment when [Ernst] reappeared amid the thunders of applause, after performing those glowing grandly conceived works of his in his most imposing style, and as a farewell gesture to his audience played the variations on the *Carnival of Venice* – a piece of sublime whimsy in which invention and technical wizardry are so skilfully blended that in the end one ceases to be astonished at anything and simply sits back, lulled by the constant rocking movement of the accompanying theme, as though the solo violin were not executing the most prodigious feats of agility and conjuring cascades of gleaming and iridescent melody the while. This fascinating display of virtuosity put to consistently tuneful ends, never fails to dazzle and enthrall the audience whenever Ernst plays it. He is like a juggler whose counters are diamonds. If old Councillor Crespel [a character from one of E.T.A. Hoffmann's *Tales*], the curious eccentric who owned the Cremona violin, could have witnessed these fantastic feats of musical ingenuity, the poor man would speedily have lost what was left of his wits; he would not then have suffered so bitterly from the death of his Antonia.
>
> These variations affect me in a strange way whenever I hear Ernst play them, as I have often since then (and only the other day in Baden.) As soon as the Venetian air appears at the touch of that magic bow, it is midnight, I am in St Petersburg once more, it is a great auditorium bright as day, experiencing again that curiously pleasurable sense of nervous fatigue one feels at the end of a splendid musical evening; there is a hum of excitement in the air, the glint of smiling faces; I fall into a romantic melancholy which I am powerless to resist, nay, which would be painful to struggle against. ... No other art has music's power to affect one retroactively. Not even the art of Shakespeare can evoke the past with this degree of poetic intensity. Only music appeals at one and the same time to the imagination, the intellect, *and* the senses; and from the reaction of senses on intellect and feelings, and vice-versa, come the phenomena which people with the right physiological mechanism are susceptible to, but to those not so endowed (otherwise known as philistines) will always remain a sealed book. [BM:538-9]

In April, Ernst had the pleasure of being introduced to Liszt's future mistress, the Princess Carolyne Sayn-Wittgenstein [FLWY:38], and then of playing two movements from *Harold in Italy* at Berlioz's last major performance on his Russian visit, on either 23 April or 5 May. Berlioz told Auguste Morel: 'Ernst played with the greatest expressiveness, in a manner as simple as it was poetic, the solo viola in *Harold*' [CGB:III:419], and the concert ended with Berlioz conducting *Romeo and Juliet*. He recalls:

> The whole thing was imperially organized: the performance, as it could hardly fail to be, was marvellous. I remember it as one of the great pleasures of my life. And I was in such good form that I had the luck to conduct without a mistake, which at that time did not often happen to me. The Grand Theatre was full. On all sides uniforms, epaulettes, tiaras, diamonds, flashed and rippled. I was recalled I do not know how many times. But I confess I paid little heed to the public that day. I sang the divine Shakespeare poem to myself; and it had so great an effect on me that after the finale I fled trembling to a room at the back of the theatre, where Ernst found me a few moments later in floods of tears. 'Ah nerves,' he said. 'I know all about it.' And he took my head on his shoulder and let me cry

like a hysterical girl for fully a quarter of an hour. Try to imagine a bourgeois from the rue Saint-Denis or a director of the Opéra (Paris, of course) witnessing such an attack. What could they possibly understand of the storm raging in the composer's heart; of his vague but potent memories of childhood and early loves and the blue Italian sky, in imagination, revived and flowing again in the glow of Shakespeare's genius; of the vision of a Juliet ever dreamed of, ever sought, never attained; of the revelation of unbounded love, infinite grief; and of his joy that his music had caught a few far-off echoes of that starry poetry of the spheres? The mind boggles at it. One can only dimly picture them, mouths agape and eyes popping with astonishment. But the first bourgeois would be sure to say, 'The man's sick – send for a glass of sugar and water'; and the second, 'Pure affectation! I shall have to put him in the *Charivari* [the Parisian satirical newspaper]'. [BM:534–5]

These later concerts, and his engaging personality, ensured that Ernst's visit was eventually viewed as a triumph. The correspondent of *Der Spiegel* concludes:

[Gradually], Ernst captivated the local public absolutely, not only as an artist but also as a human being, with his charming modesty, willingness, and kindness, to appear with his talent as assisting genius and saving angel to all the unfortunate as well as fortunate concert-givers. He is now totally popular in Petersburg, and the pole around which all musical interest and every conversation about art revolve. He could continue giving concerts until the summer, and they would all be sold out. He is truly a great artist. [EOC:20]

Although they had performed together in Brussels and Vienna, it seems to have been this Russian tour that set the seal on Berlioz's admiration for Ernst:

Let me reiterate, Ernst, who is a great musician as well as a great violinist (as well as being the most delightfully humorous man I know) is the complete, rounded artist, profoundly and predominantly expressive in everything he does, yet never neglectful of the craft, the discipline of music. He has that rare nature by which an artist combines a powerful imagination and the ability to realize his imaginative ideas unhesitatingly. He is a progressive musician and exploits all the modern resources of the art. He uses his violin to discourse poetry in the language of music, of which language he is a complete master. [BM:538]

The virtue which most impressed Berlioz was Ernst's command of rhythm. A number of writers felt that Ernst almost abandoned the rhythmic pulse in his performances. Haweis is typical:

Ernst, certainly the most Romantic player we have had since Paganini, possessed the same marvellous quality of perturbing almost everything he played until it became absolutely nothing but a melodic expression of his own wild mood. Those who remember the way in which he was wont to play one of his great solos on Hungarian airs, with orchestral accompaniments, will remember the profound meditation, almost coma, into which he seemed to fall in the middle of one of those slow and measured melodies – losing the sense of time and rhythm – allowing, as it were, his own soul to float out upon the waves of melody, which swelled and shook with sensitive thrills, holding the audience breathless, until, in the utter silence of the room, it was impossible to tell when the notes actually ceased to vibrate. [MAM:104]

Better informed authorities like Berlioz disagreed, and felt that Ernst achieved freedom *within* the fundamental pulse of a piece:

> Chopin chafed under the restraint of time, and to my mind pushed rhythmic freedom much too far. Ernst can take liberties with the beat when artistic reasons, in particular the expression of passionate feelings demand it, but he is essentially a rhythmic player, there is steadfastness in the heart of his most daring fancies. Chopin could simply not play in strict time: Ernst is capable of abandoning strict time, but only that the underlying pulse may be felt all the more strongly when he returns to it. One only needs to hear him play Beethoven's quartets to appreciate this quality in his playing. [BM:537]

This view finds support in Chorley's obituary notice:

> The secret, however, of Ernst's success ... lay in his expressive power and accent. There has been nothing to exceed these as exhibited by him on his best days. The passion was carried to its utmost point but never 'torn to tatters,' – the freest use of *tempo rubato* permitted, but always within the limits of the most just regulation. This is an excellence granted to few, – *measured* abandonment (if such a term may be employed) being one of the rarest graces in Art. ... Ernst possessed it in the highest degree. We recall ... certain readings (as those of Beethoven's second Razumouffsky Quartett, and of the Cavatina in his posthumous Quartett in B[♭] major ...) which 'stand out,' after their kind, as distinct and superior as anything to be cited in our not too long list of first class musical treasures. There is nothing of the exaggeration which the death of a great man is too apt to awake in the above praise ... [A:21/10/65:541]

By April, Vieuxtemps had gone on tour to Paris [V:33], and Ernst, in one of his characteristically touching gestures, erased any thought of ill-feeling or competition by including a performance of Vieuxtemps's *Romance* in his final concert. Having Ernst and Vieuxtemps side by side for an extended period meant that the performances of both men could be studied closely and compared. The most detailed and discerning appreciation appeared in the *Algemeine Musikalische Zeitung*:

> Ernst followed Vieuxtemps. He gave six concerts which aroused such enthusiasm that many of the audience waited for him at the exit after the concert and then accompanied him as far as the road, clapping and throwing flowers as they went. Both Vieuxtemps and Ernst are great and extraordinary virtuosos, and yet both in their performances and intentions they are substantially different. Vieuxtemps possesses an exceedingly happy physical organization and has everything which can be achieved by a strong will and assiduous study and has made it his own to such a degree that he can stand as an example of technical perfection. There has perhaps never been a staccato such as his, he only toys with it and it is not heard often enough. Even his intonation, which is always perfect even when faced with the most intricate difficulties, earns the most vivid praise. His compositions bear witness to able theoretic science, exact knowledge of the effect of instruments, educated taste, serious intentions and the emulation of classical examples. Such assets are ample to justify completely his great reputation. If he ever lacks that inner warmth, which flares upwards as enthusiasm in artistic performance, as if from the heart, and also seizes the heart of the listener, then he shouldn't be reproached, for it is a gift from heaven and cannot be gained through study.
>
> Ernst, on the other hand, does not have the faultlessness which can only come about through strict training. His intonation is not always perfectly pure despite his enormous

technical ability. He lets himself be led astray by his capricious fantasy and to take on difficulties which overstep the narrow boundaries of the violin or get close to the dangerous point where barely one in ten attempts succeed. Then it depends on his mood, whilst Vieuxtemps achieves the same effect every time without fail. All of these, however, are drawbacks which can only be found in true genius. And Ernst is such a genius, who has the warmth of feeling, enthusiasm and originality to a great extent which no amount of studying but nature alone can give. It is indisputable that he has devoted serious study to his art in all directions, this, however may have been tempered by a spiritual leaning, and has therefore protected his virtuosity from that cold unbalanced perfection, which, because it reminds one of an artistic machine, brings forth amazement but can never capture one's heart. Ernst, on the other hand, brings about the deepest most sustained effect through his noble, wonderful tone, and deeply felt, masterful phrasing in pieces like his richly lyrical *Pirate* fantasy; his *Elégie*, which, probably because of its connection with the melancholy nature of Russian national music has been particularly popular here and was demanded in every concert; or his richly spiritual, graceful *Carnival of Venice*. Vieuxtemps is a virtuoso and composer par excellence, Ernst, however, is an artist *par la grâce de Dieu.* [AMZ:6/47:Col.432–3]

In the summer of 1847, Ernst played again in Berlin (where he seems to have met Hans Christian Andersen [HCA. BC]); in September, he was in Cologne; in the autumn, instead of going to Vienna as expected, he went first to Stockholm then to Copenhagen. He played two concerts at the Theatre-Royal, and a further concert was organized at the palace. King Christian VIII, who was mortally ill, insisted on lying on a sofa in a small room next to the hall so he could hear the performance, and, during the concert, Ernst was invited through three times to receive the King's congratulations. [SMW:9/47:310; 11/47:327. AWMZ:24/11/47:810. RGM:28/11/47:39. E:119] A further pleasure of the visit, was re-establishing contact with Reinecke, who recalls:

Once again I ran into Ernst in Copenhagen, and again he devoted himself to advancing me as often as he could. This was in 1847, and in the meantime I had become Court pianist to the King of Denmark, but nevertheless the reflection from the glory of Ernst's fame was of great use to me. So he forthwith offered his assistance at the musical evenings I had originated, and on 4th December 1847, he played with me a piano quartet of my own (it appeared later as Op.34), and once more Beethoven's Kreutzer Sonata, while on 5th January, 1848, he adorned my soirée with the performance of Beethoven's C major string Quartet, Op.59. (The names of the other performers were Francke, v. Königslöw, and Sahlgreen.) [HFPV:55]

Ernst had also rehearsed Beethoven's late quartets with the same group of players, but the surviving fragment of a letter indicates that Ernst felt prospective audiences would have trouble with such works, and that he himself did not find them unproblematic:

Only if the great Beethoven's last quartets are played and studied continuously for some time can one truly appreciate them. Now we play only these wonderful works three times a week. Excellent artists such as Königslöw, Holm and Schlagren [*sic*] play with me. They are inspired by the greatness and beauty of our great immortal German master's work. If one or another of these great quartets by Beethoven is heard in Soirées before a large mixed public from time to time, people would be too surprised by it. This music so greatly surpasses all other works in this genre that in such a case either our mind or our heart is attracted momentarily. It is not a total pleasure. [NMZ:14/3/46:132; trans. E:120]

Reinecke continues by quoting a letter from Ernst whose full comprehension requires knowledge of three facts: Reinecke was not a *Kapellmeister*; Ernst was acquainted with several pieces by Reinecke, all in E♭; and Ernst's letter was blotted with snuff rather than the usual sand:

> 'Seiner Wohlgeboren dem Herrn Capellmeister Carl Reinecke (In E flat) in the capital of Denmark.
> Bless you, my dear friend! I am very sorry that we cannot dine together to-day, and still sorrier that your illness should be the cause. I will execute your commission. I enclose the Italian songs by Kullak and Eckert: They seem to me very charming and effective. But look at them and bring them back with you. We are perhaps to play them at Court to-night. Adieu. Receive the assurance of my great esteem and devoted friendship. When I assure you of this it is certainly Ernst (earnest). Copenhagen, Dec.20th 1847.'
>
> The Court concert mentioned in this letter really took place, and moreover we played the above-mentioned Fantasie by Kullak and Eckert, but I confess that I played my good friend Ernst a terrible trick on that same evening. And this is how it came about. At that time a certain tune was running riot in Copenhagen, a remarkably lively polka, the authorship of which was ascribed to Princess F., who was a very ugly old lady. This polka amused Ernst so much that he could not hear enough of it, and played it to everyone, on the violin and on the piano, and whistled and sang it everywhere he went. Now in the midst of that Court concert, when Ernst was playing his inevitable 'Carnival of Venice,' and I was accompanying him, a sudden freak seized him, and he proceeded to introduce Mozart's 'Non più andrai farfallone amoroso,' Mendelssohn's 'Auf Flügeln des Gesanges,' the *Freischütz* waltz, and every other imaginable tune one after the other, coming back every time to the chief motif of the 'Carnival', while I had to reel off the monotonous accompaniment, (consisting of only two chords) by the yard. Then there came to me the wicked idea of amusing myself on my own account, so I began to play Princess F.'s celebrated polka with my left hand. Now, Princess F. was sitting directly opposite Ernst. Suppressing his laughter with difficulty, he cast beseeching glances at me, but I pretended not to see, and hammered away unmercifully at my polka with the left hand, while the right continued the proper accompaniment. Afterwards his anger vanished in a hearty laugh, for he had a keen sense of humour, and even a liking for childish jokes. [HFPV:55]

Besides quartet performances, Ernst gave four public concerts (the last on 3 January 1848). As a direct result of his success in Copenhagen, Christian VIII decided to confer the Knights Cross of the Danish Flag on Ernst, but died before he could present it. Thus on 13 February, at a special private reception, the new King, Friedrich VII, presented the medal to the violinist on behalf of his father. [SMW:1/48:27; 3/48:80. AMZ: 22/3/48:Col.207. E:120–21]

In late February 1848, revolution broke out in Paris. Its reverberations were felt throughout Europe and they severely disrupted concert life. Ernst probably spent February and March in Denmark, waiting for the immediate crisis to blow over, and when he arrived in Hamburg in April to play two concerts on the 26th and 28th, he had been expected for four months. The theatre, unsurprisingly, was not full, but the expressive way he played his concerto was widely appreciated, even though he was clearly ill and his technique did not always seem completely at his command. [SMW:4/48:131; 5/48:158. AWMZ:11/5/48:227. E:121–2] Increasingly desperate for peace and quiet, he decided to stay with his family in Brünn, and travelled there by way of Leipzig. By July, he was feeling better, and on the 2nd of that month gave what he described as a 'successful and brilliant' concert which raised 300 florins for the unemployed of his home town. [NMZ:8/8/48:64]

His next year is best summarized by two paragraphs of a letter he wrote to Berlioz from London on 5 May 1849, evidently his first communication since their meeting in Russia in the spring of 1847:

> I don't have many things to tell you on my own account. Since we met in St Petersburg, I've been condemned, firstly by my poor health, and secondly by the political events which have stunned all of Europe, to complete inactivity.
>
> I've just spent nearly an entire year at my brother's house in Brünn. You understand that, [being] close to Vienna, the theatre of continual and also terrible catastrophes, my stay could not have been the most agreeable. I went – and that's all. My only pleasure was to find myself with my family, my only satisfaction the idea that I was some comfort to them. [AC]

The revolution and counter-revolution in Vienna had indeed been particularly bloody and painful. In October 1848, the war minister, Latour, was lynched after trying to send troops against the Hungarians, and the city was taken over by revolutionaries. The Court withdrew to Olmütz, and the two Austrian field commanders, Windischgrätz and Jellačić, moved against the capital. Windischgrätz laid siege, and on the fifth day he broke through and began his retribution. [VLR:196–7] Nine people, including the composer and writer Alfred Becher, were shot immediately; a further twenty-five were hanged in the next year of martial law, and about two and a half thousand people were arrested. However, this overlooks the huge numbers of ordinary people who died during the troubles. Their deaths are generally unrecorded, but one eyewitness reports that Jellačić's troops managed to kill fifty-seven people while conducting a house-to-house search of a single street. [VLR:198]

Like Chopin, Hallé, and many others, Ernst decided that the only major European country where a profit might be still be made from music was England which was unaffected by revolution. He left Brünn in early March 1849 and headed initially for Leipzig where he took part in a quartet concert with Joachim and David on 7 March. Four days later, he played in a concert in the Gewandhaus and gave the Leipzig premiere of his two new compositions – the concerto and *Hungarian Airs*. Moscheles was in the audience and found the experience slightly painful: 'Ernst gave a Matinée which, I grieve to say, was poorly attended. He looked wretchedly ill, but played with great energy and passionate feeling ...' [LM:II:202] The concerto was performed again on 15 March, along with a new symphony in E by Ferdinand Hiller which made a considerable impression on both Ernst and Moscheles. During the concerto, cognoscenti in the audience were awed by the rapid passages in thirds, octaves, and double harmonics – the last of these must have been improvised by Ernst, as no such notes are found in the published score. Ernst's cantilena was considered exquisite, but the great heat in the hall made it difficult to keep the upper register of the violin in tune. [RGM:25/3/49:96. SMW:3/49:110, 130. NMZ:5/4/49:156; 12/4/49:168. E:122–3]

Weimar was his next port of call, and on the day of his last concert in Leipzig, Ernst wrote to H.-A. Chélard, director of the Weimar theatre:

> Dear Friend, I've just received your friendly letter and hurry to reply that, at the concert in question, I intend to play a new Allegro de Concert, and some variations on Hungarian themes composed by myself, if these pieces don't upset the programme you've sketched for the occasion. I don't need to tell you how happy and enchanted I'd be to play some duos with the admirable Liszt, and I'd prefer the grand sonata by Beethoven, or at least two movements from this masterpiece. I also have a duo on Italian themes of great effectiveness composed by Kullack [sic] and Eckert. Moreover, I shall be in Weimar at about nine o'clock tomorrow night, so I think there will be all the time necessary to arrange the final programme. Please present my respects to M. Ziegesar [intendant of the theatre], and tell him that I had the honour to receive his letter, that I thank him for having moved the concert two days earlier, and that I will bring some pieces for violin and piano, whatever Liszt wants.
> I'll see you soon, in the meanwhile please accept my best wishes, H.W. Ernst. [PM:MLT E71.C516]

Ernst's journey to Weimar, and the small lunch party which followed, were recalled many years later by Reinecke:

> In 1848 [actually 1849] I was living in Leipzig. One day Ernst, who on the violin was not unlike Liszt on the piano, and who had been staying in Leipzig for some time, invited me to accompany him to Weimar, to pay a visit to Liszt. That I was overjoyed to be able to make the Master's acquaintance goes without saying. We got to Weimar at about midday and hastened to the Altenburg [Liszt's house]. .... Liszt welcomed Ernst most warmly, and me, the latter's protégé, with the heartwarming kindness so characteristic of him. The meal to which we were invited was not Lucullan, but it was a very good one .... When [Liszt offered us a glass of liqueur brandy] Ernst declined on my behalf with the words, 'Reinecke is a puritan who drinks nothing strong,' Liszt said: '*Enfin*, my dear Reinecke, you are quite right; I intend to give it up too.' All the same, he then took his coffee with a dash of cognac in it. [PL:250–51]

Liszt conducted Ernst's concert and wrote a report of it to Franz Kroll on 26 March 1849:

> Ernst has just been spending a week here, during which he played some hundred rubbers of whist at the Erbprinz [Hotel]. He is a noble, sweet, and delicate nature ... Last Monday, he was good enough to play, in his usual admirable manner, at the concert for the orchestral pension fund. The pieces he had selected were his new Concerto pathétique (in F-sharp minor) and an extremely piquant and brilliant caprice on Hungarian Melodies. (The latter piece dedicated to me.) The public was in good humour, even really warm... [LOFL: I:65–6]

In 1908, Arthur Abell recalled speaking to an old man who heard Liszt and Ernst play the *Kreutzer Sonata* together at this concert, and reported that 'the impression of Ernst's passionate playing was indelibly marked in his memory'. [FVP:5]

Liszt responded to Ernst's dedication of *Hungarian Airs* by dedicating his *9th Hungarian Rhapsody*, entitled *Carnival in Pesth*, to the violinist in April 1853. [FLUP:143] This was a highly appropriate gift for someone who had probably been inspired to write *Hungarian Airs* by a three-month stay with his family in Pesth, and who was most famous for writing the *Carnival of Venice*. Liszt's response to Ernst's *Concerto Pathétique* was far more deeply involved with his own creative process.

The late 1840s was a period when there was much debate about the future of form – particularly of sonata form, and the three- or four-movement form of conventional sonatas and symphonies. Schumann, for example, after criticizing the four connected movements of Moscheles' *Concerto fantastique*, wrote:

> Still, there is a lack of smaller concert pieces, in which the virtuoso can give us, at the same time, his performance of an allegro, adagio and rondo. It would be well to invent a new one, to consist of one great movement in moderate tempo, within which form the preparatory passage might take the place of a first allegro, the cantabile that of an adagio, and a brilliant close might replace a rondo. Perhaps this idea might suggest something which we would gladly see embodied in a peculiar original composition. The movement might well be written for pianoforte alone. [NZM:8/4/36:123]

We can see that Ernst's concerto exactly fits the kind of form Schumann has in mind; in fact, he may well have responded to Schumann's challenge. However, it was after conducting Ernst's concerto that Liszt too began to experiment with large-scale one-movement sonata forms, and fulfilled the prophecy of Schumann's last sentence.

The first major piano work Liszt wrote after hearing Ernst's concerto was the *Grosses Konzertsolo* probably written in 1849–50 for a Paris Conservatoire competition in 1850. (It was unlikely to have been used. Even the dedicatee, Adolf Henselt, said he found the piece too difficult. [NLE:V:X]). This was Liszt's first attempt at a one-movement sonata structure, and there are good reasons for supposing that its form was influenced by Ernst's *Concerto Pathétique*. Its opening theme – with its anacrusis, descending thirds, minor key, dots, grace notes and rhetorical triplets – is recognisably in the same language as Ernst's opening theme (exx. 14.1 and 14.2):

Example 14.1   Ernst, Concerto, op.23, bars 1–9

Example 14.2   Liszt, *Grosses Konzertsolo*, bars 1–6

In addition, the *Konzertsolo* like the concerto ends with a *grandioso* transformation of the shy second subject (bars 35–44, 371–390), and there is even a reminiscence of the solo violin when Liszt writes the extraordinary instruction 'vibrato' over bar 105. But perhaps the most telling piece of evidence in favour of Ernst's influence is that when Liszt arranged the *Konzertsolo* for two pianos in 1856, he called it *Concerto Pathétique* – the very title by which he referred to Ernst's concerto.[1] At a later period, Liszt even attempted to turn his *Concerto Pathétique* into a proper concerto for piano and orchestra, returning the work even closer to the source of its inspiration.

Liszt finished his own piano sonata in B minor, one of his very greatest works, on 2 February 1853, having begun work on it three or four months before [FLWY:150]. All authorities are agreed that the *Konzertsolo* is the immediate forerunner of this work. The *Konzertsolo* uses the same virtuoso language, the same extended one-movement form, and even shares a main theme. Consequently, there are good grounds for thinking that that Ernst's concerto had a strong indirect influence on Liszt's sonata.

Like the sonata, Ernst's concerto is based on four important themes, and, as I have already shown, there is some primitive use of thematic transformation. It is also worth noting that the concerto and the sonata share the same ambiguity of form. Ernst's concerto has been thought of both as a three-movement work, and as a single-movement work in sonata form. In the same way, Liszt's sonata can either be thought of as a three- or four-movement work compressed into one, or as a single sonata-form movement consisting of exposition, development, recapitulation and coda. [LBS:32]

---

[1] Ernst was not the first composer to write a *Concerto Pathétique*. Moscheles, for instance, had written a well-known exampple, his concerto no.7 op.93, in 1835–36.

The influence of a now obscure virtuoso concerto on one of Liszt's major piano works may now seem surprising, but it becomes less so when we consider the impact of Alkan's *Grande Sonate: Les Quatres Ages* on the B minor sonata. There was virtually no response to the appearance of Alkan's sonata because it was published in 1848 and all but obliterated by the revolution. Thereafter, it languished in complete obscurity until the Alkan revival of the 1960s. However, Liszt clearly saw a copy, and it left its imprint on his sonata. The second movement, 'Quasi Faust' involves a similar repeated note figure after bare octaves (Alkan, bars 2–4; Liszt, 13–15), and the transformation of this figure into a cantabile melody (Alkan, bars 56–64; Liszt, 153–159). Alkan also imports, in more explicit form, the Faustian struggle between God and the Devil which commentators have often found in Liszt's work (after all, the sonata's second theme is also found in Liszt's own *Faust Symphony*).

Huge numbers of sonatas were written in the 1840s, but they tended to be dully academic, and talented composers steered away from the form. As Schumann had complained, 'It is remarkable that those who write sonatas are generally unknown men; and it is also strange that the older composers, ... who grew up in the springtime of the sonata, ... cultivate the form least.' [LBS:8] Such innovation as there was, tended to be found amongst works of extreme technical difficulty (as if pushing back one kind of limit made it natural to push back others). It is therefore quite understandable that Liszt should find his formal and thematic as well as technical inspiration in two virtuoso works.

Indeed, the interplay between the solo sonata and the concerto – the most obviously virtuoso of all the conventional forms – in the decades between 1830 and 1860 is very striking. Schumann originally called his second piano sonata in F minor, op.14, *Concerto Without Orchestra*; and Alkan would go on to publish a *Concerto for Solo Piano*, op.39, nos.8, 9 and 10, in 1857. Perhaps these compositions were partly inspired by the *Kreutzer Sonata* – recently played by Ernst and Liszt – which Beethoven himself described as 'scritta in uno stilo molto concertante quasi come d'un Concerto'.

The form of Alkan's sonata (four movements which get gradually slower) has little to recommend it, and appears to have had no impact on the form of Liszt's work. But, given Schumann's speculations about one-movement form, Liszt may well have found that Ernst's concerto offered just the stimulus he needed. If so, then Ernst made a considerable contribution to the Music of the Future, and thus a considerable contribution to the history of music in the late nineteenth century.

I   Ernst's Birthplace: 58 Der Grosse Kröna, Brünn

II   The courtyard of Ernst's school, the Augustinian Monastery in Brünn

III   The young Ernst in Vienna in 1827; a lithograph by Eduard Teltsher

IV   *Duo de Violon et Piano*, a drawing by Eugène Delacroix. This is now thought to represent Ernst and Chopin rehearsing for their concert on 26 April 1841. [DFC:101]

V   The leading violinists of Paris, together with the elderly Pierre Baillot, c.1841–42; a lithograph by Nicholas Maurin. Ernst's image is based on Kriehuber's lithograph printed in Vienna is 1840

VI   Kriehuber's third portrait of Ernst, Vienna, 1846

VII   Prinzhofer's lithograph of Ernst, Vienna, 1846

VIII   *Ein Matinée bei Liszt* [A Morning at Liszt's]; a lithograph by Kriehuber, Vienna, 1846. From left to right, the sitters are: Kriehuber himself, Berlioz, Czerny, Liszt and Ernst

IX A drawing of Ernst by J.-J.-B. Laurens, Montpelier, 24 February 1853, and signed by the violinist. Illness has already given a strange cast to his face

X A photograph of Ernst taken by L. Angerer, Vienna, probably in late 1854

XI   Ernst's wife, the actress Amélie-Siona Lévy taken by Mr Kilburn, Regent Street, London, probably on her first visit to England in 1854

XII   Another portrait by Angerer of Vienna. Ernst and his wife may well be on their honeymoon in late 1854

XIII This murky image from the mid-1850s is the only known photograph of Ernst playing (or at least posing with his instrument in a playing position)

XIV A photograph of Ernst, probably taken in London in 1864, which shows the ravages of illness all too clearly

XV   A photograph from Moser's biography of Joachim, allegedly showing the quartet of the London Beethoven Quartet Society in 1859. Piatti and Joachim have signed their names; the others are written in by another hand

XVI The same photograph as it appears in Amely Heller's book on Ernst headed, 'The last quartet with Ernst in London'. '1854' should be 1864, and 'Chapelle' should be Chappell

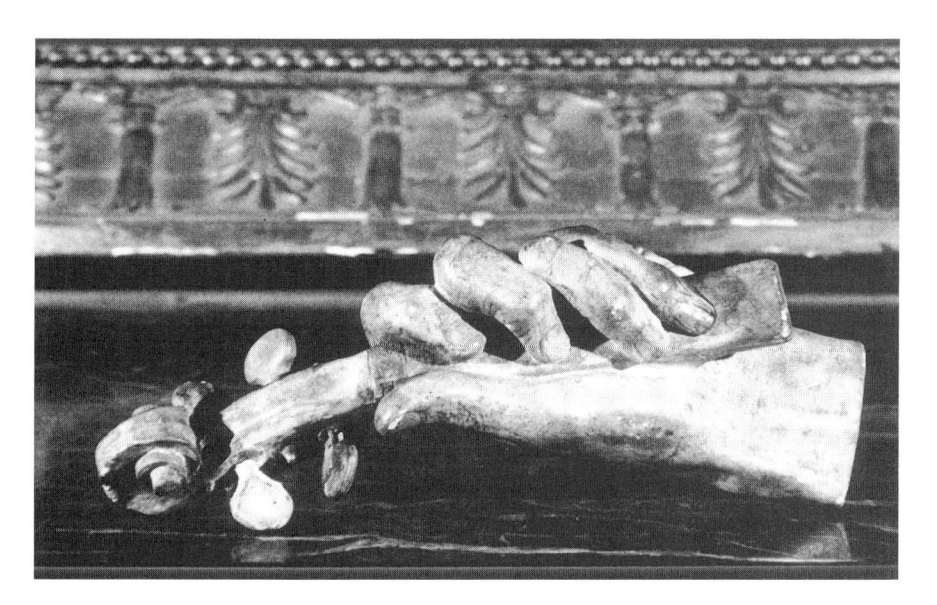

XVII One of two sculptures of Ernst's left hand made by his wife in the 1860s

XVIII The rue St François de Paule in Nice. The apartment where Ernst died is on the second floor of the last building before the right-hand corner

XIX   Ernst's grave (the third on the right) in the Castle Cemetery in Nice

XX   The bronze relief, made by his wife, on Ernst's grave

PART III
Later Tours

Chapter 15

The Elite and the Popular: 1849

From his student years in Vienna, Ernst had taken part in private performances of chamber music, and during the 1840s, he had occasionally given quartet performances at large public concerts. In London in 1849, the musical atmosphere was peculiarly favourable to the kind of chamber music that most interested him. First, there was serious interest in Mendelssohn and the late quartets of Beethoven. Second, since Ernst's last visit in 1844, two institutions had been created specifically to further the appreciation of good chamber music. The earlier to be established was the Musical Union, which I shall discuss in this chapter; the later was the Beethoven Quartet Society, which I shall discuss in the next.

For many decades, the Musical Union was the most important chamber music society in London, whose concerts, held on weekday afternoons, ran from 1845 to 1881. For thirty-six of these thirty-seven years, the society was directed by its founder, John Ella. The idea which gained him eminence was re-emphasizing in the public mind the connection between chamber music and social distinction, and he accordingly arranged a series of subscription concerts with a committee of aristocrats. It is unclear if this committee – which included, at various times, Prince Albert, the Duke of Leinster and the Duke of Cambridge – ever met, but all its members allowed their names to appear at the head of the programme, and some of them attended the concerts. This lent the Union immense social prestige, and naturally attracted members of the upper-middle classes. Next to aristocracy, Ella's greatest love was for foreign musical lions, and he was prepared to pay extravagant prices to secure their services. The reverse side of this passion was his dislike of native-born musicians, and it was said that no British pianist ever played at the Union. [JEMU:193–214]

The chamber concerts at which Ernst, Mendelssohn and Joachim played in 1844 (Ella's predilection for foreign artists is already evident), were a rehearsal for the society's inauguration, and the first official concert was given on 11 March 1845 in Blagrove's small concert hall in Mortimer Street. [JEMU:196] The Union's social prestige proved a great draw, however, and the following year it moved to the larger Willis's Rooms in St James's. [JEMU:199]

Although Ella's worship of aristocracy and artistic prestige were widely regarded as comic, he had many virtues and was a powerful educative force. He insisted on proper rehearsals for all concerts no matter how familiar the performers were with their music and each other, and he tended to use the same leading London players for the lower parts of quartets to ensure continuity. Above all, he insisted on a new standard of behaviour from audiences. Seated on his podium, he would clap his hands to signal the beginning of the concert, and those wanting to enter or leave during the concerts were expected to wait for breaks between pieces or movements. No talking was permitted during a performance and at the top of all programmes was printed: 'The greatest homage to music is silence.' Copies of the programme – containing extensive analytic notes and examples – were sent to subscribers in advance, and they would be presented with a second edition, and sometimes a supplement, at the door. Above the notes was printed another motto, from Pierre Baillot: 'It is not enough that the artist should be well prepared for the public, the public must also be well prepared for what he is going to hear.' [EO:215]

The Musical Union normally held eight matinées in a season plus a concert for the director's benefit. In 1849, Ernst played at the third, fifth and sixth concerts. In the first of these, on 1 May, he played, together with Deloffre, Hill and Piatti, Mendelssohn's quartet in E♭, op.44, No.3, and Beethoven's quartet in E minor, op. 59, No.2; and, with Hallé at the piano, Beethoven's G major violin sonata op.96. The *Illustrated London News* described this as 'one of the greatest musical treats ever experienced': 'The wondrous power of Ernst was never heard in greater perfection – the poetry of his style, and the impassioned sentiment he infused into the subjects, raised the enthusiasm of the amateurs [that is, the audience] to the highest pitch. … The scherzo of the Mendelssohn quatuor was encored with enthusiasm …' [ILN:5/5/49:290]

In the fifth concert, the programme was Haydn's quartet in G, No.81, Mendelssohn's trio in D Minor, op.49 (again with Hallé), and Beethoven's quartet in C, op.59, No.3. Ernst's playing in the Mendelssohn and Beethoven was particularly admired:

> In the Razoumoffsky quartets, the grandest and most perfect specimens of Beethoven's chamber music, Ernst stands almost alone. His breadth of style, variety of tone, and energetic boldness of execution, are peculiarly suited to this intellectual kind of music, which demands the most refined and delicate appreciation, no less than the utmost command and mechanical resource.
>
> In the C major quartet Ernst had opportunities of demonstrating this excellence in very opposite styles; the andante in A minor, a movement which has hardly been surpassed in romantic beauty, and the finale, which contains the celebrated *fugato*, the basis of the entire movement, were equally effective in his hands, the former for the poetical expression which he gave to the *cantabile*, and the latter for its sustained vigour and animation, a perfect command of light and shade being preserved amidst the most rapid execution. [MW:2/6/49:341]

The sixth concert was more ambitious. After Mozart's D minor quartet K.421, and Beethoven's early G major trio, op.1, No.2, Ernst led the first performance at the Union of Beethoven's late quartet in B♭, op.130. Ella had been nervous about its reception, but with Ernst leading the quartet he need not have worried:

> Of all modern violinists, Ernst is the one most deeply versed in the compositions of the great masters who have devoted their genius and talents to the higher forms of chamber music. German by birth [*sic*], and German by feeling, he enters into the spirit of these masterpieces with real German enthusiasm. … The result was a performance really magnificent. The audience at once showed that they were quite able to understand the beauties with which the B flat quartet is crowded, applauded every movement warmly, and encored the fantastic presto in B flat minor, which Ernst played quicker than we

have ever heard it played before, justifying his reading by the effect produced. But it was in the adagio in E flat, styled 'cavatina' by Beethoven, with whom the movement was an especial favourite, that the sympathetic tone and impassioned expression of Ernst had amplest room for development. We have rarely listened to a performance more unaffectedly beautiful. [MW:9/6/49:375–6]

For the last concert of the series, the matinée for the benefit of the director on 26 June, Ernst and Piatti (together with the pianist Mortier de Fontaine) returned to the lower slopes of Hummel's *Trio Concertante*.

Meanwhile, Ernst's old friends continued to think of him. Berlioz wrote to Morris Barnett on 28 April 1849: 'I heard that Ernst is in London, do you know him? If you see him, send him my best wishes. He's one of the artists whom I love the most, and with whose talent I am most *sympathetique*.' [CGB:III:628] Barnett may well have been one of the people who passed on Berlioz's good wishes, prompting Ernst to write to the French composer on 5 May. This letter usefully summarizes many of his solo activities since arriving in London:

> It's nearly two months ago now that I left [my family in Brünn]. In coming here, I stayed for eight days in Weimar, where I spent almost the whole time with the admirable Liszt. We often spoke of you, as two old friends talking of a good friend.
>
> I spent about eight days at Düsseldorf, where Hiller is, and had occasion to hear his oratorio, The Destruction of Jerusalem. I found many beautiful things in it. He has just composed a symphony that I had the chance to hear in Leipzig, which is very beautiful throughout, but the first movement appeared to me a work of the very first rank.
>
> I've been here in London a month. I appeared for the first time at the Philharmonic Concerts with such brilliant success that, in spite of the swarm of artists and so-called artists with which London is plagued, I yet hope to complete my business. You know how things are done here. I am not, however, going to shrink from giving a concert at my own risk and expense. It's fixed for 4th June. Before then, I've got still other engagements in London and the provinces. I don't reckon to do enough to go to California [Californie], but enough nevertheless to make me spend some time at least in rosin [colophane]. If you have the time, the ability, and above all the good will to mention me in your journal, whatever you wish, do it. I don't need to tell you that you are doing me a service that I shall be most grateful for.
>
> If, by any chance, you intend to spend time in London, you can lodge very well with me, and I promise you in addition the best coffee in the world. Ask Allard [*sic*], he went into ecstasies over my coffee, and if he praises it, offer him a friendly greeting, if not, offer it to him all the same.
>
> If you see Heller, greet him from me, and say I'll make haste to write to him on the first occasion I'll be capable of making haste. Frank sends his greetings, and I'd be pleased if you'd send me your news. With best wishes, H.W. Ernst. [AC]

The letter found Berlioz at a low moment. Music in Paris was still in the doldrums after the previous year's revolution and only someone of Meyerbeer's wealth and influence could stage a lavish and decently rehearsed production of his work. In addition, Berlioz's first wife, Harriet, was nearing the end of her life, and began to suffer from a series of minor strokes. Berlioz, as well as supporting his mistress Marie and his son Louis, had now to pay Harriet's rent and the care of two full-time maids, and this placed him under severe financial as well as emotional strain. Accordingly, composition had to take second place to the much more lucrative criticism and, while struggling to complete the *Te Deum*, he felt compelled to produce article after article largely detailing performances of dismal operas. [BSG:428–42] At least he could be sure that the infinitely sympathetic Ernst would understand all about bile, spleen and boredom:

> Dear Ernst, I thank you for your letter; I was impatient to hear from you. You are not dead. Good! I am sick to death of ennui, and disgust with Paris and all the intrigues therein; I am as savage as a bear with a sore head, I want to go away and I cannot stir, I have articles to write – ah! The plagues of Egypt are nothing in comparison with that. … What weather! It rained yesterday enough to wash the houses away. Today it is almost cold. I have a headache. Damn the article; I will not begin it; I have shrunk from it for a week, and I have not the shadow of an idea about the subject I am to write upon. What a career! Where can I find the sun and some leisure? Where can I be free to think of nothing, to sleep, to hear no more pianoforte playing, to hear no mention of [Meyerbeer's] *Prophète*, the elections, Rome, M. Proudhon, to watch the world tumbling to pieces through the smoke of my cigar, to be as stupid as eighteen deputies. …
>
> I am going out. I am going to be dull outside. I am too dull at home. Come to Paris for a while.
>
> P.S. – I have a pain in my stomach, another thing I forgot to tell you. Ah, my dear Ernst, pity me. These articles will kill me. [8 May 1849. LB:II:395–6. See also CGB: III:632–3]

Liszt was in a better mood, but still had troubles of his own. The most pressing of these was Richard Wagner who had taken part in the Dresden uprising of 1848 and was now wanted by the authorities. Liszt sheltered him for a day or two, before sending him on his way to Paris. He then began a tireless campaign to get Wagner's work staged and appreciated, and his letter to Ernst of 30 May 1849 forms part of it:

> Dear Friend, Weimar has not forgotten you, and I hope soon to be able, after the return of the Hereditary Prince whom we expect for the day of his *fête*, by 24th May at the very latest, to forward to you the token of the distinguished remembrance in which you are held. It pleases me to think it will be agreeable to you, and that it will tend to attach you more in future to people who worthily appreciate you. I should have liked to tell you sooner of this, but the inevitable delays in present circumstances postpone more than one wish.
>
> After the deplorable days in Dresden[,] Wagner came here, and only departed again to escape the warrant (*lettre de cachet*) with which the Saxon government is pursuing him. I hope that at the present moment he will have arrived safe and well in Paris, where his career as dramatic composer cannot fail to be hugely extended. He is a man of evident genius, who must of necessity force himself on the general admiration, and hold a high place in contemporary art. I regret that you have not had the opportunity of hearing his *Tannhäuser*, which is for me the most lyrical of dramas, the most remarkable, the most harmonious, the most complete, the most original and *selbstwürdig* (the most worthy of its country) both in foundation and form, that Germany has produced since Weber. Belloni has, I believe written to you on the subject of Wagner, to ask for information as to the actual state of the English Opera in London.

I have no doubt that if it were possible for Wagner to obtain from the directors a tour of performances in the course of the year for a new work (*Lohengrin*, the subject of which, being about the Knights of the Round Table who went to search for the Holy Grail, is most poetic) he would make a great sensation and large receipts by it. As soon as he tells me the news of his arrival in Paris, allow me to induce him to write to you direct if his plans not change in this matter. [LOFL:II:501–2]

Ernst's reply was not encouraging. He pointed out that there was no such institution as the English Opera. There were only two Italian companies, each of which had recently had its own financial troubles, and a German company that staged very mediocre productions. [BAL:I:118] Consequently, he could see little possibility of a performance of *Lohengrin*, and Liszt duly forwarded this news to Paris. [FLRW:686]

After several weeks in England, Ernst was feeling distinctly depressed:

My premonition about London was not mistaken. More than ever, music here is exploited in a manner that would make the most courageous and dignified artists despair.

I nonetheless gathered all my energy to give, after having played at the Philharmonic and some other concerts, a concert for myself; it took place on 4th June at the Hanover Square Rooms, and I only just managed to pay the expenses which rose to £120. People there made me repeat three of the five pieces I had announced. I was annihilated by fatigue, and the next day, I received the news of my brother's death [Nathan had died on 12 May]; you can well understand how much I had to suffer physically and morally from all these last emotions and fatigues, and even then, I am not even speaking to you about all the typically English annoyances and irritations which preceded my concert. Eventually, I went and announced at the end a second [concert] for 2nd July, that I will give with Hallé who is newly arrived in England. I hope it will be as good as the first [but] for which I don't have to pay the expenses. [7 June 1849. BAL:I:118]

Ernst's appearance at the Philharmonic – where he played his concerto and *Hungarian Airs* – had indeed been a brilliant success. Described as looking 'thinner and paler ("consequently, more interesting," the ladies will rejoin)' than when he last appeared in England in 1844, he was particularly complimented on his ability with octaves ('the rapid and tremendous passage of octaves near the end [of the concerto] ... was delivered with an aplomb, an energy, and a truth of intonation quite astonishing') and with harmonics ('his control over the manipulation of harmonics, and his unheard of capability in giving them accent and expression, were made plentifully manifest.') [MW: 21/4/49:241. *Morning Herald*: MW:28/4/49:263] 'The only drawback to an absolute perfection,' said the *Morning Advertiser*, 'is a slight tendency to sharpness in his intonation.' [MW:28/4/49:262]

Further appearances – in Manchester on 14 May, his own concert on 4 June, and at concerts given by Helen Stoepel on 28 June and Louis Jullien (from 1 June) – were equally successful. The event which shows an innovation, however, was on 2 July, when he and Hallé gave a 'Grand Evening Concert' at Hanover Square. As well as a smattering of his own pieces and, unusually, a Bach sonata for violin and keyboard, he gave his first performance of Mendelssohn's violin concerto:

> His reading of the Mendelssohn concerto was admirable throughout. He gave the first allegro much faster than we have been accustomed to hear it, and produced a fine effect by strongly contrasting the *traits de bravoure* and the *cantabile* phrases which so gracefully relieve them. The former he played with passionate impetuosity, the latter with a playful tenderness peculiarly his own. In the *cadenza* – marked *ad libitum* in the score – Ernst tripled the difficulties by introducing octaves and double notes, which, while preserving its character, materially added to its brilliancy. The slow movement was perfect, attaining the highest possible degree of expression, without a tinge of that exaggerated sentiment which, being essentially artificial, has nothing to do with nature. The sparkling and delicious *rondo*, a movement in Mendelssohn's happiest manner, was rendered with equal ability; the *staccato* passages were produced with delightful crispness, the phrasing coloured with the finest taste, and the whole finished and rounded off with the most consummate art. We have seldom listened to a concert more poetically beautiful or more thoroughly satisfactory as a display of executive skill. [MW: 21/4/49: 417–18]

Introducing a substantial contrast in speed and tone between the themes and the passagework was a nineteenth-century tendency which can still be heard in some of the recordings made early in the twentieth.

In England, Ernst sometimes found the same stiffness of manners he disliked in Berlin. He feared he may have committed a *faux pas* in his method of introducing himself to Lord Wilton, and in some distress asked Liszt's advice. [BAL:I:119–20] He found solace, however, in his developing relationship with the music critic Henry Chorley whom he had first met in 1844. 'I have not seen Chorley since I had your letter,' he wrote to Liszt, 'but I see him very often, we talk each time about you, and both of us want to see you with us. He is an excellent friend and a true *gentihomme*, I deliberately did not say gentleman because I am not in love with gentlemen, or those to whom the epithet is normally applied in this dear country.' [BAL:I:119]

More cheering news was soon in the post. Shortly after his first letter to Liszt, Ernst received the token from Weimar which the pianist had promised, the Order of the Red Eagle [BAL:I:120–21], and he would receive two further honours – Honorary Member of the Philharmonic Society at St Petersburg, and Honorary member of the Royal Academy of Arts in Stockholm – before he played at the Liverpool Festival on 27 and 30 August. [MW:4/8/49:48] At this point in the year he would normally go to Vienna for the winter season, but the bloodletting there now made this impossible. Feeling ill and exhausted after the English season [BAL:I:121], he therefore returned to France and wrote a letter to Davison reviewing his future plans:

> My Dear Friend, Here I am already 14 days in France. I spent the first 8 days in Paris. And the rest in the country in the home of old friends. It was only yesterday evening that I returned, and only this morning that I have your news, that's to say your official news in the Musical World which, certainly for me, is not worth a single word of our private conversations. I hope you don't delay for too long after receiving this letter to give a sign of life and to let me know about your present projects and those in the near future. I am definitely not planning to go to Germany. In a few days I will leave for a small excursion to Bolougne. Osborne has organized a concert there, which will be held on 26th of this month. After the concert, I plan to return here, to wait for the next London season to bring me back there, if, however, some acceptable arrangement doesn't call me there before that time …

... I am perfectly happy here, living the life of a simple soul, I don't worry about anything, and do nothing to touch my inheritance on the material side. First, it has always been my supreme happiness not to earn money with my intelligence, with my soul, or even with my fingers. This temporary insouciance will exercise a beneficial influence on my state of mind and also on my body. I'm doing infinitely better since I came here – my everyday pains have not returned since I left you. ... [16 September 1849. BL]

Davison was an exasperatingly bad correspondent, but on this occasion he seems to have responded fairly quickly. Ernst's next letter, on 23 September, shows that Davison had decided to spend some time with him in Paris after Ernst's concert on the 26th. [BL]

Their joint holiday cannot have lasted much beyond a few weeks because on 14 November Ernst was back in London playing at the fourth of the London Wednesday Evening concerts. Organized by a Mr Stammers, these were some of the most ambitious popular concerts ever staged in London. They took place in London's largest venue, the Exeter Hall which could hold 3,000 people, and were therefore extremely cheap – entrance could be obtained for as little as a shilling. In the 1848–49 season, more than 60,000 people were able to attend the series of twenty-seven concerts, and Ernst also appeared on 21 and 28 November, and 5, 12, 19 and 26 December. After a period of recuperation, it is clear that he was playing exceptionally well, and if his appearances at the Philharmonic and the Musical Union laid the foundation of his success amongst English connoisseurs, then it was these popular concerts which etched his name on the popular consciousness. The level of enthusiasm he provoked sometimes reached almost frightening intensity. On his fifth appearance at the concerts, he played his version of Mayseder's variations, with the impressive cadenza, as well as the inevitable *Carnival*. The *Musical World* reported:

> Ernst ... returned and bowed again and again; but this was not enough for the multitude – despotic as mobs are ever, despotic and inconsiderate. The hurricane continued, when Ernst had left the orchestra, with increasing vehemence, and was once more forced to return. Combined cries of 'the Carnival' and 'the cadence,' [i.e., cadenza] now rode upon the waves of the hurricane. The mob was divided. Ernst, however, obeyed the majority, and his own convenience – for really the cadenza, twice through in immediate succession was impossible – and played some variations on the 'Carnival.' ... The hall was crammed to suffocation; the heads of the audience waved about like a troubled sea. [MW: 8/12/49: 788–9]

Even though the crowd was frequently noisy, critics could still discern the quality of the performances:

> Ernst [is] the greatest living violinist ... [but his playing] depends very largely upon temperament, and hence is not always equally perfect: the assured certainty of intonation possessed by performers fathoms deep beneath him in excellence, is at moments wanting; but, when inspired by the *feu sacré* for legitimate power, silveriness of tone, depth of sentiment, elevation of taste, delicacy and facility of execution, grace, firmness and steadiness of bow, he is 'himself alone;' and those who had the good fortune to be present

at Exeter Hall last night gave expression to their feelings in irresistible shouts of applause, or murmurs of delight. [*Morning Post*: MW:17/11/49:727–8]

Some critics even felt that they could see the educative effect that the great artist was having on such a huge body of people. After the seventh concert, the critic of *The Times* wrote:

> The performances of this great violinist, no less intellectual than they are surprising, are tending to elevate the taste of the large numbers that flock to the Wednesday concerts. His influence is already beginning to be evident. The enthusiasm he excites on every occasion would seem to have weakened the *prestige* of the ballad style of music, and the encores, which, when indiscriminately awarded, have hitherto been an absolute plague at these entertainments, are apparently less frequent and are certainly less hearty and unanimous. The opposition at the present concert to some of the encores was strong, and in two or three instances successful. ... A very interesting feature of this concert was the celebrated *Septuor* in E flat by Beethoven, [led by Ernst] ... The whole of this fine work, with the exception of one of the slow movements and one of the minuets (there are two of each), was given, and the performance occupied about thirty-five minutes. This was testing the appreciation of the audience – and their patience some may add – with a vengeance; but what crowd, assembled for the express purpose of listening to music, could have heard with indifference a composition so overflowing with natural melody, performed with such fervour and unerring skill? It is gratifying to state that the *Septuor* was completely successful ... [*The Times*: MW:8/12/49:774–5]

The *Musical World* even felt that Stammers, with Ernst's assistance, could now do more to further the education of the multitude:

> It may here be asked, since Mr Stammers has such a good orchestra, why has he not a better? Since he has forty good men, why not fifty – aye, or sixty, "the Beethoven number?" Exeter Hall is large enough, and the Wednesdayites would not object. Mr Stammers could then give a symphony and make some tremble in high places. A symphony for a shilling would become the watchword and war-cry of the musical reformers ... [MW:22/12/49:804]

A word with Mr Stammers to conclude. What was the point of Mendelssohn writing the finest concerto (not excepting Beethoven's) ever composed for the violin, if Ernst does not play it? And what is the use of Mr Stammers having engaged the most accomplished violinist ever born (not excepting Paganini) if he does not invite him, nay, compel him (if force be necessary in such a cause) to play the finest of concertos at the London Wednesday Concerts? [MW:22/12/49:805]

An appearance at Mr Willy's Classical Concerts on 31 December – where he played a Beethoven sonata with Sterndale Bennett, and Mendelssohn's E minor quartet with Willy, Hill and Reed – was, unsurprisingly, Ernst's last appearance of the year.

Chapter 16

Beethoven and the Classics: 1850–51

On about 1 January 1850, Berlioz wrote to Ernst asking whether he would be prepared to play in the opening concert of a new philharmonic society he was founding in Paris. [CGB:III:675] Ernst was obliged to turn down the request. His appearances at the London Wednesday Concerts had proved so successful and remunerative that Stammers had engaged him for six further performances in the early months of 1850, and these, together with his other commitments, made even a brief trip across the Channel unthinkable. Berlioz was undoubtedly disappointed, but managed to link the violinist with his latest enterprise in two other ways. First, on 8 January, he asked if Ernst would become an honorary members of the society, and also asked him to enquire if Davison and Macfarren would consent to receiving the same honour. [CGB:III:678] There is no positive evidence that any of them accepted, but since all were close friends of Berlioz, and as the list of members would later include Meyerbeer, Liszt and Spontini, it seems unlikely that either Ernst or the Englishmen refused. Second, if Ernst the performer could not be present, then Ernst the composer could be, and Berlioz arranged for Joachim to come from London at short notice and play his mentor's *Otello Fantasy* in the inaugural concert in Ste Cécile on 19 February. [BSG:448–9]

Although the invitation to undertake a further six London Wednesday Concerts was flattering, it also presented a problem. A series of thirteen concerts in one venue in quick succession was almost unprecedented in Ernst's career and clearly placed a strain on his still limited repertoire. This must be one reason why he decided to compose a new piece for the second half of the concert series – his *Fantasie brilliante sur le Prophète* – an operatic pot-pourri based on themes from Meyerbeer's recently staged opera. Whereas Ernst's compositions of 1845–46 cautiously broke new ground, the *Fantasy* looks backwards to the kinds of music he was writing in Paris in the mid-1830s. He was a man who liked to please his public, and the musical taste of the London crowds was well behind that of central European connoisseurs.

Designed for popular consumption or not, the work proved a great success with the British critics. The *Musical World* wrote:

> The fantasia is founded on the popular airs in the *Prophète*, commencing with the beautiful prayer of Fides, 'O mio Figlio,' in F sharp minor, including, among other morceaux, the pastorale (Mario's) 'Un impero piu soave,' in B flat, I think, and the bacchanalian (Mario's) in the last scene. Ernst has arranged his fantasia for the orchestra with masterly skill and magical effect. It were a venturesome thing to declare, but I am really of opinion that he has improved on Meyerbeer in certain instances. … Of Ernst's solo performances, I am inclined to rate that of the fantasia on the Prophète among the highest; and of his

fantasias, I cannot hesitate to set his new one among the most striking and musician-like. [MW:12/1/50:18]

At the last concert of the Wednesday series – a special benefit concert for Ernst on 6 February – he bowed to Davison's urgings and played the Mendelssohn concerto. The performance was clearly wonderful: 'A grander performance was never heard upon the violin. The first movement was intensely passionate, wayward, capricious and sublime; the second exquisitely tender and expressive; the *rondo* impetuous, playful and humorous by turns, as Mendelssohn himself would have thought it …' [MW:9/2/50:78]

Once again, the reactions to Ernst's performances show how he was beginning to mould popular and critical taste. Firstly, he confirmed it was possible to play fine instrumental pieces lasting more than half and hour to a large and popular audience:

> Who will now say that Mendelssohn's concerto is too long and too elaborate for the crowded audience of the Wednesday Concerts? Ernst with his magic bow, has for ever laid at rest this objection of the unbeliever. Ernst has shown that the noblest inspirations of the musical art may be acceptable to the 'mob,' as it styled by those whose commercial interests are better served by the encouragement of tinsel and trash than by the popularisation of the most perfect works of art. [MW:9/2/50:78]

Secondly, the quality of Ernst's performance helped to establish the concerto's canonical position in England: not only did his performance highlight the Mendelssohn, but it also placed and diminished the works of Spohr, hitherto considered the acme of classical taste, perfection and importance. 'We admire the work more than any violin concerto with which we are acquainted, excepting Beethoven's. We consider it finer than any of Louis Spohr's …' [*Morning Post*: MW: 9/2/50:79]

In the last of the Wednesday Concerts, Stammers again bowed to the critics. He devoted the entire first half to works by Mozart, including the late G minor symphony, and then Ernst and Sterndale Bennett performed Mozart's E♭ sonata complete, 'long as it is, unobtrusive in style, and offering few occasions for the display of brilliant execution' – something quite unthinkable even a year earlier. [MW:50:112]

The new forums for chamber music that were established in England between 1845 and 1850 profoundly affected Ernst's repertoire. He made far fewer appearances as a soloist playing his own works, and hugely increased his chamber music repertoire and the number of his chamber music commitments. The first of these in 1850 was playing in four Classical Chamber Concerts in Manchester, organized by Hallé, and held between 21 February and 4 April. These produced the usual furore, but the reviews are interesting for two reasons. First, two of them give a particularly good description of Ernst's stage presence and playing:

> There is something in his personal appearance which immediately strikes you, that in Ernst a master mind is before you; his high intellectual forehead, and grave, thoughtful, ever pensive cast of countenance; his dark hair; his expressive eyes, which seem to emit sparks of fire when he is warmed with his subject; his slight, yet well knit frame, and easy dignified deportment, all bespeak a man of no ordinary mould; and to hear him in classical

music in a concert like this at once raises him to the very highest ranks of living violinists. [MW:2/3/50:134]

He feels and enjoys [great music] whilst he is playing, and this gives such an indescribable charm to his performance. His expression and pathos are quite unrivalled. His crescendo is almost painful from its very intensity. He seems to be forcing, as it were, the most ravishing tones from his instrument in spite of itself; and then, how he can subdue its tones to a gentle murmur – a mere whisper – the piano of pianissimos; but the *tone*, still there, fine as a gossamer thread, yet clear as a bell. [MW:16/3/50:164]

Second, there is a hint that excellent concerts of chamber music are beginning to undermine the taste for the kind of programme found in popular concerts:

A regular storm of applause both preceded and followed [the last piece], and thus ended Ernst's first concert (in Classical Chamber Music) in Manchester. It is said the 'appetite grows by that it feeds on,' and in our growing love for the classical we shall be inclined to eschew and have little relish for solo performances (written for – and calculated merely for – individual display) in future. [MW:2/3/50:135]

After their successes in Manchester, Hallé and Ernst decided to give a similar concert of classical music in Liverpool. 'Relying upon his great reputation and my rising one,' wrote Hallé, 'we [made an excellent programme and] promised ourselves a great success.' They were therefore more than a little abashed to discover there were only eleven people in the audience, four of whom were reporters. [LLCH:115–16] Ernst's reaction is described by Hallé's son, C.E. Hallé, in a memoir of his father:

My mother used to relate how on one occasion, soon after his arrival in England, he and Ernst the violinist, with whom he was touring in the provinces, arrived at a small town [*sic*] where amateurs of music were so few that scarce a dozen persons had assembled to hear them. From the artists' room they could see how small was the audience, and simultaneously exclaimed: 'Then we must play as we have never played before!' They kept their word, and at the close of the concert the impulsive, highly-strung Ernst threw himself into my father's arms, saying, 'Hallé, we never played like that in all our lives!' [LLCH:147]

More important concerts were to be found in London. As in the previous year, Ernst made a number of appearances at Ella's Musical Union. To unanimously excellent reviews, he played quartets with Deloffre, Hill and Piatti at four of the eight concerts:

9 April	7 May
Mendelssohn: composite quartet: Allegro assai appasionata from quartet in E minor op.44 no.2 Andante and Scherzo from op.81 Finale from op.44 no.2 Beethoven: Quartet in E♭, op.74 Beethoven: Sonata for violin and piano in G op.30 no.3 (Ernst and Sterndale Bennett)	Mendelssohn: Quartet in F minor op.80 Haydn: Quartet in C no.57 Beethoven: Piano trio in B♭ op.97 (Heller, Ernst, Piatti) Ernst and Heller: 3 *Pensées fugitives* (Ernst and Heller)
18 June	**2 July**
Haydn: Quartet in C no.57 Ernst and Heller: selection from *Pensées fugitives* (Ernst and Heller)	Mozart: Quintet in D [K.573] Mendelssohn: Quartet in E♭ op.44 no.3 Beethoven: Sonata for violin and piano in A op.47 (Ernst and Hallé)

But Ernst's most exciting new venture was to lead the six concerts given by the Beethoven Quartet Society. The driving force behind this organization had been Thomas Massa Alsager, a wealthy cloth-manufacturer who, although self-educated, was a deeply cultivated man of many accomplishments. A first-rate classicist, he was also a friend to Lamb and Hazlitt, and owned the copy of Chapman's translation of Homer which Keats first looked into. He also had extensive philanthropic interests, but became best known as the first financial editor and joint manager of *The Times*. Published daily from 1825, his 'money article,' became required reading for anyone with an interest in business and investment. [ODNB:I:894–5]

His overriding passion, however, was music. As already noted, he submitted occasional music criticism to *The Times*, and was said to play competently on all the instruments of the orchestra, but his major contribution to musical life in England was organizational. In about 1830, he founded the 'The Queen Square Select Society', based in his sumptuous London house at 26 Queen Square in Bloomsbury, where Beethoven's *Missa Solemnis* was performed in 1832, and the early quartets were programmed two years later. Growing enthusiasm for Beethoven's quartets amongst members of the Select Society, made Alsager decide to found the Beethoven Quartet Society in 1845. During its first series of five concerts between 21 April and 16 June 1845, given in the Beethoven Rooms at 76 Harley Street, the whole cycle of Beethoven quartets was played complete for the first time in history. A work from each period – early, middle and late – was performed in each concert, with two works from the six of op.18 being played at the fourth meeting. The only Beethoven quartet movement not played was the *Grosse Fuge*, but this is hardly surprising. It was found so off-putting and rebarbative that it had not been performed in public since its premiere in March 1826, and would have to wait until 1857 for its second public performance. That year, Ferdinand David started to play it regularly in Leipzig, but Joachim still omitted it from his complete quartet cycles in 1903–7. [FCB: 502–4, 514]

The Beethoven Society quartet was led by Sivori, accompanied – as the role was usually described – by Sainton, Hill and Rousselot, and all the performances were prepared with extreme care. The quartet rehearsed as many times as was felt to be necessary; an analytic programme, complete with musical examples was produced for each concert; pocket scores were published for each member of the audience, and the audience were expected to arrive half an hour before the concert began. [FCB:502–3]

The quality of the artists, the care taken in preparation, and upper-class patronage, ensured that the series was successful and influential, and it was repeated in 1846, with Sivori and Sainton alternating in the leader's place. Unfortunately, 1845 and 1846 were terrible years for Alsager. His wife, whom he loved dearly, had died in 1845, and in the same year he was accused of various financial irregularities at *The Times*. After thirty years' service, he was compelled to leave under a cloud, and, unable to face the first anniversary of his wife's death on 6 November, he attempted to commit suicide by slashing his throat and left wrist. He lingered for over a week, and finally died of exhaustion on 15 November. As a suicide, he had to undergo the indignities of a midnight burial. [ODNB: I:894–5]

The administration of the Society was taken over by the quartet's cellist, Rousselot, who was determined to honour Alsager's memory. A further concert series were held in 1847 (when the leadership was shared between Sainton, Joachim, Vieuxtemps and Hellmesberger) and in 1848 (when it was shared by Sainton and Molique). [LBQ:87] Ernst was announced as leading the quartet in 1849, but for some unknown reason, no concerts at all took place.

Whatever the difficulties were, they did not recur in 1850. 'A crowded audience of amateurs assembled on Wednesday night,' wrote the *Musical World*, 'to listen to the first performance of the season. The knowledge that Herr Ernst is to lead all the six performances has, of course, had a favourable effect on the subscription …' [MW:20/4/50:241] The first concert, on 17 April, consisted of Beethoven's op.18, no.1, op.59, no.3, and op.130. The great violinist did not disappoint:

> Herr Ernst has no rival in music of this elevated kind. A great master of style as of execution, he is just the artist to enter thoroughly into the spirit of those rich and varied inspirations in which the genius of Beethoven has disclosed itself in every phase of expression. Where simplicity is appropriate nothing can be more simple and unaffected than Ernst's manner of playing; while in passages demanding the most impassioned feeling he is equally in his element. [MW:20/4/50:241]

Unlike the previous series, this set of concerts also included some of Beethoven's piano trios, and on this occasion Ernst, Rousselot and Heller joined forces to play the D major trio op.70 no.1. This was the pianist's first foreign tour since taking up residence in Paris, and was probably prompted by continuing political instability and the consequent scarcity of pupils. [LMRP:56] After the first three concerts, Rousselot introduced four concerts of mixed programmes, prompting fears in the London press that not all the Beethoven quartets would be played, and that the Society's concerts would begin to lose their distinctive identity and *raison d'être*. The programmes were as follows:

Wednesday 1 May Quartet in D op.18 no.3 Quartet in F op.59 no.1 Sonata for piano and cello in G minor, Op.5 no.2 (Sterndale Bennett and Rousselot) Quartet in E♭ op.127 (Ernst, Cooper, Dando, Rousselot)	Wednesday 15 May Quartet in A op.18 no.5 Quartet in E♭ op.74 Piano trio in B♭ op.97 (Ernst, Heller and Rousselot) Quartet in C♯ minor, op.131 (Ernst, Cooper, Hill, Rousselot)
Wednesday 29 May[?] Haydn: Quartet in D major no.79 Mendelssohn: Quartet in E minor op.44 no.2 Beethoven: Piano sonata in C♯ minor op.27 no.2 (Lindsay Sloper) Quartet in F major, op.135 (Ernst, Cooper, Hill, Rousselot)	Wednesday 12 June[?] Mozart: Quartet in C [K.465] Beethoven: Quartet in A minor op.132 Beethoven: Piano sonata in D minor op.31 no.2 (Eugenie Colon) Mendelssohn: Quartet in E♭, op.44 no.3 (Ernst, Cooper, Hill, Rousselot)
Wednesday 26 June[?] Haydn: Quartet in B♭ no.78 Beethoven: Quartet in F minor op.95 Beethoven: Piano sonata in A♭ op.26 (Alexandre Billet) Mendelssohn: Quartet in D op.44 no.1 (Ernst, Cooper, Hill, Rousselot)	

The last concert of the season, a benefit for Ernst, was held on 8 July 1850. The programme was:

Beethoven: Quartet in B♭ op.18 no.6

Beethoven: Quartet in B♭ op.130

Mendelssohn: Andante and Scherzo for string quartet from op.80

Beethoven: Sonata for violin and piano in A op.47

Heller, *Études de concert*, for piano (Ernst, Cooper, Hill, Rousselot; piano: Heller)

So much chamber music laid heavy demands on Ernst, but he continued to appear as a soloist. Besides playing at the Philharmonic on 17 June [MW:22/6/50], he also played in less high-profile concerts at Greenwich, Liverpool, Dublin, and London.[1] The old *Ludovic Fantasy*, probably chosen because the opera's composer was in the audience, served its turn at the Philharmonic, and the *Elegy* and *Carnival* continued to draw rapturous applause elsewhere. His solo repertoire shows a disappointing lack

---

1 Reports of these concerts can be found in the following pages: Greenwich [MW:9/2/50:90]; Liverpool [MW:2/3/50:134]; Dublin [MW:4/5/50:271–2]; London – two concerts in Kennington [MW:2/3/50:138; 3/8/50:490]; three concerts with Osborne [MW:13/4/50:227; 4/5/50:283; 25/5/50:329]; and one each with Aguilar [MW:27/4/50:265] and Benedict [MW: 22/6/50:385–6].

of development. I suspect the problem was that, although he could learn repertoire by other composers very quickly, he still felt inhibited about playing popular repertoire which he himself had not composed, and his hectic English schedules ensured he had no time for composition.

With Heller, he left for Paris by mail train on about 7 August, but his old touring pattern was irreparably broken. Thus, instead of heading for Vienna, he went back to Brighton in the last full week of September to play at two concerts given by the German composer and violinist, Eckert. Returning to Paris on the 28th, he then travelled to Nantes for two triumphant concerts in October [MW:28/9/50:621; 16/11/50:733] and was in Paris again by 4 November. On 14 December, he arrived in London to begin his preparation for the season. [MW:14/12/50:807].

As in the previous year, Ernst's first engagement of 1851 was to perform piano trios by Beethoven and Mendelssohn at one of Hallé's Classical and Chamber Concerts in Manchester. [MW:18/1/51:42] He returned to London immediately, and on 27 January 'played magnificently' [MW:1/2/51:87] in a concert given by the Irish composer Michael Balfe in the Exeter Hall.

His main project for the first three months of the year was to undertake a provincial tour at 'enormous terms' [MW:3/8/50:490] with the singers, Angri, Tamburlink *fils*, Stockhausen, and the pianist Frank Mori. He had accepted the idea with some reluctance: 'I have even decided to accept an English-style tour [that is, one involving a number of performers],' he wrote to Liszt, , 'if it is offered on suitable terms because, as you know, it is the only way an artist can exist in this country without making himself ridiculous. Dear friend, I have refrained from this for a long time but prudence and my future decided it.' [BAL:I:119] The tour lasted for six weeks, from the 28 January to the middle of March, and included thirty-one concerts in, amongst other places, Liverpool, Manchester, Cheltenham, Dublin, Glasgow, and Edinburgh. In many of the main centres he was familiar and revered. 'Herr Ernst was most enthusiastically received,' observed a Liverpool correspondent, 'and played in his usual style of unsurpassable excellence.' [MW:15/2/51:103] 'Ernst, thin and pale,' wrote a Manchester critic, 'in mind intellectual, elevated, spiritual, with that touching tone of melancholy which pervades so many really great musical existences – the great, the unapproachable Ernst, was to us the grand attraction of the concert.' [*Manchester Guardian*: MW:12/4/51:236]

Two of the main difficulties of provincial tours were inferior orchestras and limited rehearsal time, and in Edinburgh these caused problems: 'It was apparent to everyone present that the utter unsteadiness of the orchestra greatly distressed Ernst and Angri, so much so, that the former, when encored in his fantasia on *Otello*, declined to repeat it, but gave instead a piece without accompaniment.' [MW:15/3/51:67]

In Dublin, one critic displayed the kind of confusion that had long been the butt of Davison's humour: 'We need not dwell on the matchless performance of Herr Ernst. None who have ever heard the magic tones of his violin can forget him. Were we to select any of his glorious efforts on the last evening for special praise, one might perhaps, the sinfonia [concerto?] of Beethoven, or his fantasia, introducing "the Last Rose of Summer" …' [*Freeman's Journal*: MW:15/2/51:103] This report is interesting, however, in that it shows Ernst had finished the *Fantasia on Irish Airs* he had mentioned composing in 1844. [ME:12/10/44:830]

By the time he arrived back in London, he was ill and exhausted and had to cancel an appearance at Mlle Graumann's concert where it was reported that his absence was 'a serious drawback to the entertainment.' [MW:22/3/51:188]

While Ernst remained confined to bed [MW:22/3/51:188] the rest of London was abuzz about the opening of the forthcoming Great Exhibition, which ran from 1 May to 11 October 1851. Six million people, many of them brought by rail, paid between a shilling and three guineas for entrance to the Crystal Palace in Hyde Park, where a glorious series of exhibits – hymning British enterprise, industry and character – awaited them. It was a triumph, and Prince Albert, who initially had difficulty finding a role for himself in Britain, bathed in the glorious success. German-speakers in England suddenly found themselves admired and highly popular, and it was a fashion from which Ernst benefited.

Unfortunately, the Exhibition drew people away from the normal commercial entertainments and severely affected their takings. The Italian Opera did badly, Drury Lane had to close more than once, and foreign pianists – including Pleyel, Liszt and de Meyer – stayed away. For the most part, violinists too decided to try their luck elsewhere, and those that came enjoyed mixed fortunes:

> Vieuxtemps, already as near to us Paris, preferred remaining in France, picking up a few hundreds of 20 franc pieces in the French provinces, to walking about Regent-street with his hands in his pockets. Joseph Joachim, no less wary, kept to his post at Leipsic. Sivori came; but we doubt much if that admirable violinist has gained more than enough to pay his expenses. Ernst was already in possession of the field; but even Ernst can hardly be supposed to have reaped a golden harvest. The fact is, that the Crystal Palace has absorbed both the curiosity and the money of the public, and there was nothing left to remunerate artists, foreign or native. [MW:14/6/51:369]

The elite chamber music institutions suffered, but not as badly as more popular forms of entertainment. The Beethoven Quartet Society returned to its previous plan of playing a quartet from each of Beethoven's three periods, but also planned a series of additional concerts with mixed programmes. Ernst would once again be leader. For him, one of the attractions of this London season was that he would again be in close contact with Berlioz. The composer had been asked by the French minister for trade to be part of the jury examining musical instruments at the Great Exhibition, and he had set off for England on the evening of 9 May. He stayed in the house of his friend Adolphe Duchêne, which also happened to contain the Beethoven Society's meeting room: 'Since the door of my apartment opened on to the staircase which leads to [the concert room], I had only to open my door to hear everything that was being performed. One evening I heard Beethoven's C minor trio ringing out … I opened my door wide … Come in, come in, and welcome, proud melody … God, how fine and noble it is …' [EO:217] Amongst those he would have heard rehearsing was the Society's quartet for that season:

> The leader is the German Ernst, no less! Ernst, more thrilling, more dramatic than ever. The second part is entrusted to Mr Cooper, an English violinist whose playing is always faultless and wonderfully precise, even in the most intricate passages. He does not try to shine out of place, however, unlike so many of his rivals, and he never gives to his part

more than the relative importance which the composer assigned to it. The viola player is Mr Hill an Englishman like Mr Cooper, one of the best viola players in Europe, and the owner to boot of a marvellous instrument. Lastly, the cello is in M. Rousselot's capable hands, ... [a man of the world, a man of wit, ... a knowledgeable and skilful composer, an artist in the highest sense of the world.] [EO:216–17]

The programmes for the six evening concerts were as follows:

2 April Quartet in A op.18 no.5 Quartet in E♭ op.74 Quartet in B♭ op.130	15 April Quartet in C minor op.18 no.4 Quartet in F op.59 no.1 Quartet in A minor op.132	30 April Quartet in F op.18 no.1 Quartet in E minor op.59 no.2 Quartet in E♭ op.127
14 May Quartet in G op.18 no.2 Quartet in C op.59 no.3 Quartet in C♯ minor op.131	28 May Quartet in C minor op.18 no.4 Quartet in F op.59 no.1 Quintet in C op.29	11 June Quartet in B♭ op.18 no.6 Quartet in F minor op.95 Mendelssohn: Quartet in E♭ op.44 no.3

Ernst led all of these quartets except for the concert on 28 May. Here, the quartets were led by Sivori, who had just returned from America; and the quintet was led by Sainton. Three quartet matinées were held on 24 April, 9 May and 22 May and an extra miscellaneous concert on 9 June. Sivori and Sainton alternated as leaders in the first two concerts, while in the third Ernst played Beethoven's C minor sonata for violin and piano op.30, no.2 (with Elise Künitz) and led performances of Mendelssohn's quartets op.44, nos.1 and 3. The extra miscellaneous concert is interesting because it shows that a rapprochement had at last been effected between Ernst and Sivori: they played a duet for violin and viola by Spohr together. The rest of the programme consisted of Sivori and Bottesini playing the latter's popular *Duo* for violin and double bass, Rousselot's third quintet for string quartet and bass, Beethoven's quartet op.59, no.3, and also his piano trio in C minor op.1, no.3 played by Sivori, Rousselot and Mlle Conlon. This was the group Berlioz must have listened to through his open door.

Although in uncertain health (his performance on the 30th was interrupted by a coughing fit) Ernst was still capable of playing magnificently. 'In the adagio in A♭ (No.10 [E♭ op.74]) ... Ernst fairly surpassed himself ... the fourth string, in one passage ... spoke with the voice of a desperate lover. ... [And] let us note that we never heard the grand arpeggio *trait de bravoure*, in the *allegro* of the same, so dexterously executed, and with such energy, as by Ernst on Wednesday night.' [MW:5/4/51:214] 'Ernst was never more earnest and impassioned, and never more sparkling with vivacity and animation.' [MW:3/5/51:277] 'The *canzona* [of op.132] in his hands (in spite of its Greek crudities) was transcendent. Such a thanksgiving was worthy such a cure.' [MW:19/4/51:249]

It was leading the performances in the Beethoven Quartet Society that finally convinced Joachim of Ernst's surpassing greatness:[2]

> It was only in the fifties ... in the concerts of the Beethoven Quartett society led by Ernst that I started to love and duly appreciate this violinist, whom I had known for a long time and whom I admired most highly as virtuoso and quartet player. ... [FCB:524] Those who have not heard Ernst play in his healthy days performing Sphor's *Gesangsszene*, or his own *Elegie* (so often mishandled now by incompetent players) do not know how communicative the cantilena of the violin can be. Never have I heard a more expressive tone than the one he produced in the adagios of Beethoven's Quartets Op 59 and 74. More than once did my associates feel compelled to kneel to him, or kiss his hands during rehearsal, when he could not defend himself with a grateful smile in his resigned, melancholy way; at the time of the Beethoven Society ... he was in very poor health. In short, Paganini may have been the greater virtuoso, [Joachim never heard Paganini] but he could not have played with more warmth, poetry, and esprit than Ernst. [GV:519. GMV:204–5]

These concerts were not only important for Ernst's reputation, but as part of a general movement to make Beethoven's late quartets, widely regarded as unintelligible in the 1830s and '40s, appreciated throughout Europe. There is a telling moment in Thayer's *Life of Beethoven*, when he quotes a passage from Sir Julius Benedict, who himself performed at many of Ernst's concerts:

> I heard the first public performance of Beethoven's so called 'posthumous quartets' in [Beethoven's] own presence. [The E♭ quartet op.127, played on 6 March 1825] Schuppanzigh and his companions, who had been his interpreters before were scarcely equal to the occasion: as they did not seem to understand the music themselves, they failed entirely to impart its meaning to the audience. The general impression was most unsatisfactory. Not until Ernst had completely imbued himself in the spirit of these compositions could the world discover their long hidden beauties. [TLB:III:139–40]

Despite Ernst's heavy commitment at the Beethoven Quartet Society, the Musical Union was not neglected, and he appeared at five of their ten concerts (three regular concerts and two extra meetings). He played in the following pieces:

---

2   Joachim said he was thinking of 1854/5 [GV:519] but the Beethoven Quartet Society ceased to exist after 1852. I have assumed he was thinking of this society in 1850/51, but his reference to the mid-fifties may suggest he was actually referring to Ernst's performances at the Musical Union in 1854/5. At the Beethoven Quartet Society in 1850, Ernst played op.59 nos.1 and 3, and op.74; in 1851, he played all the op.59 quartets and op.74. At the Musical Union, he played two quartets from op.59 and op.74 in 1854; and op.59 nos.1 and 2 in 1855. Ernst's health caused serious concern in 1851 and forced him to cancel several concerts, so I am inclined to think this was the year Joachim was referring to. Joachim did not play at any of these concerts, so he must have just attended the rehearsals.

8 April Haydn: Quartet in F no.48 Mendelssohn: Quintet in B♭ op.87 (with Mellon, 2nd viola) Beethoven: Sonata for violin and piano in C minor op.30 no.2 Mendelssohn: Presto Scherzando in F♯ minor for piano. (Ernst, Deloffre, Hill, Piatti; piano: Hallé)	**10 June** Mozart: Quintet in G minor [K.516] Beethoven: Piano trio in D op.70 no.1 Mendelssohn: Quartet in E♭ op.44 no.3 (Ernst, Deloffre, Hill, Seligmann; piano: Hallé)
11 June Beethoven: Quartet in B♭ op.18 no.6 Beethoven: Quartet in F minor op.95 Mendelssohn: Quartet in E♭ op.44 no.3 (Ernst, Cooper, Hill, Rousselot)	**17 June, Extra Matinée** Mozart: Quartet in D [K.499] Beethoven: Sonata for violin and piano op.24 (Ernst and Hallé) Beethoven: Quartet in E minor op.59 no.2 (Ernst, Deloffre, Hill, Piatti)
24 June, Director's Matinée Beethoven: Piano Trio in E♭ op.70 no.2 (two movements only) (Ernst, Piatti; piano: Hallé)	

The concert on 24 June had a long and miscellaneous programme, and it must have been one of the few occasions when one could hear five famous violinists – Ernst, Sivori, Vieuxtemps, Laub and Sainton – play in one concert. The lions of the Union's season were celebrated in a splendid print by Baugniet where Ernst and Hallé – seated at the front – take pride of place. [MW:21/6/51:398]

Ernst's last chamber music commitments of the season were in two concerts organized by the English pianist and composer Brinley Richards in the New Beethoven Rooms. With Piatti and Richards he played Beethoven's C minor trio, and then 'one of the most difficult and trying of Mozart's chamber pieces', the 'fine and elaborate sonata in A [K.526].' [MW:12/7/51:420] In the even more successful second concert, Ernst and Richards, besides playing the *Elegy*, performed a real novelty: Steibelt's E minor sonata for violin and piano. 'So rarely has this work been performed in public,' said the critic of the *Musical World*, 'that we may almost consider it new to the present generation, or at least unknown. Interpreted by such artists ... the effect was decided.' The critic was even more impressed by the assemblage of rank and title in the room, and, with an attention to correct address that even Ella could not have improved upon, decided to print the name of every notable in the room: ' ... The Right Hon. The Countess of Dungarvon, the Countess Reventlow, the Right Hon. The Lady Robert Grosvenor, the Baroness Braye, the Baroness de Rutzen, Lady Moreton, ... the Hon. Mrs. W. Chetwynd Talbot ... His Excellency the Count Reventlow ...' and at least a hundred others. [MW:12/7/51:437]

So many chamber performances of 'Classical Music' began to have an effect on Ernst's programmes as a soloist. Evidently encouraged by his successful performances of the Mendelssohn concerto in the previous two years, he now announced a public performance of the Beethoven concerto at his own concert on 2 June.[3] The reception could not have been more enthusiastic:

> Beethoven's concerto is a very fine composition, though the passages assigned to the solo instrument are not always thoroughly violinistic. Ernst, however, contended triumphantly with all obstacles. Where it was impossible for him to impart an individual and independent brightness to his part, lofty musical feeling came to his aid, and enabled him to realize the author's conception by becoming an important part of a great whole. On such occasions, he blended his tones with the confluent and responsive music of the orchestra with admirable skill ... [The concerto's] magnificent execution on the occasion may rank among the great violinist's grandest achievements. [*Morning Post*: MW:14/6/51:373]

The critic of the *Musical World* was stunned by the cadenzas which Ernst had written for the first and third movement, and talks about them in some detail:

> To the solo player [the concerto] offers but few points of display; hence the reason for Ernst writing the cadences. ... He wrote [them] *con amore*, and, while considering the practicalability of introducing every possible difficulty into his playing, never lost sight of the character and style of his author. ... The first cadence is of great length, but had it been twice as long it would have been doubly interesting, so wrapped up were the audience in its dazzling effect. Henceforth let no one prate of wonders. Ernst, in his new cadences has mastered impossibilities. Some of the effects are creations, no one ever heard them before. Paganini might have had a vision of them on his death-bed but posterity will owe them to Ernst. Shall we attempt to describe them? Shall we catch the rainbow, or transfix the wailing of an Aeolian harp? Enough to say that it is Ernst's most astonishing feat, and having said so, our readers may have some idea of the prodigious difficulties mastered with infinite ease by the prodigious violinist. [MW:17/6/51:355]

Given his extensive efforts on behalf of Beethoven this season, it was appropriate that Ernst and several of his distinguished contemporaries should have played at the unveiling of a new bust of Beethoven by N. Burnard on 21 June. The reception was held at the home of the Union's treasurer, Frederick Beale, and Berlioz was amongst the celebrated musicians who attended.[4] [MW:12/7/51:420]

On 1 August 1851, Ernst and his friend Eckert left for Paris [MW:2/8/51:493], and the next week, Ernst announced plans for a Swiss tour with Stockhausen. Hallé, feeling a little trapped in the smoke and rain of Manchester, wrote to Ernst, expressing mild envy, and inquiring about the progress of a string quartet Ernst had mentioned. [LLCH:239–40] But Ernst's situation was not enviable. The violinist replied by saying that the intensity of the English season had brought on a serious

---

3   The second movement of the Beethoven violin concerto ends on a chord of A, so that it leads into the D major Rondo. A fragment of manuscript score for sale on MGB shows that Ernst recomposed the ending of the slow movement of the concerto so that it ended on a chord of G. This was clearly so the slow movement could be performed alone. However, there is no record of Ernst playing this version

4   One of Ernst's last engagements in England in 1851 was playing first violin in the premiere of the string quartet in E minor by the pianist Kate Loder. This well-received performance took place in the New Beethoven Rooms on Saturday 5 July. [MW:12/7/51:446]

attack of his illness, and that, postponing his Swiss tour, he had retired to Bougival to rest and be treated by his friend Dr Roth. He hoped, however, to spend some of the time in composition. [LLCH: 245–6]

In the event, neither Roth nor Bougival could do much to alleviate Ernst's suffering. For nearly three months there was no news of him, and then a concert of his music in Paris, to be conducted by Berlioz, was announced for 22 December. But this too had to be postponed, and Ernst's continuing ill-health is the most likely reason.

Chapter 17
Amélie: 1852–53

Ernst eventually gave his concert, under Berlioz's direction at the Salle Herz on 14 January 1852. This was the first time he had given a public performance in Paris for ten years, and there was considerable anticipation. All seats for the concert were sold out long in advance, and he did not disappoint: his playing was praised, at length and as usual, for its combination of outstanding technical skill and expressive beauty. The success of this concert led to his appearance at an equally remunerative concert organized by *La France musicale* later in the month, and two further concerts were immediately organized at the Salle Herz. [FM:10/1/52:15. RGM:18/1/52:20]

The concert on 4 February was as successful as those in the previous month, and Ernst's concerto made such an impact it had to be repeated. At the next engagement, on 1 March, he felt bold enough to introduce two pieces of chamber music alongside his normal concert fare: the *Andante* and finale from the *Kreutzer Sonata* with Wilhelmine Clauss, and Mendelssohn's E minor quartet with Eckert, Maas and Chevillard. [E:159–60]

His success was indisputable, but German doubts about the nature of this success, which had long appeared in private conversations, diaries and letters, began to manifest themselves in the press:

> I cannot but say that for me Ernst was too virtuostic. After a trickily difficult *Concert-Allegro* he played again, just like many years ago, the inevitable *Otello-Fantasie* and the indeed beautiful *Élégie*, then stuffed in a *Rondo Papageno* and at last the desperate *Carnaval de Venise*. I would prefer, and many others have the same feeling, to have a small piece of genuine art instead of something formidably difficult. Of course, it does not need to be said that everything was accomplished with astonishing mastery. But I always think that the queen of instruments ought to be treated in a kingly manner … [GMP:7/3/52:75–6; trans. E:160]

At this time of year, Ernst would normally have gone to London, but after three years spent almost entirely in England he seems to have been ready for a change. Early in the year, he clearly had intentions of returning to Weimar, possibly because he wanted to hear the performance of Berlioz's *Benvenuto Cellini* which Liszt was directing. The proposal was warmly endorsed by Liszt in a letter of 31 January 1852:

> Dear Friend, I am delighted by Belloni's agreeable news that you are shortly to come here, and that you have not further postponed your intended visit to Weimar. Their Imperial and Royal Highnesses look forward very much to seeing you again, because our Court has especially pleasant memories of you. You will also find again whist partners who regard your arrival as a festival, and who can reckon with your tireless passion for the game. As

partners in Weimar this time, you can meet several acquaintances you will certainly gladly make or renew. Joachim, Cossman, Raff, and Herr von Bülow, who all sincerely rejoice with me over the prospect of the few days before us. I hope you are not displeased with the musical direction, which we are engaged in forming, and find pleasure in the innovations made during your absence. …

… Try to arrange to be here on 13th, for I place great value on Cellini taking up its deserved place on the stage. … [VN:348–9]

In spite of this encouragement, Ernst left for his delayed tour of Switzerland a few days after his last Paris concert. Joachim, who was going to London himself, was surprised and wrote to his brother: 'Ernst is in Basel! Why not in London? I was looking forward to seeing him again.' [24/3/52. BJJ:I:28] If the thought of Ernst's presence delighted Joachim, Wagner, who was passing through Basel on his way from Paris to Zurich, was rather less thrilled by the actuality: 'The man and the violinist Ernst meet here: I was recommended [to] this G to E-string beast and therefore I could not quite avoid this melancholic stringed character. He brought me instructions from Hiller which assured me … that he was my present rather than previous friend. (I seem to rankle these kinds of people: my exile casts a fatal shadow on their glance.)' [25 March 1852. WSB:IV:327]

This is obscurely expressed but one can see at least three grounds for Wagner's hostility. The first is that illness had certainly darkened Ernst's personality, and from this point onwards people find that melancholy – which was always an important element of his personality – begins to dominate his character. The second is that the reference to him as 'an E to G string beast' suggests that, as a musician, Ernst is entirely preoccupied with the technicalities of the violin rather than the wider philosophical and nationalistic issues that play such an important role in Wagner's musical outlook. The third is that he comes bearing news from Hiller, who was associated with the conservative stream of German music that would later show open opposition to the ideals of Liszt and Wagner. Writing to Liszt, however, a day or two later, whom he knew to be Ernst's friend and admirer, Wagner adopts an altogether sunnier tone: 'Apropos! Ernst was here, gave concerts and, as he told me, he decided to stay in Switzerland until the end of this month. So you would like to see him too! Bring the Princess with you!' [Late March 1852. WSB:IV:343]

One can well understand Ernst's desire to extend his stay, as the tour was turning into the kind of triumph he had experienced in Central Europe in the early 1840s. Marie Escudier summarized his success in *La France Musicale*:

Ernst is receiving in Switzerland at the present moment ovations, which seem to be echoes of those which welcomed him in Paris during the winter. On arriving at Bâle he played at a concert which had been organized for him in advance. Such was his success, that it was proposed to him by the entrepreneurs that he should give another within eight days; but the celebrated violinist had already accepted invitations from St Gallen and Winthertheer, and could not undertake to return in time. At the end of his tour, however, he has consented to give one more concert at Bâle.

From Bâle Ernst went to Zurich, and the day after his arrival he gave his first concert in the Casino. His success, we are informed by our correspondents, surpassed even the general expectations, although Ernst had been preceded by a colossal reputation. He was immediately engaged to give three concerts in the theatre. The first took place on 26th

March. All the boxes were taken by the previous evening, and the room was so crowded, that many persons were unavoidably refused admittance. What gave to this concert more than ordinary interest was the presence of the unfortunate Countess Batthyani, who was desirous of hearing the accomplished virtuoso whom Hungary had applauded and fêted in happier times. [After the siege of Pesth, her husband had been executed by the Austrians.] Since the illustrious lady had inhabited Zurich, she has not once been to the theatre. Ernst played his famous solo on Hungarian melodies, with that expression of tender poesy which always animates his execution. Tears were seen to flow from the cheeks of the Countess Batthyani and the following day she was anxious to see and speak with the great artist, who had given her such sweet and profound emotion. The touching interview produced a deep sensation in Zurich and the vicinities.

From Zurich, Ernst is to proceed to St Gallen, where all the seats had already been taken for the concert, which was announced for the following Tuesday. From St Gallen he goes to Winthertheer, and thence again to Zurich, to give his second concert in Easter week. He is also expected at Mulhouse, Berne, and some of the minor towns of Switzerland.

We follow Ernst in his artistic pilgrimage with all the interest of friendship, happy to know that his admirable talent is everywhere judged, appreciated, admired, and applauded, as it was but now in Paris. [MW:10/4/52:225–6]

In the light of this success, Ernst decided to extend his tour not simply until the end of March, but for a further six months, and he would eventually perform in Bern, Neuchâtel Lausanne Geneva, Vevey, Geneva (again), Aix-les-Bains, Chambéry, Bern (again), Zurich, and Basel. [E:162–3] He finally ended his tour in Geneva, where he played for the third time on 8 October.

By November, he had returned to France, and in that month gave two concerts at the Grande salle des concerts in Lyon, and probably two at Georges Hainl's quartet séance. At the one of the latter, Ernst – along with Cherblanc, Hainl and Pesch – played a Haydn quartet, and the actress Amélie-Siona Lévy recited work by Musset. This is the woman who would later become Ernst's wife, and this is their first recorded appearance on stage together. [GMP:28/11/52:408. SMZ:13/12/52:146. FM:2/1/53:7]

Amélie was a considerable celebrity in her own right. French dictionaries and reference books say that she was born in Mutzig (Bas-Rhin) on 14 April 1834. The place is correct, but her birth certificate shows that she was actually born on 11 April 1831 (in French handwriting, ones and fours can look confusingly similar). Her parents were Aron Lévy, described as a merchant, and his wife Rosalie Weil, both twenty-five years of age. Like many girls of her age and class, Amélie was given two forenames, 'Amélie-Siona', so that she could drop the obviously Jewish forename if she wished to assimilate. [TMU:49]

Dark, robust, round-faced and strong-featured, she was widely thought to be very attractive, and if her letters are any guide to her character she was warm, voluble, dotty about children (although she was never to have any of her own), a little too addicted to reciting French verses, and fond of teasing and the mock scold.

She came to Paris with her mother in the second half of the 1840s to study drama. The family were clearly encouraged in this ambition by the colossal success of 'Rachel' – the stage name of Élisa Félix, the daughter of a Jewish peddler from

Alsace – who had caused an immense sensation in the roles of Camille, Roxane, Phèdre and Lucrèce, and single-handedly revived the fortunes of classical French drama in the mid-nineteenth century.

Amélie studied at the Paris Conservatoire under the two great actors Provost and Mlle Mars, and appears to have made her debut at the Salle Herz – a venue normally used for music. This was the occasion on which she first impressed the French poet and critic Théophile Gautier, who wrote:

> Another concert took place in the Salle Herz, but this one offered something distinctive, it was given by Mlle Siona Lévy, a young and beautiful girl who is not a singer, not a pianist, who does not play the organ or the accordion, but devotes herself quite simply to the recital of tragic verse. In this concert, where the music occupied only one half, she recited scenes from … Racine and Corneille with a fire, a taste and an intelligence which may give the Théâtre français something to think about. [*La Presse*: 31/1/1848: TGCG: III:431–2]

Besides writing positive reviews, Gautier took a more personal interest. A letter from Amélie, written to him in early 1848, thanks him for writing a letter recommending her to the great French actress Mme Girardin, and for giving her a lesson on how to perform monologues. Successes followed. Eight months later, she won the Conservatoire's first prize for declamation [MW:1/4/54:208] and the third prize for tragedy. [DB:XII:1400] Gautier renewed his earlier praise and engaged in some tentative speculations about her future: 'The tragic crown was placed on the head of Mlle Siona Lévy, who has intelligence, a beautiful voice, expressive eyes, and great precision of intonation; by her doubly Jewish name and her talent, Mlle Siona Lévy promises to follow in Rachel's footsteps "non passibus aequis" but at an honourable distance.' [TGCG:III:432]

Behind the scenes, Gautier continued to exercise his influence, and in February 1850 wrote to his friend Arsène Houssaye, manager of the Théâtre français: 'Don't forget my protégée Siona Lévy. She will play Atalide if you want (in *Bajazet*): but try to persuade Rachel to play Eriphile in *Iphigénie*, where the young ingénue will be much better than in the Turkish masquerade. You know that tragedy consists principally in the art of putting curtains on shoulders.' [TGCG:IV:121]

Perhaps the great Mlle Rachel was not entirely keen to give a younger Jewish actress, especially one who was more conventionally beautiful, a more grateful part, and she stuck to her original intentions. Gautier accepted this with good grace and wrote on 18 March: 'Mlle Rachel will perform in *Bajazet* having Mlle Siona Lévy as Atalide. Mlle Rachel has shown the most perfect kindness in facilitating the first stage appearances of this young and intelligent person, whom we think destined for a fine career in the theatre.' [TGCG:IV:121] After the premiere on 21 March, other critics were less unstintingly positive than Gautier, but agreed that Atalide was not the part for Mlle Lévy:

> She knows how to speak clearly and gave proof of her happy qualities, notably a true sensibility. Physically, Mlle Lévy lacks power [and] her embarrassed gestures betray her inexperience; but her intelligence and agreeable appearance were appreciated. Her costume was charming. People say that Mlle Rachel is interested in Mlle Lévy. In this

case, she would be well advised to let her play some role other than Atalide, an ungrateful part, difficult in that Roxanne constantly effaces and crushes her. Iphigénee would be a good second role for her. [*La Revue et Gazette des Théâtres*: 24/3/50: TGCG:IV:490]

If Amélie found her career being advanced by Gautier, then he derived considerable satisfaction from knowing her. He had evidently cast a connoisseur's eye over her figure, and invited his friend Félix Bonnaire to do the same:

> It would be very kind if you would turn your vagabond steps towards my private and political salon on Wednesday to see a young actress in whom I discovered the possibilities of Iphigénie en Aulide. If it's possible, try to look like a respectable man who is just passing by chance. Afterwards, you can give me your opinion of the young tragedian's physique, although I reserve the right to share it later with Buloz from les deux mondès [the newspaper]. [TGCG:IV:148]

When she appeared in *Iphigénie* on 21 April 1850, *La Revue et Gazette des Théâtres* was still reserved in its judgement: 'The role of Iphigénie demonstrated the same qualities of diction that we noted on her first appearance, but also the same physical insufficiency. Her face is hardly tragic, her body is thin, but her accentuation and voice are good. The young actress is intelligent as well as willing.' [25/4/50: TGCG:IV:490] Gautier had not reviewed her appearance in *Bajazet*, but now felt called on to answer some of these criticisms:

> This young actress with a gracious face, absolutely suitable for her first appearance in tragedy, played the sweet daughter of the king of kings with a great deal of talent, intelligence, and sensibility. She well understands the religious and devotional character of the role, and kept her virginal and poetic characterization from descending into whining. Several rounds of applause proved to the young actress the public's satisfaction with her, surprised to find so much talent in one so young. [TGCG: IV:144]

She soon secured the role of première tragédienne at the Odéon – the main rival to the Théâtre français – and appeared as Palmyre in *Mohamet* in August 1850, Théodore in *L'Abbé de L'Epée* and Camille in *Horace* the following year. Gautier wrote a deeply flattering account of her stage roles in *La Presse* on 22 September 1851 [TGCG:IV:382], but perhaps his most touching tribute was the poem he sent to her. The quatrain shows that, even at this early stage, she was writing as well as reciting poetry:

> For Siona Lévy
>
> Child doubly applauded
> You sing and make verse
> And your mask of tragedy
> Is crowned with green laurels. [TGCG:IV:382]

Having firmly established her theatrical career at both the Odéon and the Théâtre français, and acquired some influential mentors, she then, much to everyone's surprise, renounced the stage. The immediate cause was '*exaltation religieuse*' [BCSW:I:179] possibly stirred up by what had befallen her brother J.B. Lévy. He had recently had a vision of the Virgin Mary, converted to the Roman Catholic priesthood, and entered a convent in Bordeaux. These events were 'for sometime the theme of public conversation.' [NMZ: MW: 4/11/65:690] Amélie also became a Catholic, and considered entering a convent, although whether anything quite so dramatic caused her conversion is unclear. [MW:4/11/65: 690; BCSW:I:179]

Ernst and Amélie are most likely to have met in Paris in early 1852, at what was clearly a difficult and confusing time of her life. They got on so well that, within a few weeks, she and her mother – acting as chaperone – decided to travel through Switzerland with Ernst. [BAL:I:305] A notice in the *Musical World* observes that 'in the *soirées de musique et de déclamation* organized by Ernst, the eminent violinist, in the principal towns and cities of the south of France, Switzerland, and more lately in Rhenish Germany, [Amélie Lévy's] recitations were everywhere received with enthusiasm.' [MW:1/4/54:230] It is true that no reviews mention her performances before the couple's arrival in Lyon, but this is probably because the reviews are largely brief items of news from foreign correspondents which do not mention supporting artists.

After their performance in Lyon, the couple set out on a joint tour of southern France: Marseilles in December, Draguignan and Nice in January 1853, Marseilles again in February, and Roignon, Nîmes and Montpellier in the same month. Ernst would play his normal crowd-pleasers and she would recite poems and speeches from plays that fitted in with the music's mood and atmosphere. Gautier's 'Variations sur le Carnaval de Venise' (actually written about Paganini's version) was frequently apt, but Musset's 'Une bonne fortune' also made frequent appearances. These joint evenings were every bit as successful as Ernst's earlier concerts:

> The amateurs of serious art have retained too pleasant a remembrance of the soirées of music and declamation given at Lyons by Herr Ernst and Mademoiselle Siona Lévy not to follow with interest the peregrinations of the two eminent artists through the principal towns of the south. The accounts which we gather, from various sources, of the artistic excursion of Herr Ernst and Madmoiselle Lévy, represent it as an uninterrupted succession of triumphs. At Grenoble, at Marseilles, at Draguignan, at Grasse, at Nice; wherever, indeed they have appeared, they have created most unequivocal sympathy, and conquered the sufferages and affections of all.
>
> At Marseilles, where Ernst was heard sixteen years ago, the two travellers met with a truly enthusiastic welcome. A promise was hailed by the idolizing public of a speedy return; and indeed, Herr Ernst and Mademoiselle Lévy have already returned to that city, and are preparing at this moment to resume the course of their triumphs, interrupted a month ago by the religious solemnities of Christmas. The Marseillaise audiences are not satisfied, night after night, with covering them with wreaths and bouquets; they besiege their hotel and perform serenades in their honour. … [*Salut Publique*: MW:19/2/53:109]

Ernst wrote to Berlioz about his triumphs, and on 7 April 1853 Berlioz replied with the news from Paris:

> My Dear Ernst, Your letter gave me great pleasure and I want to thank you very much for all the kind and flattering things you said about me in your letter from Marseilles. I know how little you like writing, and a letter from you is therefore a great prize.

We were almost hoping to see you in Paris for the end of the concert season, though it's true that, as the concerts haven't finished yet, you're free to come any time you like in the certainty that you will always find yourself in the midst of a crowd of small and middling virtuosos who clutter up the place with their usual scraping and strumming. This year especially the number of pianists has been exorbitant; a cloud of grasshoppers has descended upon Paris. So much so that Zimmerman said the other day: 'It's terrifying! Everybody these days plays the piano and everybody plays it well.' To which I replied: 'Indeed, my poor Zimmerman, we're the only two left who don't play it.' …

I shall probably be going to London; the director of Covent Garden would like me to put on my opera *Benvenuto Cellini*; and if the conditions I've just sent him are accepted I shall have to start again on the painful business of rehearsing singers.

I think I shall after all be engaged by Bénazet for a large concert in Baden in August. Might you be in that part of the world by any chance? …

Heine has just written one of his most charming impieties in the *Revue des Deux Mondes*, entitled *The Gods in Exile*. It's sparklingly witty and admirably written.

Now then, do you know you write absolutely excellent French? Who the devil gave you permission? It's indecent!

Heller's doing well and sends you his best wishes; he has some pupils and he continues to give his lessons punctiliously.

Goodbye, I feel my head spinning after writing these four small pages to you. Votre bien dévoué. H. Berlioz [7 April 1853. SLB:280–81. GBL:158–9. See also CGB:IV: 301–3]

After Marseilles, Ernst and Amélie's tour seemed to excite even more enthusiasm:

At Draguignan, their arrival caused, as it were, a revolution. From all parts of the department people came to hear them. To fête them, flower beds were despoiled, hotbeds were pillaged, even branches of laurels were thrown upon the stage, not to speak of verses and poetic epistles, through the medium of which the vivid exultation of the meridian imagination signalized itself. No sooner were Herr Ernst and Mademoiselle Lévy observed, than every body approached them, to grasp them by hand: and during the whole time of their stay in Draguignan, balls and fêtes were got up without cessation on their account.

After several concerts at Nice, which were attended with fresh ovations, the two artists returned to Marseilles, in obedience, as we hinted above, to the most pressing solicitations. Herr Ernst and Mademoiselle Siona Lévy appear to have taken up their headquarters in that city. In the intervals of soirées promised to the Marseilles, they will make an excursion to Avignon, Nîmes, Montpellier, and Toulon. They then propose to proceed to Paris, stopping at Bourdeaux and Toulouse on their way. … [*Salut Publique*: MW:19/2/53:109]

In May they were in Toulouse, in June at la Rochelle, and in Bordeaux at the end of the month. By July they were heading for Paris, and by the middle of that month they were back amongst the fresh air, pine forests and mountains of Baden. Here, on 16, 23 and 28 July, Ernst played three chamber music concerts with Ehrlich and Seligmann, appeared at two of Amélie's evenings of recitation, and aroused huge enthusiasm on two trips to Homberg. [E:167–8] His primary reason for being in Baden, however, was to play in two concerts given by Berlioz – an idea originally floated in the French composer's letter to Ernst in April. The first took place on 11 August when Berlioz conducted the opening parts of *Faust*, two duets from *Semiramide* sung by Sophie and Marie Cruvelli, Ernst's *Carnival of Venice*, a clarinet solo by Cavallini, and the *Roman Carnival Overture*. [BSG:515] The reception Ernst received could not have been more enthusiastic. As usual, he improvised new variations on the *Carnival* 'with incomparable originality and charm' [GMP:14/8/53] and the audience was as ecstatic as it had been when he played the piece a week or so before: 'One does not know how to give an idea of the kind of enthusiasm Ernst has created here. The applause was frantic and unanimous ...' [GMP:31/7/53:270] The public was equally enthusiastic if a little sparser at an all-Berlioz concert a day or two later in Frankfurt, when the composer repeated *Faust*, but this time supported it with a section from *The Childhood of Christ*, his orchestration of Weber's *Invitation to the Waltz*, and Ernst playing *Harold in Italy*.

Quite apart from her personal feelings, Amélie's new professional partnership with Ernst suited her admirably. She felt more comfortable in public reading than acting (she had won first prize for declamation at the Conservatoire but had only secured the third in tragedy), and her appearances on the professional stage had not passed without criticism. Her first instinct had been to give a poetry recital during a concert at the Salle Herz, and her partnership with Ernst allowed her to make a touring career using this kind of programme. Ernst, of course, was also hugely successful and famous, and this brought her talents to much wider notice.

In mid-September, Ernst and Amélie ran into Liszt. He was in the area finalizing plans for the Karlsruhe Festival for the following month, and had come to Baden, where the Karlsruhe Diplomatic Corps had taken up residence, to arrange travel documents for visits to France, Austria and Russia. [BCSW:I:176] In writing home to the Princess in Weimar, he includes two concise, wise, and informative paragraphs about the Ernsts:

> I also saw Ernst, who for more than a year has been greatly attached to a Rachel II, Mlle Lévi [*sic*] who abandoned her theatrical career having achieved great success for two years at the Odéon, I believe because of religious exultation as they say. She is 22, appears 19 – and is Catholic. Her brother entered a convent in Bordeaux, and his sister considered the same vocation. Ernst is seriously thinking about marrying her, but for my part I wouldn't want to advise him for or against it.
>
> There is something of a reaction amongst German artists against Ernst's reputation. The fact is that for 15 years, he has played constantly and almost exclusively the Fantasy on *Otello* and the *Carnival of Venice* which would have been fine for 3 or 4 years but not 15. He has a languid and easygoing manner which does not lack charm but which he would have done well to get rid of a long time ago. Anyway, just as he is, I like him infinitely more then 99 out of a 100 other celebrated colleagues, because there is a sort of delicate and affecting probity in him which gives him true moral courage. It is not impossible that he will establish himself in Weymar. For next winter, he is projecting a new tour of Russia – with Mlle Lévi you understand – who holds out to him the sugared almond of very high Catholicism. [24/9/53. BCSW:I:178.]

Liszt was due to conduct two concerts in Karlsruhe in early October. On 26 September, Joachim, who was playing his violin concerto in G minor at the first concert, wrote to the cellist Bernhard Cossmann from his Karlsruhe hotel: 'Ernst might come across; Monday 3rd October is the first concert.'

[BJJ:I:80] In the event, Ernst fell ill again and was unable to attend. He had to take to his bed until late October, and could only hear at second hand about the artistic riches the festival contained. The main work of the opening concert was Beethoven's *Choral Symphony*, and in the second Bülow played Liszt's fantasy on motifs from Beethoven's *Ruins of Athens* for piano and orchestra. Works by Wagner, however, were the primary focus of the festival: the *Tannhäuser* overture opened the first concert (public demand made Liszt repeat it), and some excerpts from *Lohengrin* closed the second. [FLWY:233]

Ernst was well enough to give a concert with Amélie on 26 November in Strasbourg, and, early in the New Year, in Stuttgart and Mainz. [GMP:16/10/53:369. NMZ:17/12/53:200] It was probably en route from Stuttgart to Mainz that he wrote to Liszt:

> Dear and Illustrious Friend, I find myself in the great dead city of Carlsruhe, which some persons say seems doubly dead to all those privileged to attend the recent festival to which your presence gave such animation and lustre. From this city itself I wish to convey to you my regrets at not having been able to attend and profit by so rare an opportunity of hearing under your direction the creations of our great masters, and notably those of Wagner, which have found in you so valiant a champion and intelligent an interpreter. In saying this, dear Liszt, I simply repeat the expression of Wagner himself. I had the good fortune to see him at Basel on his way back from Paris to Zurich, and you may well believe that you furnished the principal subject of our conversation. His admiration did not at all astonish me; but it was a pleasure to see him imbued with gratitude for your truly loyal and artistic conduct toward him.
>
> I also want to thank you for all your kindnesses towards the Lévy ladies, which, in the middle of all your occupations and preoccupations, were of double value. In addition, they have asked me to express anew all their gratitude, and asked to be remembered to you.
>
> My intention to arrange a concert in the theatre here failed, for the reason which il padre Milanollo warned me of, that Teresa is already playing tomorrow night. [Her sister Marie had died in 1848] I persist however in my plan of giving a concert, but in the Museumssaal, because evil tongues sharpened no doubt by the padre broccolo [broccoli] are already spreading the rumour that I have taken flight.
>
> If you don't believe in the self-love of virtuosi, I'm pleased to think you believe in the *honour of our sex*, and that your old friendship with me will welcome the favour I am going to ask of you. It is very important for the success of my plan to interest the court. I know influential people there, but at the moment I lack the most powerful of them, and that is the Count of Leiningen, to whom I don't want to present myself without a good introduction. I know how intimate you are with him, and I'm going to ask you to send me some words for him in which you also mention Mlle Siona Lévy. You can do it so much better now that you know her, after her manners, wit and distinction (given what you said to me) produced such a favourable impression on you. You don't know her talent, fair enough, but believe me, without partiality, it is remarkable. Emile Devrient [the actor], who had a chance to hear her in Baden, was astonished, filled with enthusiasm. If you can't see any obstacles to the fulfilment of this request, be so kind as to satisfy it as quickly as possible, and be sure in advance of all my gratitude.
>
> We are going from here to Stuttgart; there I will decide whether to go to Vienna or Frankfurt. One time in this last town, you may well believe that I will not fail to come and greet you in Weimar.

In waiting for your good news, I want you to receive the assurance that I have so often given you of my friendship and admiration.

Tout à vous, H.W. Ernst

Please present my respectful greetings to Madame the Princess Wittgenstein. [13 December 1853. Zähringer Hof. BAL: I:305–6]

Chapter 18

Changing Fashions: 1854–55

After Stuttgart and Mainz, the Ernsts toured several other Rhenish cities: Mannheim, Darmstadt, Wiesbaden, Frankfurt and Baden. Their success was mixed. In Stuttgart three concerts were not enough to satisfy the population's curiosity, and critics in Mainz and Wiesbaden critics praised his tone and brilliant technique. [NMZ:13/1/54:31. GMP:29/1/54:55] But in Mannheim and Wiesbaden the halls were far from full, although those that did attend were wildly enthusiastic. In addition, one critic in Mannheim felt that Ernst's repertoire was now antiquated – the time for pure virtuoso display had now passed, and violinists should concentrate on music of greater depth – while another in Wiesbaden disliked Amélie's recitations. [SMZ:13/3/54:42; 27/3/54:51. NMZ:10/3/54: 76. E:172–4]

In March, they travelled, possibly with some relief, to England via Cologne and Brussels. Ella had recently introduced a set of Musical Winter Evenings to complement the normal meetings of the Musical Union, and Ernst appeared at the fourth of these on 30 March 1854. Besides the *Elegy*, he played in Mendelssohn's quartet in E minor op.44 no.2, and Beethoven's auartet in E♭ op.74 with Goffrie, Hill and Piatti. In a programme note for the concert, Ella observed that no other executant could match Ernst in the performance of Mendelssohn. This was partly because of the power of his playing, but also because Ernst was exceptionally generous in sharing his opinions with other members of the quartet; indeed, all the bowings at the end of the scherzo were Ernst's own, and they added greatly to the effect of the movement. [RMU:6/4/54:28]

However, the German critics whom Liszt had noted, and who had dogged Ernst in Paris and on his tour of the Rhine, now reappeared in particularly lethal form in London:

> Ernst is here … he looks as usual, he plays as usual. It's clear that his Élégie is also as usual and his interpretation of this work is still always the best. Ernst is the last surviving artist of the 1830s, he brings his epoch everywhere with him and offers material for very melancholy reflection. His playing was wonderful in the past, but it is boring now. He has taste, feelings, nuances, and at the same time looks pale and feeble; he has all that was interesting in the past; but this is no longer thrilling. He is a feminine player, but today virtuosity asks for manliness. What we want are vigour, daring, energy; better coldness and substance than feeling and – dullness, if not to say triviality. I don't believe in Germany such virtuosos as Ernst are still lucky and can make money. As to what is happening here this is easy to understand: for with respect to music, England has not yet moved beyond the 1830s. [SMW:4/54:139. trans. E:175]

Why was Ernst growing so unpopular amongst German musicians? Liszt pointed out that Ernst's endless repetition of the same pieces was partly to blame, but the situation is more complex than this alone suggests.

Opposition to touring virtuosi had always been strongest in Germany. One reason for this was that, for the first seven decades of the century, Germany consisted of scores of small states and courts, all with churches, theatres and resident *Kapellmeisters*. These men, who were often versatile and highly trained musicians, frequently resented the excitement caused by visiting virtuosi, and were only too ready to point out their limited repertoire and, under the glitter, their primitive compositional techniques. [BAV:83–5] As Paris was seen as the great international centre of virtuosity, suspicion of itinerant virtuosi was also frequently fuelled by patriotic motives. The opinion of the Germans was growing increasingly influential because, during the nineteenth century, political and military power moved away from Paris and Vienna towards Germany, and musical influence moved with them. Consequently, opposition to virtuosi, which had once been a largely provincial matter, now became absorbed into the mainstream of music.

Hostility increased after 1848. Italian operatic music, and certain kinds of French operatic music, began to fall out of fashion, largely because it was seen to be the music of the repressive aristocratic classes. [VLR:202] This in turn meant that much of the virtuoso music written by Paganini, Bull and Ernst, which was built on operatic themes, began to fall out of fashion too. Its place would be taken by national music – Polish, German, Czech, Hungarian – which expressed a people's desire for liberty and unity. Since Ernst was Jewish and embraced a life of international wandering, this was not a movement to which he could easily belong.

The general public also began to grow bored with virtuosity. Instrumental technique, particularly that of the violin and piano, had made huge strides between 1820 and 1840. But by 1850 it was widely felt that little more progress could be made in this direction, and that what had once astonished now seemed arid. This was never more effectively expressed than in Hanslick's review of Bull's return to Vienna in 1858:

> Ole Bull was always given to one-sided virtuosity, to a combination of sovereign bravura and bizarre manners which might best be called 'paganinic.' Enthusiasm for this kind of thing, which leaves hearts and minds untouched and which excites only surprise, has decreased astonishingly during the last twenty years. The heaping up of technical difficulties and their ever so brilliant mastery can only give pleasure as a medium for more spiritual purpose, a transitory device for a nobler effect. We demand of a virtuoso, himself insignificant as a composer, that he places his technical abilities at the service of superior music. Now, as he did twenty years ago, Ole Bull plays his own compositions. They are, if we are not greatly mistaken, the same pieces.
>
> ... [Many] aspects of his technique are now common property. ... By way of summation we can say that his virtues are purely technical. The whole orientation of his playing has become obsolete, and it needs all his personal charm to recall it even partially to a fictitious life. [HMC:69–71]

The two greatest virtuosi of the early nineteenth century avoided this fate. Paganini had died in 1840, and Liszt had given up his virtuoso tours and settled permanently in Weimar – largely so he could concentrate on composition – in 1848.

Many of the more old-fashioned virtuosi – Gottschalk, Sivori, Hauser and Bull himself – managed to make a respectable living in America where tastes were less well developed. The idea never appealed to Ernst. In the autumn of 1845, a rich American named Doodle had offered to invite him to the States. He guaranteed that if Ernst gave concerts for four months in New York he would be able to earn $100,000, but the offer was never taken up [SMW:9/45:309], and Ernst's thoughts about going to California in his 1849 letter seem entirely whimsical.

The twin examples of Paganini and the late Beethoven helped encourage a growing demarcation between composer and performer. The demands of both roles were now so strenuous that, for the first time in history, it was coming to be felt that one man could not excel at both tasks. Liszt and Mendelssohn, of course, were outstanding in both fields, but the next generations usually allowed one role to lapse. Brahms was a first-class pianist but he gradually allowed performing to come second to composition. Bülow and Joachim composed in their youth, but their performing careers soon began to eclipse their compositional ambitions.

If the performer was not a composer, then he was clearly not competent to improvise or alter a composer's wishes as the whim took him. Consequently, leading German musicians by the 1850s had given up playing extempore fantasias, and no longer rewrote or altered composers' works to suit their own tastes. Ernst, however, continued to perform rewritten versions of Spohr and Mendelssohn concertos, frequently altered his own compositions in performance, extemporized sets of variations, and sometimes improvised additions to works of chamber music. In Germany, such practices were looked on with widespread disapproval. Wasielewski wrote: 'In certain circumstances [Ernst] did not hesitate when seeking superficial effect to add arbitrary variations (especially in chamber music) of his own to the composer's text.' [CV:92–3] Fidelity to a written text was now not simply a matter of taste; it was a matter of morals.

In addition, Ernst's compositional language was beginning to look dated. In the 1850s, a rift was opening in German musical life. This was between more conservative musicians who looked for inspiration to the Leipzig Conservatoire – the Schumanns, Hiller, David, Joachim and Brahms – and more progressive musicians who looked to Liszt at Weimar – Wagner, Berlioz, Raff, von Bülow and Cornelius. (Liszt's remark in his 1852 letter to Ernst about 'the musical direction, we are engaged in forming' clearly refers to this bifurcation.) The acrimony of this dispute, of course, further emphasized composition at the expense of performance. Ernst was irrelevant to all this, firstly because he was friends with several members of both sides, and secondly because he was largely influenced by Mendelssohn and Chopin who had both died by 1850.

By the mid-century, Mendelssohn began to look a little pallid and conservative, and an increasingly anti-Semitic atmosphere in German music made his example additionally problematic. Schumann was undoubtedly the leading composer in the Leipzig group in the early 1850s, and there are a number of anti-Semitic comments in his diary. [MR:165] And Wagner, for the Weimar group, caused outrage when he published 'Judaism in Music' in 1850. Ernst's kinship with Chopin was also questionable. He used the same musical forms as Chopin, resembled him in appearance, frequented the same Parisian salons, was a deeply expressive player, and had a strong appeal to women. In the mid-1850s, with his illness growing worse, he also began to resemble the older Chopin's exhaustion and feebleness. Unfortunately for Ernst, as the review of his concert quoted above makes clear, weakness and tubercular pallor had fallen out of fashion.

The changing format of concerts also worked against Ernst's compositions. In the old style of concert up to thirty musicians, including singers, took part, and even leading virtuosi were given slots of only ten to twenty minutes. The format was still widely used in England (indeed Philharmonic concerts up to the First World War still have something of its flavour) but on the Continent it was becoming obsolete. In the mid-1850s, Liszt's idea of a solo recital had not entirely conquered, but concerts involving only three or four performers, often all instrumentalists, were commonplace. Most of Ernst's pieces are what Clara Schumann called 'concert pieces', works of about eight to ten minutes in length. Clearly designed for the old format, they suddenly became hard to programme, not being substantial enough for a main item, and yet too much so for an encore. Even Ernst's concerto, which lasts about twenty minutes, seems too short for the modern concerto slot, and consequently its popularity declined. After all, if you are going to hire a soloist, he may as well play something more extended.

The violinist who became most strongly associated with modern German ideals was Ernst's protégé Joachim, and it was inevitable that his reputation would soon begin to menace his mentor's. As early as 1852, when Joachim was 20, we can find their rivalry in Germany being mentioned in England: 'Herr Joachim is a violinist of the first stamp, and may be fairly said to divide the championship of Germany, with the incomparable Ernst, whom, nevertheless, he resembles in nothing but in those sterling and indispensable requisites which are the basis of all artistic excellence.' [MW:8/5/52:290]

In fact, the styles of the two violinists were very different. Ernst was coming to be thought of as far too emotional. His style is characterized as 'feminine', 'mannered', 'sentimental', 'nervous', 'humorous' and 'subjective'; whereas Joachim's is 'healthy', 'manly', 'serious', 'pure', 'German' and 'objective'. A review of Joachim's first Viennese concert in 1862 makes these differences clear:

> The influence exerted on him by Mendelssohn and Ferd. David is unmistakable; his style is purely German, and has lost nothing of its essential qualities by his long sojourn in London and Paris. ... This manly seriousness preserves him, moreover, from that effeminacy which not infrequently obtains the upper hand with modern violinists, and thus his playing never degenerates into artistic mawkishness ... while it keeps aloof from the popular *tremolos* and *vibrandos* which Ernst brought into fashion, and which may be called the toilet arts of affected feeling. [*Der Wanderer*: MW:16/3/62:166]

For Ernst, contemporary German reviews imply, virtuosity is an end in itself, for Joachim it is a means for the adequate interpretation of supreme masterpieces:

> A sure mastery over his instrument, wonderful technical skill, equally perfect in every particular, and capable of comparison with that of any artist, up to Ernst and Paganini themselves, are for Joachim, as for every other instrumental performer, merely a means for the attainment of the highest object in art, namely the rendering of works of creative

masters in all their originality and peculiar spirit. The fact of his fulfilling this task with extraordinary self-abnegation; of his being able to make himself, with Protean power, the docile organ of so many different artistic individualities; and of his retiring into the background ... in a word his perfect *objectivity*, is the very rare quality which ... places him at the head of all the violinists of the present day. [*Donau-Zeitung*: MW:16/3/62:166]

This led to a fundamentally different approach to repertoire. Paganini largely played his own display pieces; the next generation (Ernst and Sivori, for example) played their own display pieces and a good deal of 'classical' repertoire; Joachim was the first violinist, after his youth, to restrict himself entirely to the classics. As early as 1849 he wrote: '...Gade came to ask me if I would play twice in the next concert here. I did not want to play old things, and (*entre nous*) such stuff as Vieuxtemps, Bériot, Ernst, and David, etc, I cannot play without disgust.' [JJ:287] His sycophantic biographer, Andreas Moser, explains why:

> It is true that Vieuxtemps and David played the Beethoven Concerto and other classical works long before Joachim's day, but they were both like Liszt, and always followed a work of depth with their poor but dazzling fantasies on some popular air, as if they wished to apologise to the audience for having so far annoyed it as to play serious music. On the other hand, by wasting their strength on the production of meaningless and unworthy music, they lost the power necessary to grasp the depth of a true work of art and the capacity to reproduce it in its true spirit. [JJ:290]

Like improvising ornaments, playing display pieces was now a moral failing which weakened, or suggested weakness in, the performer's whole character.

It must be said that Ernst and Joachim continued to hold one another in the highest possible esteem, and Ernst seems to have felt no resentment about Joachim's triumphs. A report in the *Musical World* says that Ernst was writing a new violin concerto for Joachim (although the work seems to have remained unfinished [MW:20/1/55:35]), and he certainly dedicated two important works to his protégé – the third of the *Polyphonic Studies*, and the third string quartet in C major. [MW:20/1/55:35] When Ernst fell seriously ill, Joachim tirelessly championed his new works and frequently appeared at concerts to raise money for the older man. He also took over the position which Ernst had created in England. This was noticeable as early as 1858. Chorley wrote:

> It is with regret that we must continue the bad accounts of Herr Ernst's health, which affords little hopes of his being able to resume his career as a player, for the present at least. It is fortunate for lovers of great violin-playing that Herr Joachim is in his prime and in extraordinary (not too extraordinary) favour here; – since the alternatives are not many. Consummate in point of tone and execution as M. Vieuxtemps is, he has, nevertheless, never taken a hold on the hearts of our amateurs; and after these two celebrities are mentioned, it becomes difficult to lengthen the list. [A:27/11/58:690]

The difficulty of Ernst's situation in Germany was compounded by the fact that he had spent so much time in England, and was so universally revered by the critics there. This was because, with good reason, both warring camps in Germany regarded the English critics as hopelessly reactionary, and this situation was largely the responsibility of Ernst's friends Davison and Chorley. Although these two disliked one another, and disagreed about the quality of contemporary British music, their enthusiasms were remarkably similar: they worshipped the classics (Handel, Haydn, Mozart, Beethoven, Hummel, Spohr), admired one or two lesser composers of the previous centuries (Dussek, Steibelt), but amongst contemporaries could only adore Mendelssohn and, in Davison's case, some of Mendelssohn's British disciples (Sterndale Bennett and Macfarren).

Davison detested any music he thought Romantic, and from his immensely influential positions on the *The Times* and the *Musical World* waged unceasing war against it. As his list of Romantics included Schubert, Chopin, Schumann, Liszt, Berlioz (before he got to know him) and Wagner, his attitude ensured that for nearly thirty years the main currents of European composition largely bypassed England. Thus any performer who was revered by the English critics could only be held in deep suspicion by leading German musicians.

In reactionary England, on 5 April 1854, Ernst played *Hungarian Airs* and the Mendelssohn concerto at the New Philharmonic under Lindpaintner. British critics were lavish in their praise, but in his memoirs, John Edward Cox recalled: '[He played] with immense spirit, but far from perfectly with regard to truthful intonation – a fault he never wholly overcame.' [MRLH:II:277] And a correspondent for the *Süddeutsche Musik-Zeitung* remarked that his playing was altogether too nervous, and that even some notes in easy passages were out of tune. [SMZ:15/5/54:80]

In late April, Ernst left to play in Dublin and Manchester, and appeared at a Classical Chamber Concert in the latter town on the 27th. With Hallé and Piatti he played to the audience's huge satisfaction, Beethoven's trio in D, op.70, no.1, Mendelssohn's D minor trio, the *Kreutzer Sonata*, and two of his own short pieces.

As in 1849–51, his main efforts were devoted to the Musical Union, and in this, its tenth season, he led all six concerts. The programmes were as follows:

25 April Haydn: Quartet in D no.70 Mendelssohn: Trio in D minor op.49 Beethoven: Quartet in E minor op.59 no.2 (Ernst, Goffrie, Hill, Piatti; piano: Sterndale Bennett)	9 May Beethoven: Quartet in C minor op.18 no.4 Mendelssohn: Quartet in E minor op.44 no.2 (Ernst, Goffrie, Hill, van Gelder)
23 May Mozart: Quartet in E♭ [K.428] Mendelssohn: Quartet in F minor op.80 Beethoven: Sonata in A for violin and piano op.47 (Ernst, Goffrie, Hill, Piatti; piano: Hallé)	6 June Spohr: Quintet in G op.33 no.2 (Molique, Ernst, Goffrie, Hill (2nd viola), van Gelder) Beethoven: Quintet in C op.29 (Ernst, Molique, Goffrie, Hill, van Gelder)
13 June Mozart: Quartet in D [K.525] Spohr: Trio Concertant in E minor, op.119 Beethoven: Quartet in A op.18 no.5 (Ernst, Goffrie, Hill, Piatti; piano: Hallé)	20 June Mendelssohn: Quartet in E minor op.44 no.2 Mozart: Piano Quartet in G minor [K.478] Beethoven: Quartet in C op.59 no.3 (Ernst, Goffrie, Hill, Piatti; piano: Hallé)

All of these concerts were packed, and the reviews were uniformly outstanding. Only at one point was there a hint of dissent. Reviewing the fourth concert, the critic for the *Morning Post* wrote: 'There was, however, one thing, and only one, which we did not like in this … performance: and that was Herr Ernst's interpolation of some notes of his own, a few bars from the end of the episodical Andante Scherzo in A major. In every other respect, as we have already said, the performance was perfect.' [7/6/54. E:180–81] Even in England, it would seem, German ideas about fidelity to a written text, were beginning to make headway.

Ernst played at J. Blumenthal's concert in the Dudley Gallery on 29 May, where he and Piatti took part in Blumenthal's trio, and Amélie recited a scene from Schiller's *Marie Stuart* (Ernst would later quote one of its most celebrated lines to Bulwer Lytton). In late June, he joined Bazzini to perform the latter's *Concertante* for two violins and orchestra.

After being constantly in one another's company for more than two years, Ernst married Amélie at the Register Office in Marylebone, London, on 31 July 1854. The certificate says that Heinrich Wilhelm Ernst, aged 41, a bachelor living at 8 Old Cavendish Street, an artist, and the son of Jacob Ernst, gentleman (deceased), married Siona Levy [sic], aged 22, a spinster living at 10 Welbeck Street, daughter of Aaron [sic] Levy, merchant. The ceremony was conducted by Thomas Stoner Tindall in the presence of J.W. Davison [the critic], F.J. Jelot [unidentified], Walter Stewart Broadwood [the piano manufacturer], and Rose F. Levy [sic] [the bride's mother]. [MC] That this was a civil wedding, and the fact that the phrase 'according to the rites and ceremonies of' is crossed out, suggest that Ernst had not yet taken the path to Rome, even though he was thinking about it as long ago as November 1852. [CGB:IV:219]

There is no news of Ernst in the press for the rest of 1854 and one assumes he was on his honeymoon. The couple spent at least some of the time in Paris, as we know from a letter of 3 November from Ella to Hallé: 'I am just home from a three months' ramble in Switzerland and France. I saw Chorley and Davison *separately*. I was one of the four *témoins* [witnesses] at the wedding of Berlioz, and I am happy to say that he is in better spirits, with only one wife to provide for. Ernst is enjoying a passive matrimonial existence with a florid amount of maternal eloquence *ad lib*.' [LLCH:249–50] They probably also visited Vienna. On their return, Amélie began to look after the administration of their concerts, and Frankowski left Ernst's service after more than twenty-five years.

The couple remained devoted to one another. This was a blessing because, although neither partner could know it, their marriage ceremony was the beginning of a long period of trial and suffering. Ernst's health worsened significantly in 1854, by 1857 he had to retire, and by the early 1860s he was frequently paralysed and in terrible pain. On her marriage, Amélie might reasonably have expected twenty more years of performing and celebrity, but instead she spent the next eleven years nursing an invalid. Despite the additional loss of her own career, she stood by him selflessly throughout these years: reading to him, encouraging him, tending to him, fussing over him, and he was never less than profoundly grateful for her love and care.

The Ernsts had returned to England by the middle of November 1854 so that Ernst could appear at two more Classical Chamber Concerts in Manchester on

16 November and 14 December. On 2 and 9 January, he then appeared at two of Jullien's popular concerts which had recently moved from Drury Lane to Covent Garden. In the first concert he scored a huge success with Beethoven's violin concerto ('If Beethoven had written the concerto expressly for the performer, he could not have adapted it with more art and more felicity to his fervour, his profound feeling, and true majesty of style'); and in the second, he gave an overwhelming performance of the Mendelssohn ('Perhaps on no former occasion has the German violinist – full of vigorous intellect and dreamy imagination – been heard to more conspicuous advantage.') [MW:6/1/55:10; 13/1/55:25]

It must have been around this period that the Reverend H.R. Haweis first heard Ernst. The passage from *My Musical Life* requires quotation in full (complete with asterisks), not only because it is a wonderful example of a lost prose style, but because it represents the *ultima Thule* of the Romantic dreaming which Ernst's playing always seemed to induce:

> It was my privilege to hear ERNST before he lost his cunning, not shall I ever hear his like again. He played once at Her Majesty's Opera House, when the whole assembly seemed to dream through a performance of the 'Hungarian Airs.' The lightest whisper of the violin controlled the house; the magician hardly stirred his wand at times, and no one could tell from the sound when he passed from the up to the down bow in those long cantabile notes which had such power to entrance me. ...
>
> Great, deep-souled, weird magician of the Cremona! I can see thy pale, gaunt face even now! Those dark, haggard-looking eyes, with the strange veiled fires, semi-mesmeric, the wasted hands, so expressive and sensitive, the thin lank hair and emaciated form, yet with nothing demonic about thee like PAGANINI, from whom thou wast absolutely distinct. No copy thou, – thyself all thyself – tender, sympathetic, gentle as a child, always suffering; full of an excessive sensibility; full of charm; irresistible and fascinating beyond words! Thy Cremona should have been buried with thee. ...
>
> *　　*　　*　　*　　*　　*
>
> In the night I hear it under the stars, when the moon is low, and I see the dark ridges of the clover hills, and rabbits and hares, black against the paler sky, pausing to feed or crouching to listen to the voices of the night.
>
> *　　*　　*　　*　　*　　*
>
> Alone in autumn woods, when through the shivering trees I see the angry streaks of the sunset, and the dead leaves fall across a sky that threatens storm.
>
> *　　*　　*　　*　　*　　*
>
> By the sea, when the cold mists rise, and hollow murmurs, like the low wail of lost spirits, rush along the beach.
>
> *　　*　　*　　*　　*　　*
>
> In some still valley in the south, in midsummer, the slate-coloured moth on the rock flashes suddenly into crimson and takes wing; the bright lizard darts timorously, and the singing

of the grasshopper never ceases in the long grasses; the air is heavy and slumberous with insect life and the breath of flowers. I can see the blue sky – intense blue, mirrored in the lake – and a bird floats mirrored in the blue, and over the shining water comes the sound, breaking the singing silences of nature: such things are only in our dreams!

*   *   *   *   *   *

It is thus only I can hear again the spirit voice of thy Cremona, dead master ... [MML: 31–3]

After his difficulties with the Germans over the past three years, Ernst's success at Jullien's concerts must have been heartening, and he mentions them in a letter to Hallé:

The concerts in Covent Garden are always very well attended and I'm pleased to see that I can assert myself steadfastly in front of the English public. My success is always truly enthusiastic, in the performance of classics as well as rubbishy works of my own composition... [After 17 January. MALS]

The principal purpose of this letter was to arrange the programme for a Manchester concert on 25 January. In the event, the pieces selected caused some complaints in the press. 'The programme differed from the usual routine inasmuch as *two* trios and *two* sonatas were given, which is certainly one too much – from eight to quarter past ten is quite long enough for a concert of this kind, and the above was not over until eleven.' [MW:3/2/55:70] Irritation, however, did not blind the correspondent to the excellence of the performances – 'in feeling and expression, Herr Ernst, in our opinion, surpasses all living violinists' – and he was encored twice. These chamber music concerts in Manchester were important because their success encouraged Hallé to arrange a series of orchestral concerts, and their success in turn led to the foundation of the Hallé orchestra.

Once again, Ernst had heavy chamber music commitments in London. The Beethoven Quartet Society disappeared after its 1852 season, but Ernst was contracted to play for both Ella's concert series – the Musical Winter Evenings, and the regular concerts of the Musical Union. The works in which he played were as follows:

Musical Winter Evenings

15 February	1 March
Mozart: Quartet in B♭ [K.589] 3rd and 4th Movements	Haydn: Quartet no.74
	Beethoven: Quartet in F op.59 no.1
Mendelssohn: Quartet in E♭ op.12	Beethoven: Trio in E♭ op.1 no.1
Ernst and Heller: 3 *Pensées Fugitives*	(Ernst, Goffrie, Hill, Piatti; piano: Pauer)
(Ernst, Goffrie, Hill, Piatti; piano: Pauer)	
29 March	
Beethoven: Quartet in B♭ op.18 no.6	
(Ernst, Goffrie, Hill, Piatti)	

The Musical Union

17 April Haydn: Quartet in B♭ no.78 Mozart: Quintet in G minor [K.516] Beethoven: Piano Trio in D op.70 no.1 (Ernst, Cooper, Goffrie Hill (2nd viola), Piatti; piano: Pauer)	12 June Mozart Quartet in C [K.465] Beethoven: Piano trio in B♭ op.97 Mendelssohn: Composite Quartet op.81 Ernst and Heller: 3 *Pensées Fugitives* (Ernst, Cooper, Hill, Piatti; piano: Pauer)

19 June
Haydn: Quartet in D no.63
Hummel: Quintet in E♭ op.92
Beethoven: Andante and Finale from
    Kreutzer Sonata op.47
(Ernst, Cooper, Hill, Piatti, Bottesini;
    piano: Hallé)
	26 June
	Spohr: Quartet in E♭ op.58
	Beethoven: Quartet in E minor op.59 no.2
	Beethoven: Sonata for violin and piano
	    op.24
	(Ernst, Cooper, Hill, Piatti ; piano: Mrs
	    Joseph Robinson)

All of Ernst's performances were enthusiastically received, and Davison, momentarily overcoming his dislike of Ella, was generous enough to describe the Musical Union as 'perhaps the best conducted institution for the performance of chamber music in Europe'. [MW:16/6/55:382] But an even more venerable London institution was in some trouble. As Ernst explains to Hallé:

> The Philharmonic still seems to be in great difficulties. So I was told by Sainton, and Anderson is on his travels searching for a conductor in Paris. Maybe he'll come back with a bus conductor! We thank you for your best wishes and return them. And now Adieu! And see you soon. [After 17 January. MALS]

The troubles were of two kinds. The first was that a rival organization, the New Philharmonic, had been formed by Dr Henry Wylde in 1852, and he had invited Berlioz from Paris to conduct the first season. Wylde's intention was to give a fair hearing to modern and native composers – something he felt the old Philharmonic was conspicuously failing to do. The New Philharmonic had a larger and better orchestra than the old, and Berlioz galvanized musical London with the precision and vigour of his first season. Consequently, he was invited back to conduct two concerts in 1855. [BSG:568] For a time it looked as if the old Philharmonic was in danger of being superseded. [OE:179–82]

The other difficulty for the old Philharmonic was finding a replacement for Costa, the famous conductor and orchestral disciplinarian, who had resigned at the end of the 1854 season because of excessive musical commitments elsewhere. Berlioz had been approached but was already contracted to the New Philharmonic; Lindpaitner could not obtain a sufficiently long leave of absence from Würtemberg; Spohr, as usual, could not leave Kassel. [MW:20/1/55:41; OE:183] The Society's Honorary Treasurer, George Anderson, was therefore sent abroad in conditions of some secrecy to see if he could find another conductor. A day or two after Ernst's letter to Hallé, the news broke that Anderson had gone to Zurich and secured the services, not of a bus conductor, but of Richard Wagner. [MW:20/1/55:42] This threw the London musical press, led by Davison, into a frenzy of denunciation. Wagner was the leader of the German musical radicals and was one of their most eloquent anti-Semites, he could therefore only be execrated and abhorred in London which worshipped the conservative and Jewish Mendelssohn. It is a pleasing paradox that, in 1855, the most musically conservative capital in Europe should have had two of the most radical and advanced musicians in charge of its leading orchestral institutions.

Ernst appeared with both men. On 12 March he mounted the platform with Wagner at the first of the old Philharmonic's concerts playing Spohr's *Gesangsszene*. How good the overall performance was is almost impossible to decide because critical prejudices were so deeply entrenched.

Predictably, Davison loathed Wagner's performance, and found Ernst's playing one of the few rays of light: 'The fine dramatic concerto in A minor of the "stupid" old doctor at Cassel [Wagner's alleged opinion] was gloriously executed by the poet fiddler Ernst, but loosely and coarsely accompanied by the band. Herr Wagner seemed not to know this "by heart," and in two places was "abroad." Ernst, however, knew it well "by heart;" and Herr Wagner got out of the scrape.' [MW:17/3/55:172] Chorley in the *Athenaeum* concurred: 'Dr Spohr's *Scena Dramatica*, got through heroically by Herr Ernst, was as badly accompanied as a solo can be …' [A:17/3/55:329]

On the other hand, George Hogarth, writing in the *Illustrated London News*, was full of praise, although here it must be remembered that he was also Secretary of the old Philharmonic Society, and therefore instrumental in Wagner's appointment. 'So convinced were the audience of the admirable manner in which [Wagner] had acquitted himself that, at the conclusion of the concert, he was saluted with repeated rounds of applause. It is sufficient to add, in respect to the solo performances, that Ernst in his concerto showed that in tone and expression he is still without a rival …' [ILN:12/3/55:254]. Ferdinand Praeger, who along with Sainton had originally suggested Wagner's appointment, thought that Wagner was 'the beau ideal of conducting' [WAK:235], but found Ernst's performance old-fashioned and mannered.

Ernst's appearances at the New Philharmonic were less contentious. On February 14 he played his *Pirate Fantasy* under Dr Wylde, the only complaint being that a single slight piece was insufficient to show his talent [ILN:17/2/55:155]; and on 28 March he played his *Otello Fantasy* 'as grandly as ever' with the same conductor. [MW:31/3/55:204] The highlight of the season, however, was undoubtedly his performance of *Harold in Italy* under Berlioz's baton at the sixth concert. '[The] difficult and interesting [viola] part was confided to Herr Ernst,' wrote Davison, 'who performed it with the most exquisite poetry and sentiment. The performance indeed was indebted in no slight degree to the admirable co-operation of the great German violinist.' [MW:7/7/55:436]

Ernst socialized with both conductors, but his relations with Wagner could never be warm. Ernst, as a Jew, could only be appalled by Wagner's anti-Semitism; Wagner, as a radical, could only be disgusted by the reactionary German regimes (Kassel, Hanover, Braunschweig) with which Ernst had been associated. Ernst nonetheless made an attempt to keep relations cordial. 'To-day' wrote Wagner to his first wife on 30 March, 'I dine with Ernst who has married another Jew here.'

[RMW:189] Ernst's relations with Berlioz were much better, and, in a letter to Theodore Ritter, Berlioz described the last rehearsal of *Harold in Italy*:

> Yesterday an awful rehearsal at Exeter Hall, Glover's Cantata, style very piquant but difficult, I sweated until the gutters in the Strand overflowed, and the Finale of 'Harold' … Wanderings in the London streets by moon-light, I go and rejoin my wife at Ernst's, Mme. Ernst asks me if I like Molière, ye Gods!! And in a jiffy, well I will recite or declaim something of his: A scene from the 'Misanthrope,' after which the chessmen are brought up and Ernst sits down to the table with M. Louis Blanc and there they are crouching over these stupid combinations till three in the morning … [GBL:204–5. See also CGB: V:124–5]

Louis Blanc, the French Socialist leader, and a friend of Ernst's since the 1840s, had been forced into English exile after the 'June Days' of 1848. He would not return to France until 1870.

Between his concerts with Wagner and Berlioz, Ernst toured several provincial cities including Dublin. From Morrison's Hotel in that city, he wrote Davison a charming and nostalgic letter on 18 May:

> It's the hour when you are probably already exhausted over tomorrow's edition of your paper. As for me, I am going to find some words of friendly remembrance of the town where our acquaintance became a true friendship. Ten years have flown since then, and neither the divisions nor the absences which have come between us since then have made us less affectionate. [BL]

Back in London, Ernst took part in the first chamber music concert to be held in the Crystal Palace. This was a laudable attempt to make chamber music available to the masses who could not afford the prices of the Musical Union. But the vast space and audience (more than a thousand were present, even though only season-ticket holders were allowed in) ensured the concert was a failure: 'The arrangements were not good, and it was only possible for those in the immediate vicinity of the platform to hear anything. No more than half the programme was performed.' [MW:9/6/55:366] Much more successful were appearances at John Macfarren's concert [MW:23/6/55:400] and at a morning performance organized by Mrs Anderson, the Honorary Secretary's wife, and pianist to the Queen. [MW:7/7/55:435–6]

Ernst left London for Aix in Savoy on 14 July. In August, he played at two concerts in the casino in Aix [GMP:5/8/55:455; 26/8/55:263], and in the autumn gave four concerts in Geneva. He wrote to Davison in November:

> I am sending you a little article on the three evening concerts of classical music which I gave in Geneva but since (the 27th October) I also gave a farewell concert with the assistance of Madame Jenny Goldschmidt Lind, Herr Goldschmidt and Benedict. You can well imagine it was very brilliant and that it was received with the liveliest enthusiasm. As for me, I beg to tell you, that in spite of these dangerous neighbours, I was no less well received than in my three previous concerts. [BL]

On 4 November he arrived back in Paris, and wrote to Davison the next day, asking if a tour of England would interfere with Jullien's concerts. Characteristically, Davison did not reply, and Ernst wrote again on 12 December:

> I understand your significant silence. The proof is that you have not seen me again in London, and that I have taken the decision to stay two or three months in Paris.
> ... I've accepted an engagement to play 4 evenings of classical music. I also plan to finish some compositions. In the meantime, I ask you to keep an eye on my interests in London, and to tell me if something fruitful and suitable appears for me, because I must tell you that I gave up my plan to return to England with reluctance, and it will not be long before I return there at the first opportunity. [BL]

Chapter 19

Decline: 1856–57

The concerts of classical music which Ernst mentions in his letter to Davison were the four 'Soirées de musique classique et historique' given by Lebouc and Paulin. He played, or played in, the following pieces:

15 [?] January 1856 Beethoven: Quartet in E♭, op.74 Onslow: Quintet no.9 Beethoven: Sonata for violin and piano op.47 (Ernst, Blanc, Ney, Gouffé (2nd viola), Lebouc; piano: Louise Mattmann)	29 January Mozart: Quartet in D minor [K.421] Bach: Chaconne (Ernst, Blanc, Ney, Lebouc)
12 February Mozart: Clarinet Quintet K.581 Mendelssohn: Quartet in E minor op.44 no.2: Andante and Scherzo (Ernst, Blanc, Ney, Lebouc; clarinet: Leroy)	26 February Weber: Piano Quartet J.76 Haydn: Quartet (unidentified) (Ernst, Ney, Lebouc; piano: Mattmann)

Lebouc and Paulin also arranged a concert of instrumental and vocal music on 17 February for the Association des artistes where Ernst played his *Hungarian Airs* and *Elegy*.

The most striking innovation in these concerts is Ernst's performance of Bach's *Chaconne* from the Partita no.2 in D minor. Although he was responding rather late to the programmes of David and Joachim, the critics were extravagant in their praise. *La France Musicale* wrote:

> New triumph awaited Ernst in Sebastian Bach's almost impossible *Chaconne* for the violin. ... [Though] replete with eccentricities, how fresh and elegant the ideas, how pure the form! It requires no small courage and no small self-denial to execute this piece in public. The first sensation on hearing it was that of surprise, the second of enthusiasm; and at the conclusion the demonstrations were such as are rarely witnessed. Ernst never previously, perhaps, in his brilliant and glorious career, achieved a success so flattering to his self-love as an artist. [MW:16/2/56:99]

His performances at the first concert gave less pleasure to the trained ear. The great artist Delacroix noted in his diary on 15 January 1856:

> Magnificent concert by Mme Viardot; The air from *Armide*. Ernst, the violinist, gave me pleasure; Telefsen [*sic*] said to me at the Princess's that he'd played very badly. I admitted

my inability to distinguish a great difference between different performers once they'd arrived at a certain degree of competence. I talked to him about my picture of Paganini, he said to me that, without doubt, he was an incomparable man. The difficulties and so-called tours de force in his compositions were still, for the most part, unmanageable by even the most able violinists. There's the inventor, there's the real man, the genuine article. [JD: III:126–7]

Thomas Tellefsen, a gifted pianist and pupil of Chopin, knew what he was talking about, and it is sad that comparisons with Paganini, which in the 1840s had all been in Ernst's favour, were now tending to run in the opposite direction.

Perhaps encouraged by the success of their concert in Geneva, Ernst left Paris in March to begin a six week tour of the English provinces with Jenny Lind, her husband, and Piatti. But he had returned to London by 13 May when he appeared at the fourth concert of the Musical Union. This was an important occasion because it was his first public appearance with Clara Schumann. Her husband had been placed in a sanatorium two years before, and it was now entirely her responsibility to earn money to support herself and her family. She had little desire to visit England, but tours there could be highly profitable, so on 8 April, on a miserable, rainy night, she set off for London. [CSAL:131]

Robert was now very ill, and it was a time of considerable stress. She found the English with their worship of Mendelssohn 'dreadfully behind the times', and she was appalled by English venality and haste. Even the best musicians, she felt, dulled and exhausted themselves by teaching from early morning until night, and she blamed them for their inadequate rehearsal schedules and monstrous programmes. Although she particularly disliked the way English musicians allowed themselves to be treated as inferiors by the aristocracy, she respected Ella as one of the few musicians in London to treat music with German seriousness, and was happy to appear at his concerts. [CSAL:132–5] On 13 May, Ernst, Cooper, Hill and Piatti played the following programme with her at the Musical Union:

Mozart: Quartet no.1 in G
Beethoven: 32 variations in C minor op.36, piano solo
Mendelssohn: Quartet in E major op.81 (Posth)
Mendelssohn: Piano trio in C minor, op.66

Ernst, according to Davison, 'was in glorious play', and the trio was played as if the performers had 'been born together, and had been playing together since they were born'. [MW:17/5/56:315]

For the fifth concert, the same musicians played Mendelssohn's quartet in E minor op.44, no.2 and Beethoven's quartet in A op.18, no.5, and Ernst 'never played more magnificently.' [MW:31/5/56:343] Hallé replaced Schumann as the pianist that afternoon (she had a piano recital at the Hanover Square Gardens) and played a selection of pieces by Bach. At the end of the concert, Hill, Piatti and Hallé were joined by several additional players to perform Hummel's septet in D minor.

Ernst's last appearance at the Union that season was on 10 June. Along with Cooper, Goffrie and Piatti, he played Mozart's D minor quartet K.421 and Beethoven's late quartet in B♭. Finally, the violinist and the cellist were joined by Clara Schumann to give a performance of Beethoven's piano trio in D op.70 no.1.

Letters and telegrams from Germany had been warning Clara of her husband's deterioration. She left London on 4 July, and on the 14th his doctor said he could not promise Robert would live another year. In fact, death was close at hand, and the composer died shortly after a visit from his wife on the 29th.

During these months, Ernst played at several other concerts. He performed the *Kreutzer Sonata* with Arabella Goddard (Davison's future wife) on 15 May [MW:17/5/56:316]; the 'sparkling and captivating' *Rondo Papageno* at Benedict's on 21 May, and Bohrer's on 27 June [MW:24/5/56:330; 5/7/56]; and *Hungarian Airs* 'with inimitable taste' on 7 June. [MW:12/7/56:440] Probably his most important appearances after the Musical Union, were his performances at two of Jenny Lind's concerts. He was warmly applauded when he appeared with her in early May [MW:10/5/56:295], and his 'truly magnificent' performance of Spohr's *Gesangsszene* increased the already heightened emotion at her final farewell concert – she gave three – on 30 June. [MW:5/7/56:426]

Although his schedule in 1856 was much less demanding than those he undertook in 1850–51, it was still taking a toll on his fragile health. Feeling distinctly weary, Ernst and his wife retired to Boulogne in the middle of July, but he was sufficiently recovered to take part in a concert there 'with the success he never fails to command' on 23 August. [MW:27/9/56:617] At the beginning of October, he passed through London on his way to play in a provincial tour of northern England, including a chamber music concert with Hallé and Piatti in Manchester on 6 November 1856, but he had returned to London by 27 December. [MW:27/12/56:815]

The beginning of 1857 found Ernst trying to regain his health in Brighton. Berlioz wrote to him there at the end of January, regretting that he could not come over, outlining his progress on the *Trojans*, and reviewing plans for an English performance (which in fact never materialized) of the *Childhood of Christ* – he particularly dreaded the English manner of rehearsing. [CGB:V:420–21]

In the middle of February, the *Musical World* could report that Ernst's fragile state had done little to impede his normal concert schedule:

This distinguished violinist is at present sojourning at Brighton, for the benefit of his health. He has, nonetheless, made several artistic visits to Manchester [on 8 and 22 January], Bradford, Sheffield, etc besides performing in several concerts in Brighton. Everywhere the great violinist has been received with enthusiasm. Our metropolitan *dilettanti* will be pleased to hear that the fresh sea-breezes and the clear sky of Brighton (where Ernst's fine talent has been fully appreciated and his assistance at all the first musical *réunions* has been a *sine qua non*) have quite re-established his health, and that he will shortly return to London for the season. [MW:14/2/1857:106]

Several of these Brighton concerts do appear to have been very successful, and the provincial setting allowed him to dip into his older repertoire. On the morning and evening of 6 February, as well as playing trios and sonatas by Mozart and Beethoven, he showed his 'wonderful command over the instrument' in the *Otello Fantasy*, and then brought down the house with the *Carnival of Venice*: '[He] literally astonished the audience with his prodigious *tours de force*. Tremendous applause succeeded this extraordinary performance.' [MW:21/2/1857:118] However, the state of his health was such that brilliant playing on one day could be followed by a dire performance on the next. Haweis heard him perform several easy pieces and was clearly pained by what he witnessed: 'I heard Ernst at Brighton. He played [some occasional 'Morceaux' ... shockingly out of tune ... [MML:52]] ... and I was told that he was so shaken in nerve, that playing a Beethoven quartet in private, and coming to a passage of no great difficulty, which I have often scampered through with impunity, the great master laid down his fiddle and declared himself unequal to the effort.' [MML:31–2]

Unevenness had always been a feature of Ernst's performances, and had even been seen as part of his sensitivity and charm, but now it was beginning to cause anxiety to his devotees. Some articles and obituaries note that not only was his intonation deteriorating but his tone as well. After Ernst's death, the violin dealer David Laurie wondered why Ernst's violin had acquired such a bad reputation. 'As I knew Mr Hallé had often played with the late M. Ernst in public, I asked him if it was not the case that its owner's failing health was accountable for the change in the tone, owing to his ability to bring it out, and he said no doubt it was; at any rate, there had been a vast difference in the receptions he got latterly from those of former days.' [RFD:141] A German source notes the same deterioration:

> When he was past forty, a diminution in his power and likewise in his success became apparent. The 'Carnaval de Venise,' which he still played, had lost a great deal of its attraction, and, in addition to this, Ernst's execution became more and more uncertain, his tone more and more effeminate; seldom did the old fire, the pristine energy, burst forth, though when it did, he was incomparable – a spring of deep fervid feeling gushed forth with his tones, and profound was the emotion of those who listened to them. [NBMZ: MW:4/11/65:690]

Ernst returned to London on about 9 March, and joined Goffrie, Blagrove, Piatti and Pauer at the Musical Union to play Mozart's quartet in D, K.499; Mendelssohn's quartet in E minor op.44, no.2; and Silas's trio in A op.27. At least for the moment, Ernst had clearly recovered, and his playing was said to be excellent. For the benefit of his aristocratic audience at the next concert on 5 May, Ella provided a note outlining and explaining Ernst's particular strengths as a player. The most striking of these was his use of high positions on one string if a phrase required it:

> If other violinists play Mozart, Haydn, and Spohr to satisfy us. Ernst more completely realizes our conception of the true rendering of Beethoven and Mendelssohn. Each artist, then, ... has an organization especially adapted to excel in different styles of art. This is most striking in performers on stringed instruments, where the artist instinctively adapts the timbre of each string to express suitably a particular phrase. In this judicious application of colour lies the secret of a poetical executant on stringed instruments, such as Ernst and Piatti, who dare encounter any amount of risk, rather than destroy the unity of expression with a mixed timbre. It is otherwise with the pianist; the manufacturer supplies one quality of tone pervading the whole range of notes. [RMU:5/5/57:6]

Ernst had difficulty living up to this description because he was ill before and during the concert, in which he played Beethoven's quartet in G op.18, no.2, and Mendelssohn's quartet in D major op.44, no.1. The review in the *Musical World* is one of the few occasions when a poor performance by Ernst is mentioned in the English press:

> Ernst rose from his sick bed to take part in the performance sooner than disappoint the subscribers. Evidence of his indisposition was unmistakable in the first [quartet], the slow movement of which, given with exquisite tenderness, alone revealed the great violinist. But in the grand quartet of Mendelssohn, Ernst seemed to rise 'like a giant refreshed.' His execution of the first and last movements was superb for breadth and energy ...and the plaintive andante ... revealed all his unrivalled powers of expression. [MW:9/5/57:295]

Clara Schumann, on her second tour of England, played a selection of Scarlatti sonatas and Beethoven's *Appasionata*. Davison felt her account of the first movement was 'too much tormented' and the coda to the finale over-pedalled. [MW:9/5/57:295]

With his health failing, Ernst must have been gratified to see that his compositions were retaining their popularity. Eduard Reményi had been appointed solo violinist to the Queen in 1854, and played a good deal of Ernst's music. On Monday 9 May he played the *Otello Fantasy* at a concert in Eton [ILN:14/2/57:136] and, more importantly, performed Ernst's concerto in the second Philharmonic concert on 4 May, the day before Ernst's last appearance at the Musical Union with Clara Schumann. 'Reményi,' wrote George Hogarth, 'showed himself to be a great artist, equally remarkable for beauty of tone, command of the instrument, elevation of style, and strength of expression. His success was complete; and no one was warmer in expressions of admiration than the author of the music, Ernst himself.'[ILN:9/5/57:433]

There were three further Musical Union concerts:

2 June	16 June
Mozart: String quartet in E♭ K.428	Haydn: Quartet in C no.57
Beethoven: Quartet in C minor op.18, no.4	Mendelssohn: Quartet in E♭ op.44 no.3
Beethoven: Piano trio in B♭ op.97, the Archduke	Beethoven: Sonata for violin and piano in G op.96: 3rd and 4th movements)
(Ernst, Goffrie, Blagrove, Piatti; piano: Clara Schumann)	(Ernst, Goffrie, Blagrove, Piatti; piano: Hallé)
14 July	
Haydn: Quartet in D, no.63	
Beethoven: Quartet in C op.59 no.3	
Beethoven: Sonata for Violin and piano in C minor op.30	
(Ernst, Goffrie, Blagrove, Piatti; piano: Hallé)	

Davison wrote that the *Archduke* on the 2 June did not go well, and that Clara Schumann's 'execution was by no means unimpeachable'. [13/6/57:380] But Davison's relations with Ella were worsening (the critic had recently complained about Ella excluding harsher critics from the Union's concerts) and he would stop covering these concerts himself the next year. [MW:9/5/57:295] Davison regarded Clara not only as the widow of an advanced composer he disliked, but also as an over-praised protégé of Ella's.

Between the Union's meetings, Ernst assisted at concerts given by, or held for, several other artists. On 3 June he took part in a performance of Rubinstein's string quartet in D minor in Harley Street, to help the composer who was travelling through London to publicize his compositions. The quartet was found technically demanding, especially the parts for violin and cello, but two rehearsals turned out to be sufficient. Ernst played 'finely', and 'con amore'. [RMU:16/6/57] On about 27 June, he played Beethoven's C minor sonata and the *Andante and Finale à la hongroise* from Haydn's G major piano trio at Clara Schumann's matinée. He was still clearly capable of playing excellently: 'Ernst was in his best play, and the sonata went admirably. The slow movement was exquisitely given by both artists, but the great German violinist especially shone in expressive and poetic sentiments. ... Haydn's two movements were faultlessly given, the animated *finale* terminating the concert with unusual *éclat*.' [MW:4/6/57:426]

Ernst's last appearance in London seems to have been at Edward Loder's concert on about 6 July, when he appeared on the same platform as Bottesini and Arabella Goddard. By 28 July he was in France, and in spite of the warm weather, he and his co-artists – Ascher and Reichardt – managed to attract a large crowd to the *école gratuite anglaise* in Boulogne. Soon after, Ernst left for Paris where he arrived in early August.

Despite the success of his own contribution in Boulogne, this concert was to be his last professional engagement. The illness which had dogged him from his mid-twenties, and which had made his concert life increasingly difficult, now manifested itself in a particularly acute, painful and debilitating form. We hear no news of him for seven months and then, in February 1858, the *Athenaeum* announced: 'Everyone will regret to hear that Herr Ernst is withdrawn from his professional career for the present by severe indisposition.' [A:13/2/58:216] And he had to cancel commitments already undertaken in Vienna. [GMM:91] His career as a virtuoso was at an end.

These events raise the question: what was the illness from which he suffered? As his symptoms worsened they became clearer and, before offering a diagnosis, it is worth listing them:

1) From the 1830s onwards, his unusually pale complexion is noticed. In April 1864 his face is described as shockingly yellow.
2) The first mentions of serious illness and debility occur after his competition with Paganini in 1837. He would then have been aged 24–25.
3) In June 1844, he staggers off stage, screams and passes out with pain.
4) He is always liable to play out of tune, but this becomes more pronounced after 1854. His tone also becomes feebler.
5) From 1857 onwards he suffers from great weakness in the legs, has difficulties with walking, and has to be seated when playing. His posture becomes bent, and after 1862 he is frequently paralysed.
6) From 1857 he suffers from 'frequently recurring pains and crises' [PM: MCF E715.X2]: pain in the right foot; pains in arms and fingers when

writing; heaviness in the lower back. These pains can be of tormenting and exhausting intensity.
7) He is frequently confined to bed with headache, fever, and other flu-like symptoms.
8) He suffers from severe insomnia.
9) He is subject to mental agitation and anguish. Even in his late teens he suffers from serious depressions, and during his final illness he hallucinates.
10) He suffers from 'crises of the stomach.' [HALS:D/EK:C3/133] Sometimes his digestive faculties stop working altogether.

There are three contemporary diagnoses of his condition. Ole Bull described it as gout. [OBM:239] This usually first attacks the big toe, but it can also affect the knees, wrists, fingers and other parts of the body. It can also be associated with back pain and mild feverish symptoms. However, it cannot explain his complexion, digestive difficulties, and mental problems. [NNG:1] The obituary in the *Neue Berliner Musik-Zeitung* also asserts that Ernst was suffering from gout, but goes on to say that this turned into 'paralysis of the spinal marrow'. [MW:4/11/65:690] This is not a recognized modern condition, but it might hint at Pott's Disease, a variety of tuberculosis which attacks the spinal vertebrae and causes them to soften and collapse. This can lead to compression of the spinal cord which in turn causes a rigid paralysis, pain, and other neurological problems. [EM:2–3] Again, this explains his fever, pain and difficulty with walking, but it cannot encompass his digestive problems. In his memoirs, the Russian violinist, Bezekirsky says that one of Ernst's diseases was paralysis of the spinal marrow, but that, in addition, he suffered from rheumatism. [EOC:27] The latter could explain his joint and back problems, but it leaves feverish symptoms, mental difficulties, and digestive problems untouched. [WD:1]

No contemporary, for obvious reasons, seems to have suggested syphilis, although it may be hinted at in one obituary [MW:4/11/65:690] and Abell's much later article. [FVP:5] There are no signs that Ernst suffered from the chancres associated with the first stage of the disease, nor the rash associated with the second, but if he ever had such symptoms he would certainly have kept them well hidden. However, the second stage of syphilis also causes 'headache, malaise ...vomiting, ... and slight fever', and he certainly suffered from these.[SWD:1] The third and final phase, which can manifest itself up to thirty-five years after the first infection, also includes many of Ernst's symptoms. One variety is actually referred to as *tabes dorsalis* (literally 'wasting of the back'), and the disease can also cause heart and liver damage, stomach pain, problems with the respiratory tract, anaemia, widespread damage to the nervous system, uncoordinated movement, paralysis, personality changes, and arm and leg weakness. [SWD:1–2] Many of Ernst's contemporaries would be familiar with these symptoms (Donizetti, Schumann, and Heine all died of syphilis) and I imagine that many of them thought that Ernst was suffering from the same disease.

One difficulty with these suggested ailments is that, although they can all be agonizingly painful when far advanced, they cannot explain why a young man should scream and pass out with pain when there appears to be nothing wrong with his joints or movement at all. Ernst's malady did become progressively worse, but it tended to manifest itself in the form of attacks or crises; something which is not characteristic of the diseases already considered.[1] Modern medicine suggests there is one condition which exactly fits all of Ernst's symptoms, and this is a rare disease called acute intermittent porphyria (AIP).

All forms of porphyria occur because of a problem with one of the eight steps the body uses to manufacture haem – a component of haemoglobin which is used to transport oxygen around the body. If any of these eight steps is interfered with, either by an inherited genetic mutation or by an environmental toxin, then products of the earlier steps – porphyrin intermediates – build up to toxic levels in the skin and other organs, and have to be excreted in the faeces and urine. [BTP:2]

AIP is usually a hereditary form of porphyria which can be inherited from either one or both parents and usually reveals itself after adolescence. [CPF:1] It occurs because of a deficiency in an enzyme called porphobilinogen deaminase. Although many people have this deficiency, only 10–15 per cent show symptoms of AIP. Why this is so is not well understood, but hormones, drugs, diet and environment play a part. [APF:1]

The symptoms of the condition are:

1) Sudden and severe abdominal pain. This can be so agonizing as to lead to loss of consciousness.
2) Problems with the limbs. These normally begin in the arms and shoulders but spread to the lower limbs. [MMHE:2] The problems can include numbness, involuntary muscle-spasms, tingling, severe pain, weakness and paralysis. Sometimes the patient may recover in periods ranging from a matter of days to three years. Sometimes the nerve damage is permanent. [MMHE:2]
3) Constipation and urine retention. The functions of the intestines, small bowel, and stomach can be severely impaired.
4) Insomnia. [MMHE:2]
5) Nausea, vomiting.
6) Mental changes, including hallucinations, depression, restlessness, extreme anxiety, paranoia.
7) Back pain.
8) Coma. [BMJ]

Initially, because of the lack of red blood cells, AIP causes anaemia, but the porphyrin intermediates initially collect in the liver [MMHE:1], and this means the sufferer begins to develop abnormal liver-function and sometimes cancer of the liver. [GHR:1] It is this accumulation of intermediates which damages the nerves leading to the abdomen and limbs.

Attacks can build over hours or days, and they are known to be triggered by the following factors: alcohol, tobacco, physical and mental stress, pregnancy, the menstrual cycle, infection, lack of food, and a large number of drugs.

---

1 Diagnosis at this distance is very difficult, and there are several other diseases which might explain his symptoms – some varieties of anaemia and lupus, for example.

This disease explains a number of features of Ernst's career. No source says that his 'crises of the stomach' and his screaming and fainting off-stage are one and the same phenomenon, but since the abdominal pains of AIP are agonizingly painful, the surmise seems likely. AIP's motor neuropathy begins in the arms and shoulders, and one can well see why numbness, muscle spasms, weakness, and lack of reactions would be debilitating for a violinist. It is no wonder that his tone and intonation suffered. Even Chorley, the most severe critic of his intonation, agrees that the problem was likely to be the result of an affliction, not of insufficient talent or practice:

> [His mastery was] accompanied by a singular drawback, which was probably organic, – not a defect arising from incomplete study. During his entire career, Ernst was always more or less liable to play out of tune; in this way resembling the greatest singer of modern times, Pasta, who could not, even by her indefatigable industry and indomitable will, control her tendency to imperfect intonation. [A: 21/10/65:541]

AIP comes in attacks of varying severity, and it is thus possible to understand why Ernst could play brilliantly one day and appallingly the next; indeed, sometimes his abilities varied from hour to hour. [NMZ:MW:11/11/65:705] Gradually, his muscle weakness and pains spread to his lower limbs and this eventually caused paralysis.

AIP also explains his insomnia, sense of anxiety and depression; and lack of red blood cells followed by liver damage would explain why his complexion changed from strikingly white to shockingly yellow. AIP has additional symptoms, but whether he also had darkened urine, a racing and irregular heart beat, high blood pressure, absent reflexes, and chest pain it is impossible to say. All of them seem highly likely.

His way of life was ill-adapted to his disease: he drank a good deal, his letters are full of enthusiasm for cigars, and his itinerant mode of life meant that he often ate and slept irregularly. By seeking out competition with Paganini, performing at the most prestigious concerts, and constantly embarking on long and exhausting journeys, he ensured his life was physically and mentally stressful. There is no known cure for AIP and, apart from recommending a high carbohydrate diet, modern medicine merely advises sufferers to avoid the drugs, stress and inadequate sleep which precipitate attacks. It is sobering to realize that, if he had given up the usual stimulants, and lived a more settled life, he might have enjoyed a long and unproblematic career.

This diagnosis of Ernst's disease may also throw some light on the absence of information about his mother. He would have inherited the faulty gene which causes AIP from at least one of his parents. His father, a robust man who lived to be 81, clearly did not show symptoms of the disease, and this gives some grounds for supposing he did not have it. But AIP is more common in women than men, and it is possible that Ernst's mother, who died young, both had the disease and showed the symptoms. These symptoms frequently manifest themselves during pregnancy, and women who have the disease are now often advised not to have a child within two years of the last. [BMJ:4] Ernst's mother had a succession of children before she gave birth to Ernst's younger brother Moritz, and this last pregnancy may well have proved fatal. The disease could also explain why Ernst's niece, Josephine, knew nothing of his mother, Charlotte. AIP can cause severe mental problems (as in the case of George III of England) and the memories may have been too painful to pass on.

With respect to Ernst's childhood in Brünn, it's also worth observing that AIP's symptoms can be brought on by exposure to the chemicals used in tanning and textile manufacture. [CPF:2] As Brünn was a centre for both industries, and the Ernsts' café was close to the old Kleine Krona textile works (and the no doubt highly polluted stream and river), this environment may well have triggered symptoms in both him and his mother.

PART IV
Retirement

Chapter 20

Nice, Vienna and the B♭ Major String Quartet: 1858–62

When Ernst ceased to play in public, he obviously became of less interest to newspapers and journals. Consequently, his movements over the next year or so are hard to trace. But around this time he probably spent some time in Berlin, where the following incident occurred. Joachim narrated it to his biographer, and it is a slight but characteristic example of Ernst's humour:

> While H.W. Ernst was in Bordeaux [in 1835?] he was a frequent visitor to the Biarnez' house, and [would play with Madame Biarnez]. From the way in which her parents treated and spoke of Ernst, little Enole concluded that the curly-haired violinist must be a very great personage, and she longed to ask him for a souvenir, but did not dare to do so. One evening, however, while Ernst was playing with her mother, the child softly crept up behind him, and with a pair of scissors cut off one of his curls, which she promptly hid and carefully preserved. Many years later, when the little thief had become the wife of Franz von Mendelssohn [in 1856], she met Ernst again in Berlin and confessed her childish theft. Ernst thoughtfully ran his fingers through his meagre locks, and said, 'Oh! Give it me back; for I could do with it now very well.' [JJ:307–8]

However, it is clear that he spent most of his time at spas and health resorts desperately seeking a cure, initially to allow him to play again, finally to make his life bearable. At the beginning of 1858, it was announced that Ernst was seriously ill in Brünn [RMU:9/2/58:4], and he was certainly in England later in the year. [*The Times*:23/6/62:8] Without success, he tried many of the German baths [MW:1860:696]: Ole Bull wrote to his son on 8 May 1858, 'Ernst is very ill in Baden-Baden; he, the poor man, is crippled by gout!' [OBM: 239]; there is a note from Berlioz, probably to Amélie, in the same town on 22 August [CGB:VI:583]; and in July 1859 he was in Gastein. [VW:52] But within a year of leaving the stage he had decided to make Nice the centre of his activities. [JN:9/10/10/65:2]

His sudden retirement left him in financial difficulty. '[It] is to be feared,' wrote Chorley, 'that the princely munificence with which the artist dispersed the gains made by him during his career of public exhibition left him to face sickness in its most depressing form, under narrow circumstances.' [A:21/10/65:541] In spite of this, he became involved in charitable work. One of his best informed obiturists wrote of his funeral: 'In addition to the leading inhabitants of Nice, a long line of poor, who did no less honour to the deceased, followed the corpse. Yet Ernst was anything but rich; it was not from his superfluity that he gave; he denied himself a great deal in order not to withdraw from the needy whom he had once assisted the gift to which they were accustomed.' [NMZ:MW:705] The musical highlights of the (winter) season in Nice were the concerts for *les pauvres* organized by the singer Sophie Cruvelli. Given Ernst's commitment to the poor, and his friendship with Cruvelli, it is highly likely that he was involved with these, at least to the extent of attending regularly.

Ernst's last semi-public appearance in Nice was a performance at the Villa Bermond in 1859. A correspondent of the *Musical World* met Ernst in Vienna in October 1859 and reported: 'The last time he played [in public] was to some members of the imperial family of Russia at Nice, and was then obliged to be seated during his performance. His account of the reception accorded to him by the Court, reminded me of the "pitying Duchess" in "The Last Minstrel".' [MW:696] The reference is to canto one of Sir Walter Scott's once popular epic, *The Lay of the Last Minstrel*, where the elderly and dejected harpist plays before the duchess and her daughter. The old man is no longer sure he can play adequately, but he receives gentle encouragement and gives great pleasure.

Nice was not a major musical centre, but the pianists Planté and the brothers Andreoli lived in the town; it had an opera house, and was regularly visited by celebrities including Sivori, Bottesini, and Vieuxtemps. [AMDM:268] There were also two amateur string quartet groups who played to a good standard. The first was led by the Conte de Cessoles, who occasionally gave public performances of quartets and piano trios at his residence. The second was organized by a M. Gautier, an ex-mayor of Nice, who encouraged visiting professional players to lead performances at his soirées in the old town. Ernst's name appears in the Conte de Cessoles' autograph album; and it seems highly probable that, as an internationally celebrated violin virtuoso, he would have enjoyed *sirops* and *thé à l'anglaise chez* Gautier. [AMDM:271–5] More importantly, it is likely that one of these groups gave the private premiere of Ernst's quartet in B♭ which the composer first heard 'played by a party of amateurs' in Nice. [MW:25/4/63:264]

For many years, Ernst had had ambitions to compose a string quartet, and it is mentioned in two letters from Hallé in 1851, and a short item in the *Musical World* in 1855. [20/1/55:35] In late 1859, the following report appeared in the *Athenaeum*: '[Ernst's] health has improved by his residence at Nice, and … he has been turning his retirement to account by composition.' [A:26/11/59:711] That the composition referred to was a sting quartet is confirmed by a letter from Heller written on 10 May 1860. The pianist commiserates with Ernst on the composer's lot, but congratulates him on receiving frequent performances 'in London, Dublin, and Germany', and on writing a string quartet. [RRA] The existence of two groups of accomplished amateurs meant that he could hear not only a performance of the finished piece, but also sections of the work while it was in progress.

Most modern music dictionaries and encyclopaedias report that Ernst played in the London Beethoven Quartet Society in 1859, and fathered a son called Alfred Ernst in 1860. Both are highly unlikely. The evidence for his playing in the Beethoven Society in 1859 is an alleged photograph of the quartet in Moser's biography of Joachim, and Joachim's statement to Moser that he performed in the Beethoven Society in the 1850s with Ernst leading, Wieniawski playing viola, and Piatti cello. [JJL:291–2. GV:245] Since Wieniawski first visited England in 1859, the quartet cannot have formed before that year. There seems to be no evidence that Alfred Ernst was Ernst's son, beyond the large number of encylopaedias in which the statement is repeated.

It is clear that Joachim's account of the quartet, forty years after the event, is confused. *The Times*, in an article written by Ernst's friend Davison, says that Ernst was last in England in 1858 [23/6/62:8]; and a Viennese correspondent, writing to the *Musical World* in 1859, reports that Ernst 'has been an invalid ever since he left London three years ago'. [1860:696] The dates may not align, but together they make the idea of some London performances in 1859 very unlikely. Even more conclusively, a thorough search of the musical press shows that the Beethoven Quartet Society ceased to exist after 1852.

The alleged photograph of the 1859 Beethoven Society quartet in Moser's biography, the only piece of evidence in support of Joachim's memory, has clearly been doctored. The original photograph [MGG1:XIV:1589 and EUZ:32] shows five figures not four, and if you look carefully at the version in Moser's book, you can see where the fifth figure's arm has been painted out. [See Plates XV and XVI] In Heller's book, the genuine photograph has the caption: '"Das Letze Quartet bei Ernst in London" am 6. Juni 1854' and identifies the fifth figure as 'Chapelle'; in *Die Musik in Geshichte und Gegenwart*, the photograph is labelled 'Die "Beethoven Quartet Society" ... (London 1864)'. [MGG1:XIV:1589] Other contemporary photographs allow us to identify this fifth figure as Arthur Chappell who organized Ernst's last benefit concert in London on 6 June 1864.

The '1854' in Heller's book is clearly a misprint of '1864', and the photograph is a picture of the organizer and the four great string players who took part in Ernst's second London benefit concert, where Ernst's last quartet in A major was first performed. The photograph in Moser's book was obviously altered to show a quartet of famous string players, but they never played together. Joachim frequently played with Ernst, and he certainly played with Piatti and Wieniawski in 1859 [E:206], but he never gave a public performance with all three. In his old age, his memory was either misled by the photograph that eventually found its way into Moser's book, or someone doctored the photograph to make it concur with his faulty memory. [E:204–8]

The idea that the writer Alfred Ernst was Ernst's son is more easily refuted. Alfred's birth certificate, from Perigueux, shows that Carl Eugène Alfred Ernst was born on 9 April 1860 to François Joseph Eugène Ernst, a school teacher, aged 36, and Caroline Scattner, aged 37. I suspect the muddle came about because Alfred Ernst translated Wagner and propagandized for both Berlioz and Wagner in the last decades of the century; Ernst's nephew, the singer Heinrich Ernst, was involved in Wagner productions; and Amélie would later write a number of books under the name 'A.Ernst'. Her writings and Alfred's were often confused [AG:II:900], and one can easily see how the thought that Alfred was a relative of Ernst's, possibly his son, arose.

In July 1859, the Ernsts were in Gastein, and by the autumn they were in Vienna. A report in the *Musical World* from that city reads:

> Oct 27 [1859] A hearty greeting to all his friends in England from Ernst. ... After trying many of the German baths, without any beneficial result, he has come to Vienna to

consult the medical men, who have given him hopes of a speedy restoration of his health if he follows their advice. He suffers acute pain, and is at times quite unable to stand or walk without support. I called yesterday at the house of Mad. Wertheimber, the most liberal friend of music and musicians in this musical capital, with whom Ernst and his wife are staying. The doctors had just left, and had given a favourable opinion as to the progress of his patient. Ernst was in better spirits than usual, and expressed the greatest interest to know what had been doing in the musical world of London since his absence. [MW:1860:696]

Ernst was staying at the home of Leopold and Josephine von Wertheimstein (not Wertheimber) who lived in considerable style on Vienna's Singerstrasse. Outwardly, the family seemed successful and cultivated but, in a typically Viennese fashion, their private life was riddled with neuroses and unhappiness.

Leopold von Wertheinstein was the general manager of the Rothschild's bank in Vienna who had married Josephine Gomperz in 1843 when she was 23 and he was 41. Although an amateur cellist and ardent theatre-goer in his youth, he was undemonstrative and reserved, whereas Josephine was beautiful and capricious. Soon, differences in age and temperament began to tell. They had two children – Franziska and Carl – but when tutors began to take up more of their time, Josephine's life came to seem increasingly stale and meaningless. She and the children began to suffer from psychosomatic illnesses, and they spent their time away from Vienna, wandering from spa to spa in search of cures. She seems first to have met the Ernsts in Gastein with her brother in July 1859. One of his letters reports that the pianist Theodor Leschetizky and his wife were there, together with the violin virtuoso Heinrich Ernst, 'so plenty of music is played'. [VW:52]

Josephine's troubles increased when she returned to Vienna and met Robert Lytton – the poet and son of the English novelist Bulwer Lytton – who had arrived to become Second Secretary at the British Mission. He too was unhappy. His proposed marriage to a Dutch aristocrat had just fallen through over money difficulties, and he had been obliged to sell at a loss the contents of the home he had bought for her. Miserable and frustrated, Robert and Josephine fell in love, and she considered leaving her husband. In the end, however, the thought of the children and the scandal made her break off the affair. Robert was so upset he had to leave Vienna for a time; she wrote a series of deeply melancholy poems in the 1870s about the affair, and told a friend in 1907 that their break-up had been a 'crown of thorns' she had had to wear ever since. [VW:55]

Amidst these emotional entanglements, Ernst continued to play and compose. A note in the *Athenaeum* reads: 'It will give everyone sincere pleasure to be told that Herr Ernst, ... has recovered sufficiently to be able to take his violin in hand' [A:7/4/60:481], and we can see from Bulwer's later letters that Ernst's playing moved Robert – no doubt in a rather delicate emotional state – to tears. [KA:430]

In October 1861, several music journals reported that Ernst was at work on a small opera that would be performed under Berlioz's baton at the inauguration of the Theatre at Baden in 1862. [SMW:17/10/61:591. NMZ:18/10/61:146. GMP:27/10/61:343] Marie d'Agoult said that Berlioz made considerable efforts to help Ernst and this might have been one of them [*Le Temps*:4/11/64:2]; perhaps the idea had been discussed during Berlioz and Ernst's joint stay in Baden in 1858. Just over a month after the initial reports, the *Revue et Gazette musicale* stated that the opera was now finished. But regrettably this is the last we hear of it, and the *Neue Zeitschrift für Musik* reported in early 1862 that a new comic opera by Berlioz would be used for the inauguration of the Baden Theatre. In the event, a German opera put on by the Karlsruhe opera company was used for the opening on 6 August 1862, although Berlioz's *Beatrice et Bénédict* was first performed there under Berlioz's direction, with brilliant success (at least amongst the artistic section of the audience), on 9 August. [E:209–10. BSG:682–3]

What happened to Ernst's opera it is impossible to know. There is no particular reason to think that *Beatrice et Bénédict* was written to replace it. *Beatrice et Bénédict* was originally to have been a short one-act opera, and it seems possible that Ernst's 'kleine Opera' was intended to share an evening with it. But *Beatrice et Bénédict* grew in the process of process of composition: from the original plan of nine musical numbers and the overture, it expanded into a two-act opera with fifteen different musical settings. [BSG:667–9] Did Ernst, on learning of this, decide to give way to the much greater creative talent of his friend?

Perhaps Ernst's opera never existed and the reports in the musical press are false. It certainly seems most unlikely that a man in Ernst's state of health – who found writing out a string quartet painful and exhausting – would have wished to undertake anything so arduous as composing an opera, especially as he had never composed any extended vocal music before. Perhaps he did finish it and either he or Bénazet – manager of the casino and theatre in Baden – found it unsatisfactory. The most likely explanation of all is that Ernst felt flattered by the commission, wrote a few sketches, found his health and aptitude quite unequal to the task, and abandoned the project, destroying any remaining material.

In the early months of 1861, a report gives some good news about a composition Ernst definitely did complete: 'A correspondent from Germany announces that Herr Ernst, the state of whose health precludes any hope of his being able to resume his profession, is putting the last touches to a string quartett, which will be forthwith published in Leipsic.' [A:23/2/61:268] Fittingly, the quartet in B♭, op.26, his greatest creative effort in the first years of this retirement, was dedicated to his host, the passionate cellist and neglected husband, Leopold von Wertheimstein.

The quartet is not a masterpiece, but it is an admirable and amiable work that would bear the occasional performance at a modern concert. Its major virtue is the expertise of the writing: each part is complex and rewarding and they fit together to produce a consistently varied and interesting texture.

The first movement, *Allegro moderato*, is probably the weakest. The introduction and main melody appear to have little to do with one another, the writing tends to the academic, and the second subject is a little too lightweight for its context. The second movement, *Andante con moto e molto tenerezza*, is more engaging. It has moments of Mendelssohnian charm and builds to an impressively lush and passionate climax.

The main theme of the last movement, *Allegro energico*, lacks distinction, but it forms the basis for an admirably relaxed and vigorous movement. The persistent dotted motor-rhythm in the accompaniment clearly derives from the finales of Beethoven's second Razumovsky Quartet op.59 no.2 – a particular favourite of Ernst's – and the finale to the same composer's late quartet in C♯ minor op.131.

Much the best movement in the piece is the tiny scherzo, without trio, which comes third. This *Allegretto animato e scherzando* begins with demisemiquavers on the unaccompanied viola which are soon joined by rising violins and high, skittering semiquavers. These lead to a confident second subject, and the piece ends almost before it has begun with the violin recalling, high up on the E string, the viola's demisemiquavers. The whole movement is puckish, bizarre and expertly written. It sounds like no one else, and would make a fine encore for a present-day quartet.

Ernst clearly felt that his stay in Vienna had improved his health, and by February 1862 he was feeling distinctly better. In a surviving letter from Nice to a friend in Vienna (possibly Carl von Wertheimstein, Leopold's son) he remarks: 'I only want to say that since the recovery of my dear Amélie [from a brief illness] I feel better with the exception of difficulties in walking and a certain pain in my right foot. My frequently recurring pains and crises have left me completely for weeks and I have never had greater hope than now.' [13 February 1862. PM:MCF E715.X2]

This new optimism must have come at about the same time as an offer from Hallé to have his new quartet performed in London. By May, arrangements were being completed: only the arrival of the manuscript and a decision about the precise personnel of the quartet were awaited. Ernst's health was beginning to fail again, but he still writes with considerable excitement to Hallé, expressing his gratitude for an idea which his friend had clearly suggested five years before:

> Dear Friend, I have just finished a letter to Chorley in which I begged him to tell you that I would write to you in a few days. But 'je prends mon courage à deux mains,' in spite of fatigue and excitement, and do so at once, for I will no longer delay to tell you how glad I am that you have joined the friends who are venturing upon my enterprise. You must feel a certain satisfaction in contributing to the success of a project in which, a few years ago, you took the initiative. Let me thank you today (which I hope Roth has already done for me), and at the same time assure you that my joy at your participation would have been complete had your kind offer been sent to me by yourself; although on the former occasion I thought it right for different reasons not to accept it. It is now five years since misfortune overtook me, and much has changed since then. In compliance with our friend Chorley's wish, I have already sent you my quartet by post; I hope it is now in your hands, if not, kindly claim it at Chappell's in New Bond Street. Notwithstanding the hopes attached to it, I can assure you that the appreciation, if only in part, of my work by the public would fulfil the innermost wish of my artist's heart, and be the greatest satisfaction the efforts of my career could obtain.
>
> Under your direction, and with artists so great as those London can offer, I am certain of the most perfect interpretation, and in the event of ill-success, my disillusion would be all the bitterer.
>
> I have no special remarks to make. I hope you will be able to read the score: it is very unevenly written out, according to the greater or lesser degree of my suffering. To your judgment and insight I leave it, whether the scherzo is to follow the first movement or the *andante* (as it is written); since I sent it off the thought has occurred to me to let it follow the first movement, as it would serve to make the contrast greater between the *allegro moderato* and the *andante*.
>
> But one thing more – pay special attention to the part in the last movement commencing with *poco a poco piu lento*, and continuing to the *poco a poco accell. e*

crescendo. I should like it to be played almost *rubato* and with great *abandon*. The whole of the last movement with the greatest possible swing.

    I cannot tell you, my dear Hallé, with what impatience I am expecting a letter from you. In our youth art brought us together. After five years separation and almost entire cessation of our former so intimate intercourse, she again stretches out her hand to unite us once more. May you seize it as eagerly as I! Write to me soon. With real joy I shall hear of all that concerns you and your family. Do not be chary of news, tell me of all our mutual friends, and of the present state of art in London. Your old and true friend, Ernst.

    A thousand greetings to all yours, and the same from my wife. [21 May 1862. Nice. LLCH:269–70]

A few weeks later, Hallé was able to give more details of the arrangements. The quartet was to be played at the ninety-ninth Monday Popular Concert at St James's Hall, London, on Monday 23 June 1862. Joachim was to be first violin, and Piatti would play the cello. The other two players had not yet been decided. Ernst wrote to convey his enthusiasm, but also to report a minor disaster:

Dear Friend, The good news contained in your kind letter gave me all the more pleasure [in] that it arrived at a moment when the ill-luck, that has followed me so long, had just dealt me another blow. Can you believe it, that yesterday morning, between four and five o'clock (almost the only hour in which I slept, and indeed I had a light burning until then) we were robbed, and in the very room in which we slept. The value of the articles stolen is at least 1,000 frs., and besides their material worth they were precious as remembrances. Among them a large watch, which, together with its wooden stand, was taken from under my very nose, from the table beside my bed. The whole day we had *commisionaires de police, juge d'instruction, procureur impérial, commandant des gens d'armes,* and *gens d'armes* in the house, to search the premises and take our depositions. Up to the present, the wooden watchstand has been found on the ground floor, but it has led to nothing further. It has been such a curious robbery that it gives rise to all sorts of conjectures and solves none of them. All this has excited and distressed me so much that I have spent a terrible night, and this morning early I received your letter; you can imagine how welcome it was. A thousand thanks for it, and a thousand thanks to you for all your sympathy.

    I accept with great gratitude the offer for my quartet, so delicately put … With regard to the time of publication, it would be advantageous to me if it could be deferred until late autumn, as some musical friends in Vienna propose to organise a performance of it, for which the summer season is not suitable, and it would lessen the interest of the public if the work was already printed and at everyone's disposal.

    The kind offer of a concert at which my quartet will be played, and the form which it is to take pleases me greatly, and it is a matter of course that Chappell's will have the right to perform it afterwards as often as they like. The good God grant that its reception may be such as to make them wish to exercise the right frequently … And now let me tell you that what you say of the impression my composition made upon you on reading it through, greatly pleased me, and I shall be enchanted if you think as well of it after having heard it. Write to me, I earnestly beg of you, as soon as ever you are able to tell me your opinion.

    Need I assure you that the two names Joachim and Piatti delighted my artist's heart, and that the thought of the first public performance of my work being in their hands filled me with the liveliest hopes?

    Thank them for the care they are going to bestow on me, which you have already promised in their name. In your next letter I should like to hear what artists you have chosen for the second violin and viola.

My health, I am sorry to say, is no better, and only the importance and interest of the circumstance enabled me to overcome the agitation of spirit, and the pain in my fingers and arms which long writing produces. The day before yesterday I took my first sea-bath, but could not continue them.

I close my letter with repeated thanks to my friends Chorley and Chappell; the latter's letter I have received and shall write to him soon. Hearty greetings to your dear wife and children, from myself and my wife. Your old friend, Ernst [LLCH:270–72]

Hallé arranged for the brilliant virtuoso Ferdinand Laub to play the second violin at the concert, and for Ernst's old friend Molique to play the viola. Chorley contributed a song – 'When I was a Lad', Hallé and Benedict would play the piano, Madame Sainton Dolby and Santley would sing. Davison broke precedent by advertising the concert in *The Times*. As well as giving details of the programme, he passed on some melancholy news to the general public: Ernst's condition was now deemed incurable, and it was most unlikely he would ever resume his professional career. [*The Times*:23/6/62:8]

The concert was a triumph, and Davison wrote a long review in *The Times*:

The concert last night for the benefit of Herr Ernst was successful beyond anticipation. St James's Hall was crowded in every part, and the amount realized, after all expenses paid, is stated to be upwards of £300. The entertainment itself was one of the most attractive imaginable – a genuine 'Monday Popular Concert,' one of the very best.

Of course the great feature was the quartet in B flat, for two violins, viola and violoncello, composed by Herr Ernst, and performed by MM. Joachim, Laub, Molique and Piatti. As this will no doubt be heard again in St James's Hall, we must be content at present to say that it is a work of exquisite fancy, in every moment showing the hand of a master. The execution was perfect. How, indeed, could it be otherwise on such an occasion and with such players? Movement after movement was applauded with enthusiasm, and at the end, the four distinguished musicians – who in thus paying homage to a brother artist did equal honour to themselves – were unanimously recalled.

The most flattering reception awaited the 'Élégie' (in C minor), one of the most pathetic pieces ever written – not merely by Herr Ernst, but by any composer who could be named. In saying that this performance vividly reminded us of that of Herr Ernst himself, by its impassioned tenderness, its richness of tone, its depth and variety of expression, we have paid Herr Joachim the highest possible compliment. A rapturous 'encore' was elicited – an 'encore' not on any pretext to be declined, and the earnest sincerity of which was further declared in the vehement plaudit that followed the repetition of the piece.

Three of those graceful and charming bagatelles, entitled Pensées Fugitives – the joint composition of Herr Ernst and M. Stephen Heller – entrusted to Mr Charles Hallé and Herr Laub (a violinist by the way whose visit to this country deserves more than passing notice), made up that part of the selection to which Herr Ernst contributed as a composer. These brought the concert to an end with éclat. … [*The Times*: 23/6/62:8. Paragraph breaks added]

'Please tell Davison,' wrote Ernst to a mutual friend (probably Chapell), 'that his friendly words in the 'Times' were my first news of the success of the concert. One of my friends, Mr Lehmann had the happy thought of sending them to me the day of their publication. Tell him that my heart throbbed with joy and pride at the feeling I had not been forgotten by so incomparable a friend, and so distinguished an artist and critic. I heartily greet him, bitterly grieved though I be at his five years' silence.' [FMW:251]

Delighted by this success, Ernst wrote to thank Hallé both for organizing the concert, and for sending the £100 Chappell gave him to publish the quartet. His health, however, had gone into serious decline:

> Dear Friend, I am just at present in a series of very painful days, else I should have acknowledged sooner the receipt of the £100, and not have let two days intervene before expressing my great joy at the success of the concert, and the gratitude and emotion that filled me at hearing of such widespread expression[s] of good-will and sympathy.
>
> Even today it is impossible for me to write at any length; therefore I beg you, dear Hallé, to be the interpreter of my most heartfelt thanks to all those (*à commencer par vous*) who, in one way or another, have proved their sympathy for me. As soon as I feel better, I hope to be able to write to each of them separately. The unprecedented composition of the quartet enchanted me. I beg you at the first opportunity to embrace them all four, and their instruments as well. That which my dear friend, the great master Molique, did for me, pleased me above all.
>
> I received letters from Lehmann, Chappell, and Joachim senior; greet them all for me; letters will follow, as soon as I am a bit better, to each in turn. The weather is so unusually bad here that since my first sea-bath, I have not been able to take another. Lehmann sent me the *Times*; many thanks.
>
> I can write no more. I greet you and yours a thousand times. Your old faithful,
> Ernst.
> P.S. – I am very, very ill, my dear friend. Forgive my brevity. You would oblige me much by sending me some of the papers that have notices of the concert. [29 June 1862. Nice. LLCH:272–3]

It was more than a fortnight before he was well enough to thank Joachim and give him some cheerless news about the robbery:

> Dearest Friend, I have already requested Chorley, Hallé and Chappell to express my thanks generally to all those who have been so kind and sympathetic to me.
>
> You are in the front rank of these, so let me embrace you warmly and give you a brother's thanks for brotherly conduct.
>
> You honoured me too in this, and I cannot tell you how happy it has made me to realise that your friendly action has not lessened your reputation as an artist. But as no pleasure is complete in this world, I still feel the deepest regret that I have not heard myself through you; who knows if this pleasure will ever be mine, and my regret is all the greater when I think that this strength-giving source was so close to me in Vienna, but that the modern law-giver of violin-playing refused to wave his magic wand. You have shown, too, that you are a greater magician than your illustrious predecessor, for you have worked the wonder of causing my mouth to water here when you wielded your magic bow in London. Write to me soon, as your brother promised. Nothing gives me [the] comfort of courage save the conviction that those for whom my heart has always been, and still is, full of love and admiration have not grown indifferent towards me. I have been rather better for the last few days. I have less pain, and the weather is so glorious that I can go on with my sea bathing without interruption. I hope I shall obtain some relief and sufficient strength at any rate to enable me to get through the winter fairly well.
>
> Not a thing has been found out about the robbery at our house; but the probability of its having been done by our servant seems more and more evident, now that it is too

late. She left us nearly a month ago, however, and the police do not seem anxious to open a new enquiry. Apropos the robbery, I forgot to reply to the charming and intelligent Heinrich's (I do not mean myself but your ... [brother's]) remark that it just proved how well and soundly I slept. My answer to that is that such a thing could never happen to a child of fortune like himself, that it takes an unlucky wretch like me to be awake the whole night until a quarter past four and then, when the thief was presumably growing impatient, to turn over and fall asleep from sheer weariness and pain – and allow his watch and other valuables to be stolen from his bedside table before his very behind. If it was a professional thief it was probably lucky that I did not turn round and face him at [that] moment. I can laugh over it now, because in life all unpleasant impressions grow weaker, thank God, but I can assure you that I did not have a moment's peace during the night for a week after this unfortunate occurrence. As all this is addressed more to your brother than yourself, I will send him word to be more charitable next time something like this happens (and I hope it will fall to his lot and not mine) and *Goimel zu benschen* for this time (I expect you will know what that means).[1]

I entreat you once more to write to me, and if you have composed anything new send it to me, together with your Concerto in D minor [the *Hungarian Concerto*, one of Joachim's most impressive compositions], which you promised me in Vienna.

God be with you. Your faithful, affectionate and admiring friend and brother, H.W. Ernst ... [17 July 1862. Villa Osten, Promenade des Anglais, Nice. LJJ:256–8]]

---

1 The italicized sentence is a short prayer, used by German Jews, to give thanks after recovering from an illness.

Chapter 21

Bulwer Lytton and the Last Journey to England: 1862–63

Ernst's name had not appeared in the pages of the *Musical World* since the account of his benefit concert on 28 June 1862. Now at last, on the 25 April 1863, there was something to report:

> Herr Ernst has been in England for the last ten days, staying at the mansion of a friend in Kensington. The reason why 'the most poetical of fiddlers' – as he has been styled by all who can feel the poetry of music – now favours the country with a visit, is one which encourages sanguine hopes for his recovery. By the advice, we are informed, of Sir Edward Bulwer Lytton, Herr Ernst is about to undergo what is termed 'the water cure,' at Malvern. Dr Wilson – the celebrated hydropathic doctor, who owns the principal establishment in that delightful spot – has been attending Herr Ernst since his arrival, for which purpose he came expressly up to town. Yesterday, Herr Ernst, accompanied by Madame Ernst and Dr Wilson, left for Malvern. That every musician, and every amateur will pray for a speedy and complete recovery, we need scarcely add; for never was artist more universally esteemed. [MW:25/4/63:162]

The name 'Bulwer Lytton' means little now, but Sir Edward was one of the most famous men of his age. He had some success as a politician – eventually rising to be Secretary of State for the Colonies under Disraeli – but he was chiefly celebrated as England's most successful and innovative novelist. Amongst his twenty-five three- and four-volume fictions are *The Last Days of Pompeii*, *Paul Clifford*, *The Caxtons*, *Zanoni*, *Pelham* and *The Coming Race*, and all of them sold like 'bread displayed to a hungry crowd'. [HD:12] He became Victorian England's highest paid novelist, and his innovations were frequently copied by his rivals, Dickens and Thackeray. Wagner based his first successful opera on Bulwer's *Rienzi*.

His domestic life was, however, singularly unhappy. His marriage to Rosina Doyle Wheeler broke down soon after the birth of their children, Emily (b. 1828) and Robert (b. 1831), and Rosina spent the rest of her life trying to punish Bulwer for what she regarded as his cruelty, neglect and unfaithfulness. She picketed his political campaigns, wrote books to blacken his name, and bombarded his colleagues with venomous and obscene letters. He responded in kind by harassing her publishers, having her rooms searched, and trying to get her confined to an asylum. Robert, as we have seen, survived his childhood to become a successful poet and diplomat, but Emily was less lucky. After the separation, she was entrusted to a nanny in Germany who subjected her to much ill-treatment and neglect. She developed a spinal complaint, and by the time Bulwer realized how serious it was, the situation was beyond remedy. He brought her back to a lonely existence at Knebworth – his stately home in Hertfordshire – where she received long letters from her mother which caused her to develop a morbid terror of both parents. She eventually died of typhus in London in April 1848 immediately after a visit from her mother. Bulwer was utterly crushed by her death, and it led to further acrimony between her parents, as each accused the other of causing it.

For a number of years, a distinctly battered Bulwer sought refuge from overwork, domestic tragedy and unwelcome publicity by wintering at Nice. From November 1862 until April 1863 he stayed at the Hotel Europa, and it was during this time that he met the Ernsts. Amélie's name first appears in a letter to his son written on 30 November 1862, and Bulwer, feeling his scars, is inclined to be suspicious:

> There is a nice pretty woman here who says she knows you. Madame Ernst. Wife of the violinist. She has a story which he confirms of your being affected to tears by his music. She seems a good woman. Is she? I have little faith in good women from my own judgement of them. The best seem to be good although not particularly – good to some relation in life – a lover[,] a husband – a child. Tho' they may be devils to the rest of the world, i.e., good where they love. Real goodness is goodness where you don't love. [KA:430]

But these doubts have abated by 5 January1863, and a genuine friendship has begun to form. Ernst himself is still only of interest in relation to Amélie (it is quite possible he went to fewer public gatherings), but Bulwer's thoughts have moved beyond her appearance and his own misgivings to a just appreciation of her charm and character: 'I see much of the Ernsts, whom I like much. She, a great admirer of yours, is a charming companion, full of sympathy, playfulness and natural talent, and a most devoted loving companion to him – in a way that reconciles one to a belief in wifedom.' [KA:456] By 1 February her personality is sufficiently established for him to discuss her without any reference to Robert. Bulwer focuses now on her natural talent while allowing himself a grain of criticism: 'There is a wonderful mixture of sweetness and power in Mad. Ernst's talking which interests and charms me more than any other woman I have known for many years – I should have liked her as a sister. The only time she bores me ever is her habit of reciting French verses.' [KA:463]

With the arrival of April, Ernst's own qualities have made themselves manifest, and his wife's relationship with Bulwer has become more relaxed and domestic. This is also the first time the letters mention that the Ernsts will be travelling to England with him. 'I shall leave Nice with nothing tonight except the Ernsts whom I really love like relations. He is witty and delightful and she tends me like a daughter.' [KA:498] Evidently, abstract and ungenerous moral scruples have evaporated in the face of female warmth, vivacity and tenderness.

The next relevant letter is almost entirely about the Ernsts, and although undated can be confidently ascribed to 14 or 15 April 1863. By this stage, Bulwer has become deeply appreciative of Ernst, and it is really remarkable that a man so crippled and racked with pain could inspire such affection. Amélie is no longer merely charming, talented and solicitous; she has come to hold a central place in his affections:

I arrived today and bring the Ernsts[.] He is going to try the Water Cure at Malvern which seems the sole chance left to him. I have been with him a week on the road from Nice & at one time despaired of bringing him; he was so ill – I can't say how much I love & pity & admire him, tho' I never heard him play & never care if I do except for his sake. And she is the best warmest hearted female creature I have ever known save one – and that one loved me and all women who love us are warmhearted. [KA:802-4]

However, Amélie Ernst was not only a deeply affectionate nature, but a vigorous woman with a strong sexual appetite. Alerted to this, no doubt, by the forced proximity of a journey, Bulwer encapsulated his fears in an extraordinary piece of doggerel conjured up for his son's entertainment and instruction: 'I fear she loves him too much for his [Ernst's] health & to borrow the words of a great poet whose practical and simple way of viewing things I commend to your recitation –

"Alas, the joys of Hymen
Will too often render dry them –
And – (unless they turn cold tummies
Towards their their too loving dummies),
Will reduce them into Mummies."' [KA:804]

All through this correspondence, it is difficult not to feel that Bulwer is musing on what it must be like to have such a pretty, appreciative, and loving wife, and that his interest in her libido may not have been entirely motivated by altruistic concerns. But more pragmatic matters soon obtruded: 'I have never had so anxious a charge. I will however soon give Ernst over to Wilson & if Wilson take the same view of the case I do – he will not think it hopeless & may get cured – But it is a dreadfully difficult case.' [KA:804-5]

Before Ernst was handed over to Dr Wilson's charge, there were artistic matters to attend to. Several of Ernst's musical friends and supporters knew of his imminent arrival, and arrangements were soon in place for an appropriate celebration:

> The director of the Monday Popular Concerts [Arthur Chappell], very properly considering Herr Ernst's arrival a fitting opportunity to reproduce his Quartet in B♭, – which met with so brilliant a reception last summer, and in the composition of which (together with two others, nearly finished, in A and C) solaced many a weary hour during a long and tedious illness – has announced it for performance at the 126th concert on the 27th inst. On Thursday afternoon it was rehearsed by MM. Vieuxtemps, Weiner, H. Webb, and Piatti, in the presence of the great artist and a select number of friends, at the house of Mr Benson [*sic*], where Herr Ernst has been residing. The composer, who till then only heard it played by a party of amateurs, was evidently much pleased with the attention thus paid him by Mr Arthur Chappell, and expressed his satisfaction in the warmest terms to M. Vieuxtemps and the other gentlemen of the 'quartet.' [MW:25/4/63:264]

The advertised performance – which also included piano trios by Hummel and Mozart performed by Arabella Goddard, and songs and arias by Mendelssohn and Sullivan sung by Sims Reeves – duly took place in St James's Hall. The *Athenaeum* noted that something of Ernst's spirit seemed to have rubbed off on Vieuxtemps that evening:

> Nothing is pleasanter is to be noted in the history of music ... than the willing cordiality of the violinists all Europe over to produce the quartett of the greatest of modern players, Herr Ernst. It has been given in Paris; the other day at Vienna under the auspices of Herr Hellmesberger; and it was on Monday night repeated at the Popular Concert, with M. Vieuxtemps for leader. He has never been heard to play with more, if so much, heart and expression. There was, in this performance something apart from the music, and beyond the performer's usual habits and sympathies, well seconded by his comrades. [A:2/5/63: 593]

It tells us something, either about the urgency of Ernst's case, or the fullness of Wilson's medical diary, that the party could not delay their departure for Malvern by three days so as to hear the public performance of the quartet – especially as Ernst had never heard it played before a concert audience.

I suspect there was no performance in Paris in 1863,[1] but in Vienna a committee had been formed by a group of distinguished artists to help Ernst financially, and it organized two benefit concerts. The first took place on 12 April 1863, while Ernst was travelling between Nice and London, at a private soirée in the home of the pianist Julie von Asten. [AMZ:22/4/63:314] No lesser figure than Brahms – perhaps out of respect for Joachim's early mentor – played Schumann's *Kriesleriana*, some of the *Pensées Fugitives* with Hellmesberger, and, with the addition of a cellist, a number of Beethoven's arrangements of Scottish folksongs. [KJB:II:47] But the main event of the concert was the Viennese premiere of Ernst's quartet given by the Hellmesberger string quartet. [AMZ:22/4/63:314] The evening allowed 4,700 gulders to be sent to Ernst, and the planning and performances also received some praise in the press: '[The concert] stood out advantageously because of the programme and its attractive execution.' Ernst's quartet, however, was received less enthusiastically. The report concludes: 'His fame as a composer has been little increased through the new string quartet.' [AMZ:1/5/63:458] Ernst's new more Mendelssohnian style was barely more welcome than his old Italian idiom.

The second and larger Viennese concert, which took place on 18 December 1863 at the Bösendorfer Salon, featured the premiere of a new work by Brahms: *Wechsellied zum Tanze* (words by Goethe), the first section of *Drei Quartette*, op.31, performed by Ottile Hauer, Ida Flatz, Eduard Tisch and Emil Föchgott. [JBTC:95] Some of Brahms's op.28 vocal duets were sung, and then Brahms himself and Julie von Asten played Schumann's variations for two pianos. [KJB:II:47] Another substantial sum was forwarded to Ernst.[2]

By the time reports arrived of the first Viennese concert, Ernst was already on his way to Malvern. It is not possible to discover exactly what treatment Ernst underwent, but one of the later editions of Wilson's main book, *The Water Cure: Its Principles and Practice*, outlines the treatment he gave for rheumatic gout, a complaint from which Ernst was thought to suffer:

---

1   Well over a year later, the *Athenaeum* reports: 'The *Gazette Musicale* ... has ... a just article ... on Herr Ernst's Quartetts, *heard the other day for the first time in Paris.*' [A:12/11/64:644] (My italics)

2   Kalbeck has the date of the second concert as 18 December 1862, but this seems to be a mistake. See JBTC:95.

The treatment is commenced by packing in blankets, to induce gentle, but long continued perspiration, sometimes for an hour, followed by a shallow bath at 85°[F] for three minutes, and then cooled to its natural temperature, for three minutes more; steady but gentle rubbing with towels being actively carried on during the whole period the patient remained in the bath. Before packing in the blankets[,] compresses were applied to all the afflicted joints. At noon the joints were fomented for an hour, followed by the same shallow bath, as in the morning after the sweating; when reaction was well established, the compresses were replaced. The douche was also used at the proper time. ... In these cases, when the symptoms are acute, with fever and quick pulse, a partial packing in sheet for three quarters of an hour is necessary; but as a general rule, the lamp bath or the blanket packing is one of the principal remedies. [TWC:65–6]

The 'lamp bath' was a procedure where the naked patient was placed on a chair, and a broad clotheshorse some twenty inches high was positioned around him. Blankets were then spread over the clotheshorse and the patient's body, and held in place around his neck, thus forming a tent-like structure. A lighted spirit lamp was then placed under the chair. Within three minutes the patient became very hot 'though more likely to roast than melt' – as one wag had it – and perspiration 'rolled off the skin like rain'. [MWC:28] At this point the attendant administered draughts of cold water to stop the patient overheating, before ending the procedure by plunging him into a cold bath, rubbing him dry, and dressing him for a walk. The douche, the most vigorous treatment available at the water-cures, was more disturbing – 150 gallons of cold water in three minutes were poured over the naked patient from a height of twenty feet. One dreads to think what it must have done to someone in Ernst's condition, and hopes there was no 'proper time' for such a fragile patient.

At least one of the letters Ernst wrote to Bulwer during his English sojourn can be confidently ascribed to the time he stayed in Malvern. It gives some account of his symptoms and state of health:

> Dr W. has now a better opinion on my case, everybody finds my appearance better, as for myself, I feel during two or three hours a day a little improved. I no longer have such awful nights. You see that I even have the strength and perhaps you might say the courage to write you a long and boring letter. All this appears to be progress towards better things, nevertheless my pains, the great weakness in my legs, and the other inconveniences that you know of me have only left me *very rarely*.
>
> Oh if only I were able to tell you directly that I'm doing well! Just as it would be good to shorten the description, this regiment of words about my illnesses. But it is necessary to submit to the laws of nature. Unfortunately, *there is only one health and many illnesses*. ... [Your] grateful friend. H.W. Ernst [HALS:D/EK:C18/99]

The slight signs of improvement mentioned in the letter must have continued because, on 6 August, the Ernsts returned to London. The *Musical World* noted:

> Herr Ernst was in London on Wednesday. On Thursday he left for Sir Edward Bulwer Lytton's estate at Knebworth, in Hertfordshire, where he will remain some weeks on a visit to that distinguished baronet and man of letters. On the whole, the Malvern water-cure, under the vigilant supervision of Dr Wilson, has been of use to the great artist, and he certainly looks better than when he was last among us. All musical England will pray for his speedy and complete recovery. [MW:8/8/63:507]

Making use no doubt of the excellent fifty-minute train service from Stevenage near Knebworth, Ernst made a round trip to London again around the 5 September: 'Herr Ernst has been in London for a few days attending a consultation of Doctors on his case, and has returned to Sir Edward Bulwer Lytton's seat, Knebworth, Hants [*sic*].' [MW:5/9/63:574]

For the next four months, the Ernsts stayed with Bulwer amidst the gothic turrets, gargoyles, stained glass, tapestries and armour of Knebworth. Here, Ernst and his host spent many hours driving round the countryside in Bulwer's brougham, and the monotony of their days was broken by visits from several musicians, including the remarkably gifted amateur violinist and clergyman, Francis Hudson. [IRR:149]

Bulwer's only major production of 1863 was *Caxtoniana*. This is a collection of essays, the first of which appeared in *Blackwood's Magazine* in February 1862 and the last, the twentieth, in October 1863. Like the von Wertheimsteins, Bulwer was lonely and unhappy, and the tone of the dedication makes clear just how much Ernst and Amélie had come to mean to him:

TO
HEINRICH ERNST.

MY DEAR ERNST,

Accept the Dedication of these Essays. You will recognise, in some of them, subjects on which I have, not unfrequently, conversed with you and the charming critic who so worthily bears your distinguished name.

The friendship I have formed with natures so noble as hers and your own, has added new charm to my life; and all who have the privilege to know you will comprehend the affectionate pride with which I inscribe to that friendship this grateful memorial.

E.B.L.
Knebworth, *October*, 1863 [C]

The completion of this book may well have been the excuse for a party held at Knebworth in early October. In his journal, George Eliot's common-law husband, George Lewes noted: 'November the 1st. Since my last entry ... I spent three days with Bulwer at Knebworth, discussing colonial plans ... At Knebworth there were Ernst and his wife (very charming), Louis Blanc and his brother Charles [the politician and art theorist], Herbert Wilson, Robert Lytton, and Dr. and Mrs Wagstaffe [probably a mistranscription of 'Radcliffe']. Very agreeable visit.' [GEL:IV:112]

Bulwer was ill in the autumn of 1863 (amongst other things he had an agonizing abscess of the jaw) and he left for London to consult his doctors shortly after the party mentioned above. The Ernsts' feelings for Bulwer are most clearly displayed in some of the letters which they wrote to him – often more than once a day – during his absence. Some of these are about Ernst's health and occupations: 'I thank you for putting at our disposal today and yesterday your charming little Brougham. If it didn't get rid of my pains, it at least made them more bearable, and brought about a change in ideas, which at the moment are not very cheerful' [HALS:D/EK/C18/100] But all of them show the couple's extraordinary love and affection for their patron. For example:

We're doing well in our life as the master and mistress of the castle, but to complete our well-being we lack the visit of our best friend who should be here as the most beloved and desired host. Come as soon as possible then dear Sir Edward, you will be greeted with open arms. You will find among us not only hospitality but an affection without limit. My state of health is about the same as when you left us. This morning I received a letter from Dr Read, which I shall keep for your return. My best beloved nurse was as delighted as I was by your parcel. She thanks you as I do, and sends her [in English] 'best love' like me. With very best wishes, H.W. Ernst [HALS:D/EKC18/98]

Amélie – in slightly imperfect English – tended to write more detailed reports of their doings:

Our beloved Ernst has not had a very good night again – the drops did not give him any sleep – however, he is not very unwell – writes so much that he is at the end of his paper – we will take a short drive soon. ... We do not hear from our bohemian friend D[avison]. But Robert has written again a most affectionate letter ... full of my friends from Vienna. ... No news from my mother. Mrs Benzon writes most kindly that they would come here for now for Copped Hall. [HALS:D/EK/C18/110]

In early November, the Ernsts travelled with Bulwer to Bath, and arrived at the house he had rented, number 15 in the magnificent Royal Crescent, on about the 5th. Amélie Ernst later wrote an account of an incident which took place here on 13 December. She used to include it as part of her public prose readings, and it has the slightly too-good-to-be-true quality of a well-polished and oft-repeated anecdote, but I quote it in full because it is the only detailed description of Ernst in a domestic setting.

Thalberg Magician

By Amélie Ernst

In December 1863, the picturesque town of Bath reunited a small group of intimate friends of different nations unified by that sympathy which grants intuitive understanding of natures, educations, tastes and sentiments formed by different climates. That sympathy, in a word, which melts ideas and opinions together, rounds off sharp edges, and makes the most discordant tones burst forth in complete harmony.

The illustrious English novelist, Sir Edward Bulwer-Lytton – who later became Lord Lytton – Mr Benson [sic], a rich German-American industrialist whose sumptuous library contained manuscripts as precious as those Anatole France discovered in Sylvetre Bonnard's city of books [In the novel of the same name]. His very pretty and spirited wife, the sister of Lehmann the painter, a German; my husband, a Moravian, and me, a French Alsatian.

The immensely wealthy iron and steel magnate, Ernst Schlesinger Benzon, and his wife Elizabeth, lived at 10 Palace Gardens, Kensington, which not only served as a pied-à-terre for the Ernsts when they first arrived in London, but was a regular meeting place for George Eliot, George Lewes, the Brownings, and most of artistic and literary London. Excellent concerts were held in their drawing room, and Rubinstein and Joachim played there regularly. The couple's son, 'Jubilee

Plunger' Benzon, gambled aware their entire fortune within two years of inheriting it. [GEAB:391] Amélie continues:

> Here are the dear beings, since departed, who pleased themselves at that time by spending together some beautiful winter days in mountains as green as in spring. We talked there each evening of art, literature, politics and philosophy. From these discussions Bulwer composed an entire book called: Caxtoniana, with this dedication: *To Heinrich Ernst.* [Amélie's chronology here is slightly confused.]
>
> The latter, despite his continual and intolerable pain, threw the living and brilliant sparks of his spirit and his good humour into the conversation and, when it became too serious, made it start through one of his witticisms, so gay and profound ...
>
> Cards, Dominoes, Billiards, Backgammon, Chess and Sir Edward's musical box, that's what filled a good part of these long soirees, when suddenly a new kind of pleasure offered itself.
>
> Thalberg, who was now making his last tour of England, wrote to Ernst that he would like to make use of a Sunday (a day when concerts were forbidden in this country) to come and spend a day with him. He added that he would be very happy to see Sir Edward Bulwer-Lytton at close quarters, whom he admired more than any other author, and asked as a great honour to be presented to him.

From the point of view of Amélie's story, two facts about Thalberg are important. First, he was the most ingenious of the nineteenth-century pianists, the man who amazed the public by his magical 'three-handed trick'. This involved playing an accompaniment with the left hand, adding florid decoration (usually arpeggios) with the right, and then dividing the melody, in the piano's tenor register, between the thumbs of both hands. This gave the impression of a three-handed pianist, and the public stood on its chairs to see how the trick was accomplished. Second, of all the nineteenth-century virtuosi, he was the one who was felt to have the most gentlemanly manners and appearance, the most innate aristocratic distinction, and the most unflappable sovereign calm.

> Ernst made haste to communicate this agreeable news to Sir Edward, but the latter asked him who Thalberg was. Ernst was so surprised by this question, which revealed a complete ignorance of the celebrated artist's international fame, that he replied with amusement;
>
> 'He's a famous magician.'
>
> 'Get him here at once,' said Bulwer, who loved conjurers, quacks, palmists, fortune-tellers, card-sharpers, and charlatans of all sorts and all countries, and a little time before hand had invited the de-frocked priest, L'abbé Constant to his ancestral home at Knebworth, and who would, for a fee, show you the devil in a bucket of water ...
>
> [Thalberg's] arrival was very eagerly awaited and he was presented to the great man of letters and statesman at dinner time.
>
> Bulwer sat at the head of a long table and as always had Ernst on his right so that his deafness might not impede conversation, and placed Thalberg on his left.
>
> Dinner started with an *Irish broth*, a kind of soup in which chops of mutton float. The master of the house served himself this first, fortifying dish. Plunging the spoon to the bottom of the tureen, he took care to extract one chop for each plate of soup.
>
> Thalberg, without doubt, had never seen Irish broth, because, throwing a glance towards my husband, said to him:

'Look! What absentmindedness! Sir Edward has not noticed that someone has dropped the chops into the soup. Warn him about it.'

On seeing that Ernst didn't move, Thalberg remarked to Sir Edward himself: 'Sir Edward, can you see the chops …'

He replied immediately:

'I know what you want to say monsieur – that you are going to conjure them away. I challenge you to do it. I'll watch you. Knowing that, you won't be able to do a trick here. I'd know well how to prevent you doing it.'

And in effect the evening passed for him preventing all the tricks that … Thalberg did not do.

We never saw him more satisfied with himself or in better humour.

Thalberg, very surprised, and not understanding a single baffling word of this odd remark, looked in turn at my husband and me[,] who made it appear that we did not hear, and the Bensons who were as surprised as he was.

'Eat up!' said Ernst to him. 'It's very good. It's a national dish. Don't think badly of it, and don't be astonished by anything you hear my friend say, he has his quirks; you'll see however that he's very amiable.'

But a little later, Bulwer having made a movement to reach the salt, and Thalberg having made a movement to pass the salt-cellar to him as well, was abruptly stopped:

'Don't move, it's useless, monsieur, I know very well that in place of salt it's sugar you're offering me, and that in place of powder you offer me stones, I've already seen all that – during the time my meat will go cold again, yours too, leave me to eat quietly, please do the same,' and gripping his hand with a large and kind gesture, he added:

'Besides, you're here to rest.'

Thalberg, wanting to engage the noble poet in a proper conversation, spoke to him of his vast knowledge, and Bulwer, still preoccupied with his own idea, replied:

'Yes, when it comes to tricks I know all of them,' and he recounted in support all that he'd seen done by all the Bosco's of the world; that nothing more could surprise him and that he would take malicious pleasure in foiling all attempts to try to stop him.

'And you'd be right,' Thalberg said to him[,] more and more disappointed to see the conversation take another strange turn at the moment he had prepared to hear marvels of imagination and poetry.

Ernst, impassive, made a sign to me to keep a straight face.

Suddenly, Bulwer took Thalberg by the shoulder and embraced him in a friendly way, letting his hands slide along his sleeves. Then he spread his fingers and plunged them into his own guest's sleeves, and even into the depths of his waistcoat, with such evident curiosity and such visible suspicion that Thalberg, struck suddenly by a terrible idea, said in German to Ernst and the Bensons:

'Why's he searching me? Does he fear that I might have taken his cutlery?'

'He wants no doubt,' Ernst said to him, 'to gain an understanding of the structure of a great pianist's hands and arms, so he can describe it in his next novel.'

This idea charmed Thalberg, and Bulwer delighted to have made him incapable of exercising his talents, … that he didn't have, soon became himself and talked with the charm, the richness, and the enchanting eloquence that he always had towards the end of a good dinner, without releasing Thalberg's hand. Thalberg was flattered by what he took to be a sign of friendship from one who dazzled him with witty salvos, [so] animated and imaginative that they cannot be described to someone who has not had the good fortune to have heard them.

The meal ended, and we went from the dining room to the brilliantly lit drawing-room.

As usual, the immense musical box which travelled everywhere with our host, gave us a morning serenade.

This treat offered to musicians greatly amused Thalberg. He appeared not to know this kind of instrument any better than soup with chops because he leant over the open box and watched its great gilded cylinder with a child's delight. He was rapt in contemplation, when all at once Sir Edward's singing canary, awakened by the lights and the music – excited by airs he knew by heart and in the habit of singing with the musical box in unison – burst into full-throated song.

Thalberg, dazed by this fantastic concert, dashed towards the cage where the bird, neck tense, was singing without making a movement, the wings half spread. He thought it was an automaton and, transported by admiration, asked Bulwer where he had procured such a surprising device.

As if switched off, the little canary fell asleep again and Bulwer was delighted to have tricked the trickster. He walked, full of pleasure, with Thalberg, from one end of the room. By mistake he let his handkerchief fall believing he had put it in his pocket. Thalberg saw it and hurried to pick it up.

During this time, Ernst, sitting at the chess board with Mr Benson was watching and laughed up his sleeve. Bulwer pushed away Thalberg's hand, who was returning the handkerchief in a very polite and friendly manner and saying:

'Sir Edward, it's your handkerchief. You just dropped it'

Sir Edward ignored Thalberg's bent posture and outstretched hand. Thalberg appealed to me:

'Dear madam, Sir Edward let his handkerchief fall ... I picked it up and gave it back to him, but he doesn't understand that it's his, and refuses to take it back. Help me. What should I do?'

'Speak louder,' I said to him, 'you know he's a little deaf.' He decided to do this.

'Sir Edward, it's your handkerchief ...'

But Bulwer, who did not like people shouting in his ears, strode to the other side of the room, and shouted:

'It's useless. I won't touch it. You must keep it to yourself. I know it's full of rabbits.'

Thalberg, baffled, assumed the misunderstanding was due to deafness and did not dare to take the matter further.

I will always see him with the handkerchief in his hand, searching for some piece of furniture to put it on. He caught sight in a corner of a spinet from Queen Anne's reign, relegated there with other curios. He opened it, tried the keys which responded to his fingers with a broken, quavering note, like that of an old man.

This drew us towards him.

Smiling, he sat in front of this antediluvian embryo piano, made several flourishes on the chipped and incomplete keyboard, played an octave above or below the note when a key failed, or imitated the absent sounds with his voice, his cheeks blown out like a glass-blower's.

It was amusing to see and hear. We laughed around him. But the instrument seemed to come alive beneath his magic fingers; some strings numbed by two centuries of dumbness awakened as if from a dream. The artist stirring them into life seemed to receive from them a mysterious impulse from a vanished age. He trembled, his face became serious, his hands had a truly mesmeric and supernatural quality in their movement. The galvanized instrument became melodious, and gave forth a voice that answered the soul which spoke to it.

Galvanized also, we held our breath to hear Chopin's funeral march, which I have never heard sound like this again. Thalberg was transfigured, sublime.

We were all in tears, except Bulwer who, full of joy, took Thalberg in his arms, embraced him as though to suffocate him, while shouting:

'Ah! Too bad, that last trick I couldn't prevent. You are better than all the others. Ernst was right. You are a famous enchanter, a wizard; incomparably the best slight of hand I ever saw.'

This time, we were all of his opinion and none of us contradicted him.

Thalberg was much flattered by this enthusiastic outburst; he attributed it to the magic of his own talent which could unleash a virtuoso display from a keyboard which must always remain mute to fingers other than his. He left delighted with his host, loaded down with books and manuscripts in prose and verse by the wonderful author of *Pelham*, *The Last days of Pompeii*, *Caxton* [sic], and so many other masterpieces; whom he had just been amusing like a child.

Such simplicity is often found in geniuses …

I'm quite sure that Bulwer and Thalberg have forgiven Ernst in Heaven for this characteristic 'little trick' which was never explained to them on earth – even though a woman was party to it. The same woman can hold her tongue no longer and now must tell you the story. ['Thalberg Prestigitateur.' MLP:260–67]

After the stay in Bath, Bulwer and the Ernsts did not return to Knebworth, but to Copped Hall, 'a tumbledown old house' [MHC:210] in Totteridge, Hertfordshire, where they were visited by Frederick Lehmann. Bulwer was in the habit of purchasing houses so they could be later sold at a profit, although it was rumoured in London literary circles that he bought them for his mistresses. It is not clear why they stayed here, an idea which, as we can tell from Amélie's letter to Bulwer, had been mooted several months before. Bulwer probably wanted to avoid the expense of opening up his large house, and three people in at best indifferent health had every reason to avoid the gloom and arctic interiors of Knebworth in winter.

Chapter 22

Norfolk, London, and the A Major String Quartet: 1864

For Ernst, 1864 began rather well. He moved from Copped Hall to London so he could be more closely supervised by his doctor, and the determined spell of composition his wife had noted in the autumn of the previous year continued. 'Herr Ernst,' the *Musical World* informed its readers, 'who is now in London, at the residence of Dr. —— (Cavendish Sq.) – is said to be far advanced in the composition of a new quartet in A major. Mr Aurthur Chappell will doubtless introduce it to his patrons at the Monday Popular Concerts.' [MW:9/1/64:27]

He was in good hands. The doctor in Cavendish Square – 25 Cavendish Square – was Charles Bland Radcliffe, one of the most eminent of Victorian medical men and Bulwer Lytton's personal friend as well as doctor. He was one of the earliest investigators of the role of electricity in nerve and muscle function as well as being much interested in theology. Under the care of such an eminent, dashing, and polymathic figure, a cautiously optimistic Ernst writes to Bulwer from Cavendish Square in late January or early February:

> Dear Sir Edward, I cannot tell you what a pleasure it was to notice in your letter the absence of complaints about your dreadful pain. My own pains ... have been conspicuous by their absence for most of our stay in the house of our dear doctor; my nights are generally good, and if I could walk without feeling a certain heaviness in the lower back, I would not change place with John Jones [unidentified], although I don't have his 25 years and 500 a year. There is still a hell of a way to go, and the Good Lord must be willing to take on the rest.
>
> I hope and desire with all my heart that you will soon be free of all your worries over there and you will return free from all unpleasant preoccupations to be with your friends and involved in your favourite occupations. I embrace you with all my heart. H.W. Ernst [HALS:D/EK:C/109]

For Bulwer, 'unpleasant preoccupations' usually took one form, and early 1864 was no exception. After a long spell of ill health and literary work, his interest in politics was just starting to revive when it was violently checked by the activities of his wife. He wrote to his son on 20 January:

> This morning, I received a letter from Disraeli, which conveyed the thunderbolt that L[ady] L[ytton] has resumed attacks – written, he says to my colleagues and friends, making horrible and nameless accusations. ... The horrible calamity weighs on me, but I know not what to do. Of course, it will prevent office. I cannot go through such scandals again as an official character. ... [The] thing effectively damps the ardour I was beginning to have for politics. [EBL:II:356]

The contents of the letters were indeed grim, and included the charge that he had sodomised Disraeli to achieve his cabinet post. [VML:62] Misfortune as always brought ill health, and he was depressed and debilitated for the rest of the year.

The Ernsts, meanwhile, spent a good deal of time trying to re-establish contact with old friends and acquaintances. The *Musical World* was soon able to report: 'Herr Ernst is at present on a visit to Mr Fountaine, at Narford Hall, Brandon in Norfolk. The health of the distinguished artist still, we are happy to say, progresses favorably.' [MW:13/2/64:108]

Since his Paris days, Fountaine had settled down. On 24 February 1848 he had married Caroline Burney and now had three daughters, Mary, Caroline and Emily. [BLG:334] Like his father before him, he performed his civic duties, becoming first a magistrate, then a local Deputy Lieutenant, and finally, in 1857, the High Sheriff of the county. He paid a good deal of attention to his magnificent home, building a four-storey domed tower and two new wings, and adding extensively to one of the finest Majolica collections in Europe. [BSCH:161–2] When this was eventually sold between April and July 1884, ten years after Fountaine's death, it realized the then astronomical sum of £96, 278 18s 0d – about £7 million at today's prices. [*The Times*:18/4/84–14/7/84]

The one letter that survives from Ernst to Bulwer Lytton in this period mentions Fountaine's collection as well as Bulwer's troubles:

> My Dear, Very Dear Friend, You already know from my beloved wife's letter that we arrived thanks to the care of Mr Fountaine in [King's] Lynn. I can tell you today that it was the same from Lynn to here, and my friend shows himself to be as perfect as master of the house as he was at organizing travel.
>
> My wife talked to you in detail of all the art treasures of all types contained in Mr Fountaine's house, where I see us having a very agreeable stay.
>
> Your affectionate letter gave us great happiness, and it reassures us after the miserable impression that your last visit to London left in all our hearts.
>
> We want with all our soul for you to return to London free of all disagreeable preoccupations. A time when you will never be tormented by problems other than those that give genius.
>
> I've kept well during our short stay here. I played the violin a little and drink a great deal of stout, this is not a useless precaution before reading Mr D[avison's] articles.
>
> You see that I am going to spend my time exactly like everyone else, and I hope soon to be able to play the violin a good deal and drink a little stout. And I spend my time like you, making do entirely with the articles of Mr D.
>
> Hearty greetings, your tenderly devoted friend, H.W. Ernst [HALS:D/EK:C3/127]

In the earlier part of March, the Ernsts returned to Knebworth, stopping briefly in London on the way. The *Musical World* reported:

> Herr Ernst is in London. His visit to Narford Hall (Norfolk), the magnificent seat of Mr Fountaine, has been in great measure beneficial to his health; but Dr Radcliffe, his eminent medical adviser, who himself counselled change of scene and air, now again desires to have his distinguished patient near at hand, in order that his professional attendance may be as frequent as possible. Every musician and lover of music will devoutly pray for Ernst's speedy and complete recovery. [MW:12/3/64:170]

Ernst had been deeply upset by Davison's previous lack of communication, and in the letter quoted above, Davison's work is still treated with a certain irony. This may be more on account of its ferocious conservatism and fulsome literary style than any lingering animosity, because some kind of rapprochement had clearly occurred over the winter. In March, Ernst made the tactful gesture of dedicating a recently composed piano piece to the critic's wife. 'Herr Ernst,' reported the *Musical World*, 'has composed a *nocturne*, for piano solo – to be dedicated, we understand, to Madame Arabella Goddard. It is to be published immediately – by Chappell and Co.' [MW:19/3/64] It was Charles Hallé, however, who gave the public premiere of this attractive, well-crafted piece in June 1864.

About three weeks after completing the nocturne at Knebworth, the Ernsts returned to London [MW:9/4/64:234], this time to 21 Holles Street, just off Cavendish Square. A long and detailed letter to Joachim gives details of his health and compositions, and also makes the first mention of what was to be Ernst's final benefit concert in London:

> Dear Friend, I don't know if you've learned of my long stay in England and the various experiments I've undertaken for my health. At least I can so presume, since your dear brother [Heinrich] promised me several times, that when he writes to you with my best wishes he will give you my latest news.
>
> Unfortunately there is no progress in my state of health. Several times there were signs of improvement, but the hopes that these were justified disappeared again quickly. My doctor, however, still has the greatest confidence in his treatment and thinks that up till now the bad weather has been the major barrier to its successful completion. I want to see out a few more weeks …[.]
>
> I want to use the time of my stay to organize a concert, and the first step I'll take is to ask you frankly, if, like two years ago, you would be prepared to participate in the name of artistic brotherhood. I'm convinced that you want to. It is my second quartet that I'd most like to entrust you with. It is, without forsaking the quartet style, more worthwhile for the first violin than the first [quartet] and would you like to play the *Élégie* with it[?] (The whole world goes into raptures when people speak of your performance.) These are the stable pillars on which the whole building will be based. Tell me as frankly and as soon as you can whether you can fulfil my urgent wish, and in that case which time would be best for you.
>
> I now have a 3rd quartet in progress (in C major), of which the first movement is almost finished and the Scherzo is completely finished and which, if you will do me the pleasure of accepting it, I wish to dedicate to you. In my opinion it'll be at least average, therefore the best of my stuff, and that's why it's intended for you.
>
> I don't know if Heinrich wrote to tell you that I've published 6 studies (with the title Greetings to Brothers in Art) and that I've dedicated one to you. In my opinion it's also the best, with the name: Tercet, It's been announced that the proofs from Vienna have already been sent here to Chappel [*sic*], but I haven't received them. Maybe I'll have them when you're here.
>
> I certainly don't need to tell you, how much I'm looking forward to seeing you, and if a happy moment in terms of my health allows me to hear you again on one occasion or another – especially the one when you play your new concerto. [The *Hungarian Concerto*] I didn't get your first, may I still count on it?
>
> My wife sends her best wishes, and accept hearty greetings from both of us – although we don't know her – to your wife. I urge you again to write soon, and receive

the sincere assurance of my unchanging friendship. Yours, Ernst [11 April 1864. London. SIM. Paragraph breaks added]

On the 13 April – one is continually amazed by the speed of the Victorian post – Joachim replied to Ernst's letter from Hanover:

Dear and Honoured Friend, However sorry I am that, after you were beginning to get better, your patience should again be subjected to so hard a trial, the confidence expressed by your medical man affords me consolation. I certainly had hoped, from the accounts my brother now and then gave me of you that, on the occasion so ardently desired, on my part, of our meeting again, this spring, I should have once more enjoyed the pleasure of hearing the magnificent tones of your violin! Providence, however, decrees otherwise. I am not destined, dear Master, to hear you, and thus to me, thanks to your confidence, is entrusted the noble task of making the musical world of London acquainted with your newest creation. I need scarcely say with what deep love I shall devote myself to the service of your Muse, command me as you will, and let me soon know on what day your concert can take place. I am exceedingly anxious to see your 'Etudes,' though I am really afraid of the left-hand stretches; but whatever comes from your pen I will, at all events, practice, even though I may not succeed in doing it justice. Your truly devoted friend, Joseph Joachim [MW:7/5/1864:300]

Ernst replied seven days later:

Dear Friend, I would like to embrace you for your heartfelt letter. A thousand sincere thanks. As always, I'm getting on very well with Chappell who will deal with all the arrangements for my forthcoming concert. I can't give you a day, but it will certainly be in the second half or third week of June. Look after yourself and come soon.

Today I am writing to Spina [the Viennese music publisher]. As soon as he has the proofs of my studies ready he will send them directly to Hanover. Two or three you'll like, I imagine, but don't be too strict with the last – it consists of bravura variations on the *Last Rose of Summer* – they are dedicated to Bazzini who dedicated a piece to me years ago; they are radically modern and with intention and hindsight full of variety. If you cannot forgive me for them, at least give me the pleasure of forgetting them. I hope you will be more satisfied with this. Here is the opening:

[He copies out Example 22.4 below.]

Now hearty greetings, also from my wife, and from us both best wishes to your wife.

Your true and thankful friend, H.W.Ernst.

[Ps] My health is really dreadful again. [20 April 1864. SIM. BJJ:337–8]

Along with the concerto, the six *Polyphonic Studies* are probably Ernst's most important work, and like the concerto they represent the *ne plus ultra* of technical difficulty. In Ernst's own work, they have their origin in the manuscript *Trio pour un Violon* and the *Erlking* transcription; amongst his contemporaries, they are influenced by Wieniawski's *L'Ecole Moderne* op.10 (1854) and by Bull's explorations of polyphony. Primarily, however, in their interest in counterpoint, they look back to Bach's *Sonatas and Partitas* for solo violin.

All of the studies are in major keys, and each of them is dedicated to one of Ernst's friends amongst leading virtuosi. (Ernst's dedication, 'Greetings to my Brothers in

Art' is typically more personal than Paganini's 'To the Artists', the dedication of his *Caprices*.) The first study, dedicated to Ferdinand Laub – a virtuoso famous for his technique and finger strength – is a rustic scherzo in F major. It has an extremely difficult central section in A♭, where a lyrical tune is underpinned by running semiquavers (Ex. 22.1). The melody renders the fingering and stretches required for the accompaniment deeply problematic, while the accompaniment makes it exceedingly difficult to maintain the tone and phrasing required for the melody:

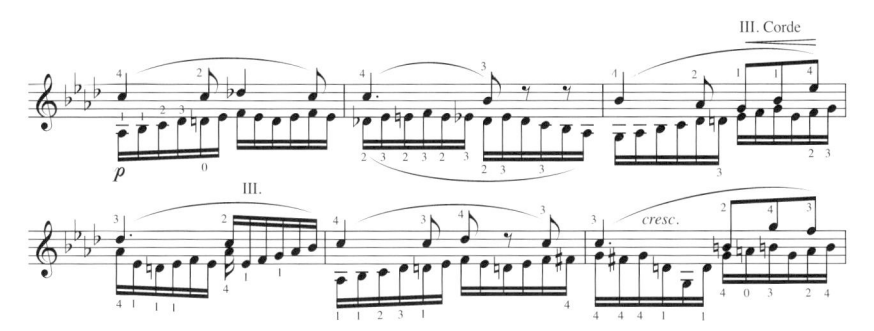

Example 22.1   Ernst, *Polyphonic Study*, no.1, bars 35–40

The second piece, dedicated to Prosper Sainton, is a study in maintaining a rhythmically ambiguous melody – is not clear whether the main pulse falls on the first or second beat of the bar – against off-beat spread chords. Some wonderfully po-faced quasi-fugal entries – deliciously at variance with the basically balletic nature of the material – lead to a digital mountain where the melody returns in a higher register accompanied by off-beat bowed chords and plucked on-beat bass notes (Ex. 22.2). It takes the same difficulty as the *Trio pour un Violon* and hugely magnifies it:

Example 22.2   Ernst, *Polyphonic Study*, no.2, bars 56–62

As we know, Ernst considered the third study, *Terzetto*, the best of the set. It is a love poem, lyrical yet full of life and movement, and more harmonically imaginative than many of Ernst's compositions. It is distinctly reminiscent of Schumann's *May, Charming May* from *Album for the Young*, op.68, and it is fittingly dedicated to Joachim who was devoted to Schumann in his last years. *Terzetto* shares the key of E major with *May, Charming May*; Schumann's piece achieves something of its miniaturized feel by rarely straying below the violin's bottom register; and above all, Ernst has learnt from Schumann how to achieve an intense lyricism combined with a touch of divine discontent by keeping semiquavers moving under notes with longer time-values. The technical demands of the piece seem to have been inspired by the third study, *L'étude*, from *L'Ecole Moderne* (Ex.22.3). This investigates the same problems of moving in parallel thirds and sixths, together with two-part similar-motion arpeggios, but Wieniawski's piece, as its title indicates, is a study pure and simple, and has none of the nostalgic charm or melodic distinction of Ernst's character sketch (Ex. 22.4):

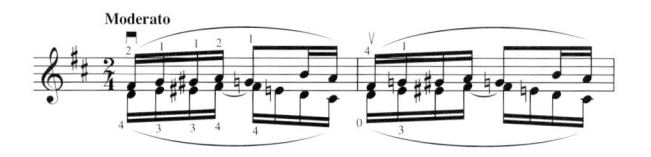

Example 22.3   Wieniawski, *Etude, L'Ecole Moderne*, op.10, no.3, bars 1–2

Example 22.4   Ernst, *Polyphonic Study*, no.3, bars 1–2

The fourth study, a glorious *moto perpetuo* in C major, at last releases the fingers of the left hand from their collaborative harness and sends them whirling up, down, and across the fingerboard. Vieuxtemps, to whom the study is dedicated, was famed for the evenness of his tone, the way his violin produced each note with chiselled exactitude, and the fact that he seemed to be able to play more notes to a bow than any other violinist. This study would show off all these qualities to excellent effect.

The fifth study, *Air de ballet* in E♭, is dedicated to Joseph Helmesberger. He was celebrated for his light, sweet-toned performances of chamber music by Beethoven and Schubert, and this study clearly suits his lyrical playing. Its position, between the furious onrush of the fourth study, and the inexhaustible virtuosity of the sixth, requires something quiet and understated, but even so, it can seem the least inspired and technically interesting of the set.

The final study – the variations on *The Last Rose of Summer* – looks backwards in a number of ways. It reverts to Ernst's favourite form of the 1830s and '40s

– introduction, theme and five variations; it is based on his earlier and unpublished *Fantasy on Irish Airs*; it recalls Paganini's *Nel Cor* variations, one of the works with which Ernst first stunned the public and its author; it hints at the last works in Paganini's *Caprices* and *L'Ecole Moderne*, both of which are sets of variations. Finally, it is Ernst's *plus ultra* response to Bazzini's *Le ronde des lutins*, which is itself a response to the *Rondo Papageno*.

The main difficulty represented by the tune is that it consists essentially of five repetitions of the same four-bar phrase, but Ernst most cunningly disguises this by using four different accompaniments and ornaments. The first variation is a study in double-stopped semiquavers, and the second is 'a floating witchery of sound' where the theme peeks through gossamer arpeggios. This variation ends with one of Ernst's most ingenious interminglings of pizzicato and arco (Ex.22.5):

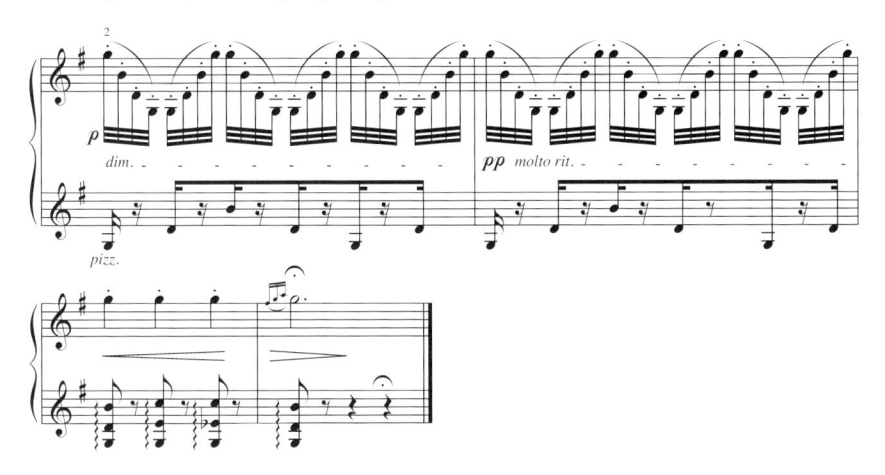

Example 22.5   Ernst, *Polyphonic Study*, no.6, variation 2, bars 39–42

The third variation is a *maestoso* in double-stopped counterpoint, which contains some remarkable melodic writing in simultaneous octaves and tenths (Ex. 22.6):

Example 22.6   Ernst, *Polyphonic Study*, no.6, variation 3, bars 11–17

However, it is the fourth variation which always causes the most astonishment. Here, the left hand plucks the tune to the accompaniment of rapidly bowed arpeggios, and harmonics replace plucked notes in the central section. The device is taken from the last study of *L'Ecole Moderne* (Ex. 22.7) – the variations on the theme from the slow movement of Haydn's *Emperor* quartet – but for a variety of reasons Ernst's composition works much better (Ex. 22.8). Ernst's faster tempo gives a more realistic impression of two violinists playing together, and the technique's necessarily low volume is better suited to Ernst's inner variation than to Wieniawski's finale.

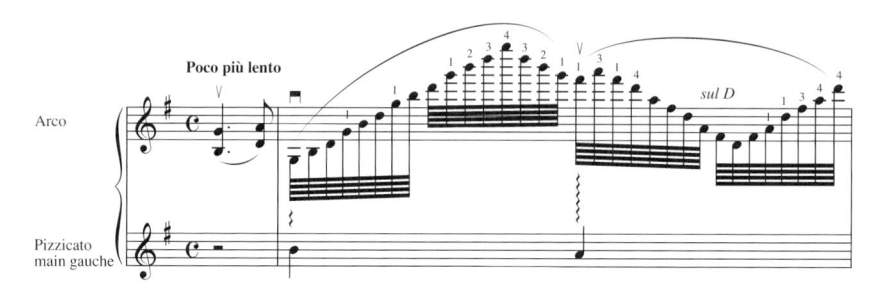

Example 22.7   Wieniawski, *Les Arpèges, L'Ecole Moderne*, op.10, no.9, variation 3, bars 1–2

Example 22.8   Ernst, *Polyphonic Study*, no.6, variation 4, bars 1–2

Ernst's own finale, is a wonderful *summa* of violin technique, including scales on one string, double harmonics, rapid artificial harmonic, and pizzicato chords. This fast scale in harmonics is particularly original (Ex. 22.9):

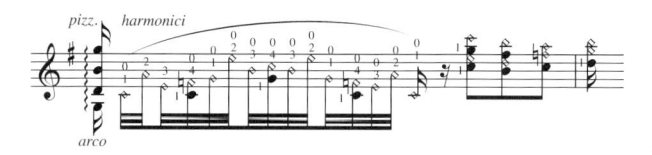

Example 22.9   Ernst, *Polyphonic Study*, no.6, finale, bars 14–15

The whole variation makes a dazzling ending to the set.

The six *Polyphonic Studies* stand between Bach's six *Sonatas and Partitas* and Ysaÿe's *Six sonates pour violon seul*. Ysaÿe certainly derives his title and the section names of the three multi-movement sonatas from Bach, but he derives his manifest virtuosity, and the single-movement form of numbers 3, 5 and 6 from Ernst. (Like

Ernst's last study, the main movement of Ysaÿe's fifth sonata has an introduction.) More importantly, the idea of dedicating each work to a friend and virtuoso – reflecting his style and perhaps hinting that he play it – is taken from Ernst's studies.

Ernst's last letter to Joachim shows that, just as in 1862, a long period of gradual improvement ended in collapse. It is probable that the stress of organizing the benefit concerts, particularly the first performances of compositions on which all his current artistic hopes rested, induced these crises. Holles Street leads into Oxford Street, and it seems quite likely that it was during this time that the seventeen-year-old Alexander Mackenzie, later famous as a composer and music administrator, caught a glimpse of the now mortally ill violinist: 'Of ... a great artist, the already dying Ernst, I had one fleeting glance when I saw him walking with evident difficulty in Oxford Street. The bent figure and probably the yellowest face ever seen on man made a lastingly painful impression on me.' [AMN:48]

In spite of Ernst's health, or perhaps because of it, a benefit ball was held for the violinist in mid-April, probably at the Benzons' in Kensington. [HALS:D/EKC18/102] Meanwhile, Chappell pushed ahead with arrangements for the benefit concert which was first advertised in the *Musical World* on 14 May 1864 [312]. This first notice stated that the concert would take place in St James's Hall on 30 May. The artists listed as playing were, Arabella Goddard, Mlle Bettelheim and Charles Santley, together with two others whose inclusion was thought to be worthy of short news items. 'Mr Sims Reeves has volunteered his invaluable services for the concert of Herr Ernst on the 20th [*sic*] inst. This is fresh proof of the sympathy that [one high artistic nature] is calculated to arouse in another. In doing honour to Ernst our good English tenor does honour to himself.' [MW: 14/5/1864:316] Even more gratifying was the announcement that an old adversary had decided to lend a friendly hand: 'Sig. Sivori leaves London for Paris to-day; he will return, however, the next week, to play as a volunteer at the next Monday Popular Concert which is announced in the name of Herr Ernst for the 30th inst. The fact does the accomplished Italian artist honour.' [MW:14/5/1864:315]

However, Ernst's concert was evidently arranged at short notice, and there were to be several nerve-racking changes of date and personnel. On 21 May the *Musical World* announced Joachim's arrival in London, and informed its readership that Sivori had left for Paris that day rather than the week before – although he was still advertised as playing. Seven days later, on the 28th, the same paper reported that Ernst's concert had been moved back to 6 June, but still promised Sivori's participation. It was not until 4 June that the full programme was announced. This did not feature Sivori, Arabella Goddard or Mlle Bettelheim who were on the original advertisement, but did include Wieniawski, Charles Hallé, Madame Leschitzka and Madame Meyer-Dustmann, who were not. Davison did his best to make amends for past neglect by printing a long passage from Berlioz's as yet unpublished *Memoirs* in praise of Ernst in the *Musical World* [MW:4/6/64:365] (although he did not bother to translate it), and by ensuring *The Times* kept the concert in the public consciousness. Perhaps because of his efforts, demand for tickets was strong, and the price of the best seats had more than doubled: from 10s 6d to 21s, and from 5s to 10s 6d (although the balcony was only 3s, and admission 1s.)

Both the female singers had strong Viennese connections. Madame Leschitzka was the first wife of the well-known pianist and pedagogue Theodor Leschitizky. The couple were part of the von Wertheinstein circle, and Ernst, as we have seen, was with them in Gastein in 1859. Louise Meyer-Dustmann, the better known of the two ladies, was a dramatic soprano and prima donna of the Viennese Court Opera from 1857 to 1875. She was a friend of both Brahms and Wagner, and when she sang Isolde in the first Viennese performance of *Tristan* she won Wagner's praise on account of her 'soulful voice and complete mastery of her role'. [JB:246]

Like the previous benefit concert, this one was to be held in London's newest concert venue, St James's Hall. Davison wrote the analytical programme note and also the longest and most detailed review. This appeared in both the *Musical World* and *The Times*.

> The concert on Monday night, for the benefit of Herr Ernst, was in all respects successful. A more brilliant audience never assembled in St James's Hall; a more varied and interesting popular programme has never been given there since these admirable entertainments were established.
>
> No stronger proof could be afforded of the high esteem and affection in which Ernst is held by his fellow artists in this country, no less than abroad, than the promptness with which so many of them of the highest eminence came forward voluntarily to do him honour. Though Herr Joachim had already proffered his invaluable assistance as leader of the new quartet and solo violinist, M. Wieniawski, one of Herr Joachim's most distinguished rivals, could not be refused; and a quartet, besides a solo, were, as a matter of course, set down for M. Wieniawski. ...
>
> That the right [compositional] stuff was in Herr Ernst was sufficiently proved by his first quartet in B♭, introduced in the year 1862 by the Monday Popular Concerts. The second quartet, in A, performed on Monday night is a decided advance on its predecessor. The design is larger and bolder, the leading ideas are more vigorous, while their development, both primitive and episodical, is more varied, spirited and masterly. The *scherzo* and *andante* especially are as original as they are striking – the first engrossing by its playful fancy, the last by its flowing melody, ingenious combinations and effective treatment of the instruments.
>
> The whole quartet – played with dedicated earnestness by Messers Joachim, L. Ries, H. Webb and Piatti – was listened to attentively and applauded with a genuine unanimity and warmth that could not be mistaken; but the movements of which the audience seemed most spontaneously to seize the meaning and recognise the merit were those we have singled out – viz, the scherzo and andante.
>
> The solo by Ernst allotted to M. Wieniawski was his prodigious 'transcription' of Schubert's 'Erl-konig' both the melody and accompaniment of which were to be expressed by the unaided fiddle; that assigned to Herr Joachim was the well known and truly beautiful Elegie. Both created an extraordinary sensation and a desire to hear them again. The 'Erl-konig,' however, was too long and too fatiguing to repeat and M. Wieniawski contented himself with bowing his acknowledgements. Not so the 'Elegie,' which Herr Joachim (accompanied by Mr Benedict) gave in a manner so like that of Ernst himself – when Ernst *was* Ernst, 'the most poetic of fiddlers' – that to many among the audience it brought back vividly the grateful memories of the past. It was quite impossible to resist the thundering encore that followed this most touching and eloquent performance; and so Herr Joachim perforce complied.

The other pieces by Herr Ernst were a grateful *notturno* for pianoforte *solis*; an English version of his *Lied*, 'Der Fischer'" (the words of Goethe being well translated by Rev. Archer Gurney); and three of the charming and always welcome *Pensées Fugitives* – the 'Reverie,' the 'Priere pendant l'orage,' and the 'Adieu.' The *nottorno* was assigned to Mr Halle, the *Lied* to Mr Sims Reeves, and the *Pensées* (adapted for the violoncello, instead of the violin) to Mr Halle and signor Piatti. Each performance afforded the utmost gratification. ... [*The Times*: 9/6/1864:19. Paragraph breaks added]

Like the quartet in C, the quartet in A was never published and the manuscript has been lost. Fortunately, the main themes have been preserved in Davison's analytical programme notes and we can derive some idea of it from these. (The relevant part of the programme is reprinted as an appendix to this book.) The themes suggest a sunnier, livelier more unbuttoned work than the earlier B♭ quartet, which makes full use of the resonant string sonorities and technical ease which the key of A major allows. The extracts indicate an appropriate harmonic simplicity, but they also suggest that the interest in counterpoint found in the *Nocturne* and *Polyphonic Studies* has become even more noticeable.

The quartet in A had three performances, and it is also possible to get some idea of the work from newspaper reviews. Only Chorley in the *Athenaeum* was inclined to be critical. Although he found the themes 'good and distinct' he also thought some of them 'overworked'. [A:11/6/1864:814] The critic of the *Reader*, on the other hand, was favourably impressed: 'Herr Ernst's new quartet was listened to with genuine pleasure. The work leaves an impression of strength, compactness, and symmetry which bespeaks a mind and imagination in full exercise of its powers.' [MW:25/6/64:406]

The *Sun* shared this opinion, and fortunately goes into considerably greater detail. Whereas Davison was most captivated – and says the audience was most captivated – by the two inner and presumably simpler movements, this critic is most forcefully struck by the more elaborate passages and by the markedly contrapuntal nature of the composition:

[The masterly new quartet is a] most original and highly imaginative composition. The symmetry of its construction, the exhilarating freshness of melody suffusing it, so to speak, like an atmosphere, the intricate involution noticeable in several of its more highly elaborate passages – created even upon that first hearing, not only upon ourselves but upon the vast majority of the audience, a profound impression. Of itself it would be an all sufficient attestation of the fact already known in this regard, that Herr Ernst is a master of the mysteries and wizardies [*sic*] of counterpoint. [MW:18/6/64:395]

All of Ernst's compositions created enthusiasm. 'A tender and beautiful *notturno*, for pianoforte, was performed with that touch of infinite grace and delicacy peculiar to Mr Hallé ... Goethe's ballad, "Der Fischer," indifferently translated by Rev. Archer Gurney, but suavely embalmed in the amber of a delicious melody by Herr Ernst, was admirably sung by Sims Reeves' and can be accounted 'one of Ernst's most sympathetically emotional compositions'. However, it is the two solo violin pieces that most impressed the critics. The *Reader* goes into ecstasies over the *Elegy* and Joachim's performance of it, while the *Sun* is astounded by Wieniawski's performance of the *Erlking* transcription, describing it as a 'wonderful composition' of 'unquestionable genius' that was 'performed with astonishing dexterity of manipulation by the wizard bow and fingers of Wieniawski'. [MW:18/6/64:395]

The informality of Ernst's next letter to Davison shows how much the relationship between them had warmed. It also indicates another change of address:

> Mon Bon, I still have not thanked you. I do it now twice over.
>
> First, and in particular[,] for the little word the day following the concert (I kiss you for that) but [also] for the tremendous words in the *Times* – and with all that I still haven't finished, because I thank you heartily for the piece in the *Times* the same day as the concert.
>
> I'll try to see you soon; my wife says the same things as me, and both of us are your true friends forever. H.W. Ernst [11 June 1864. 13 Princes Street, Cavendish Square. [BL]]

For Bulwer, the summer brought new worries. Robert had decided to marry Edith Villiers, who was not only the daughter of a political opponent, but would bring very little money into the family – and money was urgently needed for the upkeep of Knebworth and other properties. Relations between father and his son grew strained for a while, and Bulwer could only have been gratified by the balm of Ernst's parting letter:

> My Very Dear Friend, When and how will I ever be able to show all my gratitude for your constant kindness?
>
> True appreciation can never be expressed in words. In this it resembles love[;] yes, it becomes love itself when it finds a heart where it is cherished like a precious treasure rather than dreaded like a burden.
>
> It is the only prize I can offer you[,] for I say with Schiller, 'Love is love's prize.'
>
> Best wishes to you from that most devoted heart, H.W. Ernst [HALS: D/EKC18/106]]

Chapter 23

Last Days in Paris and Nice: 1864–65

In late August or early September 1864, the Ernsts began their journey home to Nice. Since his relapse in April there appeared to be little improvement in Ernst's health and he now felt both desperately pessimistic and sick. He must have reflected that it was in Nice that Paganini had died twenty-four years before, and that, after a lifetime of journeys, this was likely to be his last.

It began badly. They were supposed to pick up Davison on the way, but his notoriously impassable housekeeper initially refused them entry, and they nearly missed the boat. On board, matters improved. They met Arabella Goddard and her children, and Amélie's seasickness and Arabella's fear of drowning helped establish a firm friendship. Arriving at the Hotel Pavillion-Impérial in Bolougne, the Ernsts were delighted to discover that they were staying close to the famous soprano Adelina Patti and her agent Maurice Statchkoch returning from her first English triumphs. But on this occasion their attempt to establish a friendship proved less successful. Adelina spent a good deal of time kissing the violinist, and her agent appeared to show the deepest interest in him, but the Ernsts were mortified to discover that the glamorous couple, after a few days away, made no attempt to re-establish contact, despite occupying rooms next door. Perhaps rising stars cannot pay too much attention to those firmly in the descendent, however many stories they have to exchange about Berlioz and Bull. [8 September 1864. BL]

Ernst's health was so poor that their journey to Paris was delayed for nearly a month, and for many days he was confined to his room. When he eventually arrived in Paris, he wrote to Bulwer congratulating him on Robert's marriage, but he could not bear to write more than a few lines about his own physical condition:

> I won't talk to you in detail about my health, I know the depth of the interest you take in me, and I don't want to make you miserable. Say only that since I left London, doctors, often unfamiliar with my chronic condition, have tested me cruelly and [we are?] already a long way behind on our journey to Nice. However, my stomach has been much better since London which will allow me to regain soon, I hope, enough strength to be able to continue our journey … [9 October 1864. Hôtel de Bade, Boulevard des [Hallions?], Paris. HALS:D/EK:C18/101]

The furore in London caused by the performance of his last quartet, meant that the couple were greeted by many friends who insisted on a performance. This was arranged at short notice, and both quartets were performed in the presence of Berlioz, Heller, and Vincent Wallace, the composer of the then celebrated opera *Maritana*. Heller wrote up the concert in glowing terms for the *Review et Gazette musical*:

H.W. Ernst's Quartets

By a cruel destiny, the virtuoso [Ernst] no longer exists: he has consumed himself like the phoenix, and from his ashes he has emerged on a higher plain than the first, quite admirable though that was. This second phoenix in radiant flight is the composer.

Some days ago, we heard two of his works, two quartets for two violins, viola and cello. We do not even want to try, by a dry analysis, to give an idea of works as extensive as they are valuable. Do not look there for the amiable and charming composer of the fantasy on *Otello* or on *Il Pirate*. But you recognize the composer of the *Élégie* and the concerto, singularly developed and purified. All the promises contained in these two works are realized, and you have before you a noble artist at the height of his powers.

These quartets could only have been written by a great musician who has a hundred times played, and meditated on, the masterpieces of the genre the great masters have left us. From beginning to end, the style is invariably noble, and nowhere do we find timid complacencies designed to tickle frivolous or inexperienced ears. The beauty of these works is of the serious and severe kind which alone ensures a future for a work of art. It must not be supposed, however, that melody is not abundant: the slow movements contain song-like themes which are tender or expressive, and often passionate. The Scherzos are genuinely humorous: the first is distinguished for, we might almost say, epigrammatic brevity; the other, on the contrary is well worked out and contains instances of harmonic and rhythmic daring; neither of the two movements, however, reminds the hearer in the least of former creations of the kind, and that is a great merit. In a word: these quartets announce the complete change of the great virtuoso into the composer and deserve the deepest attention on the part of all musicians and connoisseurs.

Two young English artists, the Holmes brothers, and M. Jacquand and C. Ney, interpreted the quartets with rare talent. After a single rehearsal, they performed these difficult works with remarkable spirit and unanimity. The composer was present, and was visibly moved by the profound impression made by his return. The audience, composed of musicians, artists and connoisseurs, were very happy about it. ... [RGM:No.45:1864: 354–5]

During his last days in Paris, Ernst continued to be pressed for another performance of the quartets. Eventually one was arranged on the spur of the moment at the home of one of Joachim's relatives. The concert is especially noteworthy because this was the last occasion when Ernst played in public. There was no time to invite the usual celebrities, but fortunately Liszt's ex-mistress, the Countess Marie d'Agoult (writing under her pen name of 'Daniel Stern'), was there to record the event. Like Heller, she finds metaphors of fire and rebirth irresistible, but seems unaware that the concert was arranged so quickly that there was no time to invite Berlioz, who had, in any case, retired from criticism:

A Musical Evening

To Hector Berlioz

... It is as if the genius of virtuosity, folded in on itself and buried in silence, has undergone a metamorphosis; or that a hearth, lack-luster in appearance, suddenly shoots out a brilliant flame. Why did you not see yesterday, the great artist, his brow pale, enduring pain, but the eye bright, his hand – wasted but firm – manipulating his faithful bow, and directing by look and voice the skilful artists who are making every effort to give, as if they had conceived it, the thought of the master [?]

You did not see his physical weakness, so great a puff of wind would fell him, and his moral force, still so great that it commanded our souls, and drove those he directed where he wanted. How much you would have been touched by the sight of him, the vehement, the capricious *soloist* of former times, playing humbly and with discipline, the viola in these austere quartets passed down to him by the muse of Beethoven and Weber. My astonishment, I admit, equalled my admiration. Never could I have believed that in a state of troubles, collapse, of sufferings still unfinished through long years, he could find in himself a work as strong, as completely developed, as closely conforming to the grand laws of art and life. It is not for me to give you a musical analysis of these two quartets; all I would like to do is draw your attention most particularly to the following qualities: the integration, the solid workmanship, the unflagging originality until the last breath which forms an absolutely extraordinary contrast with the languid, nervous, unstable and tormented state of the poor invalid. There is in this phenomenon, for the moralist as much as the artist, a great subject for reflection and joy. I saw there for my part a new ground for believing in the liberty and immortality of genius. And it is why yesterday, I so much regretted not greeting you, and it is why today, I still feel with all my heart, the need to communicate with you. … [*Le Temps*:4/11/64:2]

Ernst and Amélie were last seen together by the Paris public in a box of the Comédie-Française when they attended the first night of Emile Augier's *Maître Guérin* [GD:VII:820], and were no doubt gratified by its ardent advocacy of faithful marriage. This premiere is noticed by the *Athenaeum* on 12 November 1864, and it must therefore have taken place a day or two before. As Ernst's first letter from Nice was written on 22 November, it seems reasonable to suppose that the Ernsts left for Nice in the third week of that month, probably using the new railway line to Nice which had opened in mid-October. [LUNN:24–6] On the same page of the *Athenaeum*, Chorley notes the popularity of Ernst's quartets in Paris, and also draws attention to another successful performance, led by Hubert Ries, of the B♭ quartet at a chamber concert in Berlin. [A:12/11/64:644]

Shortly after arriving in Nice, Ernst gave his news to Bulwer, taking up some military metaphors from Daniel Stern's review:

We were with a number of friends and acquaintances during the last days of our stay in Paris, but it was not only they who encumbered me, as I was also tormented by some musical authorities and a circle of amateurs to give them an opportunity to hear my quartets. The thing was arranged as well as possible on the spur of the moment and it could not have gone better. I will even tell you that because of the excitement there I found enough energy to take part as well, not as a general but as a well disciplined soldier I discharged the viola part moderately well. The sensation was tremendous, and the performances filled the most important journals in Paris.

I managed the journey from Paris well enough and in very little time. However, on arriving here I greatly regretted the demands of the journey, and it's only since yesterday that my health has entered its normal state of suffering. My stomach is much better, and with that there is always hope …

We have by chance found an excellent and very cheap apartment, with a large terrace and a covered balcony overlooking the sea. Until now we have had a fairly uneventful life that is unfortunately forced on us by my health. Don't measure it dear friend by the length of this letter. I don't permit myself this excess often; but my will can make this effort when it reaches the heart. I hope this letter finds you there. [22 November 1864. Nice. HALS: D/EK:C18/103]

The apartment, 8 rue St François de Paule, 2nd Floor, is in a six-storey building opposite a church and a chocolate shop in the old town. [See Plate XVIII.] One back from the road along the beach, the street is narrow and cool; if you look to your right as you emerge from the doorway you can see the Castle Hill; if you turn right again you can see the sea and the palm trees framed by Ernst's building and the imposing theatre.

Life in the apartment soon settled into an uneventful routine:

I go out a good deal in a wheelchair, accompanied nearly always by my dear wife, and sometimes by my mother [-in-law] and Paul [Amélie's adolescent brother], not to speak of a crowd of acquaintances who surround them.

It's still not a good idea to show my face in the Massena circle, and I don't know if I shall go back there at all this season, not so much through lack of desire as because of my health. I sometimes play whist at home with good, distinguished and agreeable players, and that only in the evening. That's enough for me at present. [4 December 1864. Nice. HALS:D/EK:C18/104]

Predictably, Davison was being a negligent correspondent, and Amélie, despite a previous threat not to write if *he* didn't, considered it worthwhile to send one last and highly informative letter.

Dear Friend, Although you haven't wanted to reply to me, I want to assume that you'll not be indifferent to some news of Ernst, and I'm going to tell you that he's not too ill at the moment, at least he has regained use of his digestive faculties since Paris and that's the great thing. Stephen Heller wrote to us that you have put his article on the quartets in the *Musical World*. Did you know that he – Ernst – played himself one evening in private, the viola part in these same quartets at the house of Joachim's uncle and aunt who were so kind to us in Paris? The quartet which is dedicated to you created, above all the others, the greatest enthusiasm. We were all friendly with one another, and the same evening Heller who, as you know, one never hears, played, and I read some very poetical verses by Musset. You would have pitied Berlioz that evening, he seemed like one risen from the dead. We asked him to come and see us here because I must tell you that by a stroke of luck we have a most spacious apartment which we could only fully enjoy if we had our friends here with us to profit from the beautiful sunshine that we have on out terrace where it's so mild that we eat outdoors every day, having the sea at our feet and the most beautiful view in front of our eyes. Ah! If you could be here to see us, what a joy that would be. That would restore our Maestro's creative impulse because he has not written anything since London. In Paris, he was so popular and feted, that he was hugely encouraged, but before everything else it was necessary to think about his bodily health, and that's better here, but he does not have perhaps the same degree of intellectual stimulation.

I am sending, thinking they will interest you, some very noble lines by Daniel Stern, on the concert where Ernst played himself. That evening, unfortunately, neither Berlioz nor Wallace, who had attended the first concert, had been invited because it was on the spur of the moment that Heinrich, having Jacquand and the young Holmes to hand, decided to play the viola and I must tell you that added to the effect – in terms of power and ideas

– of the music. What a pity you weren't there again – as usual – dear vagabond. And by the way, I must tell you that the young Holmes played easily and with astonishing skill. Now I must tell you that since Heller's article, in France, people have become stirred up about the last quartet, and have been writing to Heller from different towns in order to acquire it. So Ernst believes it's time to publish it, and I beg you to deal with the matter seriously. He will keep the copyright in all countries. So, show him that you're interested in it, write to him about it, because I know he fears that all this will burden you. All the same, you can do that for him can't you? It would be very kind if you would write something to us, we'd find it so sweet and it would give you so little trouble. You really don't know how to love those who are absent. If you were at least sending the *Musical World* one could console oneself in reading that admittedly, but my God not a single sign that you remember your friends. So tell us about yourself, your wife, your children whom we love almost as if they were ours. Adorable little creatures, kiss them for us. Would you like us to write some articles on music in Nice for you? We are ready. If you see Louis Blanc he will tell you Ernst's latest wicked jokes. I told him to tell you, because I know that you'll laugh when he tells you, and he'll make them seem funny. Ah! Would you like to return the *History of the Revolution* that you took from me[?] I need to read it Monsieur, and L. Blanc will have it sent to me. You thief! Wasn't it enough for you to be a great vagabond already? Were you finding yourself too honest?

We spoke of you in Paris with Robert Lytton who had come there to present his young and charming wife to us. They are in Greece at present. Sir Edward is ill in Hastings. I had the recent news from Radcliffe. I am certain that you won't forget them when you have some extra tickets …

And now God bless you, [In English] and we keep your love as you have ours,
Ever yours affectionate,
Amélie Ernst [15 December 1864. Nice. BL]

Davison neither replied nor ensured publication of the quartet dedicated to him, and he must in some measure be blamed for the work's loss. Consequently, it is here the correspondence ends. Berlioz showed greater interest. A week or so before sending the letter to Davison, Amélie must have sent a similar letter of invitation to the composer, detailing their large apartment and the other enticements of Nice. As she finished her letter to Davison, one of Berlioz's most splendidly splenetic replies was already in the post:

It was really very kind of you to have written to me, dear Mme Ernst, and I ought to reply in a smooth, simpering style, neatly dressed, cravat well tied, all smiles and amiability. Well I can't.

I am ill, sad, disgusted, bored, boring, idiotic, wearisome, cross and altogether impossible. It's one of those days when I wish the earth was a loaded bomb so that I might divert myself by lighting the fuse. The picture you give me of your Nice pleasures doesn't attract me in the least. I should love to see you and your dear invalid, but I couldn't accept your offer of a room. I would rather stay in a cave under the Ponchettes. There one is free to growl alongside Caliban – I know he lives there, I saw him one day – and the sea doesn't come often and fill it up: whereas with friends, even the best, one is exposed to all sorts of unbearable attentions. They ask you how you survive the night but never how you survive your boredom; they stare at you to discover whether you are sad or happy: they insist on talking to you when you are just muttering to yourself, and then the husband says to the wife: 'Do let him alone, you can see he doesn't want to talk, don't bother him,' etc.

etc. Then one takes one's hat and goes out, and on the way out bangs the door too hard, and thinks: 'Now there – what a brute. I shall be the cause of a domestic quarrel.' Now in Caliban's grotto there is none of this …

Well, never mind! Do you often stroll on the terrace and along the shady walk? And then? Do you admire the sunsets? And then? Do you breathe the sea air? And then? Do you watch the tunny fishers? And then? Do you envy the young English heiresses with their incomes of thousands of pounds sterling a year? And then? Do you envy still more the idiots without ideas or feelings who understand nothing and love nothing? And then? … Why, can't I give you all that? We have terraces and trees in Paris. There are sunsets, English heiresses, idiots – they are even more plentiful than in Nice, for the population is larger – and gudgeon to be caught with a line. One can be almost as extensively bored as in Nice. It's the same everywhere. … [14 December 1864. Paris. SLB:192–3. See also CGB:VII:169–70]

In November 1864, a grim series of events started to be played out in Nice that the Ernsts must have found an ominous portent. The Tsarevich Nicholas, the twenty-one-year-old heir to the throne of Russia, landed at Villefranche from a Russian frigate. He had just returned from becoming engaged to the Princess Dagmar in Copenhagen, and was now mortally ill with a disease of the spinal cord. By January he could no longer walk properly, and by April his condition was causing so much concern that members of his family came to his bedside on the 16th. The Tsar himself arrived five days later, and was greeted at the station by vast and silent crowds. After intense suffering, the Tsarevich died on 22 April, and fifty hussars of the French Imperial Guard mounted guard in front of the residence. A torchlight procession accompanied the body to the Russian Church, and two days later, it was moved to the frigate *Alexander-Nevsky* lying off Villefranche. As the cortege moved towards the port, the narrow streets of the old town echoed to the solemn firing of naval guns and coastal batteries. The next day, the Tsar and Tsarina, accompanying their dead son, set out to sea. [CN:328–9]

Another Russian, who must have felt profoundly affected by these events, was also able to record Ernst's condition. This was Vassily Bezekirsky, pupil of Léonard and later professor at the Moscow Philharmonic Music School. In his memoirs he recalls:

At that time (1865) in Nice the celebrated violinist Ernst was slowly dying. I frequently called upon him, and my visits evidently took his mind off his illness which was caused by two diseases; severe rheumatism and emaciation of the spinal chord. He still had sufficient strength to play the game of piquet with me, fortifying himself during the game with black coffee and cognac. The latter, he assured me, had a narcotic effect on him, allowing him to sleep soundly at least two hours out of 24. He died less than five months after my departure from Nice. In parting with me, he made me a present of his portrait, with an inscription dated June 4th. [EOC:27]

The last glimpse we catch of Ernst before his illness entered its final phase is through the eyes of a child. Her name in adulthood was D. Birnbaum and her reminiscence is published as an appendix to Samuel Wolf's English edition of Heller's book. Birnbaum was clearly the daughter of one of the Ernsts' Nice acquaintances, but otherwise there is no information about her:

I was very much afraid of the tall, pale man with the black beard. Oh, I was still too little to understand what was meant by 'the famous violinist Ernst.' I trembled before the gleam of his dark eyes and allowed myself very unwillingly to be caressed by him, in spite of the fact that he always brought me a bag of bon-bons. For he had an unusual love for children and I, the little tomboy, was his special favourite. One day he caught me, and I had to confess I was afraid of him.

'Yes, why?'

'Because you have such sad eyes,' I blurted out, 'and such a wild, black beard.'

'Well, if it's nothing else,' he said, laughing, 'then you can come to me and I will play something for you on the violin; you can dance and sing to it. Surely you like music?'

Like music? That was something incomprehensible to me, and I struggled to get away, for outside, I heard my girl friends calling to roll hoops.

'Please come,' said the artist gently, 'you shall also have some cinnamon cookies and chocolate.'

That was more tempting, but that I had been asked to come carried still more weight with me. So the following afternoon at the appointed time I tripped over to the big house where Ernst lived.

I had palpitations of the heart when the maid who had been sent along with me pulled the bell. Soon after I found myself in a large room, somewhat bare, containing a grand piano on which lay a violin. The remaining arrangement consisted of a chaise longue and about two dozen chairs. The daylight fell brightly through three large windows and made the room appear rather prosaic since neither carpets nor curtains were used as decoration. This much I noticed in spite of my seven years. Then the opposite door was opened and M. Ernst appeared on the threshold.

'Ah, my little one, there she is indeed, our dear Minna.'

With that he led me into the adjacent room to his wife, a very beautiful lady, who sat at a table with cups and leafed through a newspaper. Beside her sat a young girl, her niece. I thought I had never seen anyone lovelier. Little brown curls lay on her white forehead. She laughed in such a friendly way, and in the light pink summer dress she wore I thought I saw a fairy in her. Already I took more courage, and when I was permitted to sit on the chair beside her, whom M. Ernst called Lilli, and she poured chocolate for me, and M. Ernst laid a big piece of cake on my plate, while his wife prepared a bowl of strawberries and cream with sugar and cream for later in the afternoon, I suddenly felt all fear disappear and I ate everything to my heart's content. After we had sat at the table for half and hour, M. Ernst took my lovely neighbour by the hand.

'How would it be now for our concert? Surely we must play something for the little one?'

We all went together into the large, empty room. Mdle Lilli opened the grand piano, the violin was tuned, and an ensemble began such as I have never heard. I never thought of dancing and singing, but now I knew what music was. All at once I sprang up, ran to M. Ernst so impetuously that I almost snatched the violin out of his hand and kissed him while bright tears ran down my cheeks.

'Yes, Mouse, what is it?'

'Oh I thank you many times,' I uttered with difficulty, 'now I know that I like music, such music.'

It was quite a while before they calmed me down. The bare music room had become for me the most beautiful room, and with the greatest attention I listened to every note the bow coaxed from the strings. And when it was announced that the playing was over, I was sad as never before. Did I have a foreboding that this was his last [concert]? Soon after, the artist became very ill and died. For me, that afternoon was a holy memory. The artistic performance had awakened my musical faculties, and from then on influenced my entire later life. [EOC:21–2]

The Ernsts' financial situation continued to be alleviated by the charity of friends. Hallé and a small committee arranged another benefit concert, to be held on 23 March 1865 in the Free Trade Hall in Manchester. The main item on the programme was Beethoven's *Choral Fantasia*, but the highlight of the evening once again proved to be performances by the untiring Joachim. Ernst's own compositions continued to be enthusiastically received, and the concert allowed a 'noble sum' of money to be forwarded to Nice. [E:219–20]

In spite of the glorious weather, the death of the Tsarevich had cast a pall over Nice, and now death manifested itself in a more general form. With the great urban crowds brought by the railway came cholera, and this, coupled with the primitive and stinking conditions of Nice's drains, caused an epidemic in the later months of 1865. The authorities, distressed about its effect on the tourist trade, engaged in panicky and long overdue sanitation work, but in spite of these efforts the disease spread alarmingly quickly. It was to be fifty years before Nice's death rate was as high again – 373 died of the disease and probably as many were seriously ill – and the news of this caused the season of 1865–66 to be a disaster. [LUNN:93]

These events affected the Ernsts. Part of this sanitation work was extensive street cleaning in the old town, and Ernst's last days would have been spent listening to workmen's shouts and the clatter of shovels and pails. The Opera next door to them began to suffer. It had lost its wily director Louis Avette in March 1865 and his place had been taken by the altogether less skilful Provini [HN:II:174] who, having failed to put on any performances for several months, found his first efforts annihilated by the cholera epidemic. By October, when the season should have been at its height, the company was in serious trouble. Provini managed to persuade the performers to take a 10 per cent cut in salary, but this proved insufficient, and by November he was forced to apply to the municipal council for a subsidy. They hated the idea, but finally agreed only when they realized that, if the Opera closed, '[it] would completely destroy the success of the season that already has been so compromised'. [LUNN:94]

The death of the Tsarevich, the cholera, and the financial disaster it brought in its train, culminated for Amélie in a long-anticipated but devastating blow. Ernst died at 2 o'clock in the afternoon on 8 October [NMZ:MW:11/11/65:705]. Amélie was too grief-stricken to register the death, and Paul and his mother clearly felt the need to remain at home with her. The death was therefore registered at 10 o'clock on 9 October by Bertille Lapalu, aged 26 and a shop assistant in a tobacconist's, and Eugène Tisferand, aged 48 and the chaplain of Paul's Lycée. [GAM:128] The latter may well have been with Ernst in his last moments. On the certificate, Ernst's father is described as 'Herr Ernst, Jacob'; those registering the death knew nothing of his mother. Amélie was also too upset to communicate the news to Bulwer, and the task was entrusted to Paul:

Dear Sir, A terrible blow has just struck us, my dear brother-in-law, M. Ernst, has just succumbed to his long and sad illness. As the messenger, I hardly dare tell you of this sad blow, which I am sure will cause consternation in your noble heart.

My sister begged me to tell you that in his final moments, my brother-in-law frequently mentioned your name[;] he even believed he saw you in his rooms.

His final moments, God be thanked, were calm enough, it is as if he were simply snuffed out.

My sister will write you a longer letter, but the sadness and shock of this cruel loss has been too hard for her to communicate with his friends.

Yours sincerely, Paul Lévy [9 October 1865. Nice. HALS:D/EK:C2/132]

Bulwer, unaware of the extremity of Ernst's condition, had clearly written to him in early October. The letter arrived shortly after Ernst's death, causing Paul to write a second time.

Dear Sir, Your kind letter could not unfortunately reassure our poor Ernst, because death has taken him from us forever.

Some days after you wrote, a sad decline set in and sent him to the grave.

The funeral took place at 11 o'clock yesterday; he lies in peace in the cemetery of the Chateau. I don't want to depress you [but] I cannot tell you how miserable my sister and the rest of us are. The most constant care and attention did nothing but increase his terrible suffering[.] My sister had hope until the last moment, even the doctors could not convince her of the sad reality.

We feared for her health but happily the first and most painful moments passed[;] courage and religion helped to support her in this sad time.

I do not dwell on the subject for fear of upsetting you because he was also one of your friends. He never forgot you. How many times in his illness he spoke of you.

I believe that friends in this world will be friends in the next.

Yours sincerely,

Paul Lévy [9 [probably 10] October 1865. Nice. HALS:D/EK:C2/133]

The accounts of Ernst's last moments appear to be contradictory. The first letter says: 'His final moments, God be thanked, were calm enough, it is as if he were simply snuffed out.' The second has: 'The most constant care and attention did nothing but increase his terrible suffering.' It is of course possible that, in his first letter to Bulwer, Paul minimizes Ernst's sufferings to help reduce a friend's shock at the news. Amélie later said he died in agony; Ehrlich that he died in physical and mental torment. [CV:93] Perhaps the most likely interpretation is that Ernst did suffer horribly until immediately before the end, but when the end came it was calm and without drama.

Two days after his death, the *Journal de Nice* published a short obituary giving details of the funeral. This was probably held on 9 October: the speedy burials usual in warm climates were made even more essential by the raging epidemic: 'His funeral took place today at 11 o'clock. His coffin was followed by several friends, representatives of the press, the section leaders of the Theatre Impérial's orchestra, the head and deputy head and a deputation of musicians from the 3rd Infantry Regiment, and a line of poor. He was buried in the Castle cemetery.' [JN:9/10/10/1865:2C]

Chorley wrote a fine obituary for the *Athenaeum* of 21 October:

> The long agony – for such did the last years of Herr Ernst amount – is at last over. The *Times* of this day week [actually the 13th] recorded that his career of suffering closed at Nice on 8th of this month. This is one of the cases in which departure can only be welcomed as a relief. His long protracted bodily pain had been long known to be past the power of medicine to alleviate ... It is to be added, however, that the active kindness of those to whom his admired qualities had endeared him failed him not to the last.
>
> A more amiable man never breathed than Ernst; nor one of a better heart, a finer intelligence, and a more generous unenvying nature ... his friends will recollect him not merely by his nobility of nature, incapable of intrigue jealousy and suspicion, but also his quick and delicate sense of humour. As an artist he cannot be overrated amongst the violinists. [A:21/10/65:541]

It was to be more than a fortnight after his death before a devastated Amélie could summon the strength to write to Bulwer. The ink is sometimes blotted by tears:

> My Dear Friend, Many thanks for your kind words and your sympathy in these days of hard trial, of sorrow, and affliction. I am excessively grateful for them.
>
> I remain here in this miserable world without any consolation. I have lost the best friend I ever had. The most just, the most kind, the most merciful to me.
>
> I can say also one of the most sweet, elevated and poetical hearts who ever was. And never were two lives as united as ours, especially this last year of great pains for him, and of so great afflictions for me. I did what I could to soften this horrid suffering but at last, after a series of crises of the stomach like the one at which you were witness one day in Holles St., he could not bear any longer this *martyre* [agony] and left me alone to miss him for ever.
>
> If ever I recover some strength, some energy, I shall try to make myself as useful as possible to the dear ones I have around me and whom I make miserable now. But what I shall do I do not know, nor can I think of it. Many thanks for your kind offer of service. I am not in want of anything. I hope to hear that your health is regaining in strength and wish heartily to hear that you take good care of it especially in this season of the year. I remain here for some time. Indeed I shall be unable to go anywhere else. If you come I shall welcome you and will never forget all the kindnesses you did for him and to me, and the interest you had in his poor health. I shall lead you to his tomb, my only walk at present. I cannot believe in the happiness he has in a better world if he sees how miserable I am in this one.
>
> In the last days of my beloved husband, he was wishing news of you, and was happy to receive by kind friends the newspapers relating the opening of your Guild [for writers] in which he took a brotherly interest as your friend [and] as [an] artist. Some day I shall send a good likeness of Ernst which I made in his last days and is very like the [dear one] who is no more. Meanwhile I shall be thankful if you can give me better news of yourself.
>
> My mother and my brother (who behaved as [a] man in this sad time) unite with me in [sending] all good wishes to you.
>
> Believe me ever my dear friend, your very devoted,
>
> Amélie Ernst [24 October 1865. 8, rue St François de Paule, Nice. HALS:D/EK: C3/133]

Temporarily, Ernst's body had been placed in a vault and about a month later he was buried in a plain tomb in the Christian cemetery; this indicates that at some point after marriage – probably during his last years – he converted to Catholicism. [MW:25/11/65:744] He left his wife a collection of his manuscripts including two complete quartets, the six *Polyphonic Studies*, the A♭ piano *Nocturne*, and a grand cadenza for Beethoven's violin concerto. [RGM:12/11/65] The *Table des Successoirs et Absences* in the *Archives des Alpes-Maritimes* indicates that he left no money or possessions.

In announcing the news of his death to Berlioz, Amélie clearly mentioned the idea of raising money for a proper funerary monument. His reply is touching but pessimistic on this and many other counts:

> I would have liked to reply yesterday to your sad letter, but I was so ill I didn't have the strength. Today, writing these few lines still causes me a good deal of pain. Heller let me know the tragic news, and you know how much we share in your grief.
>
> I loved Ernst, as you know, and I loved him before you knew him. I have given proof of this in a volume of memoirs that I'm about to have printed, where you will find a letter addressed to him and an appreciation of his talent. The book hasn't yet been made public and will not be put on sale until after my death; but people can see what I thought of Ernst twenty years ago.
>
> This will be my stone for his monument. As for the other monument you mentioned, I can't do anything to help you raise it. A rich man like M. Figdor [Joachim's uncle in Paris], for example, might be willing to pay for it himself. But subscriptions never succeed in Paris. I spoke to Brandus and to Dufour and they are very much of the same opinion.
>
> As for me, who has neither health nor money, I can do nothing. Heller's position is no better. I asked D'Ortigue to write something in his next article. We have also lost another artist from amongst our friends, poor Wallace, and his widow is in the same position as you.
>
> Oh the sky is truly dark. I feel myself sinking into gloom. Are you going to stay for long in Nice?
>
> I'm sorry, I must take my laudanum and try to go to sleep. I haven't any more strength. I spend seven-eighths of my life asleep. Death is a capricious coquette.
>
> Yours, Hector Belioz [Dated 'Dimanche 20' but probably 22 October 1865. AF and CGB:VII:223]

Interestingly, the surviving manuscript is ripped into four uneven pieces. Two could be the result of an accident but four suggests deliberation: was Amélie irritated by Berlioz's inability to help or the tartness of his remark about loving Ernst before she did? If she was upset, the mood passed, and she soon set about the subscription project with a will. Funds were given by friends in Nice, particularly in the German community, and further donations were made in Vienna, London, Paris and Brünn. [E:220–21] While Ernst was still alive, Amélie, who was a sculptor as well as an actress and writer, sculpted two copies of his left hand (which would eventually find themselves in the museum in Nice), and modelled a clay relief of his face (which, when cast in bronze, would form the centrepiece of his tomb). [DPS1:II:601] The relief is probably the 'likeness' she mentions to Bulwer. The fund-raising went well, and on 8 October 1866, the first anniversary of his death, there was a small ceremony when the large roughly-finished slab, with Amélie's bronze at its centre, was dedicated. [See Plates XIX nd XX.] The place of his burial and her feelings for him, are best described in poem she wrote six years later:

> If I was dying, driven too far from his tomb,
> Oh that I should be brought back near my best beloved,
> To the country where twice the lemon tree flowers
> In its dark foliage, where the orange ripens.
> Do you know the place where I am awaited?
> On the beach at Nice, under the broad sun
> Where rises a great rock crowned with cypresses;
> It dominates the sea which comes to die at its feet
> The elegant palm trees under the languid palm leaves
> The giant olive trees covered with yellow roses,
> With bold vine branches up to their tops
> This hill all radiant ignores the winters
> The geranium fills it with perfume, and the proud acanthus,
> The spiky cacti erect themselves on its slopes
> One can see the pomegranates half-opened in the sun,
> The Japanese medlar whose fruit is like gold
> The aloes whose one flower bursts out every hundred years,
> The white jasmine, the myrtle and the scarlet carnation,
> And line of blue waves a long furrow of silver,
> To the horizon so soft, of opal so changeable
> The fishermen's boats, their luminous sails
> And the jagged mountains and the snowy peaks,
> On which the imperial crimson spreads like a cloak.
> It's there, you will see it, that my husband awaits me;
> Because my fingers, inspired by faithful memory
> Have engraved his features on rebellious bronze.
> You who loved him, you will recognise him,
> And lift[ing] his stone, friend, you will say to him
> 'Abelard! Abelard! Here is your Heloise!
> That finally in death is united with you!'
> And his arms will open to regain what is his
> And seal my heart forever in his! ['Last Vow', RFA:21–3]

Chapter 24

Epilogue

To finish, I shall briefly describe what happened to Amélie, Ernst's violin, and his family.

I

Amélie was devastated by Ernst's death, but she did everything she could to keep his memory alive. She ensured that his image was placed in important buildings, arranged memorial concerts, and saw to it that the street which runs along the side of the building where he died was named after him. (It is now the rue Robbins.) However, she needed to earn money, so she returned to her old career of giving recitations, virtually inventing the public poetry recital in France. She re-established her friendship with Gautier, who gave her some fine reviews, and befriended Alexandre Dumas, who in 1868 wrote a famous quasi-poem, *Autoportrait*, in her autograph book. [TGCG:XII:273] With such powerful backing, her readings proved highly successful, and she performed in, amongst many other places, Baden, the hall in the boulevard des Capucines, Versailles, and the Sorbonne. When Victor Hugo, from his exile in Guernsey, sent her copies of his as yet unpublished *L'homme qui rit*, crowds had to be turned away from the door.

Parallel to this career, she began to develop another as a poet. Her first collection, *Rimes françaises d'une Alsacienne* [*French Rhymes of a Woman from Alsace*], published in 1873, was a terrific success and went through five editions. This contains a number of melancholic poems about Ernst, but its popularity was largely due to the penultimate section, a deeply patriotic exploration of Prussian atrocities and French miseries during the recent Franco-Prussian War. Whereas Ernst had solved the problem of being Jewish in nationalistic Christian Europe by becoming a rootless cosmopolitan; Amélie solved it in the opposite way, embracing Catholicism and the most ardent form of French nationalism. It is as well she did not know that the *Elegy* was General von Moltke's favourite piece of music.

The war temporarily put an end to her career as a performer, and she served with considerable distinction with the ambulance service in Switzerland. [MLP: XV–XVI] On her return, she endured severe financial difficulties, and the poet Sully Prudhomme wrote an open letter to the Minister of Education saying that she should be given a position or stipend. [MLP:XIX] The appeal was turned down, but she managed to continue her career as a reader, successfully giving recitals, for example, in Lille, and in Macon to celebrate the inauguration of Lamartine's statue. [AG:II:899–900] The government eventually took some notice. The fourth edition of *Rimes françaises* was subsidized by the Ministry of Education [NB:i], and her tireless work on behalf of French diction may well have influenced the decision to make the subject compulsory in French schools.

She published several more books: *Nos bébés* [*Our Babies*], a rather twee collection of poems based on the unconscious wisdom articulated by children, in 1883; *Mes Lectures en vers* [*My Poetry Readings*], a large collection (some 640 pages) of the poems she read at her recitals, in about 1892; and *Mes Lectures en prose* [*My Prose Readings*], a similar collection of prose, in 1894.

In 1883, she had announced another collection of poetry, *Feuillets d'album et Pensées Fugitives* [*Album Leaves and Fleeting Thoughts*], a title clearly designed to honour her husband, but there is no evidence the book ever appeared. At the same time, she announced a set of memoirs – *Recueil des Notes et Souvenirs, avec documents autograph et inedits* [*A Collection of Notes and Memories, with Autograph and Unpublished Documents*] – but there is no evidence that this appeared either. [NB:i] As she knew many famous people, and the volume would have contained a good deal about Ernst, its non-appearance is a great loss.

In the 1880s she took up the visual arts again, and exhibited at the Salon of the Société des Artistes Français from 1887 onwards. [DA:IV:266]

I have not been able to discover when and where she died. The poem quoted at the end of the last chapter shows that she wanted to be buried with her husband, but the tomb contains only the bodies of Ernst and his mother-in-law, and the next plot is empty. Quite extensive searches suggest she is not buried in Nice or Paris. She was clearly desperate to be buried with Ernst and only formidable obstacles could have prevented it. Amely Heller says she was still alive, and reading at the Sorbonne, in 1904. [EOC:21] If she died in either Vienna or Alsace – places she visited regularly – during the First World War, then her body could well have been trapped behind enemy lines. Perhaps she was just one of the tens of thousands who disappeared without trace in that conflict.

II

For several years, Amélie did not want to sell Ernst's Stradivarius. She gives her reasons in a poem called 'Ernst's Violin', appropriately dedicated to the man who bought the instrument, Mr Fountaine of Narford Hall: 'You who were his living lyre, / Now you are here mute, / Shut up in your green case, / .../ Be mine at least undivided. / Only my hand will awaken you, / .../ Smash yourself in any other hand.' [RFA:18–20] However, friends persuaded her that the instrument would deteriorate unplayed, and she gave it to the violin dealer Vuillaume to sell, but named an exorbitant price. For two years, Amélie refused all lower offers, but eventually it was bought by the Scottish violin dealer, David Laurie. [RFD:137] In 1874, Madame Norman-Neruda, Lady Hallé, indicated that she wished to buy it, and a committee of aristocrats raised the asking price of £500. She bought it in early 1875, and it remained her main concert instrument throughout her career. [RFD:172]

On Lady Hallé's death in 1911 the violin was acquired by Dr Emmerich of Munich. From him, it passed into the hands of Emil Herrmann who sold it in turn to Zlatko Balokovic. The Wurlitzer Collection then acquired it from Balokovic, and they then sold it to Mrs Aurthur Crary in 1938, who bought it for the use of Miss Byrd Elliot. From here it went to Herrmann again, who sold it to the American violinist William Kroll – composer of the well known *Banjo and Fiddle* – in 1950. He recorded many pieces with it, and it can be heard, for example, in the first violin part of the Kroll Quartet's recording of Tchaikowsky's first string quartet. In 1977, as I indicated in Chapter 9, the Ernst Stradivarius was acquired by its current owner, Dénes Zsigmondy. [EOC:21] Its clear and penetrating tones can be heard in all his recordings since the date of purchase, including his collection of Romantic pieces.

III

Twenty-three people called 'Ernst' were buried between 1863 and 1940 in the New Jewish Cemetery in Brünn, where they lie amidst families bearing some of the most eminent names of the twentieth century – Popper, Epstein, Hayek, Kuhn, Korngold, Horowitz and Kafka. It is reasonable to assume that there were at least this number of Ernsts living in Brünn in 1941. But, between that date and 1943, fourteen Nazi transport trains carried the Jews of Brünn to Terezin and Minsk. Of the 10,067 deported, 670 survived. No one called Ernst now lives in Brno. Since the Jews of Hungary (the home of two of Ernst's siblings) fared little better, it is safe to assume that Ernst has no living relatives. [HJSB:7–8]

Appendix

The Main Themes of Ernst's Lost A Major String Quartet

The analytical programme for the second half of Ernst's benefit concert in St James's Hall, 6 June 1864, the 153rd Monday Popular Concert, pp.638–43. Reproduced by permission of the Royal College of Music, London.

Part II.

QUARTET (No. 2), in A major, for two Violins,
Viola, and Violoncello.   *Ernst.*

(First time of performance.)

Allegro giocoso vivace ($\mathbb{C}$)—A major.
Introduzione, moderato (C); leading to
Allegretto con moto capriccioso (6/8)—F sharp major;
  with Trio (3/4)—D flat major.
Cavatina, Andante (2/4)—D major.
Finale, allegro molto vivace (2/4)—A major.

1st Violin, Herr JOACHIM.   Viola,   Mr. H. WEBB.
2nd Violin, Herr L. RIES.   Violoncello, Signor PIATTI.

The principal themes in each movement of this quartet are subjoined according to the order of their occurrence.

Allegro (first subject—in A major).

The Main Themes of Ernst's Lost A Major String Quartet 277

639

Allegro (second subject—in E major).

Allegro (coda).

640

Capriccio (introduzione—F sharp minor).

Capriccio (principal subject—F sharp major).

Capriccio (trio—D flat major).

641

Cavatina (principal subject—D major).

Cavatina (episode).

642

Finale (first subject—A major).

It will be seen that a prominent *motivo* of the first *allegro* (as with Mendelssohn's early quartet in E flat, and pianoforte sonata in E major) forms the basis of this *coda*, as it had already formed the basis of the *coda* in the movement in which it originally appeared.

List of Works by H.W. Ernst

In some catalogues, the works of Heinrich Wilhelm Ernst (who occasionally appears as Henri Guillaume or H.G. Ernst) are confused with pieces by other composers with the same surname. The 'Gypsy Dance' for example, which appears in CPM, was probably composed by one Henri Ernst, a violinist living in Boston in the second half of the nineteenth century. [EOC:28] Similarly, the song 'Liebe Kleine Frau', attributed to H.W. Ernst and recorded by Joseph Schmidt in 1936 (BOOOO3DLW: 1995), sounds like something written in the 1930s and is most unlikely to be by the Moravian violinist.

As the list below makes clear, the opus numbers of Ernst's works are incomplete, repetitious and muddled. No works corresponding to op.2, 7 and 14 have been found.

At the end of each entry, I indicate a library where a copy (not necessarily the earliest edition) can be found. Most of Ernst's surviving music is in the British Library [BL]. The locations of the rest are indicated as follows:

BIC	Bibliothèque Inguimbertine, Carpentras, France
BLO	Bodleian Music Library, Oxford
BS	Bayerische Staatsbibliothek
CL	Conservatoire Royal de Musique de Liège
HDK	Hochschule der Künste, Berlin
LC	Library of Congress, Washington, D.C.
OBN	Österreichische Nationalbibliothek, Vienna
NL	Newberry Library, Chicago
UK	Musikwissenschaft Institut der Universität Köln
WLB	Wüttembergische Landesbibliothek, Stuttgart

Published Works with Opus Numbers

Op.4 *Variations brillantes sur un Thème de Rossini.* For violin and piano. Dedicated to the King of France. Date of composition: probably 1829. First recorded performance: Stuttgart late 1829 or early 1830. Earliest known edition: Hofmeister, Leipzig, 1834. [JP:137–9. E:225] [BL]

Op.5 *Trois Rondinos pour Violon Seul avec accompagnement d'un second Violon (ad-lib) sur des motifs favoris de Robert le Diable, Natalie et la Tentation.* Dedicated to M. le Compte de Montendre. For violin and piano/second violin. Date of composition: probably 1832–33. First recorded performance: none. Earliest known edition: Schlésinger, Paris *c*.1834. The order of the pieces varies between editions, and in some early editions, the *Rondinos* are referred to as op.3. [E:226–7] [CL]

Op.6 *Introduction et Variations brilliantes en forme de Fantasie sur le Quatuor fav. de Ludovic de F. Halévy*. For violin and orchestra/piano/string quartet/string quintet (with double-bass). Dedicated to François Schubert. Date of composition: probably 1833. First recorded performance: February 1834. Earliest known edition: Schlesinger, Berlin, 1833. [HDM. E:227–8] [CL]

Op.8 *Deux Nocturnes*. No.1: Andante spianato in A; No. 2: Andante cantabile in E. For violin and piano. Dedicated to Mr Andrew Fountaine. Date of composition: probably between 1831 and 1834. First recorded performances: probably 23 December 1834 and 13 February 1835. Earliest known edition: Hofmeister, Leipzig, *c*.1835. No.1 became the introduction to *The Carnival of Venice*. In some sources, these pieces are referred to as op.1. [BL]

Op.9 *Thème Allemande Varié*. For violin and piano. Date of composition: probably 1834 or before. First recorded performance: probably 13 February 1835. Earliest known edition: Hofmeister, Leipzig, *c*.1835. [BL]

Op. 10 *Élégie sur la morte d'un objet chéri*. For violin and piano/orchestra. Date of composition: probably after 1831. First recorded performance: 1 January 1838 (by Panofka). Earliest known edition: Hofmeister, Leipzig, *c*.1838. The *Elegy* is sometimes referred to incorrectly as op.10, no.3. The work may be a version of an adagio played by Ernst in concerts from late 1829 onwards. [E:230–31] [BL]

Op.11 *Fantasie brilliante sur la Marche et la Romance d'Otello de Rossini*. For violin and orchestra/piano. Dedicated to Joseph Böhm. Date of composition: 1837–38. First recorded performance: 1 March 1838. Earliest known edition: Schott, Mainz, 1839. [MGG1:XVI:135. E:231–2] [BL]

Op.12 *Concertino*. For violin and orchestra/piano/string quartet. Dedicated to M. Haberneck the elder. Date of composition: probably 1836–37. First recorded performance: probably 10 November or 8 December 1837. Earliest known edition: Litolff, Braunschweig, *c*.1839. [MGG1:XVI:135. E:233] [BL]

Op.13 *Deux Morceaux de Salon*: Adagio sentimentale in E and Rondino graziozo, allegretto in A. For violin and piano. Dedicated to his friends Adolphe Schönstein and Sigmund Hoffman de Hofmansthal. Date of composition: probably 1841–42. First recorded performance: April 1842. Earliest known edition: Litolff, Braunschweig 1841; J.J. Ewer and Co., London, 1841. [MW:29/4/41:237. E:233–4] The Adagio is sometimes referred to as *Nocturne Sentimentale* or *Notturno Sentimentale*. [OBN]

Op. 15 *Morceaux de Salon. Deux Romances (sans paroles)*: Allegretto molto cantabile in G minor; Agitato ma non allegro in G minor. For violin and piano, or cello and piano. Dedicated to Monsieur Auguste Franchomme. Date of composition: 1841. First recorded performance: probably winter 1841. Earliest known edition: P. Mechetti, Vienna, 1841. [GMP:29/8/41. E:234–5] [NL]

Op. 16 *Boléro. Morceau de Salon.* For violin and orchestra/piano. Dedicated to his friend Henri Panofka. Date of composition: probably early 1842. First recorded performance: August 1842. Earliest known edition: P. Mechetti, Vienna, 1842. [GMP:8/8/41:376. E:53&235–6] [HDK]

Op.17 *Polonaise.* For violin and orchestra/piano/string quartet. Dedicated to Monsieur Charles Müller, Maître des concerts à Brunswick. Date of composition: probably 1841–42. First recorded performance: April 1842. Earliest known edition: Cranz, Hamburg, 1842. [MGG1:XVI:135. E:236] [OBN]

Op.18 *Variations de Bravoure sur l'air Hollandais.* For violin and orchestra/piano/string quartet. Dedicated to Monsieur Alexis Lwoff, aide-de-camp to the Russian Emperor. Date of composition: probably 1838. First recorded performance: 21 February 1839. [BN] Earliest known edition: P. Mechetti, Vienna, 1842. [AMZ3/8/42:613. E:237–8] [CL]

Op.18 *Carnaval de Venise (Variations burlesque sur la canzonetta 'Cara mamma mia').* For violin and orchestra/piano/string quartet/string quintet (with double-bass). Dedicated to the King of Denmark. Date of composition: 1837. [MW:27/7/43:252] First recorded performance: 24 January 1840. Earliest known edition: Kistner, Leipzig, 1843. [SMW12/43:402. GMP:28/1/44:28. E:238–9] *Scordatura* is used: each string is tuned up a semitone. In the nineteenth century, this piece was sometimes referred to as op.19. [BL]

Op.19 *Introduction, Caprices et finale sur un Thème de l'Opéra Il Pirate de Bellini.* For violin and orchestra/piano/string quartet. Dedicated to Erneste Auguste, King of Hanover. Date of composition: probably 1839–40. First recorded performance: 27 January 1840. Earliest known edition: Bachmann, Hanover, 1844. [SMW:2/44:53] Irregular *scordatura* is used: the three top strings are all raised a semitone; the G string is raised to B♭. In the nineteenth century, this piece was sometimes referred to as op.20. [E:240–41] [BL]

Op.20 *Rondo Papageno.* For violin and orchestra/piano. Dedicated to Ernst's friend Maurice Wehle. Date of composition: probably 1844–45. First recorded performance: 30 April 1845. Earliest known edition: Wessel, London, 1846. *Scordatura* is used: each string is raised a semitone. In early performances this piece was referred to as *Rondo Scherzo*, and in some early editions it is listed as op.21. [E:241–2] [BL]

Op.21 (with Stephen Heller) *Grand Duo Concert sur Dom Sébastien.* For violin and Piano. Date of composition: late 1843 to early 1844. First recorded performance: none. Earliest known edition: P. Mechetti, Vienna, 1846. [AWMZ:9/4/46:170. E:242] [OBN]

Op.22 *Airs hongrois Variés*. For violin and orchestra/piano. Dedicated to Franz Liszt. Date of composition: probably 1845–46. First recorded performance: 19 April 1846. Earliest known edition: Wessels and Co., London, 1849. [MW:12/5/49:302. E:242–3] [BL]

Op.23 *Concerto Allegro-Pathétique* in F♯ minor. For violin and orchestra/piano. Dedicated to Ferdinand David. Date of composition: probably 1845–46. First recorded performance: 19 April 1846. Earliest known edition: Breitkopf and Härtel, Leipzig, 1850–51. [NMZ:21/2/51:84. E:244–5] The piece was sometimes referred to as *Allegro de Concert*, and *Concerto Pathétique*. [BL]

Op.24 *Fantasie brilliante sur le Prophète (Opéra de G. Meyerbeer)*. For violin and orchestra/piano. Dedicated to Monsieur Frédéric Klandeles. Date of composition: 1849. First recorded performance: early January 1850. First known edition: Breitkopf and Härtel, Leipzig, 1850. [MW:12/1/50:18. E:245–6] [CL]

Op.25 *Trois Morceaux de Salon pour violon avec accompagnement de piano. No.1, Allegretto con Moto. No.2, Andantino Notturno. No.3, Allegretto molto Moderato*. For violin and piano. Dedicated to Ernst's friend Bernhard Molique. Date of composition: probably 1850. First recorded performance: none. Earliest known edition: unknown publisher, 1850. [AM] Before 1859, these pieces are sometimes referred to as *Six Morceaux de Salon*. A version for cello is entitled *3 Nocturnen*. [E:246–7] [BLO]

Op.26 *Grand Caprice. Solo pour Violon sur le Roi des Aulnes de F. Schubert*. For violin solo. Dedicated to the Grand Duchess of Weimar. Date of composition: probably 1841–42. First recorded performance: early May 1842. Earliest known edition: Schott, London, 1854; Spina, Vienna, 1854. [MGG1:XVI:135. E:247–8] [BL]

Op.26 String Quartet in B♭. Dedicated to Leopold von Wertheimstein. Date of composition: the main compositional effort was clearly from late 1859 to early 1861, but Ernst is mentioned as writing a quartet in 1851 and 1855. First recorded performance: 23 June 1862. Earliest known edition: Cranz, Vienna, 1864 (although one of Ernst's letters suggests it was published by Chappell in late 1862). [MGG1: XVI:135. E:248–9] [BL]

Op.26 (with Charles Schunke) *Introduction, Variations et finale sur un Valse de Strauss (Introduction, Variations, and Finale on a Favourite Waltz)*. For violin and piano. Dedicated to General de Rumigen. Date of composition: early 1830s. First recorded performance: none. Earliest known edition: Schlesinger, Berlin, 1834. [JP:137–9. E:249–50] [CL]

Published Works without Opus Numbers

1)   (with George Osborne) *Souvenir de l'Opera La Juive de F. Halévy.* For violin and piano. Date of composition: early 1830s. First recorded performance: none. Earliest known edition: Schlesinger, Berlin, after 1835. [JP:137–9. E:257–8] No copy has been found.

2)   *Si tu ne viens.* For voice and piano. Date of composition: 1834 or before. First recorded performance: 23 December 1834. Earliest known edition: Haslinger, 1848. [NMZ:26/8/48. E:259] No copy has been found.

3)   *'Der Fischer' Ballade von Goethe.* For voice and piano. Date of composition: 1834 or before. First recorded performance: 6 June 1864. Earliest known edition: Munich, 1834. [P:137–9. E:258] In English, this ballad is translated as *The Sea*. [BL]

4)   (with Charles Schunke) *Souvenir du Pré aux Clercs. Duo brilliant.* For violin and piano. Date of composition: probably 1834. First recorded performance: 23 December 1834. Earliest known edition: Schott, Leipzig, 1836. [JP:137–9. E:258] No copy has been found.

5)   (with Charles Schunke) *Rondo über Motiven aus Oberon.* For violin and piano. Date of composition: probably 1835–36. First recorded performance: 14 February 1836. Earliest known edition: Schlesinger, Berlin, 1837. [NMZ:4/8/37. E:258] No copy has been found.

6)   (with George Osborne) *Brilliant Variations for the Pianoforte and Violin on the Favourite Air I tuoi frequenti palpiti (from Pacini's opera Niobe).* For violin and piano. Date of composition: 1835–36. First recorded performance: April 1836. Earliest known edition: Chappell, London, 1836. [E:257] [BL]

7)   *Zuh Muehle von Dr Roth in Musik gesetzt von H.W.Ernst.* For voice and piano. Date of composition: unknown. First recoded performance: none. Earliest known edition: Artistisches Institute von Gutsch and Rupp, Carlsruhe, 1842. [E:259] [BS]

8)   (with Stephen Heller) *Pensées Fugitives pour Violon et Piano.* For violin and piano. Dedicated to Dr Roth. Date of composition: 1839–42. First recorded performance: 7 April 1843. Earliest known edition: Kistner, Leipzig, 1842.
    1) *Passé* – Piu agitato, 2) *Souvenir* – Allegretto con molto colore, 3) *Romance* – Allegretto con motto, 4) *Lied* – Allegretto con motto, 5) *Agitato* – Molto vivace, 6) *Abschied* – Con motto, 7) *Rêverie* – Quasi allegretto, 8) *Un caprice* – Allegro assai, 9) *Inquiétude* – Adagio, 10) *Prière pendant l'orage* – Allegro non troppo, 11) *Intermezzo* – Allegro poco agitato, 12) *Thème original de H.W. Ernst* – Allegretto.

In England this work was published as *Les Gages d'amitié*. Confusingly, both the original violin and piano version of the *Pensées Fugitives*, and Heller's arrangement of ten of them for piano solo (Nos.1–9 and 11), were both published as Heller's op.30. [SHLW:ii. LMRP:illus.6. E:252–7] [BL]

9) *Feuillet D'Album pour violon avec accompagnement de piano*. For violin and piano. Dedicated to Mme Louise Schwendy. Date of composition: probably mid-1842. First recorded performance: August 1842. Earliest known edition: Schlesinger, Berlin, 1842. This is a transcription in D major of an étude by Stephen Heller in D♭, no.15 from his 25 études op.16. [AMZ:9/11/42:908. E:256] [BL]

10) *Lebet wohl, geliebten Blume, Gedicht von W. von Goethe*. For voice and piano. Date of composition: unknown. First recorded performance: none. Earliest known edition: Album für Gesang, Jahrg.2, 1843. [BL]

11) *Romanesca fameux. Air de Danse du 16 ème Siècle*. For violin and piano/string quartet and guitar *ad lib*/string quintet (with two violas). Date of composition: not known. First recorded performance: 12 December 1849. Earliest known edition: Schlesinger, Berlin, before 1844. [E:256–7] Liszt, Batta and Alard all arranged this dance. [BL]

12) *Valse sentimentale*. For piano solo. Date of composition: not known. First recorded performance: none. Earliest known edition: supplement to the *Maestro* No.20, Office of the *Maestro*, London, 1844. [BL]

13) *Lewewohl*. For voice and piano. Date of composition: unknown. First recorded performance: none. Earliest known edition: Schuberth and Co., Leipzig, 1852. [SMW:52:320] Possibly, 10 and 13 are the same song whose title should be *Lebewohl*.

14) *Nocturne*. For piano solo. Dedicated to Arabella Goddard. Composed: probably 1863–64. First recorded performance: 6 June 1864 (by Hallé). Earliest known edition: Chappell, London, 1864. Sometimes entitled *Nocturne Posthume*. [MW:19/3/64. E:259–60] [UK]

15) *Etudes pour le violon à plusieurs parties (Mehrstimmige Studien für Violine. Gruss an Freunde und Kunstbrüder)*. For violin solo. Date of composition: probably 1862–64. First recorded performance: none known before Ernst's death. Earliest known edition: Spina, Vienna, 1864.

Etude I: *Rondino Scherzo*, F major, dedicated to Laub. Etude II: Allegretto, A major, dedicated to Sainton. Etude III: *Terzetto*, Allegro moderato e tranquillo, E major, dedicated to Joachim. Etude IV: Allegro risoluto, C major, dedicated to Vieuxtemps. Etude V: *Air de Ballet*, Allegretto con giusto, E♭ major, dedicated to Hellmesberger. Etude VI: *Variations de Concert sur l'air national irlandais: the last rose of summer. (Die lezte Rose)*, G major, dedicated to Bazzini. [BL]

16) *Deux Valses* (from his musical remains) in A♭ and D♭. For solo piano. Date of composition: not known. First recorded performance: none. First known edition: Haslinger, Vienna, *c*.1865. [OBN]

Unpublished Works (Omitting Short Autographs)

1) *Trio pour un Violon.* For violin solo. Dated 30 April 1837. [BIC]

2) Cadenza to Mayseder's Variations in E, op.40. First recorded performance: 13 January 1840. If the work was written down it is now lost.

3) An amended cadenza to Spohr's violin concerto in A, op.47, the *Gezangsszene*. First recorded performance: 18 July 1843. If the work was written down it is now lost.

4) *Fantasy on Irish Airs*. Probably for violin and orchestra/piano. Date of composition: 1844. First recorded performance: February 1851. The manuscript is now lost, but the section incorporating *The Last Rose of Summer* was probably used as the basis for the sixth *Polyphonic Study*.

5) *Valse non dansante*. For piano solo. 2 pages. Based almost entirely on the piano introduction to Schubert's song *Auf dem Wasser zu singen*. Signed Hch. Ernst, Pesth, 31ten August 1845. [No.749 in CEAM] [LC]

6) *Moderato*. For piano solo. Album of Fanny Hürenwadel. See Discography.

7) *Glücklicher Wahn*. Words by Mühler. For voice and piano. B♭, ¾ time. [WLB]

8) An amended first-movement cadenza for the Mendelssohn violin concerto op.64. First recorded performance: 2 July 1849. If the work was written down it is now lost.

9) *Die Schönste Sprache. Lied für Fraülein Jetty Treffz In Ihren Namenstage 12th July 1849*. For soprano and piano. [Photocopy sent to author by Jan Pěčka]

10) Two grand cadenzas for the first and last movements of Beethoven's violin concerto. First recorded performance: 2 June 1851. Lost.

11) String Quartet in A major. Dedicated to J.W. Davison. Date of composition: probably 1862–64. First recorded performance: 6 June 1864. Lost (but see Appendix).

12) String Quartet in C major. Dedicated to Joseph Joachim. Date of composition: the work may be unfinished, but the scherzo was completed, and first movement almost completed, by 11 April 1864. [SIM] Lost.

H.W. Ernst: A Discography

Historical performances are placed first, whatever the date of their reissue on LP or CD. Otherwise, entries follow the order of LP or CD release. In addition to the recordings listed below, there are several fine performances on YouTube and other internet sites.

Nocturne op.8, no.1 in A
Vaclav Dvořák (violin), Michal Rezek (piano). *Dvořák and Rezek*. CD. Jan Nykrýn JN (Czech Republic). ny 24 6003-2. 2007.

Nocturne op.8, no.2 in E
Hugo Heermann (violin), F. Kark (conductor), orchestra not known. Arranged Heermann. Possibly recorded in Berlin in 1909. P514. *The Great Violinists*, *Volume 1*. CD. Symposium. 1071. 1989. Also on *The Recorded Violin*. CD. Pearl Duplicate Numbers. 1.1993.

Elegy op.10
1) Carl Flesch (violin). Edison Diamond Disc 82348. *c.*1926. 78. CD. Symposium. SYM:1032. 1994.
2) Kornelija Kalinauskaite (violin), and Halina Znaidzilauskaite (piano). LP. Melodiya S10 22741000. 1985.
3) István Kassai (piano), transcribed in 1840 by Ferenc Erkel (1810–93) under the title, *Errinnerung an H.W. Ernst: Introduction and Capriccio. Ferenc Erkel: Piano and Chamber Works*. CD. Marco Polo. 8.223317. 1990.
4) Dieter Klöcker (clarinet) and Consortium Classicum. *Introduction and Elegie* by Spohr and Ernst, arranged for clarinet and string quartet by Busoni (KiVB110). *Klarinettenquintete*. CD. Orfeo. B000005959. 1995.
5) Dieter Klöcker (clarinet) and Consortium Classicum. *Introduction and Elegie* by Spohr and Ernst, arranged for clarinet and string quartet by Busoni (KiVB110). *Busoni: Clarinet Chamber Music*. CPO. B000001RX5. 1997. Reissue of 4.
6) Ingolf Turban (violin), Giovanni Bria (piano). *Heinrich Wilhelm Ernst*. CD. Claves. CD 50-9613. 1997.
7) Lydia Mordkovitch (violin), James Kirby (piano). *Appassionata*. CD. Chandos. 10020. 2002.
8) Ilya Grubert (violin), Dimitry Yablonsky (conductor), Russian Philharmonic Orchestra. *Heinrich Wilhelm Ernst: Concerto Pathétique; Concertino*. CD. Naxos. 8.557565. 2007.
9) Ilya Gringolts (violin), Ashley Wass (piano). *Ernst*. CD. Hyperion. CDA67619. 2008.
10) Ilya Grubert (violin), Christopher Hinterhuber (piano). *Naxos Live 2007*. DVD. Naxos. B0001BQZS. 2008.

A review by Jonathan Woolf, on *Musicweb International*, January 2007, mentions two pre-war performances on 78s by Louis Zimmermann and Jan Rudényi. I have been unable to trace further details.

Otello Fantasy op.11
1) Arnold Rosé (violin). *The Great Violinists. Recordings 1910–1913*. (An excerpt of 3 minutes 42 seconds). CD.Testament. TES21323. 2001. The same performance can also be found on *Arnold Rosé: First Violin of Vienna 1909–1936*. CD. Arbiter. ABJ148. 2006.
2) David Oistrakh (violin), A. Makarov (conductor). LP. Melodiya 1946. Not issued.
3) Ruggiero Ricci (violin), Louis de Froment (conductor), Orchestra of Radio Luxembourg. *Opera Paraphrases for Violin and Orchestra*. LP. Vox Turnabout. TVS 34720. 1977.
4) Diane Steiner (violin), David Bedford (piano). *Violin Fantasias on Great Operas*. LP. Orion. ORS78313. 1978.
5) Leonidas Kavakos (violin), Peter Nagy (piano). *Leonidas Kavakos Plays Debussy, Kreisler ...* etc. CD. Delos Records. 3116. 1992.
6) Ruggiero Ricci (violin). *Fantasies Fantastiques*. CD. One-Eleven ltd. EPR-96050.1997.
7) Ingolf Turban (violin), Giovanni Bria (piano). *Heinrich Wilhelm Ernst*. CD. Claves. CD 50-9613. 1997.
8) Adam Han-Gorski (violin), Zdzislav Szostak (conductor), Slovak Philharmonic. *Opera Transcriptions for Violin*. CD. Opus Records. 9350 2000. 1998.
9) Frank Huang (violin), Dina Vainstein (piano). *Fantasies: Schubert; Ernst; Schoenberg; Waxman*. CD. Naxos. 8.557121. 2003.
10) Ruggiero Ricci (violin), Louis de Froment (conductor), Orchestra of Radio Luxembourg. *The Art of Ruggiero Ricci*. CD. Vox Classical.VOX 3611. 2005. Reissue of 6.
11) Yuki Manuela Janke (violin), pianist not known, *Debut Recital*. CD. RAM 50603. 2006.
12) Ilya Grubert (violin), Dimitry Yablonsky (conductor), Russian Philharmonic Orchestra. *Heinrich Wilhelm Ernst: Concerto Pathétique; Concertino*. CD. Naxos. 8.557565. 2007.
13) Ilya Gringolts (violin). Ashley Wass (piano). *Ernst*. CD. Hyperion. CDA67619. 2008.
14) Ilya Grubert (violin), Christopher Hinterhuber (piano). *Naxos Live 2007*. DVD. Naxos. B0001BQZS. 2008.

Concertino in D op.12.
Ilya Grubert (violin), Dimitry Yablonsky (conductor), Russian Philharmonic Orchestra. *Heinrich Wilhelm Ernst: Concerto Pathétique; Concertino*. CD. Naxos. 8.557565. 2007.

Adagio Sentimentale op.13 no.1
Sherban Lupu (violin), Peter Pettinger (piano). *Violon Diabolique*. CD. Continuum. CCD1017. 1990.

Two Romances without Words op.15 nos.1 and 2.
Ingolf Turban (violin), Giovanni Bria (piano). *Heinrich Wilhelm Ernst*. CD. Claves. CD 50-9613. 1997.

Bolero op.16
Vaclav Dvořák (violin), Michal Rezek (piano). *Dvorak and Rezek*. CD. Jan Nykrýn JN (Czech Republic). ny 24 6003-2. 2007.

Polonaise op.17
1) Sherban Lupu (violin), Peter Pettinger (piano). *Violon Diabolique*. CD. Continuum. CCD1017. 1990.
2) Willi Boskovsky (violin and conductor), Vienna Johann Strauss Orchestra. *Best Loved Classics 16*. CD. Angel Records. 724356958524. 1997.

The Carnival of Venice op.18
1) Gidon Kremer (violin), Tatayna Grindenko (violin). Variations by Paganini, Ernst and Kremer arranged for two violins. LP. Eurodisc 25182XDK. Melodiya C10 12995/8. RCA Victor Red Seal/BMO Auriola Classics. 74321969772. 1977. This disc mixes variations by Paganini, Ernst and Kremer.
2) István Kassai (piano), transcribed in 1840 by Ferenc Erkel (1810–93) under the title, *Errinnerung an H.W. Ernst: Introduction and Capriccio*. *Ferenc Erkel: Piano and Chamber Works*. CD. Marco Polo. 8.223317. 1990. The Capriccio consists of 'Cara Mamma Mia' and 9 variations loosely based on Ernst's own.
3) Sándor Lakatos (violin), and his orchestra. *Sandor Lakatos: König der Zigeunergeigen*. CD. Capriccio. 492771. 1999. Again, this performance is only loosely based on Ernst's original.

Rondo Papageno op.21
1) Sherban Lupu (violin), Peter Pettinger (piano). *Violon Diabolique*. CD. Continuum. CCD1017. 1990.
2) Ingolf Turban (violin), Giovanni Bria (piano). *Heinrich Wilhelm Ernst*. CD. Claves. CD 50-9613. 1997.
3) Ilya Grubert (violin), Dimitry Yablonsky (conductor), Russian Philharmonic Orchestra. *Heinrich Wilhelm Ernst: Concerto Pathétique; Concertino*. CD. Naxos. 8.557565. 2007.

Hungarian Airs op.22
1) Ossy Renardy (violin), Robert Walter (piano). *The Great Violinists Volume XVIII*. CD. Symposium. 1311. 2003.
2) Sherban Lupu (violin), Peter Pettinger (piano). *Violon Diabolique*. CD. Continuum. CCD1017. 1990.

3) Ruggiero Ricci (violin), James Wilhelmsen (piano). *Gypsy Melodies*. CD. One-Eleven Ltd. URS90020.1994.
4) Ingolf Turban (violin), Giovanni Bria (piano). *Heinrich Wilhelm Ernst*. CD. Claves. CD 50-9613. 1997.
5) Christophe Boulier (violin), Miklos Schön (piano). *10 pièces pour violon et piano*. CD. REM 311256 XCD (DDD).

Concerto in F-sharp minor op.23
1) Lukas David (violin), Prague Symphony Orchestra. LP. Supraphon. 1101837. 1974.
2) Aaron Rosand (violin), Louis de Froment (conductor), Orchestra of Radio Luxembourg. LP. Candide CE 31054. c.1974.
3) Aaron Rosand (violin), Louis de Froment (conductor), Orchestra of Radio Luxembourg. LP. Vox Box. CDX 5102. 1994. Reissue of 2.
4) Ruggiero Ricci (violin), Kees Bakels (Conductor). Polish Radio National Symphony Orchestra. *Wieniawski, Vieuxtemps, Ernst*. CD. One-Eleven Ltd. CD.10004.ric. 2001.
5) Ilya Grubert (violin), Dimitry Yablonsky (conductor), Russian Philharmonic Orchestra. *Heinrich Wilhelm Ernst: Concerto Pathétique; Concertino*. CD. Naxos. 8.557565. 2007.

Trois Morceaux de Salon op.25 no2.
Ingolf Turban (violin), Giovanni Bria (piano). *Heinrich Wilhelm Ernst*. CD. Claves. CD 50-9613. 1997.

Erlking Transcription/Le Roi des Aulnes op.26
1) Viktor Pikaizen. Music by Ernst, Vainberg and Mozart. LP. Melodiya CM02953-4. c.1971.
2) Joseph Swensen. *Joseph Swensen Performs works by Bach, Bartok and Ernst*. LP. Musical Heritage Society. MHS4790. 1983.
3) Gidon Kremer. *Erlkönig: Duos and Transcriptions* CD. Deutsche Grammophon. 445 820-2GH. 1995.
4) Matthew Trusler. *Matthew Trusler: A Recital of Virtuoso Violin Music from Blickling Hall*. CD. National Trust. 1995.
5) Leila Josefowicz. *Solo*. CD. Philips. 446700. 1996.
6) Ingolf Turban. *Heinrich Wilhelm Ernst*. Claves. CD. CD 50-9613. 1997.
7) Rachel Barton. *Instrument of the Devil*. CD. Cedille.41.1998.
8) Vadim Repin. *Tutta Bravura: Virtuoso Showpieces for Violin and Piano*. CD. Elektra/Wea. 25487. 1999.
9) Gidon Kremer. *Schubert: Complete Music for Violin and Octet*. CD (4 discs). Deutsche Gammophon. DG 4698372. 2002. Reissue of 3.
10) Mario Hossen. *Paganini et al: Music for Violin and Piano*. CD. Gega. GD109. 2005. This disc is also sold under the title *Paganiniana*.
11) Ilya Gringolts. *Ernst*. CD. Hyperion. CDA67619. 2008.

Six Polyphonic Studies

Individual Studies

Study No. IV: To Vieuxtemps.
Andreas Lucke. ... *für Violine solo*. CD. Cavalli Records. CCD 133. 2004.

Study No.VI. Concert Variations on the Irish Air: The Last Rose of Summer. To Bazzini
1) Yulian Sitkovetsky. *The Art of Julian Sitkovetsky*, vol.4. CD. Artek. ATK 0030. 2006.
2) Ruggiero Ricci. *Bravura!* LP. Decca. DL710172. No date.
3) Joseph Swensen. *Joseph Swensen Performs works by Bach, Bartok and Ernst.* LP. Musical Heritage Society. MHS4790. 1983.
4) Gidon Kremer. *A Paganini*. Deutsche Grammophon. CD. 415 484-2. 1986.
5) Midori. *Midori Live at Carnegie Hall*. CD. Sony. 46742. 1991 Video. Kultur Films Inc. Now on DVD 4158.
6) Maxim Vengerov. CD. Biddulph. BIDD LAW001. 1990
7) Juliette Kang. *Debut Recital*. CD. Koch Discovery. 920241. 1995.
8) Ruggiero Ricci. *A Virtuoso Recital by Ricci*. CD. One-Eleven. URS-91010. 1995.
9) Alyssa Park. *It's Me*. CD. ARS. EAN 4011407973992. 2000.
10) Wolfgang Richter. *Wolfgang Richter Plays Works by Léhar, Kreisler* ... CD. SoloMP3. 2000.
11) Scott Slapin (viola). *Two Viola Recitals*. CD. Eroica. JDT3026. 2000.
12) Pavel Šporcl. *A Paganini*. CD. Ultraphon. UP0010-2. 2000.
13) Mikhail Zemtsov (viola). CD. Natural Acoustics Stemra. NA5001CD. 2005.
14) Ryu Goto. *Debut Album*. CD. Deutsche Grammophon. 4775922. 2005.
15) Stepan Lavrov. *Violin Concerto Henri Wieniawski vol.1*. CD.DUX Warszana. DUX. 2006.
16) Yang Lui. *Songs of Nostalgia*. CD. Yang Liu. 2007.

Complete

1) Ruggiero Ricci. Ernst/Wieniawski: *6 Polyphonic Studies; 9 Study-Caprices* op.10. CD. Dynamic. CDS28. 1995.
2) Ingolf Turban. *Heinrich Wilhelm Ernst*. CD. Claves. CD 50-9613. 1997.
3) Ilya Gringolts. *Ernst*. Hyperion. CD. CDA67619. 2008.

Moderato for Piano Solo
K. Sturrock (piano). *Music for Fanny Hürenwadel*. CD. Guild. GUI7293. 2001.

Recommendations

I have not heard all the recordings listed above, but the following would make an excellent start to an Ernst collection: the four pieces on Lupu's *Violon Diabolique*; Rosand's recording of the concerto (even though the orchestral part is heavily cut); Turban and Gringolts' recordings of the complete *Polyphonic Studies*; Turban, Grubert and Gringolts' performances of the *Elegy*; Josefowicz, Rapin and Gringolts' recordings of the *Erlking* transcription; Kremer and Vengerov's performances of *The Last Rose of Summer* variations.

Bibliography of Works Quoted or Referred to in the Text

A	*The Athenaeum*
AC	Manuscript in the author's collection
ADB	*Allgemeine Deutsche Biographie* (56 vols, Leipzig: Dunder und Humbolt, 1875–1912)
AF	www.artfact.com/catalogue/viewLot.cfm (accessed 19/09/2007)
AG	Gubernatis, A. de, *Dictionaire International des Ecrivains du Jour* (3 vols, Florence: Niccolai, 1888–91)
AGM	Archiv der Gesellschaft der Musikfreunde, Vienna
AM	Amazon online catalogue (accessed 8/9/2007)
AMB	Brno City Archives (Archiv města Brna)
AMDM	Diehl, A.M., [Alice Mangold], *Musical Memories* (London: Richard Bentley and Son, 1897)
AMN	MacKenzie, Sir Alexander, *A Musician's Narrative* (London: Cassel and Company, 1927)
AMZ	*Allgemeine Musikalische Zeitung*
AO	Foster, John, *Alumni Oxonienses* 1715–1886 (4 vols, Oxford: James Parker, 1891)
APF	American Porphyria Foundation, http://www.porphyriafoundation.com/about_por/types/types)1.html (accessed 21/04/2005)
AS	Becker, Marta, (ed.), *Anton Schindler, der Freund Beethovens. Sein Tagebuche aus den Jahren 1841–1843* (Frankfurt am Main: Manskopfsches Museum für Musik und Theatergeschichte, 1939)
ASLW	Hill, W. Henry, Arthur and Alfred E., *Antonio Stradivari: His Life and Work (1644–1737)* (London: Macmillan, 1909)
AWMZ	*Allgemeine Wiener Musikalische Zeitung* (sometimes *Wiener Allgemeine Musik-Zeitung*)
AZ	Duffy, Christopher, *Austerlitz 1805* (London: Seely Service and Co, 1977)
BAL	La Mara (ed.), *Briefe Hervorragender Zeitgenossen an Franz Liszt* (3 vols, Leipzig: Breitkopf and Härtel, 1895–1904)
BAV	Gooley, Dana, 'The Battle against instrumental Virtuosity in the Early Nineteenth Century', in Christopher H. Gibbs and Dana Gooley (eds), *Franz Liszt and his World* (Princeton: Princeton University Press, 2006), pp.75–111
BC	From the catalogue (since 1971) of sold items. H. Baron, Music and Books on Music, 121 Chatsworth Road, London, NW2 4BH, UK
BCG	Filip, Aleš, *Brno City Guide* (Brno: K-Public, 2004)

BCSW	La Mara (ed.), *Franz Liszt's Briefe an die Fürstin Carolyne Sayn-Wittgenstein* (2 vols, Leipzig: Breitkopf and Härtel, 1899 and 1900)
BIC	Manuscript in Bibliothéque Inguimbertine Archives et Musées de Carpentras, France
BIHC	Sonneck, Oscar (ed.), *Beethoven: Impressions by his Contemporaries* (New York: Dover Books, 1967)
BJJ	Joachim, Joseph, and Andreas Moser (eds), *Briefe von und an Joseph Joachim* (3 vols, Berlin: Julius Bard, 1911)
BL	Manuscript in the British Library. Add.MS.70921. Letters to J.W. Davison from Heinrich and Amélie Ernst
BLD	Cooper, Martin, *Beethoven: The Last Decade 1817–1827* (Oxford: Oxford University Press, 1985)
BLG	Townend, Peter (ed.), *Burke's Landed Gentry*, 18th edn (3 vols, London: Burke's Peerage, 1972)
BLKO	Wurzbach, Constant von, *Biographisches Lexikon des Kaiserthums Oesterreich* (60 vols, Vienna: Jamaski Dittmarsch und Comp, 1856–91)
BM	Cairns, David (ed. and trans.), *The Memoirs of Berlioz* (London: Panther, 1974). This edition has now been superseded by David Cairns (ed. and trans), *The Memoirs of Berlioz* (London and New York: Everyman's Library, 2002)
BMB	Wiezl, *Beitrage zu Musikgesischte Brünn I–IX*
BMJ	http://bmj.bmjjournals.com/cgi/content/full/320/7250/1647/F2 (accessed 24/4/05)
BN	Autograph letters from Ernst in the Bibliothèque Nationale, Paris. Département de la Musique, Mus. L.a. 36, Lettres autographes, Volume 36, Erlih–Fauconnier, R 133 735
BSCH	*Burke's and Savills Guide to Country Houses*, Vol.3 *East Anglia* (3 vols, London: Burke's Peerage, 1981)
BSG	Cairns, David, *Berlioz: Servitude and Greatness* (London: Allen Lane, 1999)
BSQ	Adelson, Robert, 'Beethoven's String Quartet in E-flat Op.127: A Study of the First Performances', *Music and Letters*, 79/2 (1998): 219–43
BTP	http://www.sciam.com/article.cfm?article (accessed 25/4/2007)
C	Bulwer Lytton, Edward, *Caxtoniana* (London: George Routledge and Sons, 1875)
CEAM	Albrecht, Otto E., *A Census of Autograph Music Manuscripts of European Composers in American Libraries* (Philadelphia: University of Pennsylvania Press, 1953)
CF	Eisler, Betina, *Chopin's Funeral* (London: Abacus Books, 2003)
CGB	Citron, Pierre, (ed.), *Correspondance générale d'Hector Berlioz* (8 vols, Paris: Flammarion, 1972–2003)
CLMD	Olivier, Daniel (ed.), *Correspondance de Liszt et de Madame D'Agoult* (2 vols, Paris: Bernard Grasset Editions, 1933–34)
CN	Antier, Jean-Jacques, *Le Compte de Nice* (Paris: Editions France-Empire, 1992)
COZ	http://www.cozio.com/Instrment (accessed 16/11/06)

CPF	Canadian Porphyria Foundation http://www.cpf-inc.ca/affets.htm (accessed 25/04/05)
CPL	de Courcy, Geraldine, *Chronology of Paganini's Life* (Bonn-Wiesbaden: Rud. Erdmann, Musikverlag, c.1961)
CPM	*Catalogue of Printed Music in the British Library to 1980* (62 vols, London, Paris: K.G. Saur, 1981–87)
CSAL	Litzmann, Berthold, *Clara Schumann: An Artist's Life*, trans. and abridged Grace E. Hadow, (2 vols, London: Macmillan, 1913)
CV	Ehrlich, A., *Celebrated Violinists, Past and Present*, trans. Robin Legge, (London: E. Donajowski, 1897)
CVA	Smith, Ronald, *Alkan: The Man, The Music* (London: Kahn and Averill, 2000)
CZ	Zamoyski, Adam, *Chopin* (New York: Doubleday, 1987)
D	Deutsche, S., 'Ernst,' in Franz Gräffer (ed.), *Jüdicher Plutach* (2 vols, Vienna: Urlich Kopfsen, 1848)
DA	*Benezit Dictionary of Artists* (14 vols, Paris: Gründ, 2006)
DBF	D'Amart, Roman (ed.), *Dictionnaire de Biographie Francaise* (19 vols, Paris: Librairie Letouzey et Ane, 1932–2001)
DFC	Johnson, Lee (ed.), *Eugène Delacroix: Further Correspondence* (Oxford: Oxford University Press, 1991
DGM	Pohl, Richard, *Die Geselleschaft der Musikfreunde ... und ihr Conservatorium* (Vienna: Wilhelm Baunmüller, 1871)
DH	Saphir, M.G., *Der Humorist* [Vienna], 65 (30 March 1840): 257–9
DL	Döhring, Sieghart, 'Dresden and Leipzig: Two Bourgeois Centres', in Alexander Ringer (ed.), *The Early Romantic Era: Between Revolutions: 1789 and 1848* (Englewood Cliffs: Prentice Hall, 1990), pp.141–59
DML	Uhiŕ, Dušan, 'Die Mährische Landeshauptstat um 1800 und die Brünner Augustiner-Eremiten', *Bohemia*, 38 (1997): 22–36
DNB	*The Dictionary of National Biography* (63 vols, Oxford: Oxford University Press, 1917)
DOW	[Dostoevsky, F.], *Dostoevsky's Occasional Writings*, trans. David Magarshack (Evanston: Northwestern University Press, 1997)
DPS1	Benezit, F. (ed), *Dictionnaire des Peintres, Sculpteurs, Dessinateurs et Graveurs* (8 vols, Paris: Librairie Grund, 1949)
DS	Deutsch, O.E., *Schubert: A Documentary Biography*, trans. E. Blom (London: Dent, 1946)
DV	Dubourg, George, *The Violin* (London: Robert Cocks and Co., 1878 [1852])
E	Elun, Fan, 'The Life and Works of Heinrich Wilhelm Ernst (1814–1865) with Emphasis on his Reception as Violinist and Composer', unpublished PhD thesis, Cornell University, 1993
EBL	Lytton, V.A.G., *The Life of Edward Bulwer, First Lord Lytton* (2 vols, London: Macmillan, 1913)
EBR	Droz, Jacques, *Europe Between Revolutions 1815–1848* (London: Fontana Press, 1985)

ECL	Moore, Jerrold Northrop, *Edward Elgar: A Creative Life* (Oxford: Oxford University Press, 1987)
EJ	Roth, Cecil, and Geoffrey Wigoder (eds), *Encylopedia Judaica* (16 vols, New York: Macmillan, 1971–72)
EM	'Pott's Disease', emedicine from *Web*MD (accessed 15/10/07)
EO	Berlioz, Hector, *Evenings in the Orchestra*, ed. David Cairns, trans. C.R. Fortescue (Harmondsworth: Penguin Books, 1963)
EOC	Heller, Amely, *H.W. Ernst in the Opinion of his Contemporaries*, ed. Samuel Wolf, trans. Roberta Franke (Linthicum Heights: Swand Publications, 1986)
EUZ	Heller, Amely, *H.W. Ernst im Urteile seiner Zeitgenossen* (Brno: Selbstverlag, 1904)
F	Fétis, F.J., (ed.), *Biographie Universalle des Musicians*, 2nd edn, (10 vols, Paris: Firmin-Dibot et Cie, 1883)
FCB	Mahaim, Ivan, trans. Evi Levin, 'The First Complete Beethoven Quartet Cycles, 1845–1851: Historical Notes on the London Quartett Society', *The Musical Quarterly*, 80/3 (1996): 500–524
FCPW	Atwood, William G., *Fryderyk Chopin: Pianist from Warsaw* (New York: Columbia University Press, 1989)
FHM	Hiller, Ferdinand, trans. M.E. von Glehn, *Mendelssohn, Macmillan's Magazine* Vol.XXIX (November 1873 – April 1874)
FLPD	Burger, Ernst, *Franz Liszt: A Chronicle of his life in Pictures and Documents*, trans. Stewart Spencer (Princeton: Princeton University Press, 1989)
FLRW	Kesting, Hanjo (ed.), *Franz Liszt – Richard Wagner Briefwechsel* (Berlin: Insel Verlag, 1988)
FLSL	Williams, Adrian (ed. and trans.), *Franz Liszt: Selected Letters* (Oxford: Clarendon Press, 1998)
FLUP	Legány, Dezső (ed.), *Franz Liszt: Unbekannte Presse und Briefe aus Wien 1822–1886* (Budapest: Corvina Kiadó, 1984)
FLVY	Walker, Alan, *Franz Liszt: The Virtuoso Years 1811–1847* (Ithaca, New York: Cornell University Press, 1983)
FLWY	Walker, Alan, *Franz Liszt: The Weimar Years 1848–1861* (Ithaca, New York: Cornell University Press, 1989)
FM	*La France musicale*
FMBB	Roth, Hans-Joachim, and Reinhard Szeskus (eds), *Mendelsson Bartholdy, Felix: Briefe aus Leipziger Archiven* (Leipzig: Verlag für Musik, 1972)
FMW	Davison, Henry, *From Mendelssohn to Wagner: being the Memoirs of J.W. Davison, Forty Years Music Critic of The Times* (London: W.M. Reeves, 1912)
FS	McKay, Elizabeth Norman, *Franz Schubert: A Biography* (Oxford: Oxford University Press, 2001)
FVP	Abell, Arthur M., 'Famous Violinists of the Past VIII: Heinrich Ernst and Charles De Beriot', *The Musical Courier* (9 September 1908): 5
G1	Sadie, Stanley (ed.), *The New Grove Dictionary of Music and Musicians* (20 vols, London: Macmillan, 1980)

G2	Sadie, Stanley and John Tyrrell (eds), *The New Grove Dictionary of Music and Musicians*, 2nd edn (29 vols, London: Macmillan, 2001)
GAM	Boistier, D., (ed.), *Guide des Alpes-Maritimes et de la Principalité de Monaco* (Nice: no publisher, 1875)
GB	Green Books. Autographs of letters to Mendelssohn kept in the Bodleian Library, Oxford
GBL	Ganz, A.W., *Berlioz in London* (London: Quality Press, 1950)
GCW	Hanslick, Eduard, *Geschichte des Konzertwesens in Wien* (2 vols, Vienna: Wilhelm Braümuller, 1869–70)
GD	Larousse, Pierre (ed.), *Grand Dictionaire du XIX Siècle* (17 vols, Paris: Larousse and Boyer, 1866–77)
GEAB	Haight, Gordon S., *George Eliot: A Biography* (London: Oxford University Press, 1978)
GEL	Haight, Gordon S. (ed.), *The George Eliot Letters* (9 vols, New Haven: Yale University Press, 1954–78)
GHR	http://ghr.nlm.nih.gov/condition=acuteintermittentporphyria (accessed 29/06/2006)
GM	Orel, Vitezslav, *Gregor Mendel: The First Geneticist*, trans. Stephen Finn (Oxford: Oxford University Press, 1996)
GMM	d'Elvert, Christian Ritter, *Geschichte der Musik in Mähen und Oester-Schlesien mit Rücksicht auf die allgemeine böhmische und österreichische Musik-geschichte* (Brünn [Brno]:1873)
GMP	*Gazette musicale de Paris*
GMV	Schwarz, Boris, *Great Masters of the Violin* (New York: Simon and Schuster, 1983)
GMW	Pergera, R., *Gesellschaft der Musik in Wien* (Vienna: no publisher, 1912)
GP	Schonberg, Harold C., *The Great Pianists* (London: Gollancz, 1974)
GSL	Kutsch, K.J., and Leo Riemens (eds), *Grosses Sänger-Lexicon*, (4 vols, Bern and München: K.G. Saur, 1997)
GV	Moser, Andreas, *Geschichte des Violinspiels* (Berlin: Max Hesses Verlag, 1923)
GVC	Tiilikainen, Jukka, 'The Genesis of the Violin Concerto', in Daniel M. Grimley (ed.), *The Cambridge Companion to Sibelius* (Cambridge: Cambridge University Press, 2004), pp.66–80
GVP	Bachmann, Alberto, *Les grands violonistes du passé* (Paris: Fischbacher, 1913)
H	*The Harmonicon*
HALS	Hertfordshire Archives and Local Studies, County Hall, Hertford.
HB	Heine, Heinrich, *Briefe*, ed. Friedrich Hirth (6 vols, Mainz: Florian Kupferherg Verlag, 1949–50)
HCA	www.ruc.dk/isok/schriftserier/brevregistrant/nordske/andersen (accessed 19/9/2007)
HD	Sutherland, John, '"Ho, Diomed": Bulwer-Lytton, the Great Unreadable', *Times Literary Supplement*, 28 July 2000:12
HDM	*Deutsche Misikbibliographie* (Leipzig: Hofmeister, 1829–)

HFPV	Reinecke, Carl, trans. E. Standfield, 'A Half-Forgotten Prince of Violinists', *Monthly Musical Record*, 1 March 1896: 54–6
HJ	Johnson, Paul, *A History of the Jews* (London: Phoenix, 1995)
HJSB	Klenovsky, Jaroslav, '[A] Historical Survey of Jewish Settlement in Brno', *Centropa Quarterly*, 6/4 (2005): 1–9
HL	Sibelius, Jean, *The Hämeenlinna Letters: Scenes from a Musical Life 1874–1895*, ed. Glenda D. Gross, trans. Stephen Finn (Helsinki: Schildts, 1996)
HM	Taylor, A.J.P., *The Habsburg Monarchy 1809–1918* (London: Hamish Hamilton, 1961)
HMC	Hanslick, Eduard, *Musical Criticisms: 1864–99*, ed. Henry Pleasants (Harmondsworth: Peregrine Books, 1963)
HN	Latouche, Robert, *Histoire de Nice* (2 vols, Nice: Ville de Nice, 1951)
HPSL	Foster, Myles Birket, *The History of the Philharmonic Society of London 1813–1912* (London: John Lane, 1912)
HS	Heine, Heinrich, *The Salon: Lectures on Art, Music, Popular Life and Politics in Paris*, trans. Charles Godfrey Leland (London: Heinemann, 1905)
HWE	Leone, Dr, *H.W. Ernst: Eine biographische Skizze* (Vienna: J.P. Sollinger, 1847)
IC	Sainati, Edward, 'Idol Correspondence', *The Strad* (August 1985): 264–6
ICEC	Freudenberger, Herman, *The Industrialization of a Central European City: Brno and the Fine Woollen Industry in the 18th Century* (Edington: Pasold Research Fund Ltd, 1977)
IGT	*Iris im Gebiete der Tonkunst*
ILN	*Illustrated London News*
IMP	http://www.imp.cz?EN/Brno?years5.html (accessed 28/10/2004)
IRR	Stanford, Charles V., *Interludes: Records and Reflections* (London: John Murray, 1922)
JB	Avins, Styra, *Johannes Brahms: Life and Letters* (Oxford: Oxford University Press, 1997)
JBM	Iggers, Wilma Abeles (ed.), (*The Jews of Bohemia and Moravia: A Historical Reader*, trans. Wilma A. Iggers, Káca Pólacková-Henley and Kathrine Talbot (Detroit: Wayne State University Press, 1992)
JBTC	McCorkle, Margit L., *Johannes Brahms: Thematisch Biographisches Werkzeichnis* (Munich: G. Henle Verlag, 1984)
JD	[Berlioz, Hector], 'Revue Musicale, Ernst: Son Premier Concert', *Journal des Débats*, 27 January 1852
JDD	Delacroix, Eugène, *Journal de Eugène Delacroix* (3 vols, Paris: Librairie Plon, 1893–95)
JDGZ	*Josef Danhauser (1805–1845) Gemälde und Zeichnungen* [Exhibition Catalogue 1983] (Vienna: Osterreichischer Bundesverlag, 1983)
JDN	*Jahrbücher der Deutschen National-Verin fur Musik und ihre Wissenschaft*

JEMU	Bashford, Christina, 'John Ella and the Making of the Musical Union', in Christina Bashford and Leanne Langley (eds), *Music and British Culture: 1785–1914: Essays in Honour of Cyril Ehrlich* (Oxford: Oxford University Press, 2000), pp.193–214
JJ	Moser, Andreas, *Joseph Joachim*, trans. Lilla Durham (London: Philip Welby, 1901)
JJL	Moser, Andreas, *Joseph Joachim: ein Lebensbild* (2 vols, Berlin: Verlag der Deutschen Brahms-Gesellschaft, 1908–10)
JLR	Janáček, Leoš, *Letters and Reminiscences*, ed. Bohumír Štědroň, trans. Geraldine Thomsen (Prague: Artia, 1955)
JN	*Journal de Nice*
JP	Pěčka, Jan, 'Heinrich Wilhelm Ernst', unpublished thesis in the Philosophy Faculty of the J.E. Purkyně University, Brno (1958)
JSE	Berlin, Isaiah, 'Jewish Slavery and Emancipation,' in Norman Bentwich (ed.), *Hebrew University Garland* (London: no publisher, 1952), pp.18–42
KA	Knebworth Archive, Hertfordshire: www.knebworthhouse.com
KJB	Kalbeck, Max, *Johannes Brahms* (4 vols, Berlin: Deutsche Brahms Gesellschaft, 1908)
KL	Gittings, Robert (ed.), *Letters of John Keats* (Oxford: Oxford University Press, 1985)
KS	Tolstoy, Leo, *The Kreutzer Sonata and Family Happiness*, trans. Anon. (London: Walter Scott, no date)
LB	Mainwaring, Dunstan H., (ed.), *The Life and Letters of Berlioz*, trans. Daniel Bernard (2 vols, London: Remington and Co., 1882)
LBM	*La Belgique musicale*
LBQ	Bashford, Christina, 'The Late Beethoven Quartets and the London Press, 1836–ca.1850', *The Musical Quarterly*, 84/1 (2000): 84–122
LBS	Hamilton, Kenneth, *Liszt: B Minor Sonata* (Cambridge: Cambridge University Press, 1996)
LFMB	Mendelssohn Bartholdy, Carl and Paul (eds), *Letters of Felix Mendelssohn Bartholdy*, trans. Lady Wallace (London: Longman, 1863)
LIB	Ignatieff, Michael, *A Life of Isaiah Berlin* (London: Chatto and Windus, 1998)
LJH	Hollander, Hans, *Leoš Janáček: His Life and Work*, trans. Paul Hamburger (London: John Calder, 1963)
LJJ	Bickley, Nora (ed. and trans.), *Letters from and to Joseph Joachim* (New York: Vienna House, 1972)
LJV	Vogel, Jaroslav, *Leoš Janáček: His Life and Works* (London: Paul Hamlyn, 1981)
LLCH	Hallé, C.E. and M., (eds), *Life and Letters of Sir Charles Hallé* (London: Smith, Elder and Co., 1896)
LM	Moscheles, Charlotte, *Life of Moscheles*, trans. A.D. Coleridge, (2 vols, London: Hurst and Blackett, 1873)
LMJF	Piggot, Patrick, *The Life and Music of John Field 1782–1837: Creator of the Nocturne* (London: Faber and Faber, 1973)

LMRP	Eigeldinger, Jean-Jacques (ed.), *Lettres d'un musician romantique à Paris* (Paris: Flammarion, 1981)
LOB	Smith, Mortimer, *The Life of Ole Bull* (Princeton: Princeton University Press, 1943)
LOFL	La Mara (ed.), *Letters of Franz Liszt*, trans. Constance Bache (2 vols, London: Grevel and Co., 1894)
LRW	Ellis, William Ashton, *Life of Richard Wagner* (6 vols, London: Kegan Paul, Trench, Trübner and Co., 1900)
LS	Brown, Clive, *Louis Spohr: A Critical Biography* (Cambridge: Cambridge University Press, 1984)
LSB	Sterndale Bennett, James, *The Life of William Sterndale Bennett* (Cambridge: Cambridge University Press, 1907)
LUNN	Haug, C. James, *Leisure and Urbanism in Nineteenth-Century Nice* (Lawrence: University of Kansas Press, 1982)
MALS	Manuscript letter in Manchester Archives and Local Studies, Central Library
MAM	Haweis, H.R., *Music and Morals* (London: Longmans, Green and Co, 1898)
MC	The marriage certificate of Ernst and Amélie-Siona Lévy, 31 July 1854, Marylebone, London
MCF	Flesch, Carl, trans. Hans Keller, *The Memoirs of Carl Flesch* (London: Rockcliff, 1957)
ME	*Musical Examiner*
MGB	http://momtagnanabooks.com/Ernstquote.gif (accessed 01/03/00)
MGG1	Blume, Friedrich (ed.), *Die Musik in Geschichte und Gegenwart* (14 vols, Basel: Bärenreiter Kassel, 1949–68)
MGG2	Finscher, Ludwig (ed.), *Die Musik in Geschichte und Gegenwart*, 2nd edn (27 vols, Basel: Bärenreiter Kassel, 1994)
MHC	[Lehmann, Frederick and Nina], *Memories of Half a Century*, ed. R.C. Lehmann (London: Smith, Elder and Company, 1908).
MI	Kiowsky, Hellmuth (ed.), *Märhische Impressionen: Brünn – Ein Deutsches Schicksal im Schnittpunkt Zweier Kulturen* (Brünn: Centaurus Verlag, 2006)
MKM	Bull, Ole, *Min Kjaere Moder: En kjaerlighets erklaering*, ed. Ladislav Reznicek (Bergen: John Griegs Forlag, 1980)
MLP	Ernst, Amélie, *Mes lectures en prose* (Neuchatel: Attinger frères, 1894)
MLBV	Hanson, Alice M., *Musical Life in Biedermeier Vienna* (Cambridge: Cambridge University Press, 1985)
MMHE	http:/www.merck.com/mmhe/sec12/ch160/ch160c.html (accessed 29/06/2006)
MMI	Scholes, Percy A., (ed.), *The Mirror of Music 1844–1944: A Century of Musical Life in Britain as Reflected in the Pages of the Musical Times* (2 vols, Oxford: Novello and Oxford University Press, 1947)
MML	Haweis, H.R., *My Musical Life* (London: Longmans, Green and Co., 1902)

MP	Pellico, Silvio, *My Prisons*, trans. I.G.Capaldi SJ (London: Oxford University Press, 1963)
MR	Nichols, Roger, (ed.), *Mendelssohn Remembered* (London: Faber, 1997)
MRLH	Cox, John Edward, *Musical Recollections of the Last Half-Century* (2 vols, London: Tinsley Brothers, 1872)
MSAH	Ella, John, *Musical Sketches Abroad and at Home* (London: 1878)
MW	*The Musical World*
MWC	Harcup, John Winsor, *The Malvern Water Cure* (Malvern: Winsor Fox Photos, 1992)
NB	Ernst, Amélie, *Nos Bébés* (Paris: Librairie des Bibliophiles, 1883)
NBMZ	*Neue Berliner Musik-Zeitung*
NHB	nhb.com/berlioz/berlioz –vupar.html (accessed 15/10/07)
NHH	Niedersächsisches Hauptstaatsarchiv, Hanover, Dep.103, XXXVII, Nr.212
NJC	Records of the New Jewish Cemetery, Brno
NLE	Boronkay, Antal, (ed.), *New Liszt Edition*, Vol.5 (Basel, London: Bärenreiter; Budapest: Editio Musica Budapest, 1983)
NMZ	*Niederreinische Muzik Zeitung für Kunstfrende und Künstler*
NNG	*Facts about Gout*, http://www.niams.nih.gov/hi/topics/gout/ffgout.htm (accessed 25/04/07)
OB	Haugen, Einar, and Camilla Cai, *Ole Bull: Norway's Romantic Musician and Cosmopolitan Patriot* (Wisconsin: University of Wisconsin Press, 1993)
OBM	Bull, Sara C., *Ole Bull: A Memoir* (Boston and New York, 1882)
ODNB	Matthew, H.C.G, and Brian Harrison (eds), *The Oxford Dictionary of National Biography* (60 vols, Oxford: Oxford University Press, 2004)
OE	Nettel, R., *The Orchestra in England: A Social History* (London: Cape, 1946)
ON	Manuscript in the Österreichische Nationalbibliothek
OR	Ruppius, Otto, *Über den Ursprung von H.W. Ernsts Elegie*, from his *Westlichen Blütter*; quoted EUZ, pp.50–51
P	Sheppard, Leslie, and Herbert R. Axelrod, *Paganini* (Neptune City, NJ: Paganiniana Publications, 1979)
PAPV	Guhr, Carl, *Paganini's Art of Playing the Violin*, trans. Sabilla Novello and C. Egertonlowe (London: Novello, 1913). Original edition: Mainz, Paris, Antwerp: Schott, 1830
PG	de Courcy, Geraldine, *Paganini, the Genose* (2 vols, Norman: University of Oklahoma Press, 1957). Reprint: New York: Da Capo, 1977
PHB	Braam, Gunther, *Portraits of Hector Berlioz*, ed. Richard Macnutt and John Warrack, trans. John Warrack, New Berlioz Edition, vol.26 (Kassel: Bärenreiter, 2003)
PL	Williams, Adrian, *Portrait of Liszt: By Himself and his Contemporaries* (Oxford: Clarendon Press, 1990)
PM	Manuscript in the Pierpont Morgan Library, New York.
PWFC	Atwood, William G., *The Parisian Worlds of Frédéric Chopin* (New Haven and London: Yale University Press, 1999)

R	*Recession* [Vienna]
RFA	Ernst, Amélie, *Rimes Françaises d'une Alsacienne* (Paris: Sandoz et Fischbacher, 1879)
RFD	Laurie, David, *The Reminiscences of a Fiddle Dealer* (Boston: Houghton Mifflin and Co., 1925)
RGM	*Review et Gazette musicale de Paris*
RJBD	Register of Jewish Births and Deaths, Central State Archives, Prague (Statni Ustredni Archiv v Praze)
RM	*Revue musicale*
RMU	*Record of the Musical Union*
RMW	Ellis, William Ashton, (ed.), *Richard to Mina Wagner: Letters to his First Wife* (2 vols, London: Grevel and Co., 1909)
RMZ	*Rheinische Musik-Zeitung für Kunstfreude und Künstler*
RRA	rrauction.com (accessed 10/12/06)
S	Jensen, Eric, *Schumann* (Oxford: Oxford University Press, 2005)
SA	Spohr, Louis, trans. Anon, *Louis Spohr's Autobiography* (London: Longman, 1865). This one-volume edition retains the page numbering of the two-volume edition
SB	Tawaststjerna, Erik, *Sibelius*, trans. Robert Layton (3 vols, London: Faber and Faber, 1976)
SCFC	Sydow, Bronislaw Edward, and Arthur Hedley (eds and trans.), *Selected Correspondence of Fryderyk Chopin* (London: Heinemann, 1962)
SCI	http://www.sci.muni.cz/about/brno.htm (accessed 28/10/2004)
SE	Flaubert, Gustave, *Sentimental Education*, ed. and trans. James Baldick (Harmondsworth: Penguin, 1975)
SHLW	Barbedette, M., *Stephen Heller: His Life and Works,* trans. Robert Brown-Borthwick (London: Ashdown and Parry, 1877)
SIM	Manuscript in Staatliches Institut für Musikforschung Preussischer Kultursitz, Berlin
SL	Archives of Stadt Leipzig: Der Oberbürgermeister
SLB	Searle, Humphrey, (ed. and trans.), *Hector Berlioz: A Selection from his Letters* (London: Gollancz, 1966)
SMD	Nauhaus, Gerd, (ed.), and Peter Ostwald (trans.), *The Marriage Diaries of Robert and Clara Schumann* (London: Robson Books, 1994)
SMM	Ritter, Fanny Raymond, (ed. and trans.), *Music and Musicians: Essays and Criticisms by Robert Schumann* (London: William Reeves, 1877)
SMW	*Signale für Musikalische Welt*
SMZ	*Süddeutsche Musik-Zeitung*
SP	*Situations-Plan der Landes-Hauptstadt Brünn, Franz Dolezal*, 1858
SPP	MacDonald, Claudia, 'Schumann's Piano Practice: Technical Mastery and Artistic Ideal,' *Journal of Musicology*, 19/4 (2002): 527–63
STB	Schumann, Robert, *Tagebücher*, ed. Georg Eismann and Gerd Nauhaus (3 vols, Leipzig: VEB Deutsche Verlag für Musik, 1971–87)
SVS	Spohr, Ludwig, *Violin School*, ed. Henry Holmes (London: no publisher or date). Originally published in German in 1832

SWD	Syphilis (Professional Guide to Diseases (Eighth Edition)) WrongDiagnosis.com http://www.wrongdiagnosis.com/s/syphilis/book-diseases-7a.htm (accessed 25/04/2007)
TGC	Abell, Arthur M., *Talks with Great Composers* (New York: Citadel Press, 1994)
TGCG	Laubriet, Pierre (ed.) *Théophile Gautier: Correspondance Générale 1846–1867* (12 vols, Geneva: Libraire Droz, 1988–2000)
TLB	Thayer, A., *Life of Beethoven*, ed. Alan Pryce-Jones, (3 vols, London: Centaur Press, 1960)
TM	Todd, R. Larry, *Mendelssohn: A Life in Music* (Oxford: Oxford University Press, 2003)
TMM	Reid, Charles, *The Music Monster* [A life of J.W. Davison] (London: Quartet Books, 1984)
TMU	Brownstein, Rachel M., *Tragic Muse: Rachel of the Comédie-Française* (Washington: Duke University Press, 1995)
TW	Wliczkowski, Tobias, 'Heinrich Wilhelm Ernst: En stor violinist I skuggan av Paganini', umpublished thesis Uppsala University, 2006
TWC	Wilson, James, *The Water Cure: Its Principles and Practice*, 4th edn (London: Trubner, 1857)
UDS	Dressel, Dettmar, *Up and Down the Scale: Reminiscences* (London: Selwyn and Blount, 1937)
V	Ginsbeurg, L., *Vieuxtemps*, trans. I. Levin, ed. H.A. Axelrod (New York: Paganiniana Publications, 1984)
VBC	Wiesmann, Sigrid, 'Vienna: Bastion of Conservatism', in Alexander Ringer (ed.), *The Early Romantic Era: Between Revolutions: 1789 and 1848* (Englewood Cliffs: Prentice Hall, 1990), pp.84–108
VC	Kawabata, Maiko, 'Virtuoso Codes of Violin Performance: Power, Military Heroism, and Gender (1789–1830)', *19th-Century Music*, 28/2 (2004): 89–107
VIM	von Wasielewski, W.J., *Die Violine und Ihre Meister* (Leipzig: Breitkopf und Härtel, 1927)
VLR	Barea, Ilsa, *Vienna: Legend and Reality* (London: Secker and Warburg, 1966)
VML	Mitchell, Leslie, *Bulwer Lytton: The Rise and Fall of a Victorian Man of Letters* (London: Hambledon and London, 2003)
VMW	Auer, Leopold, *Violin Masterworks and Their Interpretation* (New York: C. Fischer, 1925)
VN	Prod'homme, J.G., (ed.), 'Vergessenes und Neues von Hector Berlioz', *Die Musik*, 6 (1906–7): 341–9
VPAT	Auer, Leopold, *Violin Playing As I Teach It* (New York: Dover Publications, 1980)
VW	Holzer, Rudolf, *Villa Wertheinstein: Haus der Genien und Damonen* (Vienna: Bergland Verlag, 1960)
WAK	Praeger, Ferdinand, *Wagner as I Knew Him* (London: Longman and Green, 1892)

WCV   Wittgenstein, Ludwig, *Culture and Value*, ed. G.H. von Wright, revised edn (Oxford: Blackwell,1998)
WD   http://wrongdiagnosis.com/r/rheumatism/symptoms.htm (accessed 25/04/2007)
WE   Wardroper, John, *Wicked Ernest: The truth about the man who was almost Britain's King* (London: Shelfmark Books, 2002)
WSB   Strobel, Gertrude, and Werner Wolf, *Richard Wagner: Sämtliche Briefe* (7 vols, Leipzig: Deutsche Verlag für Musik, 1967–88)
WWP   Jacobs, Robert L., and Geoffrey Skelton (eds and trans.), *Wagner Writes from Paris* (London: George Allen and Unwin, 1973)
YL   Załuski, Iwo and Pamela, *Young Liszt* (London: Peter Owen, 1997)
ZOB   *History of the Jewish Community in Brno*, www.zob.cz/historieen.html (accessed 28/10/04)

Index

Page numbers in bold indicate music examples

1830 Revolution 46
1848 Revolution 7, 54, 153, 159–60, 164, 169, 170

Abell, Arthur M. 161
   on Ernst 9, 47–8, 219
acute intermittent porphyria (AIP) 220–22
Adolphus, Prince, Duke of Cambridge 124
Agoult, Countess Marie d' 99, 125, 228, 260
   see also Stern, Daniel
Aguilar, Emanuel 180n.1
AIP, *see* acute intermittent porphyria
Aix 63, 64, 210
Aix-la-Chappelle 134
Aix-les-Bains 191
Alard, (Jean-) Delphin 169
Albert, Prince (of Saxe-Coburg-Gotha; husband of Queen Victoria) 114, 132, 133, 167, 182
Albrechtsberger, Johann Georg 32
Alexander, Charles, Grand Duke of Weimar 102
Alexander II, Tsar 264
Alfred I, Prince of Windischgrätz 160
Alice, Princess (daughter of Queen Victoria) 114
Alkan, Charles-Valentin 1, 5n.1, 71
   WORKS
      Concerto for Solo Piano (op. 39) 164
      Grande Sonate: Les Quatres Ages (op. 33) 164
Allgemeine Musikalische Zeitung 30
   on Ernst 43, 45, 157–8
Allgemeine Zeitung 83
Alsace 3, 192, 272
Alsager, Thomas 7, 116, 178–9
Altenburg, the (Weimar) 161
Altenburg, Duchess of 107
Altenburg, Duke of 107
Altenburg, Princess of 107
Altona 109

Amati violins 98
Amsterdam 72, 73, 102
Andersen, Hans Christian 158
Anderson, George 208
Anderson, Mrs George 210
Andreoli, Carlo 226
Andreoli, Guglielmo 226
Angers 56
Angleterre, Hôtel d' (Copenhagen) 110, 111
Angri, Elena 181
anti-Semitism 3, 4, 8n.3, 123, 201, 209 *see also* Nazism, holocaust
'Antient Concerts' (London) 130
Antwerp 72
Apollo-Saal (Vienna) 33
Appony, Count 72
Arnhem 73
Arnim family 105
Artôt, Alexandre Joseph 55, 88, 89, 95, 114
Asch, Baron von Fr. 104
Ascher, Joseph 218
Association des artistes (Paris) 213
Asten, Julie von 238
Athenaeum 261
   on Ernst 6, 131, 209, 218, 226, 228, 237–8, 238n.1, 257, 261, 268
   see also Chorley, Ernst's obituary
Athénée Musicale (Paris) 49
Atlas 119
Auber, Daniel
   WORKS
      Fra Diavolo 23
      La Muette de Portici 23
Auer, Leopold 28
   on Ernst 145
Augier, Emile
   Maître Guérin 261
Augsburg 40, 43, 81
Augundson, Torgeir 49
Augustinian monastery of St Thomas (Brünn) 7, 22–4, Plate II
Ausgarten (Vienna) 36

Austerlitz, Battle of 18, 21
Austria café (Brünn) 18, 19, 222, Plate I
Austrian Empire/Austria 15–17, 19, 77–81, 101, 135–6, 196
Avette, Louis 266
Avignon 59, 63, 195

Babbington, Dr (in London) 130
Bach, Johann Sebastian 128, 147, 214
    WORKS
        Chaconne from Partitia No. 2 in D minor (BWV 1004) 213
        concerto for three pianos in D minor (BWV 1063) 130, 133
        sonatas
            sonata for violin and keyboard 171
            Sonatas and Partitas for solo violin (BWV 1001–6) 77, 250, 254
Bacher, Dr Joseph 39
Bachmann, Alberto
    on Ernst 2
Baden (state of) 46
Baden-Baden 40, 42, 46, 48, 91, 155, 195, 197, 199, 225, 228–9, 271
Baden Theatre (Baden-Baden) 228–9
Baillot, Pierre 50, 55, 86, 168, Plate V
Baja 77, 80–81
Balfe, Michael William 181
    WORKS
        The Bohemian Girl 128
Balokovic, Zlatko 272
Bank of England 128–9
Barnett, Morris 169
Basel 190, 191, 197
Bath 241–5
Batta, Alexandre 71, 89
Batthyani, Countess 191
Baugniet, Charles (artist) 185
Bavière, Hôtel de (Leipzig) 139
Bazzini, Antonio 70, 109, 134, 136, 250
    WORKS
        Concert Allegro (op. 15) 136, 139
        Concertante for two violins 205
        Le Ronde des Lutins (op. 25) 136, 253
Beale, Frederick (publisher) 131, 186
Beauvau Hotel (Nice) 60
Becher, Alfred 160
Beethoven, Ludwig van 1, 5, 7, 28–33 *passim*, 36, 37, 38, 75, 83, 85, 88, 94, 144, 145, 148, 149, 201, 204, 216, 252, 261
Heilingenstadt Testament 33
WORKS
    32 variations in C minor (WoO 80) piano solo 214
    Andante Favori (WoO 57) 55
    Arrangements of Scottish Folksongs 238
    Choral Fantasia (op. 80) 266
    Coriolan Overture (op. 62) 23
    Fidelio (op. 72) 16, 32, 85
    Mass 23
    Missa Solemnis (op. 123) 16, 30, 178
    quartets 28, 29, 36, 62, 157, 158, 167, 178–84 *passim*, 216
        quartet in F (op. 18, No. 1) 179, 183
        quartet in G (op. 18, No. 2) 183, 217
        quartet in D (op. 18, No. 3) 180
        quartet in C minor (op. 18, No. 4) 134, 183, 204, 217
        quartet in A (op. 18, No. 5) 180, 183, 204, 214
        quartet in B♭ (op. 18, No. 6) 180, 183, 185, 207
        Razumovsky Quartets (op. 59) 84, 134, 157, 168, 184, 184n.2, 229
            quartet in F (op. 59, No. 1) 180, 183, 184n.2, 207
            quartet in E minor (op. 59, No. 2) 76, 168, 183, 184n.2, 185, 204, 208, 229
            quartet in C (op. 59, No. 3) 158, 168, 179, 183, 204, 217
        quartet in E♭ (op. 74) 178, 180, 183, 184, 184n.2, 213
        quartet in F minor (op. 95) 180, 183, 185
        quartet in E♭ (op. 127) 29, 31, 129, 180, 183, 184
        quartet in B♭ (op. 130) 128, 157, 168, 180, 183, 214–15
        quartet in C♯ minor (op. 131) 130, 180, 183, 229

quartet in A minor (op. 132) 180, 183
Grosse Fuge in B♭ (op. 133) 178
quartet in F (op. 135) 29, 180
string quartet 91
quintet in C (op. 29) 128, 183, 204
romances
    Romance in G (op. 40) 150
    Romance in F (op. 50) 149
septet in E♭ (op. 20) 174
sonatas 84, 174, 215
    cello and piano sonata in G minor (op. 5, No. 2) 180
    violin and piano sonata in F (op. 24) 185, 208
    violin and piano sonata in C minor (op. 30, No. 2) 133, 183, 185, 217, 218
    violin and piano sonata in G (op. 30, No. 3) 178
    violin and piano sonata in A (op. 47), *Kreutzer* 70n.1, 79, 89, 96, 110, 133, 158, 161, 164, 178, 180, 189, 204, 208, 213, 215
    violin and piano sonata in G (op. 96) 168, 217
    piano sonata in A♭ (op. 26) 149, 180
    piano sonata in C♯ minor (op. 27, No. 2) 180
    piano sonata in D minor (op. 31, No. 2) 180
    piano sonata in F minor (op. 57), *Appasionata* 217
    piano sonata in B♭ (op. 106), *Hammerklavier* 149
    piano sonata (op. 111) 33
symphonies 61, 129
    symphony no. 1 in C (op. 21) 23
    symphony no. 3 in E♭, *Eroica* (op. 55) 23
    symphony no. 7 in A (op. 92) 30, 36, 71
    symphony no. 9 in D minor, *Choral* (op. 125) 30, 87, 197
trios 181, 215
    piano trio in E♭ (op. 1, No. 1) 207
    piano trio in G (op. 1, No. 2) 168
    piano trio in C minor (op. 1, No. 3) 182, 183, 185
    piano trio in D (op. 70, No. 1) 179, 185, 204, 208, 215
    piano trio in E♭ (op. 70, No. 2) 185
    piano trio in B♭ (op. 97) 76, 178, 180, 208, 217
    violin concerto (op. 61) 85, 86, 88, 129, 174, 176, 181, 186, 203, 206, 269
Beethoven Quartet Society (London) 1, 167, 178–80, 182–4, 207, 226–7
Beethoven Rooms (London) 178
Belgians 88
Belgium 101–2, 117
Bellini, Vincenzo 54
    WORKS
        Tu-vedrai 74
Belloni, Gaëtano 124, 170, 189
Bénazet, Edouard 195, 229
Benedict, Julius 2, 130, 131, 180n.1, 210, 215, 232, 256
    on Ernst 184
Bennett, William Sterndale 113, 116, 174, 176, 178, 180, 204
Benzon, Elizabeth 241, 243, 255
Benzon, Ernst Schlesinger 237, 241–2, 243, 244, 255
Benzon, 'Jubilee Plunger' 241–2
Bergen 50
Bériot, Charles de 9, 47, 55, 75, 78, 85, 88, 89, 93, 102, 126, 203, Plate V
    WORKS
        first violin concerto in D (op. 16) 139
Berlin 69, 77, 93–6, 99, 103, 104, 106, 123, 150, 151, 153, 158, 172, 225, 261
Berlioz, Hector 1, 6, 39, 47, 48, 50n.1, 53, 56, 57, 74, 75, 79, 86, 89, 101–2, 104–5, 114, 153, 160, 175, 182, 183, 187, 189, 195–6, 201, 204, 205, 208, 209, 210, 215, 225, 227, 228–9, 259, 260, 262, 263–4, 269
    on Ernst 1, 4, 8, 9, 21, 27n.1, 54, 56, 144–5, 154–7 *passim*, 169–70, 255
    WORKS
        choral
            Te Deum (op. 22) 170
            Damnation of Faust (op. 24) 195, 196

  Hungarian March (from op. 24)
   136
  Childhood of Christ (op. 25)
   196, 215
 operas
  Benvenuto Cellini (op. 23) 189,
   190, 195
  Beatrice et Bénédict (op. 27)
   229
  The Trojans (op. 29) 215
 symphonies and overtures
  King Lear Overture (op. 4) 105
  Roman Carnival Overture
   (op. 9) 196
  Fantastic Symphony (op. 14) 53
  Symphonie funèbre et
   triomphale (op. 15) 101
  Harold in Italy (op. 16) 1, 53,
   101, 102, 135, 155, 196,
   209, 210
  Romeo and Juliet (op. 17) 57,
   155–6
Berne 191
Bettelheim, Caroline 255
Beust, Count von 103
Bezekirsky, Vassily 219, 264
Biarnez, Enole 225
Biarnez, Madam (harpist) 225
Billet, Alexandre 180
Birnbaum, D. 264
Bizet, Georges 21
Blackwood's Magazine 240
Blagrove, Henry 114, 130, 132, 133, 216,
 217
Blagrove's concert hall (Mortimer Street,
 London) 167
Blanc (violinist, in Paris) 213
Blanc, Charles 240
Blanc, Louis 8, 210, 240, 263
Blanchard, Henri
 on Ernst 98
Blumenthal, J. 205
Bocklet, Karl Maria von 30
Böhm, Frau 28, 29
Böhm, Joseph Michael 27–30, 31–6 *passim*,
 38, 39, 54, 80, 128, 145
 WORKS
  violin concerto in D 33, 43, 64
Böhm quartet 26, 29–30
Bohrers, the 106, 215
Bois-le-duc 73

Bonnaire, Félix 193
Bordeaux 55, 71, 195, 196, 225
Borsi (*prima donna*, in St Petersburg) 154
Bösendorfer Salon (Vienna) 238
Bott, Jean 150
Bottesini, Giovanni 183, 208, 218, 226
 WORKS
  Duo for violin and double bass 183
Boucher, Alexander 51, 61, 63
Bougival 187
Bouilly, Jean-Nicolas
 L'Abbé de L'Epée 193
Boulogne 121, 122, 172, 215, 218, 259
Brabant 73
Bradford 215
Brahms, Johannes 9, 32, 145–7, 201, 238,
 256
 WORKS
  concertos
   piano concerto in D minor
    (op. 15) 140, 146, **146**
   violin concerto (op. 77) 147,
    147
  Four Duets (op. 28) 238
  Serenade in D (op. 11) 145–6, **146**
  Three Quartets (op. 31) 238
  Wechsellied zum Tanze (op. 31,
   No. 1) 238
Brandus, Gemmy 269
Braunschweig 74, 95, 104, 108, 122, 124,
 125, 209
Braunschweig, Duke of 107, 108, 122
Breda 73
Bremen 107
Breslau 78, 94–5
Brighton 181, 215–16
Britannia 119
British Library (London) 70
British Mission (Vienna) 228
Brno, *see* Brünn
Broadwood, Walter Stewart 205
Browning, Elizabeth Barrett 241
Browning, Robert 241
Bruch, Max 88
Brumow, Charlotte, *see* Ernst (née
 Brumow), Charlotte
Brünn 2, 3, 7, 10, 15–17, 18–25 *passim*, 34,
 37, 56, 77–8 *passim*, 135, 160, 222,
 225, 269, 273
Brussels 86, 89, 101–2, 104, 116, 156, 199
Bull (née Villemot), Félice 51

Bull, Ole 48, 49–51, 54, 57, 64, 75, 109–11 *passim*, 114, 200–201, 250, 259
  on Ernst 50, 55, 219, 225
Bülow, Hans Guido von 190, 197, 201
Bulwer Lytton, Edward, *see* Lytton, Edward Bulwer
Burnard, N. 186
Burney, Caroline, *see* Fountaine (née Burney), Caroline
Busch, Chamberlain von 106
Busoni, Ferruccio 70
Buys, Mlle. (singer, in Holland) 73

California 169, 201
Cambridge, Duke of 167
Carafa, Michele
  WORKS
    Nathalie 53
Carl, Prince of Prussia 107
Carlsbad 105, 150
Caroline, Queen of England 108
Carpentras 74
Casino (Aix) 210
Casino (Baden-Baden) 229
Casino (Zurich) 190
Castil-Blaze, François-Henri-Joseph 89
Catholicism 6, 15, 29, 194, 196, 269, 271
Cavallini, Ernest
  WORKS
    clarinet solo 196
Celle 106, 107
Česká Lípa, *see* Leippa
Cessoles, Conte de 226
Chambéry 191
Chapman, George 178
Chappell, Arthur 227, 232, 233, 237, 247, 255, Plate XVI
Chappell & Co. (publishers) 3, 230, 231, 249, 250
Charivari 156
Charles VI, Emperor 16
Charles XIV, King of Sweden 107
Chélard, Hyppolyte 161
Cheltenham 181
Cherblanc, Jean-Louis 191
Cherubini, Luigi 23, 32
  WORKS
    Coronation Mass 23
Chevillard, Pierre-Alexandre 189
Chopin, Frédéric 1, 7, 51, 52, 53–4, 55, 56, 60n.1, 71, 86, 89–90, 100, 143, 144, 145, 149, 157, 160, 201, 202, 204, 214, Plate IV
  WORKS
    Ballade in F (op. 38) 90
    concertos 143
    funeral march (from op. 35) 245
    mazurkas 90
    Polonaise in A (op. 40, No. 1) *Military* 90
    scherzo in C♯ minor (op. 39) 90
    sonatas
      piano sonata in B♭ minor (op. 35) 143
      piano sonata in B minor (op. 58) 143
Chorley, Henry Fothergill 172, 203–4, 205, 230, 232, 233
  on Ernst 203, 209, 221, 225, 257, 261
  Ernst's obituary 1, 157, 268
Christian VIII, King of Denmark 109, 158, 159
Christianity 7, 16, 17, 22, 271 *see also* Catholicism
Cinti-Damoreau, Laure-Cinthie 56, 89, 90
Classical Chamber Concerts (Manchester) 1, 176–7, 181, 204, 205–6
Clauss, Wilhelmine 189
Clement, Franz 84, 85
Cohen, Hermann 55
Cologne 102, 134, 158, 199
Colon, Eugenie 180
Comédie française (Paris) 261
Concert Hall (Harmonie) (Kiel) 109
Concerts Thubaneau (Marseilles) 61, 62
Congress of Vienna 17
Constant, L'Abbé 242
Cooper, Henry C. 180, 182, 183, 185, 208, 214
Copenhagen 107–10 *passim*, 118, 158–9, 264
Copped Hall (Totteridge) 241, 245, 247
Corneille, Pierre 192
  Horace 193
Cornelius, Peter 201
Cossmann, Bernhard 190, 196
Costa, Giacomo 116
Costa, Michael 208
Courier de L'Europe 121
Court Journal 119
Court Opera (Vienna) 256
Court orchestra (Lübeck) 73

Court orchestra (Parma) 59
Court orchestra (Vienna) 28
Court Theatre (Copenhagen) 110
Court Theatre (Vienna) 28
Covent Garden (London) 127, 130, 195, 206, 207
Cox, John Edward 204
Cranz, August 107
Crary, Mrs Arthur 273
Crefeld 134
Cremona violins 155, 206, 207
Cruvelli, Marie 195–6
Cruvelli, Sophie 196, 226
Crystal Palace (London) 182, 210
Custine, Marquis de 72
Czech nationalism 17, 200

Dagmar, Princess of Demark 264
Damcke, Berthold 154
Dando, Joseph 180
Danhauser, Josef
 Die Brautschau 78n.2
 Die Schachpartie 78n.2
Dantan, Jean Pierre 10, 48, 56, 59, 62, 63, 64
Darmstadt 109, 199
David, Ferdinand 8, 75, 76–7, 96, 128, 129, 134, 139, 160, 178, 201, 202, 203, 213
Davison, J.W. 2, 6, 115–16, 119, 120, 123, 124, 127, 130, 134, 172–3, 175, 176, 203–4, 205, 208–11 *passim*, 213, 214–15, 217–18, 232, 241, 248, 249, 255, 257, 258, 259, 262–3
 on Ernst 5, 115, 126, 133, 181, 209, 214, 227, 232
Débats 153
Delacroix, Eugène
 on Ernst 213–14
Delft 72
Deloffre, Louis Michel 9, 168, 177, 185
Delsarte, François 89
Denmark 106, 107, 159
Denmark, Queen of 107
Dennstedt 96
Der Spiegel 153, 154, 156
Despréaux, Jean-Étienne 56
Dessau 98
Dessau, Duke of 107
Detmold, Johann Hermann 122
Deutsch, S. 9

Deventer 73
Devrient, Emile 197
Dickens, Charles 235
Dietz's Nouvelle Salle de Concert (Paris) 51
Dilligenzia (The Hague) 72
Disraeli, Benjamin 235, 247–8
Doesburg 73
Döhler, Theodor 110–11, 133
 WORKS
  Nocturne in D♭ 110
Dolby, Charlotte 133
Domanovecz, Nicholas Zmeskall von 31
Donizetti, Gaetano 54, 219
Dont, Jacob 28
Doodle (American millionaire) 201
Dörffel, Alfred
 on Ernst 134
Dorpat 77, 153
Dostoevsky, Fyodor 154
 on Ernst 154
Draguignan 63, 194, 195
Dresden 21, 40, 44, 76, 77, 93, 135, 150, 151, 170
Dressel, Dettmar 41
Dreyschock, Alexander 113, 122
Drury Lane (London) 182, 206
Dublin 127, 130, 180, 181, 204, 210, 226
Dublin Philharmonic 127
Dubourg, George
 on Ernst 2, 4–5
Duchêne, Adolphe 182
Dudley Gallery (London) 205
Dufour (Paris) 269
Dumas, Alexandre 271
 Autoportrait 271
Dussek, Jan Ladislav 204
Düsseldorf 96, 98, 134, 169
Dustmann, Louise Meyer 255, 256

Eckert, Karl Anton and Kullack 181, 186, 189
 WORKS
  Fantasy on Italian Songs 159, 161
Edinburgh 181
Ehrlich, A. 195, 267
Elberfeld 134
Elgar 137–8, 144, 147
 WORKS
  La Capricieuse (op. 17) 138
  Etudes Characteristiques (op. 24) 138

Violin Concerto (op. 61) 138, **138**, 144
Violin Sonata (op. 82) 138, **138**
Eliot, George 240, 241
Ella, John 7, 128, 129, 132, 133–4, 167–8, 177, 185, 199, 205, 207, 208, 214, 217–18
  on Ernst 9, 216
Elliot, Miss Byrd 273
Elun, Fan
  on Ernst 10–11
Elvert, Christian Ritter d'
  on Ernst 9, 39
Emmerich, Dr (from Munich) 272
Ems 46
Enescu, George 1
England 1, 7, 56, 59, 109, 116, 126–34, 160, 189, 199, 202–11, 214–18, 225, 227
Erard, Sébastien 83
Erbprinz Hotel (Weimar) 161
Ernest Augustus, King of Hanover 74, 106–7, 108–9, 114, 123–4, 125, 126
Ernst, Adolf (brother of Heinrich Wilhelm) 14, 18, 21
Ernst, Adolf (husband of Josephine Ernst) 10n.5
Ernst, Alfred 226–7
Ernst (née Lévy), Amélie-Siona 14, 191–7, 205, 215, 225, 227, 230, 235, 236–7, 239–45, 248–9, 259–70, Plates XI and XII
  after Ernst's death 271–2
  'Ernst's Violin' 272
  Feuillets d'album et Pensées Fugitives 272
  'Last Vow' 270
  marriage to Ernst 205
  Mes Lectures en prose 272
  Mes Lectures en vers 272
  Nos bébés 272
  Recueil des Notes et Souvenirs, avec documents autograph et inedits 272
  Rimes françaises d'une Alsacienne 271
  'Thalberg Magician' 241–5
Ernst, Barbara 10n.4, 17–18, 20, 21
Ernst, Caroline 14, 24, 107, 108
Ernst (née Brumow), Charlotte 10, 14, 18, 20, 221–2
Ernst, François Joseph Eugène 227
Ernst, Franz (grandfather of Heinrich Wilhelm) 14, 17

Ernst, Franz Anton (František Antonin, violinist and composer) 21nn.2–3
Ernst, Franziska 14, 18, 21, 59, 136
Ernst, Heinrich (son of Josephine Ernst) 10, 14
Ernst, Heinrich (son of Moritz Ernst) 21, 227
Ernst, Heinrich Wilhelm
  acquires Stradivarius 98
  at Augustinian monastery of St Thomas (Brünn) 22–4
  at Bath 241–5
  benefit concerts for 100, 176, 180, 227, 230–33, 235, 237–8, 249–50, 255–7, 266, 275–81
  birth date of 19–20
  at Copped Hall 245
  death of 266–7
  diagnosis of illness 218–22
  early childhood 21–2, 222
  and Ernst (née Lévy), Amélie-Siona
    pre-marriage 191–7
    marriage 205
    after marriage 215, 235–45, 248–9
    last days 259–66
  family history 10n.4, 17–19
  family tree 14
  funeral 267
  as Hanoverian Concertmaster 107, 108, 122–4, 125–6
  at Knebworth 239–40, 248–9
  literature on 9–11
  in London 113–20, 167–74, 175–86, 199, 204–5, 206–10, 214–18, 239, 240, 247, 249–50, 255–8
  at Malvern 235, 237, 238–9
  in Marseilles 59–65
  at Narford Hall 248
  and nationalism 7, 139, 149
  in Nice (retirement period / last days) 225–6, 230–34, 236, 261–70
  in Paris 49–57, 61, 64, 70, 71, 73, 81, 83–91 *passim*, 98–100, 122, 125–6, 134, 149, 172–3, 181, 186–7, 189, 205, 211, 213–14, 218, 259–61
  sexuality of 47–8
  and socialism 7
  siblings of 10n.4, 19–21, 24–5
  TOURS
    of Austrian Empire/Austria 77–81, 135–6, 150–51

of Belgium 101–2
of England 126–34, 167–74,
175–86, 204–5, 210, 214–18
of France 55–6, 59–65, 70–72,
120–22, 125–6, 134, 172–3,
181, 194–5, 197, 205, 210–11,
215, 218
of Germany 40–48, 74–7, 93–4,
95–8, 105–9, 134, 150–51, 158,
194, 195–7, 199
of Holland 72–3, 102–5
of Ireland 127, 130, 180, 181, 204,
210
of Poland 94–5
of Russia 153–8
of Scandinavia 109–11, 158–9
of Scotland 181
of Switzerland 52–3, 186–7,
190–91, 194, 205, 210
in Vienna (retirement period) 226,
227–30
at Vienna Conservatoire 27–36, 37–9,
41
WORKS
Adagio 42
Bolero (op. 16) 90, 91
*Brilliant Variations on the Favourite
Air: I Tuoi frequenti palpiti* 56
cadenzas for Beethoven violin
concerto 269
Carnival of Venice (op. 18) 1, 54,
55, 65, **65**, 76–80 *passim*, 84,
85, 113, 114, 118–21, 125, 127,
131, 135, 151, 153, 155, 158,
159, 162, 173, 180, 189, 196,
215, 216
Andante 118–21
Concertino in D (op. 12) 64–5, 75–9
passim, 87
Concerto in F♯ minor (op. 23) 1,
139–49, **140–48** *passim*, 159,
160, 161, 162, **162**, 171, 189,
202, 209, 250, 260
Elegy (op. 10) 1, 41, 42, **69**, 69–70,
72, 74–9 *passim*, 84, 90, 101,
106, 107, 110, 113, 127, 129,
131, 133, 145, 147, 149, 158,
180, 184, 185, 189, 199, 213,
232, 249, 256, 257, 260
Erlking transcription (*Le Roi des
Aulnes*, op. 26) 8, 54, 97, **97**,
103, 104, 106, 113, 133, 250,
256, 258
Fantasy on Dom Sébastien 99, 125
Fantasy on Irish Airs 134, 181, 253
Fantasy on Le Pré aux Clercs 53
Fantasy on le Prophète (op. 24) 175
Fantasy on a theme from Oberon 56
Feuillet D'Album 99
'Der Fischer' 257
Hungarian Airs (op. 22) 136–9, **137**,
138, 149, 156, 160, 161, 162,
171, 191, 204, 206, 213, 215
The Last Rose of Summer 8, 74, 97,
181, 250, 252
Ludovic Fantasy (op. 6) 52, 53, 55,
133, 180
Morceaux de salon: Deux Romance
(op. 15) 90, 118
nocturnes
Two Nocturnes (in A and E)
(op. 8) 55, 56, 98, 136, 257
*Nocturne et Rondo Gracioso
(Deux Norceaux de Salon:
Adagio Sentimentale et
Rondo Grazioso)* (op. 13) 95
Nocturne for piano solo 249,
257, 269
opera 228–9
Otello Fantasy (op. 11) 29, 70–80
passim, 84, 93, 101, 104, 109,
114, 128, 137, 139, 145, 175,
181, 189, 196, 209, 215, 217,
260
Pensées Fugitives (*Les Gages
d'amitié*) 73–4, 99–100, 104,
110, 178, 232, 238, 257, 272
Pirate Fantasy (op. 19) 74, 76, 78,
125, 133, 149, 158, 209, 260
Polonaise (op. 17) 96
Polyphonic Studies 1, 74, 203, 249,
250–55, **251–4**, 257, 269
quartets
quartet in B♭ (op. 26) 226,
229–33, 237–8, 249, 256,
257, 261
quartet in A 227, 247, 249, 256,
257, 259–63 *passim*, 276–81
quartet in C 203, 249, 257,
259–62 *passim*
La Romanesca 54
Rondinos (op. 5) 52

Rondo Papageno (*Rondo Scherzo*)
    (op. 20) 105, 136, 137, 149, 189,
    215, 253
  second elegy 111
  Thème Allemand varié (op. 9) 55
  Trio pour un Violon 74, 250, 251
  *Variations brilliante sur un Thème
    de Rossini* (op. 4) 44
  Variations on a Dutch Air (op. 18)
    73, 136
Ernst, Jakob 10n.4, 14, 17–19, 20, 21, 24,
    27, 37, 55–6, 79, 205, 221, 266
Ernst, Joachim 14, 18, 21
Ernst, Johann 10, 14, 18, 20, 24–5, 37, 59,
    79, 80, 102–3, 104, 106, 107, 127
Ernst, Joseph 14, 18, 20, 24, 107, 108
Ernst, Josephine 10, 10n.5, 14, 221
Ernst, Katharina 14, 18, 20
Ernst, Ludwig 10, 14
Ernst, Marianna 14, 18, 21
Ernst, Moritz 14, 18, 19, 20, 21, 221
Ernst, Nathan/Samuel 14, 18, 20, 24–5,
    171
Ernst-Kayser, *see* Kayser, Josephine
Erstekaffeehaus (Vienna) 28
Escudier, Léon
  on Ernst 90
Escudier, Marie
  on Ernst 190
Eton 217
Europa, Hotel (Nice) 236
Ewer (publisher) 95
Examiner 121
Exeter Hall (London) 173–4, 181, 210

F., Princess of Denmark 159
Félix, Élisa, *see* 'Rachel'
Fétis, François-Joseph 101
Field, John 52
Figdor, Fanny 128
Figdor, Mons. (Joachim's uncle in Paris)
    262, 269
Figdor, Nathan 80
Filtsch, Charles 113
Fink-Lohr, Madame (singer, in Holland) 73
Finland, *see* Turku
First World War 272
Fischoff, Joseph 39, 108
Flatz, Ida 238
Flaubert, Gustave 72
Flotow, Friedrich von
  WORKS
    Martha 74
Föchgott, Emil 238
Fontaine, Mortier de 169
Fountaine, Andrew 55, 98, 126, 248, 272
Fountaine (née Burney), Caroline 248
Fountaine, Emily 248
Fountaine, Hanna Green 98
Fountaine, Mary 248
France 6, 48, 55–6, 120–22, 125–6, 134,
    153, 172, 182, 191, 194, 196, 205,
    218
France Musicale 42, 59, 90, 120, 189
  on Ernst 132, 190, 213
Franchomme, Auguste 52, 70, 90
Francis I, Emperor 15, 16
Franck, Albert 84, 85
Franck, Eduard 84, 85
Francke (string-player, in Copenhagen) 158
Franco-Mendès, Jacques 102
Franco-Prussian War 271
Franke, Roberta 10
Frankfurt 40, 44, 45, 46, 48, 50, 103, 105,
    196, 197, 199
Frankowski (known as 'Frank') (Ernst's
    secretary) 47–8, 57, 59, 60, 78, 104,
    106, 111, 153, 169, 205
Frederick Wilhelm IV, King of Prussia 93,
    96, 97, 107
Free Trade Hall (Manchester) 266
Frege, Livia 134
Freidrich Wilhelm, Electoral Prince of
    Hesse-Kassel 44, 46–7
French nationalism 271
French Revolution 16
French Theatre (Amsterdam) 72, 73
Freund, Dr (in London) 114
Friedrich VII, King of Denmark 159
Froberville, Eugène 85, 99
Frölich, Franz Joseph 44

Ganz, Moriz 94
Gastein 225, 227, 228, 256
Gautier, Mons. (Mayor of Nice) 226
Gautier, Théophile 116, 192–4, 271
  'Variations sur le Carnaval de Venise'
    194
Gazette musicale 52, 99
  on Ernst 53, 55, 56, 238n.1
Gelder, van (cellist, in London) 204
Geneva 52, 191, 210, 214

Geneva Conservatoire 52
Genoa 116
Genoa Conservatoire 116
Gentleman's Concert (Manchester) 127
George, Crown Prince of Hanover 106, 107, 108–9
George I, King of England and King of Hanover 108
George II, King of England 108
George III, King of England 108, 222
George IV, King of England 108
German (language) 15, 17
German Hospital (London) 113, 114
German musicians and musical ideas 200–205 *passim*
German nationalism 200
Germanization 17
Germany 40–48, 64, 74–7, 93–4, 95–8, 101, 105–9, 134, 172, 194, 199–204 *passim*, 225, 226
Germi, Luigi 36, 59, 62, 63
Geschichte der Gerwandhaus Konzerte
    on Ernst 134
Gesellschaft der Musikfreunde (Vienna) 27, 29, 33, 37
Gévénof, Alexandre 153
Gewandhaus (Leipzig) 74–5, 76, 93, 128, 134, 160
Ghys, Joseph 71, 118n.1
Girardin, Mme Delphine de 192
Glasgow 181
Gloucester Cathedral 137
Glover, Howard 116
Gluck, Cristoph Willibald
    WORKS
        Orfeo 16
Glücksburg, Duchess of 109–10
Goddard, Arabella 215, 218, 237, 249, 255, 259
Godfroy's (Vienna) 108
Goethe, Johann Wolfgang von 121, 238, 257
Goffrie (violinist, in London) 130, 199, 204, 207–8, 214, 216, 217
Goldberg (violinist, from Vienna) 83
Goldschmidt, Otto 33, 210, 214
Gomperz, Josephine, *see* Wertheimstein, Josephine von
Gorcum 73
Gottschalk, Louis Moreau 201
Gouffé (viola-player, in Paris) 213
Grand Theatre (St Petersberg) 155

Grande salle des concerts (Lyon) 191
Grasse 194
Graumann, Mathilde 181
Graz 135, 150
Great Exhibition (1851) (London) 182
Greenwich 180
Grenoble 194
Griepenkerl, Wolfgang 105, 124
Grimm brothers 124
Grisi, Giulia 55
Grün, Jakob 28, 29, 123
Grünwald, Adolph 28
Guarnerius violins 98, 116, 126
Guasco, Carlo 154
Gueldre 73
Guhr, Carl 45, 50, 85
Gulomy, Jerome 129
Gurney, Archer 257
Gutmann, Adolf 71

Haberneck, François-Antoine 55, 64, 87, Plate V
Habsburgs 15–17
Hackel, Anton 33, 38
Hague, The 72, 73, 102, 103
Hainl, Georges 191
Halle 98
Hallé, C.E.
    on Ernst 177
Hallé, Charles 3, 7, 48, 69, 83, 113, 122, 160, 168, 171, 176, 177, 181, 185, 204, 205, 207, 208, 214, 216, 217, 226, 230–33 *passim*, 249, 255, 257, 266
    on Ernst 6, 9, 89, 113, 117, 133
Hallé, Lady, *see* Neruda, Wilhelmina
Hallé orchestra (Manchester) 207
Halvéy, Fromental
    WORKS
        La Tentation 53
Hamburg 6, 74, 75, 96–7, 107–8, 122, 134, 159
Handel, George Frideric 38, 204
Hanover 2, 74, 75, 106–8, 122–4, 125–6, 145, 150, 209, 250
Hanover Square Gardens (London) 130, 214
Hanover Square Rooms (London) 114–15, 133, 171
Hanslick, Eduard 31, 200
Harlem 72
Harmonicon, The 38
    on Ernst 33–4

Härtel, Dr (publisher) 134
Hartmann, Viktor 71
Haslinger (publisher) 80
Hauer, Ottile 238
Hauman, Théodore 55, 56, 71, 88–9, 95, 106, 114, 118
Hauptmann, Moritz 128
Hauser, Miska 80, 201
Hausmann, Robert 129, 130
Haweis, Rev. H.R.
　on Ernst 1, 4, 156, 206–7, 216
Haydn, Joseph 5, 23, 31, 38, 204, 216
　WORKS
　　quartets 84, 191, 213
　　　quartet in F (No. 48) (op. 50, No. 5) 185
　　　quartet in C (No. 57) (op. 54, No. 2) 178, 217
　　　quartet in D (No. 63) (op. 64, No. 5) 208, 217
　　　quartet in D (No. 70) (op. 71, No. 2) 204
　　　quartet in G minor (No. 74) (op. 74, No. 3) 207
　　　Emperor quartet (No. 77) (op. 76, No. 3) 254
　　　quartet in B♭ (No. 78) (op. 76, No. 4) 180, 208
　　　quartet in D (No. 79) (op. 76, No. 5) 180
　　　quartet in G (No. 81) (op. 77, No. 1) 168
　　trios
　　　piano trio (No. 25) in G, *Gypsy Rondo* 218
Hazlitt, William 178
Hebrew 17
Heidelberg 40, 46
Heifetz, Jascha 1
Heine, Heinrich 83, 87–90 *passim*, 122, 124, 125, 131, 195, 219
　on Ernst 1, 4, 125–6
　WORKS
　　Buch der Lieder 83
　　Gedichte 83
Heine, Salomon 83
Heller, Amely 272
　on Ernst 10, 19, 24, 227, 264
Heller, Stephen 60n.1, 72, 73, 74, 84, 85, 89, 99–100, 169, 178, 179, 180, 181, 195, 226, 232, 259, 260, 262, 263, 264, 269, 272
　WORKS
　　24 studies for piano (op. 16) 99
　　Etudes de concerts 180
　　Fantasy on Dom Sébastien 99, 125
　　Feuillet D'Album 99
　　Pensées fugitives (*Les Gages d'amitié*) 73–4, 99–100, 104, 110, 178, 232, 238, 257, 272
　　piano sonata (op. 9) 99
Hellmesberger, George, the Elder 28, 80, 148, 179
Hellmesberger, Joseph, the Elder 238, 252
Henselt, Adolf von 9, 162
Herrmann, Emil 272, 273
Herz, Henri 109
Hesse-Kassel 2, 44, 46, 47, 126 *see also* Kassel
Hiezinger Theater (Vienna) 80
Hill, Henry 130, 168, 174, 177, 180, 183, 185, 199, 204, 207–8, 214
Hiller, Ferdinand 8, 52, 76, 190, 201
　WORKS
　　The Destruction of Jerusalem (op. 24) 169
　　symphony in E (op. 67) 160
Hoenemann, Captain von 106
Hoffmann, E.T.A. 4, 155
Hoffmann, Sigmund 78, 95
Hoffmeister (publisher) 44
Hofoperntheater orchestra (Vienna) 148
Hoftheater (Dresden) 76
Hoftheater der Christiansburg (Copenhagen) 111
Hogarth, George 209, 217
Holland 72–3, 75, 100, 101, 102–5, 117
Holm (string-player, in Copenhagen) 158
Holmes, Alfred 260, 262–3
Holmes, Henry 260, 262–3
holocaust, *see* Nazism, holocaust
Holz, Karl 28, 31, 32
Homberg 195
Homer, George Chapman's translation of 178
Houssaye, Arsène 192
Hudson, Francis 240
Hugo, Victor
　L'homme qui rit 271
Hummel, Johann Nepomuk 5, 32, 143, 204, 237
　WORKS
　　quintet in E♭ (op. 92) 208

septet in D minor (op. 74) 214
  Trio Concertante 169
Hungarian music 29
Hungarian nationalism 29, 80–81, 136–9
  passim, 200
Hungary 77, 80–81, 191, 273
Hyde Park (London) 182

Illustrated London News 116–17, 168, 209
Imperial Chapel (Vienna) 31
Imperial Theatre (St Petersburg) 153
Institute musical (Orléans) 56
Ischl 150
Italian Opera (London) 182

Jacquand M. 260, 262
Janáček, Leoš 23
Janin, Jules 74, 83, 94
Jellačić, Count Josip 160
Jelot, F.J. 205
Joachim, Heinrich 234, 249–50
Joachim, Joseph 11, 24, 27, 28–9, 43, 45,
    47, 61, 70, 77, 80, 93, 98, 106n.1,
    109, 123, 127, 128–9, 132, 134, 145,
    148n.1, 150, 160, 167, 175, 178,
    179, 182, 184, 184n.2, 190, 201,
    202–3, 213, 226–7, 231–4 *passim*,
    238, 241, 249–50, 252, 255–7
    passim, 260, 262, 266, 269, 276,
    Plates XV and XVI
  on Ernst 1, 129, 190, 225
  WORKS
    concertos
      violin concerto in G minor
        (op. 3) 196
      Hungarian Concerto (op. 11)
        140, 234, 249
John of Capistrano 16
Josepgstadt Theatre (Vienna) 33
Joseph II, Emperor 16–17
Journal de Nice 267
Journal des débats 104, 120
Judaism and Jews 6, 7, 8n.3, 18–19, 25, 29,
    38, 54, 123, 191, 192, 200, 201, 209,
    234n.1, 271, 273
  and Nazi holocaust 2, 273
  persecution of 3, 16–17
  see also anti-Semitism
Judée, Lieutenant Émile-Jacques 72–3
Jullien, Louis 171, 206, 207, 211

Kalisch 95
Karlsruhe 40, 46, 81, 196–7
Karlsruhe Diplomatic Corps 196
Karlsruhe Festival 196–7
Karlsruhe opera company 229
Karntnerthortheater (Vienna) 33, 37, 79
Kassel, 44, 47, 49, 105, 208, 209 *see also*
    Hesse-Kassel
Kayser, Josephine (Ernst-Kayser after
    marriage) 14, 21
Keats, John 5, 178
Kensington Palace (London) 123
Kiel 107, 109, 110, 111
Kistner (publisher) 99
Kittl, Johann Friedrich 104
Kleine Krona (Brünn) 222
Knebworth 236–7, 239–40, 242, 245,
    248–9, 258
Königsberg 153
Königslöw, von, the Younger 158
Königstadt 77
Königstadter (Berlin) 77
Konow, Walter 147
Kozeluch, Leopold 32
Krakow 135
Kreisler, Fritz 138
Křenová 16, 18, 19
Kreutzer, Rodolphe 32, 34, 55
Kriehuber, Josef 39, 148–9
  Ein Matinée bei Liszt 149, Plate VIII
Kroll, Franz 161
Kroll, William 273
  WORKS
    Banjo and Fiddle 273
Kroll Quartet
  Tchaikovsky's string quartet no. 1 in D
    (op. 11) 273
Kullak, Theodor and Eckert
  WORKS
    Fantasy on Italian Songs 159, 161
Künitz, Elise 183

La Rochelle 195
La Scala (Milan) 28
Lablache, Luigi 55
Lafitte Hôtel (Paris) 55
Lafont, Charles 55, 91, 109
  WORKS
    sixth violin concerto 33
Lamartine, Alphonse de 271
Lamb, Charles 178

Lamennais, Felicité 7
Lamm Hotel (Vienna) 79
Landhassal (Vienna) 33
Lanner, Joseph 38
Lapalu, Bertille 266
Laub, Ferdinand 148n.1, 185, 232, 251
Launier 44
Laurie, David 216, 272
Lausanne 191
Le Havre 56, 63, 64, 134
Lebouc, Charles Joseph 213
Lehmann, Frederick 232, 233, 241, 245
Leicester, Duke of 167
Leiden 72, 103
Leiningen, Count of 197
Leippa (Česká Lipa) 18
Leipzig 7, 44, 48, 74–5, 76–7, 85, 96–9 *passim*, 104, 105, 110, 128, 129, 134, 136, 139, 150, 160, 161, 169, 178, 182, 201, 229
Leipzig Conservatoire 128, 201
Lemberg 135
Lemoine, Henri (publisher) 72, 118
Léonard, Hubert 264
Leone, Dr 64
    on Ernst 9, 10, 19, 20, 24, 40, 42, 44, 47, 49, 77–8
Leonhard (violin teacher, in Brünn) 22, 27
Leopold I, King of Belgium 102
Leroy (clarinettist, in Paris) 213
Leschetizka, Madame 255, 256
Leschetizky, Theodor 228, 256
Lévy, Amélie-Siona, *see* Ernst, Amélie-Siona
Lévy, Aron 14, 191, 205
Lévy, J.B. 14, 193–4
Lévy, Paul 262, 266–7
Lévy, Rose F. 14, 205, 241, 262, 266, 272
    see also Weil, Rosalie
Lewes, George 240, 241
Lichtenthal church (Vienna) 31
Lille 70, 71, 72, 271
Lind, Jenny 33, 210, 214, 215
Lindpaitner, Peter von 204, 208
Linke, Josef 28, 30, 32
Linz 81, 150, 151
Lipinski, Karol 34, 50, 75, 76, 114
    WORKS
        Variations de Bravoure (op. 22) 43
        violin concertos 50n.1
            violin concerto no. 3 in E minor (op. 24) 139
            violin concerto no. 4 in A minor (op. 32) 139
Liszt, Franz 1, 7, 33, 48, 52, 53, 54, 55, 56, 70, 71, 77, 78, 79, 81, 89–90, 93, 94, 97, 100, 102, 104, 105, 109, 124, 125, 135, 145, 149, 155, 161–4, 169–72 *passim*, 175, 181, 189, 190, 196–8, 199–204 *passim*, 260, Plate VIII
    on Ernst 1, 8, 9, 161
    WORKS
        Fantasy on Beethoven's Ruins of Athens (S. 389) 197
        Faust Symphony (S. 108) 164
        Grosses Konzertsolo (S. 176) 162–3, **163**
        Hungarian Rhapsody no. 9 (Carnival in Pesth) (S. 244) 162
        piano sonata in B minor (S. 178) 1, 163–4
Litolff, Henri 95
Liverpool 127, 130, 172, 177, 180, 181
Liverpool Festival 172
Loder, Edward 218
Loder, Kate
    WORKS
        string quartet in E minor 186n.4
London 7, 43, 56, 63, 64, 85, 86, 88, 95, 99, 111, 113–20, 126–34 *passim*, 167–74, 175–86, 189, 190, 195, 202, 204–5, 206–10, 211, 214–18, 226, 227, 230–33 *passim*, 239, 240, 247, 249–50, 255–8, 259, 269
Long's Hotel (London) 118
Lotto, Isidore 147
Louis Ferdinand, Prince of Prussia 94
Low Countries 59, 88, 101
Lower Rhine Festival (Düsseldorf) 96
Lübeck 73
Ludholm, M. 50
Lwoff, General Alexï 153
Lycée (Nice) 266
Lyon 59, 60, 64, 191, 194
Lytton, Edward Bulwer 2, 5, 205, 228, 235–7, 239–45, 247–8, 258, 259, 263, 266–7, 268, 269
    Caxtoniana 240, 242
    The Caxtons 235
    The Coming Race 235
    The Last Days of Pompeii 235
    Pelham 235

Rienzi 235
Zanoni 235
Lytton, Emily 235–6
Lytton, Robert 228, 235–6, 240, 241, 258, 259, 261, 263
Lytton (née Doyle Wheeler), Rosina 235–6, 247–8

M. Dr (in Hanover) 106
Maas (viola-player, in Paris) 189
Macfarren, George 113, 127, 130, 175, 204, 210
Mackenzie, Alexander 255
Macon 271
Mainz 197, 199 *see also* Mayence
Majolica ceramics 248
Malibran, Maria 85, 88
Malvern 235, 237, 238–9
Manchester 7, 126, 127, 131, 171, 176–7, 181, 186, 204, 205, 207, 215, 266
Manchester Guardian
 on Ernst 126, 181
Mangold, Alice (A.M. Diehl after marriage) 117
Mannheim 40, 46, 199
Maréchal de Turenne Hotel (The Hague) 72
Maria Alexandrovna, Tsarina 264
Maria Theresa, Empress 15
Marinoni, Madame (singer, in Holland) 73
Marlow 116
Mars, Anne-Boutet 192
Marschner, Heinrich 74, 75
Marseilles 44, 59–65, 194–5
Marxsen, Eduard 32
Massena (Nice) 262
Mattmann, Louise 213
Maurer, Louis
 WORKS
  Concertante for four violins 51, 80, 132, 134
Mayence 134 *see also* Mainz
Mayer, Charles 91
Mayseder, Joseph 22, 28, 30–31, 32, 33, 34, 35, 36, 43, 70, 84
 WORKS
  Grosses Konzertstück (op. 47) 139
  piano trio in B 33
  Polonaises 53
  Rondeau for violin 33
  trio for violin, piano and cello 71

Variations in E (op. 45) 31, 33, 75, 114, 173
Méhul, Étienne 32
 WORKS
  Joseph and his Brethren 23
Melbye, Anton 111
Mellon (viola-player, in London) 185
Mendel, Gregor 22
Mendelssohn, Felix 1, 7, 31, 75, 77, 85, 93–4, 96, 101, 106n.1, 108, 127–34 *passim*, 139, 167, 176, 201, 202, 204, 206–9 *passim*, 214, 216, 237
 on Ernst 9, 76
 WORKS
  A Midsummer Night's Dream Overture (op. 21) 130
  Antigone (op. 55) 96
  'Auf Flügeln des Gesanges' (op. 34, No. 2) 159
  concertos
   piano concerto in G minor (op. 25) 110
   violin concerto (op. 64) 77, 88, 93–4, 128, 139, 171–2, 174, 176, 204, 206
  octet (op. 20) 134
  presto scherzando in F♯ minor for piano (op. 5) 185
  quartets
   quartet in E♭ (op. 12) 5, 76, 207
   quartet in D (op. 44, No. 1) 180, 183, 217
   quartet in E minor (op. 44, No. 2) 133, 174, 178, 180, 189, 199, 204, 213, 214, 216
   quartet in E♭ (op. 44, No. 3) 168, 178, 180, 183, 185, 217
   quartet in F minor (op. 80) 178, 180, 204
   quartet movements (op. 81) 178, 208, 214
  quintet in B♭ (op. 87) 185
  trios 181
   piano trio in D minor (op. 49) 96, 128, 129, 168, 204
   piano trio in C minor (op. 66) 214
Mendelssohn, Franz von 225
Ménestrel, Le 90
Mensching, Dr (in Hanover) 106
Menuhin, Yehudi 1

Merk, Josef 32
Metternich, Prince 16, 81
Meyer, Charles 91
Meyer, Leopold de 127
Meyerbeer, Giacomo 93, 96, 169, 175
    WORKS
        Prophète 170, 175
        Robert le Diable 53
Milanollo, Marie 109, 128, 197
Milanollo, Teresa 109, 128, 197
Milstein, Nathan 1
Mittau 153
Molique, Wilhelm Bernhardt 75, 114, 204, 232, 233
Moltke, Field Marshall Helmuth von 41, 271
Monday Popular Concerts (London) 231–2, 237–8, 247, 255, 256, 275
Montebello, Count of 51, 55
Montendre, Comte de 53
Montpellier 64, 194, 195
Moravia 15–17, 77
Moravian Familiant Law 3, 16, 24
Moravian Toleration Edict 16, 22
Morel, Auguste 101, 155
Mori, Frank 114, 181
Morning Advertiser
    on Ernst 8, 171
Morning Herald
    on Ernst 171
Morning Post 23, 116, 119–21 *passim*, 129
    on Ernst 5, 113–14, 205
Morrison's Hotel (Dublin) 210
Moscheles, Ignaz 53, 56, 64, 113, 127, 130, 131, 133, 134, 160
    WORKS
        concertos
            piano concerto no. 6, *Concerto fantastique* (op. 90, No. 6) 162
            piano concerto no. 7, *Concerto pathétique* (op. 93) 163n.1
Moscow Philharmonic Music School 264
Moser, Andreas 203, 226–7
    on Ernst 38
Mozart, Leopold
    Versuch einer grünlichen Violinschule 22
Mozart, Wolfgang Amadeus 5, 15, 23, 31, 32, 38, 50, 81, 148, 149, 204, 216
    WORKS

operas 16
    'Non più andrai farfollone amoroso' from *The Marriage of Figaro* (K. 492) 159
    Don Giovanni (K. 527) 23
    Magic Flute (K. 620) 23, 32
piano concerto in D minor (K. 466) 149
quartets 28
    quartet No. 1 in G (K. 80 or 387) 214
    quartet in D minor (K. 421) 168, 213, 214
    quartet in E♭ (K. 428) 204, 217
    quartet in B♭ (K. 458) 5
    quartet in C (K. 465) 208
    piano quartet in G minor (K. 478) 204
    quartet in D (K. 499) 216
    quartet in D (K. 525) 204
    quartet in B♭ (K. 589) 207
quintets
    quintet in G minor (K. 516) 185, 208
    quintet in D (K. 573) 178
    clarinet quintet (K. 581) 213
symphony in G minor (K. 550) 175
violin and piano sonatas 215
    sonata in E♭ (K. 380 or 481) 176
    sonata in A (K. 526) 76, 185
trios 215, 237
Mr Willy's Classical Concerts (London) 174
Muikvereins hall (Vienna) 33
Mulhouse 191
Müller, C. 75
Munich 39, 40, 42, 43, 81, 272
Museumssaal (Karlsruhe) 197
Musical Courier 47
Musical Examiner 115, 118–21 *passim*
    on Ernst 115
Musical Union (London) 1, 138, 167–8, 173, 177, 184–6, 184n.2, 199, 204, 207, 208, 210, 214–15, 216, 217–18
Musical Winter Evenings (London) 199, 207
Musical World 115, 119, 130, 131–2, 185, 203, 204, 226, 227, 255, 256–7, 262, 263
    on Ernst 4, 114–15, 117–18, 126, 131, 173–4, 175–6, 179, 186, 215, 217, 226, 235, 239, 247–9 *passim*

Musikzeitung 28
Musorgsky, Modest
   WORKS
      Pictures at an Exhibition 71
Musset, Alfred de 191, 262
   'Une bonne fortune' 194
Mutzig 191

Nachez, Tivadar 147
Nancy 71
Nantes 56, 181
Napoleon 18, 19, 61
Napp, F.C. 22
Narford 3
Narford Hall 98, 248, 272
Nassau, Duke of 107
National Socialism, *see* Nazism
National Theatre (Brünn) 22
nationalism 7, 17, 29, 190, 271
Nazism
   holocaust 2, 273
Neale Cornelius 123–4
Nedele, Philipp 22
Neruda, Wilhelmina (Lady Hallé) 23, 272
Netherlands, *see* Holland
Neu Rausnitz (Nového Rousiova) 17, 18, 20
Neuchâtel 191
Neue Berliner Musik-Zeitung
   on Ernst 6, 219
Neue Zeitschrift für Musik
   on Ernst 75–6, 229
Neuling, Vincent 31
New Beethoven Rooms (London) 185, 186n.4
New Jewish Cemetery (Brünn) 273
New Philharmonic (London) 138, 204, 208–9
New York 201
Ney, C. 213, 260
Nice 3, 6, 59, 60, 62–4 *passim*, 194, 195, 225–6, 230–34, 236, 259, 261–70, 272
Nice Museum 39, 269
Nicholas, Tsarevich 264, 266
Nîmes 64, 194, 195
Norfolk 3, 98, 248
Norway 49
Nového Rousiova, *see* Neu Rausnitz
Nuremberg 40, 44
Nymwegne 73

Odéon (Paris) 193, 196
Odeon Hall (Amsterdam) 73
Offenbach, Jacques 127
Oldenburg 107
Olmütz 135, 160
Onslow, George
   WORKS
      quintet (No. 9) 213
Opera (Nice) 266
Opéra (Paris) 64, 156
Opéra-comique (Paris) 53, 55, 132
Oranien, Prince of 102
Orléans 56, 73, 83, 85, 125
Ortigue, Joseph Louis d' 269
Osborne, George 55, 56, 70, 172, 180n.1
Overysel 73

Paganini, Niccolò 1, 7, 8, 11, 20, 21n.3, 34–6, 38–48 *passim*, 49, 50, 53, 54, 55, 56, 59–65 *passim*, 75, 80, 84, 85, 87, 88, 89, 94, 104, 105n.1, 109, 114–22 *passim*, 125–8 *passim*, 131, 139, 140, 144, 148, 156, 174, 184, 186, 194, 200–203 *passim*, 206, 214, 218, 211, 259
   WORKS
      Caprices (op. 1) 34, 38, 39, 43, 50, 251, 253
         no. 9: in E, *La Chasse* 38
         no. 24 54
      concertos
         violin concerto no. 1 in D (op. 6) 136
         violin concerto no. 2 in B minor (op. 7) 35
      Duet for One Violin 45, 50
      Moses variations 60
      Nel cor variations 45, 50, 85, 253
      sonatas
         sonata on the G-string 63
         Sonate Militaire 35
      variations on a theme from *La Cenerentola* 35
Panofka, Heinrich 42, 69, 70, 73, 78, 83, 84, 91, 114, Plate V
   WORKS
      Cantabile 84
Pape, Henri concert hall/salons (Paris) 71, 74
Paris 7, 39, 40, 41, 42, 44, 46, 48, 49–57, 59, 61, 63, 70, 71, 73, 81, 83–91, 94, 98–100, 116, 122, 124, 125, 127,

128, 132, 134, 149, 157, 159, 169, 170, 172–3, 175, 181, 182, 186–7, 189, 190, 191, 195, 197, 199, 200, 202, 205, 208, 211, 213–14, 218, 238, 259–61, 269, 272
Paris Conservatoire 61, 64, 87, 139, 162, 192, 194, 196
Parma 59
Pasta, Giuditta 221
Patti, Adelina 259
Pau 71
Pauer, Ernst 207, 208, 216
Paulin (concert organizer, in Paris) 213
Pavillion-Impérial, Hotel (Boulogne) 259
Pavlovna, Anna, Queen of Holland 102
Pays Bas, Hotel de (Amsterdam) 73
Pěčka, Jan
   on Ernst 10
Pesch (string-player, in Lyon) 191
Pesth 21, 27, 59, 80, 85, 135, 136, 162, 191
Philharmonic Society (London) 31, 56, 62, 64, 88, 113, 126–33 *passim*, 169, 171, 173, 180, 202, 208–9, 217
Philharmonic Society (Paris) 175
Philharmonic Society (St Petersburg) 172
Piatti, Alfredo 168, 169, 177, 178, 185, 199, 204, 205, 207–8, 214–17 *passim*, 226, 227, 231, 232, 237, 256, 257, 276, Plates XV and XVI
Pixis, Johann Peter 28
Pixis, Théodore 153
Planté, François 226
Platten, Count 106
Plessen, Countess 110
Pleyel, Ignaz 54
Pleyel, Marie (Camille) 78, 182
Pleyel's salons (Paris) 54, 89
Pohl, Richard
   on Ernst 9, 38, 39
Poland 94–5
Polish nationalism 200
Pollak, Herr (painter and relative of Ernst) 78
Pollitzer, Adolf 138
Pologne, Hôtel de (Dresden) 76
Posen 78, 95
Potsdam 96
Pott, August 129
Poulson, J.H. 50
Praeger, Ferdinand 209
Prague 17, 93, 94, 135

Pressburg 78, 80–81, 135, 136
Presse, La 193
Prinzhofer, August 150
Promberger, Joseph 154
Proudhon, Pierre Joseph 170
Provence 63
Provini (opera director, in Nice) 266
Provost (actor, in Paris) 192
Prudhomme, Sully 271
Prume, François 75, 93
Prussia 271
Puccini, Giacomo 136

Queen Square Select Society (London) 178

'Rachel' 191, 192, 196
Racine, Jean 192
   Bajazet 192–3
Radcliffe, Dr Charles Bland 240, 247, 248, 263
Raff, Joseph Joachim 190, 201
Rákóczy March 80–81
Read, Dr (in Hertfordshire) 241
Reader 257
Recio, Marie 101
Redern, Count 94, 106, 123
Redoutensaal (Brünn) 77
Redoutensaal (Stuttgart) 43
Redoutensaal (Vienna) 33, 34, 54, 78, 79, 148
Redulta, The (Brünn) 15
Reed, W.H. 137
Reed (cellist, in London) 174
Reeves, Sims 237, 255, 257
Reichardt, Alexander 218
Reinecke, Carl 5, 48, 158–9
   on Ernst 9, 109–11, 139, 158, 161
   WORKS
      piano quartet (op. 34) 158
Rellstab, Ludwig 93
Reményi, Ede (Eduard Hoffmann) 28, 29, 145, 217
Revue des Deux Mondes 195
Revue et Gazette musicale 71, 72, 90, 118, 120
   on Ernst 90, 229, 259–60
Revue et Gazette musicale des Théâtres 193
Revue musicale
   on Ernst 52
Richards, Brinley 185
Richelmi (singer, in Paris) 51

Richter, Jean Théodore 94
Ries, L. 256, 261, 276
Riga 86, 153
Ritter, Theodore 210
Robinson, Mrs Joseph 208
Rode, Pierre 27, 28, 33, 55
    WORKS
        Caprices 28
        concerto in B minor 43
Roignon 194
Röller, Eduard
    on Ernst 45–6
Rome 170
Ronstand quartet 62
Rosenhain, Jacques 34, 83
Rossi, Carlo 129
Rossi quartet 62
Rossini, Gioacchino 23, 38, 54, 56, 129
    WORKS
        Otello 70
        Semiramide 195
        variations on a theme of 43
        Zelmira 44
Roth, Dr (friend of Ernst and Heller) 60, 64, 84, 85, 187, 230
Rothschilds 3
Rotterdam 72, 102, 105
Rouen 56, 64, 71
Rousselot, Scipion 7, 179, 180, 183, 185
    WORKS
        third quintet for string quartet and bass 183
Royal Academy of Arts (Stockholm) 172
Royal Academy of Music (London) 137
Royal Chapel (Munich) 42
Royal Opera (Berlin) 94
Royal Riding School (Copenhagen) 111
Royal Singspielakademie, Hall of (Berlin) 96
Royal Society of Musicians (London) 131
Royal Theatre (Copenhagen) 110
Rubini, Giovanni Battista 55, 104
Rubinstein, Anton 1, 241
    WORKS
        string quartet in D minor 218
Rudolf, Archduke 37
Ruppius, Otto
    on Ernst 40–42
Russia 85, 88, 104, 107, 125, 139, 151, 153–8, 196
Russian imperial family 226, 264 *see*
    also Alexander II, Tsar; Maria Alexandovna, Tsarina; Nicholas, Tsarevich
Ryan, Desmond 116

Sahlgreen (string-player, in Copenhagen) 158
Sainati, Edward
    on Ernst 10
Saint-Lubin, Leon de 33, 35
Saint-Saëns
    WORKS
        Introduction and Rondo Capricioso 136
Saint-Simon, Henri de 7
Saint-Simonism 83
Sainton, Prosper 132, 133, 179, 183, 185, 208, 209, 251
Sainton Dolby, Madame 232
Salle Ste Cécile (Paris) 175
Salle Chantereine (Paris) 55, 56, 70, 71
Salle Cluyesander (Brussels) 101
Salle Herz (Paris) 120, 125, 189, 192, 196
Salle Pleyel (Paris), *see* Pleyel's salons
Salles des Concerts (Boulogne) 122
Salvi, Lorenzo 154
Salzburg 81
Sand, George 89
Santini, Vincenzo Felice 55
Santley Charles 232, 255
Saphir, M.G.
    on Ernst 24
Sarasate, Pablo de 109
    WORKS
        Carmen Fantasy (op. 25) 71
        Zigeunerweisen (op. 20) 139
Sauret, Émile 147
Saxony, King of 77
Saxony, Queen of 77
Sayn-Wittgenstein, Princess Carolyne 155, 190, 196, 197
Scandinavia 107
Scarlatti, Domenico
    WORKS
        sonatas 217
Scattner, Caroline 227
Schauspielhaus (Darmstadt) 109
Schewennigen 102
Schikaneder, Emanuel 32
Schikaneder's Freihaus Theater (Vienna) 32
Schiller, Friedrich 6, 258

Marie Stuart 205, 258
Schindler, Anton 5, 83–5, 86, 87, 89, 94
    on Ernst 83–5, 87
Schlésinger, Elisa (née Foucault) 72–3, 83
Schlesinger, Heinrich 99
Schlésinger, Maurice 48, 53, 72–3, 74, 78, 86, 99, 103
Schönstein, Adolphe 95
Schroeder-Devrient, Madame 49
Schubert, Franz 7, 29, 32, 35, 38, 204, 252
    WORKS
        Erlking (D. 328) 54, 97, 103, 104, 106, 113, 133, 250, 256, 258
        mass in F (D. 105) 31
        piano trio in E♭ (D. 929) 30
        quartet in G (D. 887) 30
Schultz, Fräulin (Frau) von 107, 124
Schumann (née Wieck), Clara 1, 20, 96, 122, 129, 134, 201, 202, 214–15, 217–18, 219
Schumann, Robert 45–6, 47, 48, 54, 71, 75, 76, 110, 134, 145, 162, 163, 201, 204, 214–15, 219, 252
    on Ernst 1, 46–7, 75–6
    WORKS
        Kriesleriana (op. 16) 238
        May, Charming May (from *Album for the Young* op. 68) 252
        piano sonata in F minor (*Concerto Without Orchestra*) (op. 14) 164
        variations for two pianos (op. 46) 238
Schunke, Charles 53, 56
Schuppanzigh, Ignaz 28, 29, 30–31, 32, 36, 84, 184
Schuppanzigh quartet 28, 29, 31, 36
Schwartz, Aloys 33
Schwartz, Boris
    on Ernst 10, 84
Scott (of Antwerp) 72
Scott, Sir Walter
    The Lay of the Last Minstrel 226
Second World War 2, 3
Seligmann, Hippolyte Prosper 185, 195
Sellis, Joseph 123–4
Semper, Gottfried 76
Serwaczyński, Stanislaus 80
Seville 21n.3
Seyfried, Ignaz 30, 32, 34, 36, 37, 38, 39, 50
    WORKS
        Der Friede 32

Shakespeare, William 5, 155–6
Sheffield 215
Shelley, Percy Bysshe 116
Sibelius, Jean 144, 147
    WORKS
        Violin Concerto (op. 47) 140, 144, 147–8, **148**
Sibylla Polyxena of Montana, Countess 22
Signale für Musikalische Welt 109, 148
Silas, Edward
    WORKS
        trio in A (op. 27) 216
Sina (violinist, from Vienna) 87–8
Singer, Edmund 28
Sivori, Camillo 8, 93, 95, 114, 116–21, 122, 125, 126, 127, 129, 131–3, 148, 179, 182, 183, 185, 201, 203, 226, 255
Sloper, Lindsay 180
Smithson, Harriet 101
Snel, Jean-François 101
socialism 7
Società Armonica (London) 127, 130
Société des Artistes Français (Paris) 272
Société des Musiciens (Paris) 122
Société Philharmonic (Marseilles) 61
Société Royale de la Grande Harmonie (Brussels) 101
'Soirées de musique classique et historique' (Paris) 213
Sommer, Johann 21, 22
Sophie, Princess of Holland 102
Sorbonne (Paris) 271, 272
Southampton 134
Spina (publisher) 250
Spohr, Louis 5, 44, 47, 49, 50, 70, 77, 85, 98, 105, 105–6n.1, 109, 113, 114, 126, 128, 150, 176, 201, 204, 208, 209, 216
    WORKS
        duet for violin and viola 183
        quartet in E♭ (op. 58) 208
        quintet in G (op. 33, No. 2) 204
        Trio Concertante in E minor (op. 119) 204
        violin concerto no. 8 in A minor (op. 47), *Gesangsszene* 114, 128, 129, 150, 184, 209, 215
Spontini, Gaspare 175
St Gallen 190, 191
St Jakob (Brünn) 16

St James's Hall (London) 231–2, 237, 255, 256–7, 275
St Petersburg 6, 54, 74, 91, 94, 95, 103, 116, 122, 147, 153–8, 160
St Stephen's Cathedral (Vienna) 31
Stammers, Mr (concert organizer, in London) 173–4, 175, 176
Standard 116
Statchkoch, Maurice 259
Staudigl, Joseph 130
Steibelt, Daniel 204
    WORKS
        sonata for violin and piano in E minor 185
Stern, Daniel (Marie d'Agoult) 260, 261–2
Stern, Isaac 1
Stockhausen, Julins 181, 186
Stockholm 147, 158
Stoepel, Franz 53
Stoepel, Helen 171
Stoepel's salons (Paris) 53
Stoltz, Rosina 55
Stör, Carl 75
Strad 10
Stradivarius instruments
    cellos
        'Hausmann' 98
    violins 149
        'Emperor'/'Kubelick' 98
        Ernst's 11, 24, 98, 272–3
        'Fountaine' 98
        'Plotenyi' 98
Strasbourg 40, 81, 197
Straus, Ludwig 28
Strauss, Johann, the elder 38
    WORKS
        Erinnerung an Ernst oder: Der Carneval in Venig 80
Stuttgart 40, 43, 44, 81, 197, 199
Suche (violin teacher, in Vienna) 30
Süddeutsche Musik-Zeitung 204
Sullivan, Arthur 237
Sun 257
Suppé, Franz von 32
Sweden 107
Switzerland 52–3, 99, 186–7, 194, 205, 210, 271
syphilis 219
Szigeti, Joseph 1

Tamburlink *fils* 181

Tarnow 135
Tchaikovsky, Pyotr Ilyich
    WORKS
        string quartet no. 1 in D (op. 11) 273
Telegraph 116
Tellefsen, Thomas 213, 214
Thackeray, William Makepeace 235
Thalberg, Sigismond 5, 70, 71, 109, 129, 130, 133, 241–5
    WORKS
        Moses Fantasy (op. 33) 71
Thaler, A. 22
Thayer, Alexander Wheelock
    Life of Beethoven 184
Theatre an der Wien (Vienna) 32
Théâtre des Italiens (Paris) 49, 52, 55
Théâtre du Palais-Royal (Paris) 56
Théâtre français (Paris) 192, 193
Theatre Impérial (Nice) 267
Theatre-Royal (Stockholm) 158
Theatre Zeitung 29
Tiilikainen, Jukka 147
Times, The 2, 116, 119, 121, 178, 179, 204, 227, 233, 255, 256–7, 258, 268
    on Ernst 130, 174, 232
Tindall, Thomas Stoner 205
Tisch, Eduard 238
Tisferand, Eugène 266
Tolstoy, Leo
    The Kreutzer Sonata 70
Toulon 63, 195
Toulouse 64, 195
Tournai, battle of 108
Trollope, Fanny 38
Trouville 72
Truc, Arsene 62
Turku 147

United States of America 63, 138, 183, 201
University of Göttingen 124
Urhan, Chrétien 53

Versailles 271
Vevey 191
Viardot, Pauline 89, 213
Victoria, Queen of England 108, 114, 129, 210, 217
Vienna 7, 15, 17, 27–36, 37–40, 42, 45, 47, 77–80 *passim*, 85, 128, 135, 139, 150, 151, 156, 158, 160, 172,

181, 197, 200, 202, 205, 218, 226, 227–30, 238, 241, 269, 272
Vienna Conservatoire 3, 24, 27–36, 37–9, 41, 50
Vienna Opera 31
Vieuxtemps, Henri 4, 9, 55, 69, 70, 75, 76, 85–8, 102, 109, 139, 153–5, 157–8, 179, 182, 185, 203, 226, 237–8, 252
   WORKS
      Romance 157
      violin concerto no. 1 in E (op. 10) 85–6, 87, 88, 139
Villa Bermond (Nice) 226
Villefranche 264
Villemot, Madame 51
Villiers, Edith 258, 263
Viotti, Giovanni Battista 27, 50, 71
Voltaire
   Mohamet 193
Vrugt (singer, in Holland) 73
Vuillaume, Jean-Baptiste 116, 272
Vuillaume violins
   copy of Guarneri 116

Wagner, Richard 1, 8n.3, 21, 86–7, 94, 116, 170, 201, 204, 208–10, 227
   on Ernst 190
   'Judaism in Music' 8n.3, 201
   WORKS
      Christoph Colombe Overture 86
      Lohengrin 171, 197
      Tannhäuser 170, 197
      Tristan and Isolde 256
Wagram, battle of 19, 21
Wagstaffe, Dr and Mrs, *see* Radcliffe, Dr Charles Bland
Wallace, Vincent 259, 262, 269
   WORKS
      Maritana 259
Walton, William 88
Warsaw 94, 95, 103
Wasielewski, Wilhelm Joseph von 201
Watson, Charlotte 59, 63
Wauxhall d'Eté (Paris) 52
Webb, H. 237, 256, 276
Weber, Carl Maria von 31, 170, 261
   WORKS
      Euryanthe (op. 81) 111
      Der Freischütz 16, 159
      Invitation to the Waltz (op. 65) 196
      Oberon 23

piano quartet (op. 18) 213
Wednesday Evening Concerts (London) 173–4, 175–6
Wehle, Maurice 33
Weil, Rosalie 14, 191 *see also* Lévy, Rose, F.
Weimar 7, 75, 96, 103, 104, 105, 134, 161, 169, 170, 172, 189–90, 196, 197, 200, 201
Weimar, Crown Prince of 103
Weimar, Grand Duchess of 103, 104
Weiner (violinist, in London) 237
Weiss, Franz 28
Wenzels, the 106
Wertheimstein, Carl von 228, 230
Wertheimstein, Franziska von 228
Wertheimstein, Josephine von 228, 240, 256
Wertheimstein, Leopold von 228, 229, 240, 256
Wessel and Cocks (publishers) 99
Wheeler, Rosina Doyle, *see* Lytton, Rosina
Wieck, Clara (Clara Schumann after marriage) 109
Wieck, Frederik 48
Wielhorski, Count Michel 153
Wiener Musikzeitung 27
Wieniawski, Henryk 9, 96, 138, 226, 227, 255–7 *passim*, Plates XV and XVI
   WORKS
      L'Ecole Moderne (op. 10) 250, 252, **252**, 253, 254, **254**
      Faust Fantasy (op. 20) 71
Wiesbaden 199
Wilczkowski, Tobias
   on Ernst 11
Wilhelm II, King of Hesse-Kassel 44, 47
Wilhelm, Prince of Prussia 107
Wilhelmj, August 41, 70, 137–8, 147
William II, King of Holland 102
William III, King of Holland
   as Crown Prince 102–3
William IV, King of England 108, 114
Willis's Rooms (London) 167
Willy (violinist, in London) 133, 174
Wilson, Dr 235, 237–9, 240
   The Water Cure 238–9
Wilson, Herbert 240
Wilton, Lord 172
Windischgrätz, Prince Alfred I of 160
Windsor Castle 129
Winter, Peter 32
Winthertheer 190, 191

Wittgenstein, Hermann 128
Wittgenstein, Ludwig 128
Wittgenstein, Paul 128
Wolf, Pierre-Etienne 52, 100
Wolf, Samuel
   on Ernst 10, 45, 264
Wordsworth, William 5
Wranitzky (violin teacher, in Vienna) 30
Wurlitzer Collection 272
Württemberg 208
Württemberg, Prince of 107
Würtzberg 40, 44
Wylde, Dr Henry 208, 209

Yiddish 17
Ysaÿe, Eugène
  WORKS
    Sonates pour violon seul 1, 254–5

Ziegesar, Baron Ferdinand von 161
Zimballist, Efraim 140
Zimmerman, Pierre 71, 195
Ziwolle 73
Zsigmondy, Dénes 98, 273
Zurich 190–91, 197, 208